BEST-EVER RECIPES

BOOKS Family Circle

E·D·I·T·O·R·I·A·L

Editor, Family Circle Books: Carol A. Guasti
Assistant Editor: Kim E. Gayton
Editorial Assistant: Kate Jackson
Project Editor: David Ricketts
Copy Editor: Laura Crocker
Book Design: MBS + K
Cover Photo: Fran Brennan
Typesetting: Vicki Almquist, Jean Brassard, Alison Chandler, Caroline Cole, Maureen Harrington, Brian Kaman
Editorial Freelancers: Celeste Bantz, Kristen Keller

M·A·R·K·E·T·I·N·G

Director, Family Circle Books & Licensing: Margaret Chan-Yip
Fulfillment/Planning Coordinator: Carrie Meyerhoff
Administrative Assistant: Dianne Snively

PHOTOGRAPHY CREDITS   **Fran Brennan:** Cover, page 167. **Tom Eckerle:** Page 232. **Joshua Green:** Pages 46, 49, 50, 53, 55, 124, 127, 130, 137. **Ronald G. Harris:** Page 139. **Jenifer Jordan:** Page 257. **Rita Maas:** Pages 8, 15, 27, 40, 43, 66, 145, 176. **Rudy Muller:** Page 204. **Steven Mark Needham:** Pages 11, 16, 18, 20 22, 24, 29, 37, 38. **Carin Riley:** Pages 84, 86, 88, 95, 98, 102, 110, 169, 240-241, 247. **Bill Robbins/L.A.:** Pages 156, 160. **Ron Schwerin:** Page 153. **Jerry Simpson:** Page 248. **Michael Skott:** Pages 5, 7, 58, 69, 71, 74, 162, 165, 178, 208, 222, 235, 241. **William Stites:** Pages 188, 190, 194, 199, 215, 216, 220. **Tom Sullivan:** Pages 77, 79, 230. **René Velez:** Pages 184, 250. Cover photo courtesy of Houston Metropolitan magazine, City Home Publishing, Inc.

Published by The Family Circle, Inc.
110 Fifth Avenue, New York, NY 10011

Copyright® 1989 by The Family Circle, Inc.

Manufactured in the United States of America

10 9 8 7 6 5 4 3 2 1

Library of Congress Cataloging in Publication Data
Main entry under title:

Family circle best-ever recipes.
Includes index.

89-85778

ISBN 0-933585-15-2

Other Books By Family Circle

The Best of Family Circle Cookbook series
(Pub. Dates: 1985 - 1989)

Busy Cook's Book

Good Health Cookbook

Make It Country

The Family Circle Christmas Treasury series
(Pub. Dates: 1986 - 1989)

Favorite Needlecrafts

Hints, Tips & Smart Advice

❖ ❀ ❖

To order **FamilyCircle** books, write to Family Circle Books,
110 Fifth Avenue, New York, NY 10011.

To order **FamilyCircle** magazine, write to Family Circle Subscriptions,
110 Fifth Avenue, New York, NY 10011.

TABLE OF CONTENTS

4

HOLIDAY WINGDINGS 124

5

ON THE LIGHT SIDE 162

6

MICROWAVE MAGIC 188

7

FINISHING TOUCHES 222

INTRODUCTION

*T*oday it seems more and more of us have less time to shop and cook. At the same time, we've never been more health conscious, so we want quick food that's good for us. And yet, we also want to make special food for holidays, we want to get together with friends for weekend dinners, we want to occasionally indulge in dessert. To answer all these needs, we created Family Circle's *Best-Ever Recipes* — the one cookbook that answers all the "wants" in our busy, active lives.

We begin with a chapter on quick and easy weekday meals, designed to get you out of the kitchen *fast*. There's a complete menu for each main dish, to help plan your meals and your grocery shopping. Another time-saving option is the microwave oven — an option which has gone from novelty to necessity in many households. Our section on microwave cooking and baking gives you new recipes and time-saving techniques.

When time is not at such a premium, our chapter devoted to weekend cooking — brunches, dinner parties and fun gatherings — is just the ticket. For the holidays, you'll find recipes for a wonderful Thanksgiving dinner, delicious Christmas cookies, a marvelous spring buffet, and more. And because there are days when satisfying your sweet tooth is a must, we have a section on scrumptious desserts: some baked, some frozen, some low-cal — and all delicious.

Despite the whirl of our busy lives, we're still concerned with today's health buzzwords: cholesterol, sodium, calories and saturated fats. That's why every one of our recipes is flagged with its low-calorie, low-cholesterol, low-sodium or low-fat values. And each recipe has a complete nutritional analysis. You'll also find a chapter devoted to health concerns: the lowdown on lean meats and how to cook with them, plus wonderful, light recipes and nutritious, guilt-free snacks. In the last few years, we've witnessed an increasing abundance of fresh fruits and vegetables in the markets. So we provide information and recipes on how to use old favorites, as well as the new varieties of mushrooms, squashes, potatoes and onions available.

Turn the page for more guidelines on healthful eating; below is the criteria used for categorizing the nutrient flags of different dishes.

Criteria for Low-Calorie, Low-Sodium, Low-Cholesterol and Low-Fat Dishes

The limit for these guidelines goes up to and includes the number.

Low-Calorie		Low-Sodium		Low-Cholesterol	
Main dish	350 cal.	Main dish	140 mg	Main dish	75 mg
Side dish	100 cal.	Side dish	100 mg	Side dish	15 mg
Snack	100 cal.	Snack	65 mg	Snack	7 mg
Condiment	25 cal.	Condiment	50 mg	Condiment	5 mg
Dessert	150 cal.	Dessert	50 mg	Dessert	25 mg

Low-Fat No more than 30% of the calories in a dish should be attributable to fat. To calculate this, apply the following: Grams of fat in the recipe x 9 calories (9 calories in 1 milligram fat) divided by total calories in dish x 100 = percentage of calories attributable to fat.

Recommended Dietary Allowances (RDA)
The Committee on Dietary Allowances of the National Academy of Sciences/National Research Council publishes and frequently revises the Recommended Dietary Allowances (RDA) which set standards for the daily nutritional needs of healthy males and females at various stages in their lives. Consult the chart below for recommended dietary guidelines.

Calories
What *is* a calorie? The term "calorie" is used to describe the *measure of energy* derived from the foods we eat. When the number of calories consumed exceeds the amount needed by the body, the excess calories are transformed into fat. Stored fat may be used by the body during times of stress, but an overabundance of fat just sits in the body. In a well-balanced diet, about 8% to 12% of the calorie count should come from protein, no more than 30% from fat (primarily poly- or monounsaturated), and the rest should come from complex carbohydrates.

DAILY NUTRITION COUNTDOWN CHART
Refer to the nutrient value listings on each of our recipes and then use the following guidelines to ensure a well-balanced, healthful diet.

	Average Healthy Adult	
	Women	Men
Calories[1]	2,000	2,700
Protein[2]	44 g (176 cal)	56 g (224 cal)
Fat[3]	66 g (594 cal)	90 g (810 cal)
Sodium[4]	1,100-3,300 mg	1,100-3,300 mg
Cholesterol[5]	300 mg	300 mg

Calories that do not come from protein or fat should be derived from complex carbohydrates found in whole grains, fresh fruits, vegetables, pasta, etc.

[1]RDA [2](8%-12% of calories) RDA [3](30% of calories) Amer. Heart Assoc. and Nat'l Acad. of Science
[4]USDA [5]Amer. Heart Assoc.

Protein
We know that a healthy diet must include protein. But how much protein should we eat? Nutritionists seem to agree that a diet high in complex carbohydrates, low in fats and with moderate consumption of protein is the ideal diet both for weight control *and* for good health.

A "protein" is a long chain of amino acids. Protein is a component of all body cells, antibodies and enzymes, and is essential for the growth, repair and maintenance of healthy cells. Proteins from most animal sources — meat, fish, eggs, poultry and dairy products — usually are "complete," meaning they have a complete chain of the amino acids needed for a healthy diet. Proteins from plant sources usually are incomplete and need to be paired with complementary proteins to provide all the necessary amino acids — ie., rice with beans or peanut butter with milk.

Fat
Despite bad press, not all fat is bad. Fat provides energy, helps the body maintain its heat and assists in the absorption of fat-soluble vitamins, such as vitamin E. However, fat has more calories than a similar amount of either carbohydrates or protein, so a little goes a long way.

Fat is made up of three types of linked fatty acids: saturated, polyunsaturated and monounsaturated. Saturated fat is found primarily in animal sources, but also is present in some plant sources, such as palm and coconut oils — these are the high-cholesterol fats. Polyunsaturated fat is found primarily in vegetable sources and some fish sources such as herring, salmon and mackerel. Monounsaturated fat also is primarily from plant sources and is found in olive and peanut oils, for example.

What does all this mean? Evidence seems to suggest that polyunsaturated fats may help to reduce the amount of cholesterol by increasing the ratio of HDLs (high density lipoproteins) in the blood. These cholesterol-carrying particles actually help sweep excess cholesterol out of the bloodstream. Saturated fats, on the other hand, may increase the ratio of LDLs (low density lipoproteins) in the blood. These LDLs deposit excess cholesterol in the arteries, which may result in plaque on blood vessel walls, subsequent hardening of the arteries and cardiovascular disease. Monounsaturated fats also seem to have a beneficial effect on cholesterol levels. Recent studies of Mediterranean populations where use of olive oil is common show the incidence of cardiovascular disease is very low in this region.

Carbohydrates
Let's hear it for carbohydrates! They provide efficient energy, are comparatively low in calories and leave you with a satisfied "full" feeling — great news for dieters.

All carbohydrates are composed of sugars, arranged in various combinations. Simple carbohydrates are made of three single sugars: glucose, fructose and galactose, found in fruits and cane sugars, or in combinations of two single sugars.

Complex carbohydrates are combinations of simple sugars arranged in long and intricate chains. They fall into three categories: starch, which is broken down by the body to use as its chief source of energy; glycogen, which is excess glucose that is stored in the liver; and cellulose, the woody, stringy part of plants known as fiber (essential to the proper functioning of the digestive tract). Potatoes, whole-grain breads and cereals, rice, pasta, legumes, fruits and vegetables are all good sources of "complex" carbohydrates.

There are no recommended levels of daily intake for carbohydrates. But it is believed that an increase of complex carbohydrates and moderation of simple sugars (such as honey and table sugar) is beneficial to the diet.

Sodium

All animals need salt, and humans are no exception. Sodium, which makes up 40% of the salt molecule, is a major component of the fluid surrounding the cells in the body. Sodium is necessary to regulate the balance of water in body tissues and is active in muscle contraction. It touches off the heartbeat and controls its rhythm. But as crucial as sodium is, we need surprisingly little of it to function.

Excess sodium in the diet is considered to be a contributing cause of high blood pressure, heart disease, hypertension (a risk factor in strokes) and kidney failure. Processed foods generally contain high levels of sodium and many people oversalt food both while cooking and at the table. With sodium, as with most minerals, moderation is the key.

The U.S. Dept. of Agriculture (USDA) recommends 1,100 to 3,300 milligrams (1.1 to 3.3 grams) of sodium a day for both the average healthy adult male and female.

Cholesterol

Cholesterol seems to be the buzz word of late; many people are concerned with its adverse effects. It may surprise you to learn that most of the cholesterol in your body is produced by your liver. Cholesterol is an essential part of cell membranes, is used in building nerve sheaths and is the raw material for manufacturing hormones.

According to Harvard Medical School research, the body is capable of producing all the cholesterol it needs — without getting it from food sources. Excess levels of cholesterol in the blood have been linked with the increased likelihood of heart disease, atherosclerosis (clogged arteries) and stroke. The most concentrated form of cholesterol is the egg yolk, as well as organ meats — liver, kidney, brains. Also, any whole-milk dairy product, most red meats and some seafood are culpable.

The American Heart Association recommends no more than 300 milligrams daily for both the average healthy adult female and male.

Guidelines for Good Eating

How do you balance all of this nutritional information? In addition to the RDA, the USDA and the U.S. Dept. of Health and Human Services have suggested several guidelines for a sensible eating plan. But as research continues, these guidelines, as well as the RDA, are subject to change. The best defense is a well-informed attack: keep up-to-date on the latest medical and nutritional findings. If you have specific dietary problems, or are taking any prescription medication, consult a physician before planning your diet.

Eat a wide variety of foods. Plan your meals around the basic food groups: breads, cereals and grains; meat, poultry and fish; milk and milk products; fruits and vegetables. Vary the selection daily to ensure that you are receiving all the necessary nutrients.

Maintain a desirable weight. Consult your physician to decide upon your optimum weight. If you need to lose weight, avoid fad diets which promise a rapid weight loss. Such radical changes in weight can be dangerous. Instead, aim for a 1 to 2 pound loss per week. Avoid obesity, which has been linked to cardiovascular diseases, diabetes and other diseases.

Avoid excess fat and cholesterol in your diet. Pay attention to hidden fats in your meal planning. Choose lean cuts of red meat, increase your use of poultry and fish, and explore methods of cooking that add little or no extra fats. Remember that legumes are an excellent, low-fat source of protein, especially when combined with other proteins, such as rice.

Milk and milk products are important for their calcium content, but use low-fat and skim varieties. Use your judgement with egg consumption: the cholesterol is almost entirely in the yolk, so try making an omelet with one whole egg and just the white of a second.

Try to avoid overuse of prepackaged, processed foods. You'll be saving yourself from extra sugars, salt, cholesterol and fats.

Select high-fiber foods. Foods high in complex carbohydrates, such as whole-grain breads and cereals, vegetables, fruits and legumes are an excellent source of vitamins, minerals and fiber, and will leave you with a well-satisfied, "full" sensation.

Avoid excess sugar. Any necessary sugars are easily obtained by eating fresh fruit. Excess sugar increases the risk of tooth decay and calorie overload.

Avoid excess sodium. Processed foods, cheeses, cured meats, snack foods, baking soda, baking powder and table salt all contain sodium. Salt added during cooking often is unnecessary (except when baking) and can easily be replaced with herbs and spices. Don't add salt at the table.

Study food labels. Every time you pick up a can or package of food, read the label to check the levels of added sugar and salt. Check the oils used in processing to avoid saturated fats.

If you drink alcoholic beverages, do so in moderation. Liquor is high in calories and low in nutrients.

Weekday Whirl

4

1

"There's just no time to cook!" This phrase has become a familiar refrain in recent years.

With the busy, active lifestyles of the nineties — work, volunteer organizations, school functions, exercise classes, etc. — there's less time to devote to shopping and cooking.

While fast food, take out and frozen dinners seemingly provide the answer for busy cooks, our current knowledge of nutrition, diet and healthy eating habits tells us this just isn't so. We yearn to cook the kind of meals for our families that our parents and grandparents provided for theirs — from scratch, with fresh, wholesome ingredients.

How can the family who does it all have it all? We've designed this chapter to fit the way in which you live during the week. We offer over 45 dinner menus with recipes, food information and tips to save you time in the kitchen. And every one of the main dishes can be prepared in 30 minutes or *less*. The selection includes everything from a simple "East Meets West" featuring Shrimp Lo Mein (recipe, page 40) to a sensational "Chicken Continental" with Chicken and Spinach in Tarragon Sauce (recipe, page 14). The menus give you suggestions for appetizers, side dishes and desserts. In many cases, we also provide the recipes for these go-withs.

Take the guess work out of weekly meal planning and make the weekday whirl a little calmer. Use our menus to help plan your shopping trips; use our recipes to create terrific meals. What could be easier?

A luscious meal for any night of the week: Turkey and Apples in Brandy Cream Sauce (recipe, page 19), topped off with poached pears in Raspberry Sauce (recipe, page 263).

POULTRY

Quick to prepare, full of nutrition and still relatively easy on your budget — what could be better?

CHICKEN AND PASTA ALFREDO

Makes 4 servings.

Nutrient Value Per Serving: 799 calories, 43 g protein, 38 g fat, 70 g carbohydrate, 530 mg sodium, 250 mg cholesterol.

1	package (12 ounces) fettuccine	1	cup frozen peas
¼	pound mushrooms, quartered	2½	cups cooked chicken pieces (about 1 pound)
3	green onions, sliced	½	teaspoon salt
2	tablespoons unsalted butter	½	teaspoon freshly ground pepper
1	cup heavy cream	⅓	cup grated Parmesan cheese

1. Cook the fettuccine following the package directions.
2. Meanwhile, sauté the mushrooms and the green onion in the butter in a large skillet until they are tender, for about 3 minutes.
3. Add the cream to the skillet. Bring the mixture to boiling. Lower the heat and gently boil, uncovered, until the mixture is slightly reduced, for about 5 minutes. Add the peas, chicken, salt and pepper to the skillet. Cook, stirring occasionally, until the chicken mixture is hot.
4. When the fettuccine is cooked, drain it. Transfer the fettuccine to a large serving bowl. Pour the chicken mixture over the fettuccine. Sprinkle with the Parmesan cheese. Toss gently to mix well.

VERMICELLI WITH CHICKEN, ARTICHOKES AND OLIVES

A great, uncomplicated dish you can make in practically no time at all — and so delicious you'll want to make it again and again.

LOW-CHOLESTEROL • LOW-FAT

Makes 4 servings.

Nutrient Value Per Serving: 499 calories, 37 g protein, 14 g fat, 56 g carbohydrate, 807 mg sodium, 66 mg cholesterol.

	Pinch salt	1	can (14½ ounces) chicken broth
8	ounces vermicelli		
2	tablespoons olive oil plus a splash	¼	cup brandy
		1	package (9 ounces) frozen artichoke hearts
1	pound boned, skinless chicken cutlets, cut into 3 x ½-inch strips	1	tablespoon Dijon-style mustard
¼	cup all-purpose flour	20	black olives

Pasta du Jour

Antipasto Salad (recipe, page 119)
Chicken and Pasta Alfredo*
Italian Bread
Grapes

Chicken with Mediterranean Pasta

Carrot and Celery Sticks
Vermicelli with Chicken, Artichokes and Olives*
Panfried Plum Tomatoes (recipe, page 114)
Individual Flans

Cheers for Chicken

Every time you eat chicken you get a complete array of amino acids to fuel the growth of fresh, new skin cells. You also get a good supply of niacin, the B vitamin that helps all cells obtain the energy they need to stay healthy. A 3-ounce serving of chicken can provide half your daily requirement for niacin. Plus, with all its nutritional advantages, chicken also is low in calories.

❖   ❖   ❖

" We may live without poetry, music and art; We may live without conscience, and live without heart; We may live without friends; we may live without books; But civilized men cannot live without cooks. "
—*Edward Robert Bulwer-Lytton, Earl of Lytton*

1. Fill a large pot with hot water and bring it to boiling over high heat. Add the salt and the vermicelli, and stir constantly until the boiling resumes. Cook until the pasta is al dente, tender but firm to the bite. Drain the pasta. Return the pasta to the pot and toss it with the splash of oil.
2. Meanwhile, combine the chicken strips with the flour in a plastic bag and shake to coat the chicken. Heat the 2 tablespoons of oil in a large, heavy skillet over medium-high heat. Add the chicken in a single layer and cook for 3 to 5 minutes, or until it is golden brown. Turn over the chicken with tongs and cook for 1 minute more, or until the chicken is cooked through. Transfer the chicken to a plate and cover it with a sheet of aluminum foil to keep it warm.
3. Add the coating flour remaining in the bag to the skillet. Brown for 1 minute, stirring constantly. Whisk in the broth and the brandy, and bring the mixture to boiling.
4. Stir in the frozen artichokes and simmer the mixture for 4 minutes. Stir in the mustard, chicken and juices from the plate, pasta and olives. Cook for 2 minutes, or until the mixture is heated through. Serve.

Easy, delicious and quick to make, Vermicelli with Chicken, Artichokes and Olives is sure to become a family favorite.

7

CHICKEN PARMIGIANA WITH TOMATO SAUCE

Makes 4 servings.

Nutrient Value Per Serving: 694 calories, 45 g protein, 25 g fat, 72 g carbohydrate, 1,300 mg sodium, 144 mg cholesterol.

Tomato Sauce:
1   medium-size onion, chopped
1   tablespoon olive oil
1   clove garlic, finely chopped
1   can (28 ounces) whole Italian tomatoes, undrained and cut up
1   teaspoon dried basil, crumbled
½   teaspoon dried oregano, crumbled
3   tablespoons tomato paste
¼   cup dry red wine
     OR: dry white wine

Chicken Parmigiana:
1   egg
2   tablespoons milk
¾   cup dry Italian bread crumbs
½   cup grated Parmesan cheese
4   boned, skinless chicken breast halves, pounded (1 pound)
4   tablespoons olive oil
8   ounces spaghetti, cooked according to package directions

A Taste of Italy

Roasted Red Peppers in Olive Oil
Chicken Parmigiana with Tomato Sauce*
Sautéed Shredded Zucchini
Fresh Fruit

Simple Chicken Soup

Combine one large carrot, shredded, with 2 tablespoons of sliced green onion, half of a finely chopped large tomato, half of a finely chopped small avocado and 1 teaspoon of finely chopped parsley in a small bowl. Mix the ingredients well. Divide the mixture equally into 4 individual soup bowls. Bring 1 can (13¾ ounces) of chicken broth and ⅔ cup of water to boiling in a small saucepan. Pour the broth mixture over the vegetables. Season with freshly ground black pepper to taste, if you wish. Garnish with 8 thin lime slices.

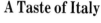

Chicken Parmigiana with Tomato Sauce is wonderfully easy to prepare. We serve it with sautéed shredded zucchini.

1. Prepare the Tomato Sauce: Sauté the onion in the oil in a medium-size, heavy saucepan over medium heat until the onion is softened, for about 3 minutes. Add the garlic and sauté for 1 minute. Stir in the tomatoes with their liquid, the basil, oregano, tomato paste and red or white wine. Bring the mixture to boiling. Reduce the heat slightly and boil gently until the sauce is thick, for 15 to 20 minutes.

2. Meanwhile, prepare the Chicken Parmigiana: Whisk the egg with the milk in a shallow dish. Combine the bread crumbs with ¼ cup of the Parmesan cheese on a piece of wax paper. Dip the chicken cutlets first into the egg mixture, then into the bread crumb mixture to coat the cutlets.

3. Heat 2 tablespoons of the oil in a large, nonstick skillet over medium heat. Add 2 cutlets and cook until each underside is crisp and golden brown, for 2 to 3 minutes. Turn, brown the other sides and cook through, for about 2 minutes. Drain the cutlets on paper toweling. Add the remaining 2 tablespoons of oil to the skillet, and repeat with the remaining cutlets.

4. Place the cutlets and the spaghetti on 4 individual dinner plates and top with the sauce. Sprinkle with the remaining Parmesan cheese.

CHICKEN THIGHS TERIYAKI

LOW-CALORIE • LOW-FAT

Broil for 12 to 14 minutes.
Makes 4 servings.

Nutrient Value Per Serving: 191 calories, 26 g protein, 5 g fat, 10 g carbohydrate, 709 mg sodium, 104 mg cholesterol.

½ cup sake OR: white wine	2 tablespoons sugar
¼ cup reduced-sodium soy sauce	1½ pounds skinless chicken thighs
2 tablespoons chopped, peeled fresh gingerroot	1½ teaspoons cornstarch
1 large clove garlic, chopped	1 teaspoon vinegar
	Orange slices, for garnish

1. Blend the sake or white wine, the soy sauce, ginger, garlic and sugar in the container of an electric blender. Strain the liquid into a self-sealing plastic bag, and discard the solids in the strainer.

2. Using a sharp knife, score the smooth side of each chicken thigh into a ½-inch diamond pattern; the score marks should be about ¼ inch deep. Add the chicken to the marinade and seal the bag. Refrigerate the chicken for 4 to 24 hours.

3. Place the oven rack 5 inches from the heat source. Preheat the broiler.

4. Line the broiler pan with aluminum foil. Remove the chicken from the marinade and place it, scored side down, in the center of the broiler pan. Set aside the marinade.

5. Broil the chicken for 7 minutes. Turn over the chicken and broil for another 5 to 7 minutes, or until the chicken is cooked through.

6. Meanwhile, measure the marinade. If necessary, add enough water to make ¾ cup. Place the marinade in a small, heavy saucepan. Stir in the cornstarch until it is dissolved. Cook the cornstarch mixture over medium heat, stirring, until it is thick and boiling. Remove the saucepan from the heat. Stir in the vinegar.

7. Transfer the cooked chicken to 4 individual dinner plates. Pour the pan juices into the sauce and spoon the sauce over the chicken. Garnish the chicken with the orange slices.

Tasty Teriyaki

Chicken Thighs Teriyaki*
Sesame Broccoli and Yellow Peppers (recipe, page 91)
Lemon Sherbet

More Than One Way to Skin a Chicken

To take the skin off a whole chicken in a jiffy and make it less fatty, remove the wings and cut the bird down the breastbone. Lay it out flat with the back up and pull off the skin.

9

CHICKEN THERMIDOR

Chicken replaces costly lobster in this classic dish. To make it even easier on you, our version is made with a store-bought, rotisserie-cooked chicken.

LOW-CALORIE

Broil for 3 to 4 minutes.
Makes 4 servings.

Nutrient Value Per Serving: 335 calories, 36 g protein, 15 g fat, 12 g carbohydrate, 720 mg sodium, 108 mg cholesterol.

1 **2-pound cooked chicken**	½ **teaspoon dried tarragon, crumbled**
1 **tablespoon butter**	¼ **teaspoon salt**
½ **cup chopped onion (1 medium-size onion)**	**Pinch freshly ground pepper**
1 **stalk celery, chopped**	½ **cup grated Parmesan cheese**
¼ **cup all-purpose flour**	1 **jar (4 ounces) pimientos, drained and sliced**
1 **cup chicken broth**	**Paprika**
½ **cup milk**	**Parsley sprigs, for garnish**
½ **cup dry white wine**	
1 **teaspoon dry mustard**	

1. Preheat the broiler.
2. Pull the chicken meat from the bones and discard the skin and bones; you should have 12 to 16 ounces of chicken. Slice the chicken meat and divide it among 4 individual, flameproof au gratin dishes, or 1 large one.
3. Melt the butter in a medium-size saucepan. Add the onion and the celery, and sauté over medium-high heat until the vegetables are softened, for about 3 minutes. Stir in the flour to coat the vegetables evenly. Add the broth, milk and wine. Cook, stirring constantly, until the mixture comes to boiling. Reduce the heat to low. Stir in the mustard, tarragon, salt and pepper. Simmer for 2 to 3 minutes. Add the Parmesan cheese. Reserve 2 tablespoons of the pimiento for garnish, and stir the remaining pimiento into the sauce. Spoon the sauce evenly over the chicken slices. Lightly sprinkle the chicken with the paprika.
4. Broil the chicken until the top is speckled brown and bubbly, for 3 to 4 minutes. Garnish with the parsley sprigs and reserved pimiento. Serve immediately.

HONEY LIME BROILED CHICKEN

Full of tangy taste and easy to prepare — our favorite combination!

Bake at 450° for 20 minutes; broil for 11 minutes.
Makes 4 servings.

Nutrient Value Per Serving: 394 calories, 41 g protein, 20 g fat, 10 g carbohydrate, 397 mg sodium, 132 mg cholesterol.

1 **teaspoon grated lime zest (green part of rind only)**	½ **teaspoon salt**
	¼ **teaspoon ground hot red pepper**
Juice of 1 lime (2 to 3 tablespoons)	1 **chicken (3 pounds), quartered**
2 **tablespoons honey**	

Chicken à la Gourmet

Chicken Thermidor*
Honey-Glazed Peas
Pound Cake with Berries in Syrup

Fowl Play

There is no important difference between a chicken labeled a fryer and one labeled a roaster when each weighs 3½ to 4 pounds. Buy the fryer, since they usually are cheaper.
■ If soup chickens are not available, or are too expensive, try using a fryer to make soup.
■ You can save money on chicken by buying a whole frying chicken or turkey on sale, cutting it into parts yourself and boning the breast for cutlets.
■ Chicken backs, rib cages, gizzards and necks make a rich, full-flavored pot of soup for just pennies a serving.

❖   ❖   ❖

Finger-Lickin' Chicken

Honey Lime Broiled Chicken*
Roasted Sweet Potato Wedges
Tossed Green Salad
Raspberry Fool (recipe, page 227)

Team Work

For today's busy two-career couples and families with teenage children, division of labor is a must. Once a week, sit down and write out complete menus for the week ahead. Make a list of things to buy, what can be done in advance and what should be started by whomever arrives home first. By having a thorough "plan of attack," you'll save time and energy in the kitchen — and by sharing the burden of meal preparation, you'll have more time to spend together.

❖ ❖ ❖

1. Preheat the oven to hot (450°).
2. Stir together the lime zest, lime juice, honey, salt and ground hot red pepper in a small bowl until the ingredients are well mixed. Place the chicken, skin side down, in a shallow baking pan and brush it with half the lime mixture.
3. Bake the chicken in the preheated hot oven (450°) for 10 minutes. Turn over the chicken and brush it with the remaining lime mixture. Bake for 10 minutes more. Turn over the chicken and brush it with the pan juices.
4. Increase the oven temperature to broil. Broil the chicken 4 to 5 inches from the heat source for 8 minutes, basting once. Turn the chicken skin side up and baste it with the pan juices. Broil for 3 minutes more. Serve.

An easy-on-you dinner: Honey Lime Broiled Chicken with glazed, roasted sweet potatoes.

CHICKEN BREASTS WITH RASPBERRY SAUCE

LOW-CALORIE • LOW-CHOLESTEROL

Makes 4 servings.

Nutrient Value Per Serving: 216 calories, 23 g protein, 9 g fat, 11 g carbohydrate, 273 mg sodium, 65 mg cholesterol.

4	boned, skinless chicken breast halves (about 1¼ pounds)	¼	teaspoon dried thyme, crumbled
2	tablespoons all-purpose flour	2	teaspoons cornstarch
1½	tablespoons vegetable oil	2	tablespoons butter, cut up
1	package (12 ounces) dry-pack frozen raspberries, thawed	2	tablespoons red wine vinegar
		2	teaspoons lemon juice
		1	teaspoon sugar
¾	cup chicken broth	⅛	teaspoon salt

1. Combine the chicken with the flour in a plastic bag and shake to coat the chicken. Sauté the chicken in the oil in a large, heavy skillet over medium-high heat for 3 to 4 minutes, or until the chicken is browned. Turn over the chicken with tongs, lower the heat to medium and sauté for 3 to 4 minutes more, or until the chicken is cooked through. Transfer the chicken to a warmed platter. Discard the fat from the pan and wipe the pan.

2. Reserve ¼ cup of the raspberries. Add the remaining raspberries, ½ cup of the broth and the thyme to the skillet. Bring the raspberry mixture to boiling. Lower the heat and simmer for 2 to 3 minutes, or until the raspberries are reduced to a saucy consistency.

3. Push the raspberry mixture through a strainer with the back of a spoon, and discard the seeds. Return the raspberry purée to the skillet.

4. Stir together the cornstarch and the remaining ¼ cup of broth in a small bowl until the mixture is smooth. Stir the cornstarch mixture into the raspberry purée. Bring the combined mixture to boiling, stirring. Lower the heat and simmer for about 2 minutes, or until the mixture thickens. Remove the skillet from the heat and stir in the butter, vinegar, lemon juice, sugar, salt and reserved raspberries.

5. Ladle the sauce onto 4 warmed individual dinner plates. Slice the chicken breasts lengthwise. Fan the slices over the sauce.

CHICKEN YAKITORI

LOW-CALORIE

Broil for 5 minutes.
Makes 4 servings.

Nutrient Value Per Serving: 234 calories, 34 g protein, 8 g fat, 4 g carbohydrate, 467 mg sodium, 141 mg cholesterol.

¼	cup reduced-sodium soy sauce	¼	teaspoon ground ginger
1½	tablespoons light brown sugar	2	cloves garlic, peeled and crushed
1	tablespoon chicken broth	1½	pounds boned, skinless chicken thighs
1	tablespoon vegetable oil		

A Taste of Spring Chicken

Chicken Breasts with Raspberry Sauce*
Basil Green Beans
Chocolate Angel Cake
(recipe, page 239)

Orient Express

Chicken Broth with Carrot Curls
Chicken Yakitori*
Hot Cooked Rice
Almond Cookies
(recipe, page 255)

1. Combine the soy sauce, brown sugar, broth, oil, ginger and garlic in a medium-size bowl.
2. Cut the chicken into 3 x ½ inch strips. Add the strips to the marinade and toss to coat them. Cover the bowl with plastic wrap and refrigerate the chicken for several hours, or overnight.
3. Preheat the broiler.
4. Thread the chicken onto eight 8- to 10-inch-long skewers. Place the skewers in the broiler pan.
5. Broil the chicken 6 inches from the heat source for 3 minutes. Turn over the chicken and reverse the broiler pan. Broil for 2 minutes more, or until the chicken is cooked through. Serve 2 skewers per person.

TURKEY-STUFFED CHICKEN ROLLS

LOW-CALORIE

Makes 4 servings.

Nutrient Value Per Serving: 342 calories, 51 g protein, 12 g fat, 5 g carbohydrate, 498 mg sodium, 137 mg cholesterol.

8	ounces ground uncooked turkey	¼	teaspoon red pepper flakes
¼	cup packaged bread crumbs	1	small clove garlic, finely chopped
½	cup dry white wine	1	egg white
2	tablespoons chopped parsley	4	boned, skinless chicken breast halves (about 1½ pounds), pounded to ¼-inch thickness
½	teaspoon fennel seeds, crushed		
½	teaspoon salt	1	tablespoon vegetable oil
¼	teaspoon freshly ground black pepper		

1. Combine the turkey, bread crumbs, ¼ cup of the wine, the parsley, fennel seeds, salt, black pepper, red pepper flakes, garlic and egg white in a medium-size bowl. Mix with your hands to blend the ingredients. Spoon one fourth of the stuffing onto each chicken cutlet. Roll up the cutlet tightly, jelly-roll fashion, from a long side and secure it with wooden picks.
2. Heat the oil in a large, heavy skillet over medium-high heat. Add the chicken rolls, seam side down, and brown them. Turn over the rolls. Add the remaining ¼ cup of wine. Cover the skillet, reduce the heat and simmer for 10 to 12 minutes, turning once. Let the rolls stand for a few minutes.
3. Transfer the rolls to a board. Remove the wooden picks. Cut the rolls into ½-inch-thick slices and arrange the slices on 4 individual dinner plates. Drizzle the slices with the pan juices.

Two-In-One Poultry Rolls

Turkey-Stuffed Chicken Rolls*
Green Beans with Mushrooms
(see Tip, below)
Sliced Tomatoes
Chunky Apple Cake
(recipe, page 231)

Green Beans with Mushrooms

Place a steamer rack over 1 inch of boiling water in a medium-size saucepan. Add 1 pound of green beans, ends trimmed. Cover the saucepan and steam for 4 minutes. Add 8 ounces of mushrooms, sliced, and steam them for 2 to 3 minutes more. Transfer the beans and the mushrooms to a medium-size serving bowl. Combine 1 tablespoon of hot water with 2 teaspoons of Dijon-style mustard in a small bowl and pour the mixture over the vegetables. Add 1 tablespoon of butter and toss to coat the vegetables. Season with salt and pepper to taste.

❖　❖　❖

CHICKEN AND SPINACH IN TARRAGON SAUCE

A fabulous meal in one dish! Thaw the frozen spinach in the refrigerator during the day and drain it well before using.

LOW-CALORIE

Makes 4 servings.

Nutrient Value Per Serving: 346 calories, 28 g protein, 19 g fat, 17 g carbohydrate, 546 mg sodium, 98 mg cholesterol.

1 pound boned, skinless chicken thighs or breasts, sliced thinly across grain	1 clove garlic, finely chopped
6 tablespoons all-purpose flour	½ teaspoon dried tarragon, crumbled
3½ tablespoons vegetable oil	1½ cups chicken broth
1 medium-size onion, chopped (½ cup)	1 package (10 ounces) frozen leaf spinach, thawed and drained*
	2 teaspoons lemon juice

1. Combine the chicken slices with 3 tablespoons of the flour in a plastic bag and shake to coat the chicken.

2. Heat 2 tablespoons of the oil in a large, heavy skillet over medium-high heat until very hot. Add all the chicken and stir to separate the slices. Sauté, without turning or stirring, until the chicken is well browned, for about 3 minutes. Turn over the slices and cook for 1 minute, or just until the chicken is done. Transfer the chicken to a serving platter.

3. Add the remaining 1½ tablespoons of oil to the skillet. Add the onion and sauté until it is softened. Add the garlic and sauté for 30 seconds more. Stir in the remaining 3 tablespoons of flour. Stir in the tarragon and the broth until they are well combined. Cook, stirring constantly, until the mixture comes to boiling. Lower the heat and simmer for 2 to 3 minutes. Stir in the spinach and the chicken, and cook, stirring constantly, just until they are heated through.

4. Remove the skillet from the heat. Stir in the lemon juice. Serve immediately.

***Note:** You can use 1 pound of fresh spinach instead of frozen spinach, if you wish. Rinse, cook and drain fresh spinach before adding it to the skillet.*

Chicken Continental

Chicken and Spinach in Tarragon Sauce*
Buttered Noodles (see Tip, below)
Steamed Peas
Stewed Apples in Creamy Rum Sauce (recipe, page 224)

Buttered Noodles

Bring a large pot of lightly salted water to boiling. Add 8 ounces of egg noodles and return to boiling, stirring constantly. Cook until the noodles are al dente, tender but firm to the bite. Drain the noodles well and return them to the pot. Add 2 tablespoons of unsalted butter, ½ to 1 teaspoon of freshly ground pepper and ½ teaspoon of salt, and toss well. Serve immediately.

❖ ❀ ❖

Tarragon

An herbaceous perennial plant with slender, aromatic, dark green leaves, tarragon has an anise-like flavor. Native to Siberia, tarragon belongs to the composite (sunflower) plant family. There are two species; the French variety is widely cultivated.

■ Fresh, young leaves can be used in salads, or steeped in vinegar or salad dressing.

■ Fresh or dried leaves are delicious with chicken, eggs, fish and sauces.

❖ ❀ ❖

CLASSIC CHICKEN CURRY

LOW-CALORIE • LOW-CHOLESTEROL • LOW-FAT

Makes 4 servings.

Nutrient Value Per Serving: 236 calories, 31 g protein, 6 g fat, 13 g carbohydrate, 386 mg sodium, 68 mg cholesterol.

1	cup frozen peas (half 10-ounce package)	1/8	teaspoon ground hot red pepper
1	medium-size onion, chopped	5	whole cloves
1	tablespoon chopped, peeled fresh gingerroot	2	tablespoons all-purpose flour
1	tablespoon vegetable oil	1	cup chicken broth
1	clove garlic, finely chopped	1	pound boned, skinless chicken breasts, cut across grain into 1/4-inch slices
2	teaspoons curry powder		
1	teaspoon ground coriander	1/2	cup plain yogurt
1/2	teaspoon ground cumin		

1. Place the frozen peas in a small, heat-proof bowl and pour enough boiling water over the peas to cover them. Let the peas stand.

2. Sauté the onion and the ginger in the oil in a large skillet over medium heat until they are softened, for about 4 minutes. Add the garlic and cook for 1 minute. Stir in the curry powder, coriander, cumin, ground hot red pepper, cloves and flour. Cook, stirring, for 30 seconds. Stir in the broth and cook, stirring, until the mixture is thickened and bubbly. Reduce the heat and simmer for 5 minutes, stirring. Add the chicken. Simmer just until the chicken is cooked, for 2 to 3 minutes.

3. Combine 1/4 cup of the cooking liquid with the yogurt in a small bowl. Stir the yogurt mixture into the skillet. Add the drained peas to the skillet. Heat the curry to serving temperature.

Curry in a Hurry

Classic Chicken Curry*
Rice Pilaf
Sliced Papaya
Coconut Cream Pudding

Curry

By itself, the term refers to a highly spiced sauce or stew that originated in India. Curry also is the spice blend used to make the sauce or stew. The blend often is referred to as curry powder and is a combination of turmeric, (which gives curry its characteristic bright yellow color), fenugreek, cumin, cilantro, ginger and ground hot red pepper.

■ In the United States, curry is a commercially blended product whose taste varies from brand to brand; some brands are quite hot, others are more aromatic.

■ In India, the spices for a curry dish are blended just prior to use.

❖   ❖   ❖

Lusciously warming, Classic Chicken Curry will take the chill off the coldest winter's night.

MEXICAN TURKEY LOAF

LOW-CALORIE • MICROWAVE

Bake at 375° for 45 minutes; or microwave at full power for 7 minutes.
Makes 4 servings.

Nutrient Value Per Serving: 241 calories, 23 g protein, 13 g fat,
8 g carbohydrate, 435 mg sodium, 145 mg cholesterol.

1	pound raw ground turkey	3	tablespoons cornmeal
1	medium-size onion, finely chopped (½ cup)	1	egg, slightly beaten
1	clove garlic, finely chopped	2	teaspoons chili powder
		½	teaspoon salt
1	canned green chili pepper, finely chopped (about 2 tablespoons)	¼	teaspoon dried oregano, crumbled
		⅛	teaspoon freshly ground pepper

Mid-Week Fiesta

Mexican Turkey Loaf*
Stewed Tomatoes and Corn
(recipe, page 115)
Cannellini Beans
Tossed Green Salad
Lemon Pudding

Try spicing an old favorite south-of-the-border style: Mexican Turkey Loaf with Stewed Tomatoes and Corn.

1. Preheat the oven to moderate (375°). Lightly grease a baking pan.
2. Mix together the turkey, onion, garlic, chili pepper, cornmeal, egg, chili powder, salt, oregano and pepper in a medium-size bowl. Shape the mixture into a loaf about 7 inches long. Place the loaf in the prepared pan.
3. Bake the loaf in the preheated moderate oven (375°) for 45 minutes. Let the loaf stand for 5 minutes before slicing it.

Microwave Instructions
(for a 650-watt variable power microwave oven)

Ingredient Changes: Add paprika to sprinkle on top of the loaves.
Directions: Mix together the ingredients as in Step 2 above. Shape the mixture into 4 equal-size balls, each about 3 inches in diameter. Space the balls evenly in a microwave-safe 10-inch pie plate. Sprinkle the tops with the paprika. Cover the balls loosely with wax paper. Microwave at full power for 7 minutes, rotating the plate one quarter turn after 4 minutes. Let the balls stand for 2 minutes.

TURKEY STOCK

A great way to use the remainder of the big bird. This hearty stock can be used in a variety of dishes, including Turkey Minestrone (recipe, page 18). Freeze extra stock to use later in soups, stews and casseroles.

LOW-CALORIE • LOW-CHOLESTEROL • LOW-SODIUM

Makes about 2 quarts.

Nutrient Value Per Cup: 48 calories, 1 g protein, 2 g fat, 7 g carbohydrate, 9 mg sodium, 0 mg cholesterol.

1	turkey carcass with some meat left on	1	large sprig parsley
4	quarts water	1	bay leaf
2	carrots, sliced	2	teaspoons dried basil, crumbled
2	celery stalks, sliced	1	teaspoon dried thyme, crumbled
1	medium-size onion, sliced		
1	large clove garlic, sliced		

1. Using a cleaver or large knife, cut slashes in the turkey carcass, or cut the carcass into pieces. Place the carcass in a large kettle or Dutch oven.
2. Add the water, carrot, celery, onion, garlic, parsley, bay leaf, basil and thyme. Bring the mixture to boiling over high heat. Reduce the heat to low. Simmer the stock, partially covered, for 3 to 4 hours, skimming and discarding any foam from the surface as it forms.
3. Cool the stock slightly, and carefully strain it through a colander lined with a double thickness of dampened cheese cloth. Discard the solids. Chill the stock and, if you wish, remove the fat from the top. Freeze extra stock in plastic freezer bags. Or fill ice cube trays with extra stock, transfer the frozen cubes to freezer bags and store the stock cubes in the freezer.

TURKEY MINESTRONE

*You can use just about any vegetables, leftover or fresh, in this hearty soup.
And any variety of pasta will do just fine.*

Makes 8 servings (about 2 quarts).

Nutrient Value Per Serving: 160 calories, 10 g protein, 5 g fat,
22 g carbohydrate, 443 mg sodium, 16 mg cholesterol.

1	medium-size onion chopped (½ cup)	4	cups Turkey Stock (recipe, page 17)
1	tablespoon olive oil	1	bay leaf
1	clove garlic, finely chopped	¼	teaspoon dried basil, crumbled
1	celery stalk, cut into ¼-inch pieces	¼	teaspoon dried oregano, crumbled
1	carrot, thickly sliced	1	teaspoon salt
2	cups cooked vegetables, such as cut green beans, corn and/or peas	¼	teaspoon freshly ground pepper
		1	cup diced cooked turkey
1	can (16 ounces) whole tomatoes, undrained and cut up	1	small zucchini, cut into ¼-inch-thick slices
½	cup small elbow macaroni	4	tablespoons grated Parmesan cheese

Pizza Party

Turkey Minestrone*
Sweet Pepper Pizza
(recipe, page 35)
Sliced Poundcake with
Strawberries in Syrup

Make a Note of That!

*As soon as you run out of a
stock item, jot it down on a
list you keep handy in the
kitchen. Your brain power
should be used for more
important things than trying
to remember whether you
need to buy flour or canned
chicken broth.*

A heart-warming meal your
family will love, any night of the
week: Turkey Minestrone and
Sweet Pepper Pizza.

1. Sauté the onion in the oil in a large saucepan over medium heat until the onion is softened, for about 3 minutes. Add the garlic and cook for 30 seconds more. Add the celery and the carrot and sauté for 1 minute more. Add the cooked vegetables, the tomatoes with their liquid, macaroni, Turkey Stock, bay leaf, basil, oregano, salt and pepper. Bring the mixture to boiling, reduce the heat to low and cook for 5 minutes. Add the turkey and the zucchini. Cook just until the zucchini and the macaroni are tender, for about 3 to 5 minutes.
2. To serve, ladle the minestrone into individual soup plates. Sprinkle the minestrone with the Parmesan cheese.

TURKEY AND APPLES IN BRANDY CREAM SAUCE

Easy and elegant, this dish is a one-skillet wonder.

LOW-CALORIE • LOW-FAT

Makes 4 servings.

Nutrient Value Per Serving: 277 calories, 28 g protein, 10 g fat, 17 g carbohydrate, 344 mg sodium, 77 mg cholesterol.

1	pound turkey breast cutlets (about 4 large)	½	cup chicken broth
3	tablespoons all-purpose flour	¼	cup apple-flavored brandy
2	tablespoons olive oil	¼	cup dairy sour cream
1	large green apple, peeled, cored, cut into 8 rings	¼	teaspoon salt
1	cup sliced green onions	⅛	teaspoon freshly ground pepper
1	clove garlic, chopped	⅛	teaspoon ground nutmeg
			Apple wedges, for garnish (optional)

1. Combine the turkey cutlets with the flour in a plastic bag and shake to coat the turkey.
2. Heat the oil in a large, heavy skillet over medium-high heat. Pat off excess flour from the turkey. Working in batches, if necessary, add the cutlets to the skillet and cook for 2 to 3 minutes, or until each underside is golden brown. Turn the turkey with tongs. Reduce the heat to low and cook for 2 minutes more. Transfer the turkey to a warmed plate and cover the plate with aluminum foil.
3. Add the apple rings, green onion, garlic, broth and brandy to the skillet. Cover the skillet and cook the mixture over medium heat for 5 minutes, or until the apple rings are tender.
4. Remove the skillet from the heat. Stir in the sour cream, salt, pepper and nutmeg. Add the turkey and heat through, if necessary.
5. Divide the turkey and sauce evenly among 4 individual dinner plates. Garnish with apple wedges, if you wish.

Elegant Turkey Dinner

Turkey and Apples in Brandy Cream Sauce*

Brussels Sprouts and Carrot Curls

Poached Pears in Raspberry Purée

Brandy: A Fine Wine

Brandy is made by distilling wine and aging it. Besides grapes, other fruits — apples, peaches, pears, plums, cherries, blackberries — can be mashed and fermented to make brandy, but these brandies must be labeled as such.

■ The variations in aroma, taste and other characteristics of brandies result from the type of wine used, the distilling procedure and the type of wood casks in which the brandy is aged.

■ Brandies of different ages are blended. "Three-Star" indicates a blend of brandies with about five years of aging but not less than two years. "V.S.O.P." (Very Superior Old Pale), is a blend of brandies aged at least four years and up to ten years.

COTTAGE PIE

This casserole is a great way to use holiday leftovers, but it is wonderful made from scratch, too. You can vary the ingredients to suit your family's tastes, and to include the leftovers you happen to have on hand.

LOW-CHOLESTEROL

Bake at 400° for 35 to 40 minutes.
Makes 4 servings.

Nutrient Value Per Serving: 505 calories, 28 g protein, 21 g fat, 57 g carbohydrate, 1,356 mg sodium, 62 mg cholesterol.

1 medium-size onion, chopped (½ cup)	2 cups diced turkey
1 tablespoon vegetable oil	2 cups diced mixed vegetables, such as carrots, corn, green beans and/or peas
1 clove garlic, finely chopped	
1 tablespoon all-purpose flour	½ teaspoon salt
1 teaspoon rubbed sage	⅛ teaspoon freshly ground pepper
1 can (8 ounces) whole tomatoes, drained	4 cups mashed potatoes
¾ cup turkey gravy (see Tip, at right)	¼ teaspoon ground nutmeg
	Cranberry sauce (optional)

1. Place the oven rack in the top third of the oven. Preheat the oven to hot (400°).

2. Sauté the onion in the oil in a medium-size, heavy skillet over medium heat until the onion is softened, for about 3 minutes. Add the garlic and cook for 30 seconds more. Stir in the flour and the sage, and cook for 30 seconds. Add the tomatoes, gravy, turkey and vegetables. Bring the mixture to boiling. Remove the skillet from the heat. Add the salt and the pepper. Turn the filling into an 8 x 8 x 2-inch baking dish and set aside.

Country Supper

Cottage Pie*
Whole Cranberry Sauce
Rainbow Salad with Mustard
Lemon Dressing
(recipe, page 118)
Peach Halves with Cinnamon

Turkey Gravy

If a recipe calls for turkey gravy and you don't have any on hand, try the following recipe: Melt 1 tablespoon of butter in a small saucepan over medium heat. Whisk in 1 tablespoon of flour and cook, stirring constantly, for 1 minute. Gradually whisk in ¾ cup of chicken broth and cook, stirring constantly, for 3 to 5 minutes, or until the gravy has thickened. Stir in 2 to 3 drops of browning-and-seasoning sauce, or enough to achieve the desired color.

❖ ❖ ❖

A classic recipe, Cottage Pie is an ideal way to create something wonderful out of ordinary "leftovers".

3. Beat together the potatoes and the nutmeg in a medium-size bowl. Spoon the potato topping over the filling in the baking dish, smoothing and making decorative swirls on the topping with the back of a spoon. Place the baking dish on a baking sheet to catch any spillovers.

4. Bake the casserole in the preheated hot oven (400°) until the top is golden brown, for 35 to 40 minutes. Cool the casserole for 15 minutes before serving it. Serve with cranberry sauce, if you wish.

TURKEY TAMALE PIE

This pie will be soft and spoonable if it is served immediately. If it is made ahead, the pie will set and can be cut into wedges.

LOW-CALORIE • LOW-CHOLESTEROL

Makes 4 servings.

Nutrient Value Per Serving: 346 calories, 19 g protein, 16 g fat, 33 g carbohydrate, 869 mg sodium, 54 mg cholesterol.

½ cup yellow cornmeal	½ teaspoon dried oregano, crumbled
½ cup chicken broth	½ teaspoon ground cumin
⅓ cup plain lowfat yogurt	⅛ teaspoon freshly ground pepper
½ teaspoon salt	
1 medium-size onion, finely chopped (½ cup)	1 can (14½ ounces) whole tomatoes, undrained
1 teaspoon vegetable oil	1 cup frozen corn kernels
1 clove garlic, finely chopped	½ cup sliced pitted ripe olives
8 ounces ground turkey	½ cup (2 ounces) shredded medium-sharp Cheddar cheese
1 tablespoon chili powder	

1. Combine the cornmeal, broth, yogurt and ¼ teaspoon of the salt in a small bowl. Set aside the yogurt mixture.

2. Sauté the onion in the oil in a medium-size, nonstick skillet over medium heat, stirring occasionally, for 3 to 4 minutes. Add the garlic and cook for 30 seconds more. Crumble the turkey into the skillet. Sprinkle with the chili powder, oregano, cumin, pepper and remaining ¼ teaspoon of salt. Cook, stirring, until the meat no longer is pink, for 2 to 3 minutes.

3. Add the tomatoes with their liquid, crushing them with a wooden spoon. Add the corn and bring the turkey mixture to boiling. Lower the heat to simmer. Pour two thirds of the yogurt mixture into the simmering turkey mixture. Stir the combined mixture and simmer for 3 minutes. Smooth the top of the mixture and scatter ¼ cup of the olives over it. Drizzle the remaining yogurt mixture over and sprinkle with the Cheddar cheese. Cover the skillet and simmer the mixture over very low heat, without stirring, for 15 to 20 minutes, or until it is set. Sprinkle the remaining olives over the top.

4. Remove the skillet from the heat and let the pie stand, covered, for 10 minutes. Serve the pie hot, or let it cool completely and cut it into 8 wedges.

Easy-as-Pie Turkey Dinner

Turkey Tamale Pie*
Romaine Salad with Creamy Avocado Dressing
(recipe, page 121)
Banana Pudding
(recipe, page 228)

Tamale: Savory or Sweet

A Mexican specialty, a tamale is made by spreading masa (the corn dough used for making tortillas) on a corn husk, wrapping this around a savory or sweet filling and steaming it.

• Savory fillings include red chili and meat, green chili and cheese, cracklings, pork, poultry and beans.

• Sweet fillings include fruits and nuts, raisins and sweetened cinnamon-spiced beans. Sweet tamales are eaten as snacks, for breakfast and as desserts.

• Making tamales involves a number of steps. That's why tamales are considered party or special holiday fare.

❖ ❖ ❖

BEEF & PORK

From good and hearty casseroles to light and delicious stir-fries, these are the recipes for the meat-lovers in your family.

STEAK AND POTATO BROIL

LOW-CHOLESTEROL

Broil for 8 minutes for medium-rare.
Makes 4 servings.

Nutrient Value Per Serving: 516 calories, 25 g protein, 32 g fat, 32 g carbohydrate, 372 mg sodium, 60 mg cholesterol.

⅓ cup vegetable oil
3 tablespoons distilled white vinegar
¼ cup chopped parsley
1 teaspoon prepared mustard
½ teaspoon salt
½ teaspoon freshly ground pepper
½ teaspoon paprika
1 clove garlic, finely chopped
1 flank steak (1 pound)
4 medium-size potatoes, cooked (1½ pounds)

All-American Night

Steak and Potato Broil*
Steamed Peas
Confetti Slaw (recipe, page 119)
Oatmeal Nut Squares
(recipe, page 246)

A stick-to-your-ribs meal! After marinating, Steak and Potato Broil is ready in minutes.

1. Combine the oil, vinegar, parsley, mustard, salt, pepper, paprika and garlic in a small bowl, and mix the ingredients well. Place the steak in a shallow glass dish and pour the marinade over it. Cover the dish and refrigerate the steak for about 8 hours.
2. Preheat the broiler.
3. Lift the steak out of the marinade and place it on the rack in the broiler pan. Quarter the potatoes and roll them in the marinade. Place the potatoes around the steak.
4. Broil the steak and potatoes 3 inches from the heat source, turning once, for 8 minutes for medium-rare steak.
5. To serve, place the steak and potatoes on a cutting board. Slice the steak across the grain into thin slices.

BEEF AND BEAN BURRITOS

Refried beans vary in quality and consistency. If you start with a thicker consistency, thin with water or broth to the consistency of applesauce.

Makes 4 servings.

Nutrient Value Per Serving: 651 calories, 33 g protein, 24 g fat, 73 g carbohydrate, 1,231 mg sodium, 79 mg cholesterol.

1	**can (16 ounces) refried beans**	1	**clove garlic, finely chopped**
¾	**teaspoon ground cumin**	¼	**teaspoon salt**
¾	**teaspoon dried oregano, crumbled**	¼	**teaspoon freshly ground pepper**
2	**ounces shredded medium-sharp Cheddar cheese (½ cup)**	8	**fresh flour tortillas (7-inch diameter)**
12	**ounces lean ground beef**	½	**cup canned tomato sauce**
1	**medium-size onion, chopped (½ cup)**		**Liquid red pepper seasoning**

1. Spoon the refried beans into a small, heavy saucepan. If they are thick, add about 1 tablespoon of water. Add ¼ teaspoon each of the cumin and the oregano. Heat the refried beans over medium heat, stirring frequently, until they are hot. Stir in ¼ cup of the Cheddar cheese.
2. Heat a medium-size heavy skillet over medium heat. Crumble the beef into the skillet. Add the onion, garlic and remaining ½ teaspoon each of cumin and oregano. Cook the mixture over medium heat, stirring frequently, until the beef is cooked through, for about 4 minutes. Stir in the salt and the pepper.
3. Heat a griddle or large, heavy skillet over medium heat. Add the tortillas, 2 or 3 at a time, and warm them, turning them frequently and sprinkling with water to freshen them if dry, until they are soft and pliable.
4. Spread ¼ cup of the refried beans mixture over a tortilla, leaving a border around the edge. Spread ¼ to ⅓ cup of the beef filling on the tortilla in a line slightly off center. Spoon on 1½ tablespoons of the Cheddar cheese, 1 tablespoon of the tomato sauce and the liquid red pepper seasoning, to taste (a few drops will be enough). Fold one side of the tortilla over the beef filling, fold in the two ends and roll over the tortilla to enclose the filling. Place the tortilla, seam side down, on a serving platter. Repeat with the remaining ingredients to make a total of 8 burritos. Serve the burritos hot.

Burritos Ole!

Beef and Bean Burritos*
Avocados in Vinaigrette
Buttered Corn Wheels
Mango Lime Mousse
(recipe, page 253)

Beef

Beef provides complete protein, with 8 essential amino acids, to your diet. It also is a good source of iron and zinc.

■ Fresh beef should be bright to deep red in color. When first cut, beef is dark purplish-red. When exposed to air, the cut surfaces turn bright red due to an oxygen reaction.

■ Store beef in the coldest part of the refrigerator, or in a meat storage drawer. Prepackaged meat can be stored as purchased in the refrigerator for 2 days, or in the freezer for up to 2 weeks. For longer freezer storage, be sure to overwrap prepackaged beef with freezer-safe wrap.

❖ ❖ ❖

CORNED BEEF AND CABBAGE SKILLET

All the wonderful flavors of Ireland in one simple dish — the perfect meal to warm a winter's night.

Makes 4 servings.

Nutrient Value Per Serving: 363 calories, 25 g protein, 17 g fat, 27 g carbohydrate, 960 mg sodium, 80 mg cholesterol.

4	medium-size potatoes (1¼ pounds), peeled and cut into ½-inch cubes
2	tablespoons vegetable oil
1	large onion, coarsely chopped (1 cup)
12	ounces cabbage, coarsely shredded (5 cups)
1	can (12 ounces) corned beef, crumbled
½	teaspoon caraway seeds
½	teaspoon freshly ground pepper
¼	teaspoon salt

Luck O' the Irish

Corned Beef and Cabbage Skillet*
Thymed Carrots and Celery (recipe, page 92)
Soda Bread
Ice Cream

Cabbage

A versatile and inexpensive vegetable, cabbage is available year-round. It is a cousin of broccoli, cauliflower, Brussels sprouts and collards. Cabbage is an excellent source of vitamin C, is full of dietary fiber and has only 20 calories per 3½-ounce cooked serving.

■ A variety of cabbage was eaten by the ancient Romans and Greeks, and the Chinese and Koreans have cultivated the vegetable for centuries. Its origin has been traced to a wild species that grows in the eastern Mediterranean and western Asian areas.

■ Cabbage can be eaten fresh or cooked. It also can be preserved by pickling or salting. Sauerkraut is the most popular form of preserved cabbage.

✦   ✧   ✦

A new variation on an old favorite, all in one skillet: Corned Beef and Cabbage. And the perfect accompaniment? Thymed Carrots and Celery.

1. Sauté the potatoes in the oil in a large, nonstick skillet over medium heat, stirring often, until the potatoes are tender and lightly browned, for about 10 minutes. Add the onion and sauté for 1 minute more.

2. Add the cabbage, corned beef, caraway seeds, pepper and salt, and mix all the ingredients well. Lower the heat, cover the skillet and cook for 12 to 15 minutes, or until the mixture is hot and lightly browned on the bottom.

3. To serve, cover the skillet with a large serving plate and flip the corned beef and cabbage onto the plate.

MEXICAN-STYLE MACARONI AND CHEESE

A combination of cumin, chili powder and hot red pepper adds an authentic south-of-the-border kick to plain old macaroni and cheese.

Makes 4 servings.

Nutrient Value Per Serving: 613 calories, 30 g protein, 31 g fat, 52 g carbohydrate, 837 mg sodium, 94 mg cholesterol.

6 ounces elbow macaroni	1 can (28 ounces) whole tomatoes in thick purée
1 tablespoon olive oil plus a splash	1 teaspoon sugar
1 large onion, peeled and cut into 1-inch cubes (1½ cups)	½ teaspoon salt
	¼ teaspoon freshly ground pepper
2 large cloves garlic, finely chopped	⅛ teaspoon ground hot red pepper
1½ teaspoons chili powder	4 ounces shredded medium-sharp Cheddar cheese (1 cup)
1¼ teaspoons ground cumin	
¼ teaspoon ground cinnamon	¼ cup chopped parsley
12 ounces lean ground beef	

1. Cook the macaroni in a large pot of boiling salted water, following the package directions. Drain the macaroni. Return the macaroni to the pot and toss it with the splash of oil to lightly coat it.

2. Meanwhile, sauté the onion in the 1 tablespoon of oil in a large skillet over medium heat, stirring frequently, until the onion is softened, for about 6 minutes. Add the garlic and sauté for 30 seconds.

3. Stir in the chili powder, cumin and cinnamon, and cook for 30 seconds. Add the beef and cook, stirring to break up the meat, for about 4 minutes, or until the beef no longer is pink. Add the tomatoes with their purée, the sugar, salt, pepper and ground hot red pepper. Bring the mixture to boiling, breaking up the tomatoes with a spoon. Lower the heat and simmer for 15 to 20 minutes, or until the mixture is slightly thickened and the flavors have blended well.

4. Stir in the cooked macaroni, tossing to coat it. Cook just until the macaroni is heated through. Stir in the Cheddar cheese and the parsley. Serve the macaroni immediately.

Mexican Macaroni

Romaine Salad with Creamy Avocado Dressing (recipe, page 121)

Mexican-Style Macaroni and Cheese*

Chocolate Granita (recipe, page 251)

La Comida de Mexico

"Mexican food" is a blend of many culture's cuisines: The Mayans and Aztecs based their dishes on corn, beans, squash and chili peppers. The Spanish brought rice, olives, beef, pork and almonds. Seafood, from the Gulf of Mexico and the Pacific, as well as native foods such as turkey, avocado, tomato and pumpkin, added even more variety to the melting-pot cuisine of Mexico.

■ Dishes from the American Southwest are adaptations of classic Mexican dishes, and represent a very small portion of authentic Mexican cooking.

■ Tacos, enchiladas and tamales, staples of Tex-Mex cuisine, are called antojitos, or "little whims," in Mexico.

❖ ❖ ❖

THAI-STYLE KEBABS

LOW-CALORIE • LOW-CHOLESTEROL

Broil for 6 to 8 minutes.
Makes 4 servings.

Nutrient Value Per Serving: 235 calories, 25 g protein, 11 g fat, 10 g carbohydrate, 236 mg sodium, 62 mg cholesterol.

1 pound trimmed, lean, boneless beef sirloin, cut into 1-inch cubes	18 small mushrooms (8 ounces)
½ cup dry white wine	2 tablespoons chunky-style peanut butter
2 tablespoons lemon juice	1 clove garlic, finely chopped
1 teaspoon dried basil, crumbled	1 tablespoon reduced-sodium soy sauce
2 small sweet red peppers (5 to 6 ounces each), cored, seeded and cut into eighths	1 teaspoon sugar

1. Combine the beef cubes, wine, lemon juice and basil in a self-sealing plastic bag, and seal the bag. Marinate the beef in the refrigerator for 12 hours, or overnight.
2. Preheat the broiler. Drain the beef, reserving the marinade. Thread the beef, red peppers and mushrooms alternately on six 12-inch skewers that have been soaked in cold water. Arrange the skewers on the broiler pan.
3. Broil the kebabs 4 inches from the heat source, turning once, for 6 to 8 minutes for medium-rare.
4. Combine the peanut butter, garlic, soy sauce, sugar and the reserved marinade in a small saucepan. Stir in any drippings from the kebabs. Bring the mixture to boiling over medium heat. Pour the sauce over the kebabs.

TOSTADA PIE

Bake at 450° for 15 minutes.
Makes 4 servings.

Nutrient Value Per Serving: 521 calories, 26 g protein, 34 g fat, 28 g carbohydrate, 994 mg sodium, 94 mg cholesterol.

12 ounces lean ground beef	1 can (16 ounces) whole tomatoes, in thick purée
1 cup chopped onion (1 large onion)	1 can (4 ounces) diced green chili peppers, undrained
1 clove garlic, finely chopped	8 tostada shells, quartered
½ teaspoon ground cumin	1 can (16 ounces) pinto beans, rinsed and drained
½ teaspoon dried oregano, crumbled	1 cup shredded Cheddar cheese (4 ounces)
½ teaspoon salt	Lime slices, for garnish (optional)
⅛ teaspoon freshly ground pepper	Parsley sprigs, for garnish (optional)
2 tablespoons all-purpose flour	

Exotic Kebobs

Thai-Style Kebobs*
Orzo with Parsley
(see Tip, below)
Broccoli with Water Chestnuts
Mandarin Orange Slices

Orzo with Parsley

Bring a large pot of water to boiling. Add 8 ounces of orzo (1¼ cups) and return to boiling, stirring constantly. Cook, stirring often, for 8 to 10 minutes, or until the orzo is tender but firm to the bite. Drain the orzo and return it to the pot. Stir in 1 tablespoon of vegetable oil, 3 tablespoons of chopped parsley and ½ teaspoon of salt.

❖ ❖ ❖

Tex-Mex Pie

Sliced Avocado with Vinaigrette
Tostada Pie*
Zucchini, Corn and Pepper Sauté
(recipe, page 105)
Poundcake with Diced Mango

1. Place the rack in the top third of the oven; preheat to very hot (450°).
2. Crumble the beef into a large, heavy skillet over medium-high heat. Add the onion and the garlic, and cook for 5 to 8 minutes, or until the beef no longer is pink. Drain off the fat. Add the cumin, oregano, salt, pepper and flour. Cook, stirring, over medium heat for 1 minute. Add the tomatoes with their purée and the chili peppers with their liquid, breaking up the tomatoes. Cook for 3 minutes, or until the filling has thickened.
3. Arrange half the tostada shells in an 8-inch square nonaluminum baking dish. Layer on half the pinto beans, half the beef mixture and half the Cheddar cheese. Repeat with the remaining ingredients.
4. Bake the pie in the preheated very hot oven (450°) for 15 minutes, or until it is heated through. Garnish with lime slices and parsley sprigs.

BLUE CHEESE BURGERS

Makes 4 servings.

Nutrient Value Per Serving: 485 calories, 33 g protein, 29 g fat, 22 g carbohydrate, 578 mg sodium, 104 mg cholesterol.

1¼ pounds lean ground beef	4 hamburger buns
3 ounces blue cheese, crumbled	Additional blue cheese, crumbled, for garnish
1 teaspoon vegetable oil	Onion slices, for garnish

1. Divide the beef into 8 equal portions. Pat each portion into a 4½- to 5-inch patty. Sprinkle the blue cheese evenly on 4 of the patties, leaving a ½-inch border. Top each with a plain patty and pinch the edges together to seal. Shape each into a single 4-inch patty.
2. Heat a large, heavy skillet over medium-high heat. Lightly coat the skillet with the oil. Add the burgers and cook until the undersides are browned, for about 2 minutes. Turn and cook the burgers for 2 minutes more. Do not overcook. Serve the burgers on the buns with the additional crumbled blue cheese and onion slices.

Burgers Supreme

Blue Cheese Burgers*
Mashed Potatoes
Sweet and Sour Cabbage and
Carrots (recipe, page 93)
Chocolate Cake

Blue Cheese

Probably the best-known variety of blue-veined cheese is French Roquefort. This cheese is cured from sheep's milk, and made exclusively in the caverns of Roquefort. Other French blue cheeses are made from cow's milk, or a mixture of cow's, sheep's and goat's milk.

Surprise your family by serving Blue Cheese Burgers with Sweet and Sour Cabbage and Carrots.

FLANK STEAK SALAD

LOW-CALORIE • LOW-CHOLESTEROL

Makes 4 servings.

Nutrient Value Per Serving: 341 calories, 25 g protein, 23 g fat, 8 g carbohydrate, 234 mg sodium, 69 mg cholesterol.

Dressing:

½	**cup plain lowfat yogurt**
½	**cup dairy sour cream**
2	**tablespoons reduced-calorie mayonnaise**
½	**teaspoon dried basil, crumbled**
½	**teaspoon dried oregano, crumbled**
¼	**teaspoon ground cumin (optional)**
1	**flank steak (1 pound)**
1	**tablespoon olive oil**

1	**clove garlic, finely chopped**
3	**medium-size tomatoes (12 ounces), cut into ½-inch dice**
1	**cup thinly sliced green onions (8 medium-size green onions)**
¼	**cup chopped parsley**
⅛	**teaspoon salt**
⅛	**teaspoon freshly ground pepper**
4	**romaine lettuce leaves**

1. Prepare the Dressing: Combine the yogurt, sour cream, mayonnaise, basil, oregano and, if you wish, cumin in a small bowl, and stir to blend the ingredients. Cover the bowl and refrigerate the dressing until serving time.
2. Cut the flank steak in half lengthwise and then cut it across the grain into ⅛-inch slices. Heat half the oil in a large, heavy skillet over medium-high heat. Add half the steak slices and half the garlic. Stir-fry for about 2 minutes, or until the steak no longer is pink. Remove the steak and garlic with a slotted spoon. Repeat with the remaining oil, steak and garlic. Return all the steak and garlic to the skillet and remove the skillet from the heat. Stir in the tomatoes, green onion, parsley, salt and pepper.
3. Place a romaine lettuce leaf on each of 4 individual dinner plates. Top each with one fourth of the warm salad. Serve with the dressing.

BROILED PORK CHOPS

Broil for 10 to 12 minutes.
Makes 4 servings.

Nutrient Value Per Serving: 446 calories, 37 g protein, 29 g fat, 8 g carbohydrate, 436 mg sodium, 127 mg cholesterol.

8	**thin pork chops (2 pounds)**
1	**can (8 ounces) tomato sauce**
1	**tablespoon plus 1 teaspoon cider vinegar**

1	**tablespoon plus ½ teaspoon light brown sugar**
¼	**teaspoon ground ginger**
⅛	**teaspoon ground hot red pepper**

1. Preheat the broiler. Place the chops on the broiler rack in a single layer.
2. Combine the tomato sauce, vinegar, brown sugar, ginger and ground hot red pepper in a small bowl, and stir well. Spread the sauce over the chops.
3. Broil the chops 6 inches from the heat source, without turning, until they are cooked through, for 10 to 12 minutes. Check the chops after 6 minutes and reverse the position of the broiler pan, if necessary; do not turn over the chops. Serve the chops immediately.

Stir-Fry Salad

Flank Steak Salad*
Sautéed Corn and Sweet Peppers
(recipe, page 93)
Honeydew Wedges

Pound Per Pound

To save time and money, buy meat and poultry in quantity when the price is right and the meat looks good; then overwrap it in freezer-safe aluminum foil, date the package and freeze it. (Keep track of the "regular" prices so you can tell if you're really getting a bargain or not.)

❖   ❖   ❖

Pork Chops Pronto

Broiled Pork Chops*
Apple and Potato Mash
(recipe, page 106)
Tossed Green Salad
Rainbow Sherbet

GLAZED PORK CHOPS AND APPLES

These tasty chops and apple slices are glazed with concentrated apple juice.

Makes 4 servings.

Nutrient Value Per Serving: 725 calories, 26 g protein, 44 g fat, 58 g carbohydrate, 1,054 mg sodium, 127 mg cholesterol.

4 **thin pork chops, each about ½ inch thick (1¼ pounds)**	2 **teaspoons Dijon-style mustard**
2 **teaspoons vegetable oil**	½ **teaspoon salt**
2 **large Granny Smith apples**	⅛ **teaspoon freshly ground pepper**
1 **can (6 ounces) frozen unsweetened apple juice concentrate**	2 **cups stuffing, prepared according to package directions**

1. Brown the pork chops in the oil in a medium-size skillet over medium heat, turning occasionally, for 8 to 10 minutes. Transfer the chops to a warmed plate.

2. Peel, core and cut the apples crosswise into about ¼ inch thick rings. Add the rings to the skillet and cook for 2 to 3 minutes, or until the rings are lightly browned. Add the apple juice concentrate and bring it to boiling. Stir in the mustard, salt and pepper. Remove the skillet from the heat.

3. Spoon about ½ cup of the stuffing onto each of 4 individual dinner plates. Top with a pork chop. Serve with the glazed apple slices, and spoon extra glaze over the chops.

The mellow flavor of autumn's star fruit makes Glazed Pork Chops and Apples a favorite for cool weather dining.

29

STIR-FRIED PORK AND VEGETABLES

Makes 4 servings.

Nutrient Value Per Serving: 449 calories, 24 g protein, 32 g fat, 17 g carbohydrate, 627 mg sodium, 79 mg cholesterol.

2	tablespoons reduced-sodium soy sauce	2	tablespoons vegetable oil
2	tablespoons chili sauce	2	medium-size onions, cut into wedges
1	tablespoon rice wine vinegar	1	medium-size carrot, cut into julienne sticks
2	teaspoons cornstarch	½	sweet red pepper, cored, seeded and cut into thin strips
½	cup chicken broth		
2	teaspoons sugar		
¼	teaspoon freshly ground pepper	1	large clove garlic, finely chopped
1	pound boneless pork, cut into strips about 2 x ¼ x ¼ inches	¾	pound cabbage, coarsely chopped

1. Combine the soy sauce, chili sauce, vinegar and cornstarch in a small bowl. Stir in the broth, sugar and pepper. Set aside the soy mixture.
2. Stir-fry the pork in 1 tablespoon of the oil in a large skillet until the pork is browned on all sides. Remove the pork from the skillet with a slotted spoon and set it aside.
3. Add the remaining tablespoon of oil to the skillet. Add the onion, carrot, red pepper and garlic, and stir-fry for 2 minutes. Add the cabbage and stir-fry for 2 minutes. Add the pork. Stir the soy mixture and add it to the skillet. Stir-fry until the mixture thickens and boils. Serve immediately.

SICILIAN RAGOÛT

Makes 4 servings.

Nutrient Value Per Serving: 444 calories, 21 g protein, 29 g fat, 26 g carbohydrate, 635 mg sodium, 141 mg cholesterol.

12	ounces lean ground beef	1	tablespoon olive oil
½	cup soft bread crumbs	1	can (16 ounces) whole tomatoes, undrained
¾	teaspoon fennel seeds, crushed	1	tablespoon all-purpose flour
¼	teaspoon salt		
¼	teaspoon freshly ground pepper	1	can (10 ounces) garbanzo beans, drained
1	egg, slightly beaten		

1. Using your fingers, mix together the beef, bread crumbs, ½ teaspoon of the fennel seeds, the salt, pepper and egg in a medium-size bowl. Shape the mixture into walnut-size balls.
2. Heat the oil in a Dutch oven or large skillet. Add the meatballs and brown them on all sides.
3. Pour off 3 tablespoons of the tomato liquid from the can and reserve it. Break up the tomatoes and add them to the pot along with the remaining tomato liquid and the remaining ¼ teaspoon of fennel seeds. Bring the mixture to boiling. Lower the heat, cover the pot and simmer for 15 minutes.

Pork Medley

Stir-Fried Pork and Vegetables*
Hot Cooked Rice
Steamed Broccoli
Poached Pears with Ginger
(recipe, page 228)

Big Batch

When cooking rice, prepare an extra-large batch and store the leftover rice in the freezer in freezer-safe storage bags, two servings to a bag. The next time you want to serve rice, pull the needed number of bags out of the freezer and heat them in a steamer basket over boiling water.

❖　❖　❖

Mediterranean Feast

Sicilian Ragoût*
Couscous
Tossed Green Salad
Orange Wedges with Coconut

4. Stir together the reserved tomato liquid and the flour in a small bowl until the mixture is smooth. Stir the flour mixture into the pot. Cook, stirring constantly, until the combined mixture thickens and boils. Stir in the garbanzo beans. Heat the ragoût to serving temperature.

SESAME NOODLES WITH PORK AND VEGETABLES

Colorful fresh vegetables team up with the exotic flavors of the Orient in this wonderfully-textured main dish.

LOW-FAT

Makes 4 servings (about 2 quarts).

Nutrient Value Per Serving: 402 calories, 23 g protein, 11 g fat, 52 g carbohydrate, 572 mg sodium, 89 mg cholesterol.

A Loving Touch

With busy schedules that have your whole family off and running at a moment's notice, it's easy to lose touch with one another. Designate dinner as "family time." It doesn't have to take an entire evening—even half an hour can allow everyone their moment in the spotlight, to keep the rest of the crowd up on current events in the family. To make this time more festive, buy a bunch of daisies, light some candles and set out pretty place mats.

These small touches can mean a lot to your loved ones.

8 ounces medium-wide egg noodles
1 teaspoon Oriental sesame oil
3 teaspoons vegetable oil
8 ounces trimmed, lean, boneless pork loin, sliced thinly and cut into ¼-inch strips
1 large onion (6 ounces), peeled and cut into ¼-inch wedges
1 medium-size sweet red pepper, trimmed and cut into ¼-inch strips
1 tablespoon finely chopped or grated peeled fresh gingerroot
1 clove garlic, finely chopped
1 teaspoon curry powder
3 small zucchini (5 ounces each), sliced ¼ inch thick
1½ cups chicken broth
1 tablespoon cornstarch
1 tablespoon reduced-sodium soy sauce
4 large green onions, sliced (½ cup)

1. Bring a large pot of lightly salted water to boiling (prepare the other ingredients while waiting). Cook the noodles in the boiling water, following the package directions. Drain the noodles and return them to the pot. Stir in the Oriental sesame oil. Cover the pot.
2. Heat 2 teaspoons of the vegetable oil in a large, heavy skillet or wok over medium-high heat. Add the pork and stir-fry just until it is cooked through, for about 2 minutes. Remove the pork with a slotted spoon. Add the remaining teaspoon of vegetable oil to the skillet. Add the onion and the red pepper, and stir-fry for 2 minutes. Add the ginger, garlic and curry powder, and stir-fry for 1 minute. Add the zucchini and stir-fry for 1 minute. Remove the skillet from the heat.
3. Stir together the broth, cornstarch and soy sauce in a small bowl. Add the cornstarch mixture to the vegetables and cook over medium heat, stirring constantly, for 1 minute, or until the sauce thickens and boils. Add the noodles, green onion and pork. Heat the mixture to serving temperature. Serve immediately.

MEXICAN PORK CHOPS

LOW-CHOLESTEROL

Makes 4 servings.

Nutrient Value Per Serving: 359 calories, 30 g protein, 13 g fat, 34 g carbohydrate, 389 mg sodium, 72 mg cholesterol.

4	thick (¾ inch) lean center-cut pork chops (about 1½ pounds)
1	tablespoon vegetable oil
1	large onion, chopped (1 cup)
1	large clove garlic, finely chopped
1	medium-size sweet green pepper, cored, seeded and cut into ½-inch squares
½	medium-size sweet red pepper, cored, seeded and cut into ½-inch squares
1	tablespoon chili powder
2	tablespoons cornmeal OR: 1 tablespoon flour
½	teaspoon dried oregano, crumbled
½	teaspoon ground cumin
1	can (16 ounces) stewed tomatoes
1	package (10 ounces) frozen whole kernel corn Salt and freshly ground pepper, to taste
1	lime, cut into 4 wedges

1. Trim any excess fat from the pork chops. Pour the oil into a heavy skillet just large enough to hold all the chops in a single layer, and place the skillet over medium-high heat. When the oil is very hot, add the pork chops and sear them for about 2 minutes. Turn the chops and brown them on the other side. Cook the chops, turning several times, for about 4 minutes more on each side, or just until the chops are cooked through. Remove the chops to a plate.

2. Add the onion to the skillet and sauté over medium-high heat until the onion is softened, for about 3 minutes. Add the garlic and sauté for 1 minute. Add the green and red peppers, and sauté for 2 to 3 minutes. Stir in the chili powder, cornmeal or flour, oregano and cumin, and cook for 30 seconds. Add the tomatoes and cook, stirring constantly, until the sauce thickens and boils. Reduce the heat and simmer for 3 to 4 minutes. Add the corn and cook for 2 minutes.

3. Return the chops and juices from the plate to the skillet. Spoon some sauce over the chops and heat them just to serving temperature. Season with the salt and pepper. Serve the chops hot with the lime wedges.

PEPPERONI QUESADILLAS

LOW-CHOLESTEROL

Bake in toaster oven at 400° for 12 minutes.
Makes 4 servings.

Nutrient Value Per Serving: 373 calories, 15 g protein, 18 g fat, 37 g carbohydrate, 614 mg sodium, 36 mg cholesterol.

2	ounces sliced pepperoni, chopped
4	ounces shredded Monterey Jack OR: Cheddar cheese
1	can (4 ounces) chopped mild green chili peppers, drained
1	package (10 ounces) flour tortillas (8 tortillas)

Fiesta Pork

Mexican Pork Chops*
Quesadillas (see Tip, below)
Green Salad with Vinaigrette (recipe, page 117)
Custard

Quesadillas

Preheat the broiler. Line a large baking sheet with aluminum foil. Place 4 flour tortillas on the foil, slightly overlapping them if necessary. Scatter ½ cup of shredded Monterey Jack cheese (2 ounces) over the tortillas and sprinkle with half a medium size sweet red pepper, coarsely chopped, 2 thinly sliced green onions and, if you wish, 1 sliced pickled jalapeño pepper. Drizzle 1 to 2 tablespoons of mild or hot taco sauce over the tortillas. Broil the quesadillas for 1 to 2 minutes, or just until they are bubbly and lightly browned. Serve the quesadillas immediately.

❖ ❖ ❖

Mexican Melts

Pepperoni Quesadillas*
Tomato Wedges with Avocado Slices
Chocolate-Topped Apple Raisin Squares (recipe, page 249)

1. Sprinkle the pepperoni, Monterey Jack or Cheddar cheese and the chili peppers on 4 tortillas, dividing evenly. Leave a ½-inch border around the edge of each tortilla. Cover each tortilla with one of the remaining tortillas. Wrap each quesadilla in aluminum foil.

2. Bake 2 foil packets at a time in the hot toaster oven (400°) for 12 minutes, or until the quesadillas are hot. While the second 2 packets are baking, keep the first 2 packets warm by placing them on top of the toaster oven. Cut the quesadillas into wedges and serve.

PORK CHOPS CACCIATORE WITH PENNE

LOW-CHOLESTEROL

Makes 4 servings.

Nutrient Value Per Serving: 600 calories, 27 g protein, 28 g fat, 59 g carbohydrate, 1,062 mg sodium, 65 mg cholesterol.

8 ounces penne OR: ziti	1 clove garlic, finely chopped
2½ teaspoons salt	1½ cups small mushrooms, quartered
2 tablespoons olive oil	
4 center-cut pork chops, cut ½ inch thick (about 1 pound)*	½ cup dry white OR: red wine
1 large onion, sliced into thin rings	2 teaspoons dried basil, crumbled
1 large sweet red pepper, cut into ¼-inch strips	1 can (16 ounces) whole tomatoes in thick purée
1 large sweet green pepper, cut into ¼-inch strips	2 teaspoons sugar
	¼ teaspoon freshly ground pepper

1. Bring a large pot of hot water to boiling. Add the penne or ziti and 2 teaspoons of the salt, and cook until the pasta is al dente, tender but firm to the bite. Drain the pasta and return it to the pot. Add 1 tablespoon of the oil and toss to coat the pasta. Cover the pot to keep the pasta warm.

2. Meanwhile, heat the remaining tablespoon of oil in a large, heavy skillet over medium-high heat. Add the pork chops and sear on each side for 1 to 2 minutes, or until the chops are lightly browned. Lower the heat to medium and panfry the chops, turning them frequently, for 4 to 6 minutes, or until they are cooked through. Transfer the chops to a plate. Discard all but 1 tablespoon of the fat from the skillet.

3. Add the onion to the skillet and sauté for 3 minutes. Add the red and green peppers, and sauté for 3 minutes. Add the garlic, mushrooms, white or red wine and the basil. Cover the skillet and cook for 6 minutes, or until the peppers have softened. Add the tomatoes with their purée, the sugar, the remaining ½ teaspoon of salt and the pepper, and simmer for 3 minutes.

4. Return the chops and juices from the plate to the skillet. Heat the chops through, for about 2 minutes. Serve the chops hot over the cooked penne.

Note: An equal weight of thinly cut chops can be substituted for ½-inch chops, yielding two chops per serving.

Zesty Pork Chops

Pork Chops Cacciatore
with Penne*
Tossed Green Salad with Cherry
Tomatoes
Mulled Wine Granita
(recipe, page 250)

Quick Boil

Pasta is the perfect choice for a time-crunched cook: It takes only minutes to prepare, it's full of complex carbohydrates, adds a boost of protein to your meal and it pairs well with just about anything. To cut down on preparation time, fill your pot with hot tap water; it comes to a boil in a shorter time than cold water. And be sure your pot has a tight-fitting lid — the trapped heat hastens the boiling.

❖ ❖ ❖

ZUCCHINI PARMIGIANA

LOW-CHOLESTEROL

Broil for 3 to 5 minutes.
Makes 4 servings.

Nutrient Value Per Serving: 359 calories, 25 g protein, 22 g fat,
19 g carbohydrate, 664 mg sodium, 73 mg cholesterol.

8 ounces lean ground beef	1 can (28 ounces) plum tomatoes, undrained
½ cup chopped onion	
1 clove garlic, finely chopped	4 large zucchini (8 ounces each)
1½ teaspoons dried basil, crumbled	1 cup shredded mozzarella cheese (4 ounces)
1 teaspoon fennel seeds crushed	½ cup grated Parmesan cheese
½ teaspoon dried oregano, crumbled	

1. Fill a large pot with hot tap water and salt the water lightly. Cover the pot and bring the water to boiling over medium-high heat.

2. Meanwhile, crumble the beef into a medium-size, heavy saucepan over medium-high heat and cook for 1 to 2 minutes. Add the onion and the garlic, and sauté until they are softened, for 2 to 3 minutes. Stir in the basil, fennel seeds and oregano. Remove the saucepan from the heat.

3. Drain the tomatoes in a sieve over a large bowl to catch the liquid, and press the tomatoes with a wooden spoon to break them up and release more liquid. Add the tomatoes along with ½ cup of the liquid to the saucepan, discard the remaining liquid. Bring the mixture to boiling over medium heat. Reduce the heat slightly, and gently boil the sauce to thicken it slightly and blend the flavors, for about 15 minutes.

4. Meanwhile, trim the ends from the zucchini and slice the zucchini lengthwise into ¼-inch-thick strips.* Add the zucchini all at once to the boiling water. Cover the pot, return the water to boiling and cook for 2 to 3 minutes. Remove the zucchini with a slotted spoon to a colander and drain them. Drain the zucchini again on paper toweling.

5. Arrange the zucchini in an 8-inch square flameproof baking dish. Spoon the sauce over the zucchini. Sprinkle the zucchini evenly with the mozzarella and Parmesan cheeses.

6. Broil the zucchini 6 inches from the heat source for 3 to 5 minutes, or until the cheeses are bubbly and browned.

__Note:__ The zucchini can be cut into thinner strips to reduce blanching time.

34

A Taste of Italy

Zucchini Parmigana*
Ziti with Buttered Bread Crumbs (see Tip, below)
Carrot and Celery Sticks
Grapes and Pear Halves

Ziti with Buttered Bread Crumbs

Fill a large pot with hot tap water and salt it lightly, or use the water the zucchini was blanched in for Zucchini Parmigiana. Cover the pot, place it over high heat and bring the water to boiling. Add 8 ounces of ziti and return to boiling, stirring constantly. Cook, following the package directions and stirring often, until the ziti is al dente, tender but firm to the bite. Drain the ziti in a colander. Return the ziti to the pot and toss it with 2 teaspoons of olive oil.

Melt 2 tablespoons of butter in a small skillet over low heat. Add 1 clove of garlic, finely chopped, and sauté for 30 seconds. Add ¼ cup of packaged bread crumbs and sauté, stirring, until they are browned and toasted, for 2 to 3 minutes. Toss the crumb mixture with the ziti, and serve immediately.

❖   ❖   ❖

ITALIAN BREAD PIZZA

LOW-CHOLESTEROL

Broil for 6 minutes
Makes 4 servings.

Nutrient Value Per Serving: 509 calories, 23 g protein, 29 g fat, 40 g carbohydrate, 1,351 mg sodium, 64 mg cholesterol.

1	large loaf Italian bread, cut in half horizontally and crosswise	16	slices pepperoni
½	cup spaghetti sauce	8	oil-cured black olives, halved and pitted
2	cups shredded mozzarella cheese (8 ounces)	2	tablespoons grated Parmesan cheese
¼	cup roasted red peppers, drained, cut into strips	1	teaspoon olive oil
		½	teaspoon dried oregano, crumbled

1. Place the bread on the broiler rack. Broil the bread 4 inches from the heat source for 2 minutes on each side, or until the bread is crisp.
2. Spread the toasted bread with the sauce. Sprinkle the mozzarella cheese over the sauce. Top with the red peppers, pepperoni, olives, Parmesan cheese, oil and oregano, dividing the ingredients among the slices.
3. Broil the pizzas for 2 minutes, or until the cheese is melted and bubbly.

SWEET PEPPER PIZZA

LOW-CALORIE • LOW-CHOLESTEROL • LOW-FAT

Bake at 425° for 15 minutes.
Makes 4 servings (one 12-inch pizza).

Nutrient Value Per Serving: 284 calories, 12 g protein, 9 g fat, 36 g carbohydrate, 643 mg sodium, 22 mg cholesterol.

1	small sweet green pepper, cut into ¼-inch-thick rings	¼	teaspoon dried basil, crumbled
1	small sweet red pepper, cut into ¼-inch-thick rings	¼	teaspoon dried oregano, crumbled
1	tube (10 ounces) refrigerated ready-to-use pizza crust dough	⅛	teaspoon salt
½	cup spaghetti sauce carbonara	⅛	teaspoon freshly ground pepper
		1	cup coarsely shredded mozzarella cheese (4 ounces)

1. Preheat the oven to hot (425°).
2. Bring water to boiling in a large saucepan. Add the green and red pepper rings. Reduce the heat to low, cover the saucepan and cook for 2 to 3 minutes, or just until the peppers are tender. Drain the pepper rings.
3. Unroll the pizza dough onto a baking sheet. Pinch, pull and stretch the dough, turning under the 4 corners, to make a 12-inch circle with a slightly raised edge. Brush the dough with the pizza or spaghetti sauce. Sprinkle on the basil, oregano, salt and pepper. Scatter the pepper rings over the sauce. Top with the mozzarella cheese.
4. Bake the pizza in the preheated hot oven (425°) for 15 minutes, or until the crust is lightly golden and crisp.

SEAFOOD

Fish and shellfish are virtual treasure troves of nutrition and great taste.

TUNA AND RICE WITH TOMATOES

LOW-CALORIE • LOW-CHOLESTEROL • LOW-FAT

Makes 4 servings.

Nutrient Value Per Serving: 196 calories, 15 g protein, 6 g fat, 20 g carbohydrate, 515 mg sodium, 18 mg cholesterol.

1 **package (10 ounces) frozen boil-in-bag Italian-style rice**	1 **tablespoon Dijon-style vinaigrette**
1 **can (6½ ounces) solid white tuna, drained**	4 **medium-size ripe tomatoes**
1 **medium-size sweet red pepper, chopped**	8 **Boston lettuce leaves** **Black olives, for garnish** **Cucumber slices, for garnish**

1. Prepare the rice following the package directions.
2. Mix together the rice, tuna, red pepper and vinaigrette in a bowl.
3. Cut each tomato vertically into 6 wedges to within ½ inch of the bottom. Carefully spoon out the center pulp and seeds. Stuff the tomatoes with the rice mixture, spooning the mixture evenly among the tomatoes. Serve the stuffed tomatoes on a serving platter lined with the lettuce leaves. Garnish with the black olives and the cucumber slices.

TUNA PUTTANESCA ON ROTELLE

LOW-CHOLESTEROL • LOW-SODIUM • LOW-FAT

Makes 4 servings.

Nutrient Value Per Serving: 418 calories, 19 g protein, 14 g fat, 52 g carbohydrate, 37 mg sodium, 8 mg cholesterol.

1 **medium-size onion, chopped**	¼ **teaspoon freshly ground pepper**
1 **clove garlic, finely chopped**	8 **ounces rotelle pasta**
2 **tablespoons olive oil**	1 **can (6½ or 7 ounces) tuna, drained and coarsely flaked**
1 **can (16 ounces) tomatoes in thick purée**	2 **tablespoons chopped parsley**
¼ **cup pitted black olives, chopped**	
¼ **cup stuffed green olives, chopped**	

Terrific Tuna

Tuna and Rice with Tomatoes*
Black Olives and Cucumber Slices
Sesame Bread Sticks
Spumoni Ice Cream

Saucy Tuna Pasta

Tuna Puttanesca on Rotelle*
Fried Zucchini Spears
(recipe, page 104)
Italian Bread
Raspberry Jam Squares
(recipe, page 248)

Tuna

A member of the mackerel family, tuna is marketed in the United States primarily in cans. Fresh tuna can be found in fish markets along the East and West coasts.

■ In Japanese cuisine, fresh tuna is used to make sushi and sashimi; dried tuna is used as a seasoning in soups, rice dishes and with vegetables. Fresh tuna also is popular in Spain, Portugal, Italy and southern France.

■ Canned light meat tuna comes from yellowfin, skipjack or small bluefin tuna. White meat tuna comes only from albacore tuna. Use light tuna for mayonnaise-dressed salads, casseroles or any recipe where appearance is not important. Use the more expensive white tuna for antipasto platters and vinaigrette salads. Both are equally nutritious, although tuna packed in water contains about half the calories of tuna packed in oil.

■ Tuna is packed three ways: solid, chunk and flake. Solid-packed tuna has large pieces of tuna, chunk tuna has about 3 chunks of tuna that are filled in with small bits, and flake tuna is made up entirely of small bits or fragments.

❖ ❀ ❖

1. Sauté the onion and the garlic in the oil in a medium-size saucepan until the vegetables are tender but not browned. Break up the tomatoes slightly with a spoon and stir them, with their purée, into the saucepan along with the black and green olives and the pepper. Bring the mixture to boiling. Lower the heat. Partially cover the saucepan and simmer the sauce for 15 minutes, stirring occasionally.

2. Meanwhile, cook the rotelle following the package directions. Drain the rotelle and keep them warm.

3. Stir the tuna into the tomato sauce. Combine the sauce with the rotelle in a serving bowl and toss to mix them. Sprinkle with the parsley.

Tuna Puttanesca on Rotelle is a colorful dish that's full of flavor. We serve it with Fried Zucchini Spears (recipe, page 104).

NEW ENGLAND CLAM CHOWDER

LOW-CHOLESTEROL

Makes 4 servings.

Nutrient Value Per Serving: 364 calories, 14 g protein, 17 g fat, 39 g carbohydrate, 608 mg sodium, 52 mg cholesterol.

3	slices lean bacon, cut into ½-inch dice (2½ ounces)	1	can (6½ ounces) minced clams, drained and liquid reserved
1	medium-size onion, chopped	1	bottle (8 ounces) clam broth
2	tablespoons all-purpose flour	3	large red-skinned potatoes (about 1¼ pounds), peeled and cut into ½-inch cubes
¼	teaspoon dried thyme, crumbled	3	to 4 drops liquid red pepper seasoning (optional)
¼	teaspoon freshly ground pepper		
3	cups milk		

1. Cook the bacon in a large saucepan over medium heat for 3 minutes, or until the bacon is golden brown. Add the onion and sauté until it is softened, for 2 to 3 minutes. Stir in the flour, thyme and pepper. Stir in the milk.

2. Add the reserved canned clam liquid, the bottled clam broth and the potatoes to the saucepan. Bring the mixture to boiling over medium heat, stirring constantly. Lower the heat. Partially cover the saucepan and simmer until the potatoes are tender, for 8 to 10 minutes.

3. Add the clams and simmer just until they are heated through, for about 2 minutes. Stir in liquid red pepper seasoning, if you wish.

Note: The chowder can be prepared a day in advance through Step 2.

A Cape Cod Supper

New England Clam Chowder*
Warm Spinach with Cider
Vinaigrette (recipe, page 120)
Oyster Crackers
Cinnamon Baked Apples

Clams

Clams are bivalved mollusks. Many varieties of clams are found along the Atlantic, Pacific, and Gulf coasts.

■ Clams can be fried, served raw on the half-shell, steamed or used to make chowders or fritters.

■ Clams are available in the shell, or shucked and canned, whole or minced. Fresh clams are sold by the dozen; buy only those with tightly closed shells. Refrigerate fresh clams and use them within 2 days of purchase. Bottled clam juice is available to use in making soups and chowders.

■ To prepare fresh clams, place them in a container of salted water (⅓ cup of salt to 1 gallon of water) mixed with ¼ cup of cornmeal for several hours so that they will cleanse themselves of sand. Then, using a stiff brush, scrub the clams well and open them with a clam knife.

❖ ❖ ❖

Thick, hearty and delicious, New England Clam Chowder will warm everyone in your family right down to their toes.

SALMON AND POTATO SOUFFLÉS

Bake at 375° for 25 minutes.
Makes 4 servings.

Nutrient Value Per Serving: 395 calories, 32 g protein, 25 g fat, 9 g carbohydrate, 967 mg sodium, 483 mg cholesterol.

3	tablespoons butter	1	can (15½ ounces) salmon, drained
2	green onions, thinly sliced	½	teaspoon salt
1½	cups milk	¼	teaspoon ground hot red pepper
⅓	cup instant mashed potato granules	1	tablespoon lemon juice
6	eggs, separated		

1. Preheat the oven to moderate (375°). Grease and lightly flour four 2-cup soufflé dishes.
2. Melt the butter in a medium-size saucepan. Add the green onion and stir to coat it. Add the milk and bring the mixture to boiling.
3. Remove the saucepan from the heat. Add the potato granules, stirring until they are thickened. Stir in the egg yolks, 2 at a time.
4. Break up the salmon and blend it into the egg mixture. Add the salt, ground hot red pepper and lemon juice.
5. Beat the egg whites in a medium-size bowl until stiff peaks form. Gently fold the egg whites into the salmon mixture. Turn the salmon mixture into the prepared dishes.
6. Bake the soufflés in the preheated moderate oven (375°) for 25 minutes, or until they are puffed and golden brown. Serve at once.

HERBED FISH FILLETS

LOW-CALORIE

Bake at 450° for 10 to 15 minutes.
Makes 6 servings.

Nutrient Value Per Serving: 207 calories, 29 g protein, 9 g fat, 1 g carbohydrate, 201 mg sodium, 93 mg cholesterol.

1	tablespoon margarine Juice of 1 lemon	1	very small clove garlic, crushed (optional)
1	tablespoon chopped fresh oregano OR: 1 teaspoon dried oregano, crumbled		Salt, to taste (optional)
		2	pounds fish fillets, such as flounder, sole, trout or catfish

1. Preheat the oven to hot (450°).
2. Melt the margarine in the oven in a baking dish large enough to hold the fish fillets in one layer. Stir in the lemon juice, oregano and, if you wish, the garlic and salt.
3. Arrange the fish fillets in the butter mixture and turn to coat them on both sides.
4. Bake the fish in the preheated hot oven (450°), basting frequently with the pan liquid, for 10 to 15 minutes, or just until the fish flakes easily when lightly touched with a fork. Serve the fish with the pan liquid.

SHRIMP LO MEIN

Makes 4 servings.

Nutrient Value Per Serving: 437 calories, 27 g protein, 15 g fat, 47 g carbohydrate, 673 mg sodium, 193 mg cholesterol.

8   ounces medium-size egg noodles
1   tablespoon Oriental sesame oil
2   teaspoons cornstarch
2   tablespoons reduced-sodium soy sauce
1   tablespoon dry sherry wine OR: rice wine
1   tablespoon catsup
¾   cup chicken broth
1   tablespoon finely chopped, peeled, fresh gingerroot
1   clove garlic, finely chopped
2   tablespoons vegetable oil
1   pound shrimp (20 to 25 shrimp per pound), thawed if frozen, peeled and deveined
¾   cup sliced green onions

1. Cook the noodles in a large amount of lightly salted water in a large pot, following the package directions, just until the noodles are tender. Drain the noodles, place them in a bowl and toss them with the Oriental sesame oil.
2. Meanwhile, stir together the cornstarch, soy sauce, sherry or rice wine and the catsup in a small bowl until the mixture is smooth. Stir in the broth. Set aside the sauce.
3. Sauté the ginger and the garlic in the vegetable oil in the same pot the noodles were cooked in over medium-high heat for 10 seconds. Add the shrimp and the green onion, and stir-fry for 2 minutes, or until the shrimp are cooked. Add the noodles and stir-fry for 1 minute. Stir the sauce and add it to the pot. Stir the noodle mixture until the sauce thickens and comes to a boil. Return the noodle mixture to the bowl and serve immediately.

East Meets West

Wonton Soup
Shrimp Lo Mein*
Oriental Radish Salad
(recipe, page 118)
Orange Sherbet

Seafood Sensations

The word is out: seafood is low in fat and cholesterol, and provides good-quality protein, B vitamins and minerals. In addition, fish contains Omega-3 fatty acids, which appear to lower the chances of developing heart disease and high blood pressure.

Even more good news: fish and shellfish are quick and easy to cook by steaming, baking, poaching, sautéing or microwaving them. But don't overcook seafood, or the flesh will become tough.

Take a ride on the Orient Express with this stir-fried Shrimp Lo Mein served with Oriental Radish Salad (recipe, page 118).

SOLE WITH PLUMS AND APRICOTS

Fresh, ripe plums and apricots are simmered in port wine to create a vibrantly colored, savory sauce that enhances the delicate flavor of the fish.

LOW-CALORIE • LOW-SODIUM • LOW-FAT

Makes 4 servings.

Nutrient Value Per Serving: 241 calories, 32 g protein, 8 g fat, 8 g carbohydrate, 140 mg sodium, 97 mg cholesterol.

4	sole fillets (about 6 ounces each) OR: 4 snapper or cod fillets	¼	pound ripe plums, pitted and quartered
2	tablespoons margarine	1	tablespoon port wine
1	large shallot, finely chopped	1	teaspoon sugar
¼	pound ripe apricots, pitted and quartered		Salt and freshly ground white pepper, to taste
			Flat-leaf Italian parsley sprigs, for garnish

1. Rinse the fish fillets and pat them dry with paper toweling.

2. Melt 1 tablespoon of the margarine in a medium-size saucepan over medium heat. Add the shallot and cook for 2 to 3 minutes, or until it begins to soften.

3. Add the apricots, plums and port wine. Stir the mixture and cover the saucepan. Cook the mixture, stirring occasionally, for 15 minutes, or until the fruit is soft.

4. Transfer the fruit to the container of a food processor or electric blender. Cover and whirl until the mixture is a very smooth purée. Return the purée to the saucepan. Stir in the sugar and the salt and white pepper. Keep the sauce warm over low heat.

5. Melt the remaining tablespoon of margarine in a large skillet over medium heat. Add the fish fillets in one layer and sauté them for 4 to 5 minutes, or until they are opaque on one side. Carefully turn over the fish with a spatula and sauté them for 2 to 3 minutes more, or just until they are opaque throughout.

6. Ladle the sauce onto 4 warmed individual dinner plates, and spread the sauce out on each plate. Place the fish on the sauce. Garnish with the Italian parsley.

Feast of Fruit and Fish

Sole with Plums and Apricots*
**Roasted Potatoes, Peppers and Onions with Rosemary
(recipe, page 108)**
Apple Gingerbread with Nutty Cream Cheese (recipe, page 254)

Fresh Fish

When selecting fresh fish, the first thing to do is smell the fish. All fresh fish should smell sweet and clean.

■ Whole fish: Look for bright, glossy, smooth skin with few scales missing; bright, bulging eyes with dark corneas (contact with ice may cause clouding of the eyes); and moist, vivid red gills. Avoid fish with rib bones separating from the flesh.

■ Fish fillets and steaks: They should look translucent, lustrous and moist. Avoid fish that is discolored, brown around the edges, separating or sitting in liquid.

PASTA & VEGETABLES

RICOTTA-FILLED SHELLS

Bake at 400° for 15 minutes.
Makes 4 servings.

Nutrient Value Per Serving: 547 calories, 26 g protein, 26 g fat, 53 g carbohydrate, 1,173 mg sodium, 136 mg cholesterol.

20	jumbo pasta shells	¼	cup chopped parsley
1	container (15 ounces) ricotta cheese	½	teaspoon dried oregano, crumbled
1	egg yolk	¼	teaspoon salt
½	cup grated Parmesan cheese	⅛	teaspoon freshly ground pepper
⅓	cup finely chopped ham	2	cups spaghetti sauce

1. Place rack in the top third of the oven. Preheat the oven to hot (400°).
2. Cook the shells in a large pot of boiling water, stirring occasionally, for 10 to 12 minutes, or until they are al dente, tender but firm; drain.
3. Stir together the ricotta cheese, egg yolk, ¼ cup of the Parmesan cheese, the ham, parsley, oregano, salt and pepper in a medium-size bowl. Spoon about 1½ tablespoons of the ricotta filling into each shell; do not overfill the shells.
4. Spread ¼ cup of the spaghetti sauce in a 12 x 8 x 2-inch glass baking dish. Arrange the shells in a single layer in the dish. Top with the remaining sauce. Sprinkle with the remaining ¼ cup of Parmesan cheese.
5. Bake the shells in the preheated hot oven (400°) for 15 minutes, or until they are hot and bubbly.

GARDEN FRITTATA

LOW-CALORIE

Broil for 2 to 3 minutes.
Makes 4 servings.

Nutrient Value Per Serving: 254 calories, 11 g protein, 14 g fat, 21 g carbohydrate, 195 mg sodium, 411 mg cholesterol.

2	medium-size red-skinned potatoes, unpeeled and diced	6	eggs
1½	tablespoons olive oil	2	tablespoons dry white wine OR: water
1	medium-size sweet red pepper, diced	2	tablespoons chopped parsley
1	medium-size sweet green pepper, diced	1	teaspoon dried basil, crumbled
1	medium-size onion, chopped	¼	teaspoon dried oregano, crumbled
½	cup diced celery	¼	to ½ teaspoon salt
1	clove garlic, chopped	⅛	teaspoon freshly ground pepper

Sensational Stuffed Shells

Ripe Olives and Celery Sticks
Ricotta-Filled Shells*
Broccoli with Garlic
(recipe, page 91)
Bananas Marion
(recipe, page 253)

Ricotta

Ricotta is made in Italy from skimmed sheep's buttermilk or the whey left over from other cheeses, such as Pecorino Romano. American ricotta is made from whole or skimmed milk; it has the consistency of a smooth cottage cheese with the flavor of cream cheese.

❖ ❖ ❖

Viva Vegetarian

Garden Frittata*
White Bean Salad
Italian Bread
Poires Cardinales
(recipe, page 254)

1. Cook the potatoes in the oil in a medium-size, nonstick skillet over medium heat, tossing, until the potatoes are browned and almost tender, for about 10 minutes. Add the red and green peppers, the onion, celery and garlic, and cook for 5 minutes more.

2. Whisk the eggs with the wine or water in a small bowl. Mix in the parsley, basil, oregano, salt and pepper. Pour the egg mixture over the vegetables. Reduce the heat to low and cook, without stirring, for 10 to 15 minutes, or until the frittata is almost set; the top still will be wet. Meanwhile, preheat the broiler.

3. Broil the frittata for 2 to 3 minutes, or just until the top is set. Invert the frittata onto a serving plate. Cut the frittata into quarters and serve.

Note: *To cook the frittata completely on the stove top, cover the skillet for the last 5 minutes of cooking to set the eggs.*

Our Garden Frittata is bursting with red potatoes, red and green peppers and herbs.

43

VEGETARIAN BAKED ZITI

LOW-CHOLESTEROL • LOW-FAT

Bake at 375° for 25 minutes for large casserole, or 20 minutes for small casseroles.
Makes 4 servings.

Nutrient Value Per Serving: 493 calories, 22 g protein, 15 g fat, 71 g carbohydrate, 1,010 mg sodium, 23 mg cholesterol.

1 medium-size sweet green pepper, seeded and diced	½ teaspoon salt
1 medium-size sweet red pepper, seeded and diced	½ teaspoon freshly ground pepper
2 tablespoons olive oil	¼ teaspoon dried oregano, crumbled
2 large onions, coarsely chopped	½ pound fresh spinach, cleaned and stemmed
2 large cloves garlic, finely chopped	½ cup frozen corn
¼ pound mushrooms, chopped	Nonstick vegetable cooking spray
1 can (16 ounces) whole tomatoes, undrained	8 ounces ziti, cooked according to package directions
1 can (8 ounces) tomato sauce	1 container (8 ounces) part-skim ricotta cheese
¼ cup dry red wine	¼ cup grated Parmesan cheese
1 teaspoon dried basil, crumbled	

1. Sauté the green and red peppers in 1 tablespoon of the oil in a large skillet, stirring often, until the peppers are barely tender. Remove the peppers with a slotted spoon and set them aside.

2. Add the remaining tablespoon of oil to the skillet. Add the onion and the garlic and sauté, stirring often, until they are soft. Add the mushrooms and sauté, stirring often, for 2 minutes more.

3. Break up the tomatoes with a fork and add them, with their liquid, to the skillet along with the tomato sauce, wine, basil, salt, pepper and oregano. Bring the mixture to boiling. Lower the heat and simmer, uncovered, until the mixture is slightly thickened, for about 20 minutes. Add the spinach and the corn. Cook, stirring constantly, until the spinach wilts.

4. Preheat the oven to moderate (375°). Coat the inside of one 2-quart casserole dish or the insides of four 2-cup casserole dishes with nonstick vegetable cooking spray.

5. Combine the ziti, tomato mixture, ricotta cheese and two thirds of the green and red peppers in a large bowl. Stir gently to mix the ingredients well. Spoon the ziti mixture into the large casserole dish or individual casserole dishes. Sprinkle with the Parmesan cheese.

6. Bake the ziti in the preheated moderate oven (375°) for 25 minutes for the large casserole dish, or 20 minutes for the small casserole dishes. Garnish with the remaining green and red peppers.

Pasta Perfect!

Vegetarian Baked Ziti*
Herbed Italian Bread
(see Tip, below)
Tossed Green Salad
Peach Halves with Raspberry Yogurt

Herbed Italian Bread

Preheat the oven to moderate (375°). Combine 2 tablespoons of softened butter with 1 tablespoon of finely chopped parsley, 1½ teaspoons of grated Parmesan cheese and 1¼ teaspoons of crumbled dried oregano in a small bowl until the ingredients are well mixed. Cut one 8-ounce loaf of Italian bread into slices about 1 inch thick. Spread one side of each slice with the butter mixture. Place the slices, buttered side up, on a baking sheet. Bake the slices in the preheated moderate oven (375°) for 8 to 10 minutes, or until they are golden brown. Serve immediately.

❖ ✿ ❖

RAVIOLI MARINARA

LOW-CHOLESTEROL

Makes 4 servings.

Nutrient Value Per Serving: 400 calories, 19 g protein, 17 g fat, 45 g carbohydrate, 1,174 mg sodium, 45 mg cholesterol.

1	large onion, finely chopped (about 1 cup)	½	teaspoon leaf basil, crumbled
2	tablespoons olive oil	¼	cup chopped parsley
2	cloves garlic, finely chopped	¼	teaspoon salt
1	can (35 ounces) plum tomatoes, undrained	¼	teaspoon freshly ground pepper
2	teaspoons sugar	1	pound cheese ravioli
		¼	cup grated Parmesan cheese

1. Sauté the onion in the oil in a heavy, medium-size skillet over medium heat, stirring occasionally, until the onion is softened, for about 7 minutes. Add the garlic and cook for 30 seconds more.
2. Add the tomatoes with their liquid, breaking up the tomatoes. Add the sugar and basil, and bring to boiling. Lower the heat and simmer, stirring occasionally, for 25 to 30 minutes, or until the sauce is reduced to 3½ cups. Stir in 2 tablespoons of the parsley, the salt and pepper. Set aside.
3. Cook the ravioli in a large pot of boiling water, following the package directions. Drain the ravioli and return it to the pot. Add the sauce and cook just until heated through. Serve the ravioli with the marinara sauce spooned over it. Sprinkle with the remaining parsley and the Parmesan cheese.

PENNE WITH TOMATOES

LOW-CHOLESTEROL

Makes 4 servings.

Nutrient Value Per Serving: 582 calories, 17 g protein, 15 g fat, 96 g carbohydrate, 155 mg sodium, 0 mg cholesterol.

10	ripe plum tomatoes (2 pounds)	¼	teaspoon salt
¼	cup good-quality olive oil	⅛	teaspoon freshly ground pepper
1	clove garlic, chopped	1	pound penne
¼	cup coarsely chopped fresh basil		Whole fresh basil leaves, for garnish

1. Blanch the tomatoes in boiling water for 10 seconds. Drain the tomatoes and run them under cold water. Peel the tomatoes, cut in half lengthwise and remove the seeds. Slice them into wedges lengthwise and set aside.
2. Heat the oil in a large skillet or Dutch oven over medium-high heat. Add the garlic and sauté, stirring constantly, for about 1 minute, or until the garlic begins to brown. Add the tomatoes, basil, salt and pepper. Cover the skillet, lower the heat and simmer the mixture for about 8 minutes, or until the tomatoes are tender but not falling apart.
3. Meanwhile, cook the penne in a large pot of boiling water until it is al dente, firm but tender to the bite. Drain the penne.
4. Add the penne to the tomatoes and cook over high heat for 1 minute, stirring constantly. Serve hot, garnished with the whole fresh basil leaves.

Weekend
Extravaganzas

2

If your weekdays are devoted to quick-and-easy meals, you can still roll up your sleeves and create "culinary masterpieces" on the weekends!

One of the nicest ways to enjoy the weekend is a luxurious Sunday breakfast. Get the whole family involved — even your little ones can help set the table. We offer you a whole pantry of breakfast goodies to chose from: a marvelous Farmer's Omelet, scrumptious Puffed Oven Pancake, muffins and a wonderful assortment of breads — Apple Pecan, Cherry Orange, Banana and more! Recipes for brunch start on page 49.

For a taste of the exotic, try our "A Taste of Tapas," based on classic Spanish buffet cuisine. With dishes such as sautéed eggplant Caponata (recipe, page 60), Tortilla de Papas (recipe, page 62) and spicy Shrimp à la Gallega (recipe, page 64), your culinary trip to Spain is a guaranteed success.

When the thermometer starts to climb, take some of the heat out of the kitchen with simple but elegant grill fare for company: Bruschetta (recipe, page 66), Grilled Vegetable Salad with Pasta Aglio-Olio (recipe, page 67) and a Lemon and Rosemary Marinated Mixed Grill (recipe, page 68).

You'll also find recipes for an Autumn Harvest Dinner, a Mexican Fiesta, and a Welcome Spring Buffet. In today's fast-paced world, the weekends are more important than ever to take the time you don't have during the work week to slow down, relax and indulge.

Rhubarb Citrus Coffee Cake (recipe, page 52) is the perfect waker-upper with a fresh pot of fragrant coffee.

BREAKFAST CLUB

There are few things we like better than sleeping late on the weekends and then having a leisurely breakfast with the family. Here's a menu full of eye-opening delights, from quick breads and muffins to farm-fresh omelets. So rise and shine!

FARMER'S OMELET

How ya gonna keep 'em down on the farm? After one bite of this mouth-watering omelet, they'll be there to stay.

LOW-CALORIE

Makes 6 servings.

Nutrient Value Per Serving: 295 calories, 16 g protein, 22 g fat, 7 g carbohydrate, 365 mg sodium, 408 mg cholesterol.

8 **eggs**	⅛ **teaspoon freshly ground white pepper**
3 **tablespoons unsalted butter or margarine, melted**	1 **large cooked potato, peeled and diced (about 1 cup)**
¼ **cup sweet yellow and red pepper squares**	1 **cup shredded Cheddar cheese (4 ounces)**
1 **tablespoon chopped green onion**	¼ **cup chopped ham**
¼ **cup chopped tomato**	¼ **cup chopped crisp cooked bacon (3 slices)**

1. Beat the eggs with 1 tablespoon of the melted butter or margarine in a large bowl, and set aside.

2. Heat a medium-size skillet or omelet pan over medium heat. Add the remaining 2 tablespoons of melted butter. Add the yellow and red pepper squares, and sauté for 1 minute. Add the green onion and sauté for 1 minute, or just until the green onion is tender. Add the tomato and the white pepper, and sauté for 1 minute more.

3. Meanwhile, stir the potato, Cheddar cheese, ham and bacon into the beaten egg mixture.

4. Pour the egg mixture into the skillet, spreading it evenly. Reduce the heat to low and cook for 3 to 4 minutes, or until the eggs are almost set, using the spatula to lift the edges of the omelet gently and let the uncooked eggs flow onto the bottom of the pan.

5. Gently loosen the omelet and slide it onto a plate larger than the skillet. Invert the skillet over the omelet, and invert the plate and skillet, so the top side of the omelet now is in the bottom of the skillet. Cook for 3 minutes more, or until no loose egg mixture remains. Gently slide the omelet onto a large serving plate. Cut the omelet into 6 wedges and serve.

Menu

Farmer's Omelet*
Puffed Oven Pancake*
Cherry and Orange Bread
(recipe, page 50)
Ham and Egg Bake
(recipe, page 51)
Rhubarb Citrus Coffee Cake
(recipe, page 52)
Blueberry Muffins
(recipe, page 53)
Poppy Seed Bread with
Orange Glaze
(recipe, page 54)
Banana Bread
(recipe, page 55)
Apple Pecan Bread
(recipe, page 56)
Fresh Fruit Juices,
Coffee and Tea

"You can't make an omelet without breaking eggs."
—Anonymous

Pancake Pizzazz

Give your favorite pancake recipe a special weekend touch with a filling or topping: pink and white grapefruit and orange sections sprinkled with powdered sugar, warm applesauce spiced with cinnamon, or finely ground toasted walnuts mixed with cinnamon and sugar (the sugared walnut mixture is especially delicious with our Puffed Oven Pancake, recipe at right).

Puffed Oven Pancake looks like it took hours, but it's really a cinch to make!

PUFFED OVEN PANCAKE

LOW-CALORIE

Bake at 450° for 15 to 20 minutes.
Makes 4 servings.

Nutrient Value Per Serving: 346 calories, 14 g protein, 19 g fat, 28 g carbohydrate, 255 mg sodium, 443 mg cholesterol.

6 eggs, slightly beaten	**Maple or fruit syrup**
1 cup all-purpose flour	**OR: 10X (confectioners'**
1 cup milk	**powdered) sugar**
3 tablespoons butter, melted	**OR: cut-up fruit, for**
Pinch salt	**topping (optional)**

1. Preheat the oven to hot (450°). Generously grease a 13 x 9 x 2-inch baking dish.
2. Mix together the eggs and the flour in a medium-size bowl. Add the milk, butter and salt. Mix the ingredients well. Pour the batter into the prepared dish.
3. Bake the pancake in the preheated hot oven (450°) for 15 to 20 minutes, or until it is puffed. Cut the pancake into 4 serving pieces. Serve the pancake with maple or fruit syrup, 10X (confectioners' powdered) sugar and/or cut-up fresh fruit, if you wish.

CHERRY ORANGE BREAD

Bake at 350° for 1 hour and 20 minutes.
Makes 1 large tube bread (16 slices).

Nutrient Value Per Slice: 325 calories, 4 g protein, 13 g fat,
49 g carbohydrate, 188 mg sodium, 82 mg cholesterol.

3 cups plus 2 tablespoons
   all-purpose flour
1½ teaspoons baking powder
½ teaspoon ground
   cinnamon
¼ teaspoon ground ginger
⅛ teaspoon salt
   Grated zest of 1 orange
   (orange part of rind only)
1 cup (2 sticks) butter,
   softened
2 cups plus 2 tablespoons
   granulated sugar

3 eggs
½ cup orange juice
2 cups pitted fresh sweet
   cherries OR: 2 cups
   canned cherries (one and
   a half 16-ounce cans),
   drained OR: 2 cups
   frozen cherries, thawed
   and drained well
10X (confectioners'
   powdered) sugar,
   for topping (optional)

1. Preheat oven to moderate (350°). Grease and flour a 10-inch tube pan.
2. Stir together 3 cups of the flour, the baking powder, cinnamon, ginger, salt and orange zest in a medium-size bowl.

The Fresh Test: Baking Powder

The leavening power of baking powder diminishes with age, so always test for freshness before using it. Place ½ teaspoon of baking powder in ¼ cup of hot water. If the water bubbles actively, the baking powder is fresh.

❖ ❖ ❖

Cherry Orange Bread is so luscious, it needs no butter!

3. Beat together the butter and 2 cups of the granulated sugar in a medium-size bowl until light colored. Beat in the eggs, one at a time. Stir in the flour mixture alternately with the orange juice.

4. Combine the cherries with the remaining 2 tablespoons of flour and 2 tablespoons of granulated sugar in a small bowl.

5. Fold the cherries into the batter. Pour the batter into the prepared pan and smooth the top.

6. Bake the bread in the preheated moderate oven (350°) for 1 hour and 20 minutes, or until a wooden pick inserted in the center comes out clean. Cool the bread in the pan on a wire rack for 10 minutes. Run a thin knife around the edges of the pan. Remove the bread from the pan to the wire rack to cool. Store the bread at room temperature wrapped in plastic wrap or aluminum foil. Sprinkle the top of the bread with 10X (confectioners' powdered) sugar, if you wish.

HAM AND EGG BAKE

A delicious dish you make the night before.

LOW-CALORIE

Bake at 325° for 40 minutes.
Makes 12 servings.

Nutrient Value Per Serving: 325 calories, 19 g protein, 23 g fat, 10 g carbohydrate, 532 mg sodium, 501 mg cholesterol.

1	cup chopped cooked ham (about 6 ounces)	3	tablespoons all-purpose flour
1	large onion, chopped (1 cup)	2	cups milk
6	tablespoons butter	1½	cups grated Cheddar cheese
1	cup sliced mushrooms (about 4 ounces)	2	cups soft bread crumbs (about 4 slices)
20	eggs, slightly beaten	¼	cup chopped fresh herbs, such as oregano, tarragon or parsley
¼	teaspoon ground hot red pepper (optional)		

1. Sauté the ham and the onion in 3 tablespoons of the butter in a large 12-inch skillet until the onion softens but does not brown, for 5 minutes. Add the mushrooms and sauté until they are slightly softened, for 5 minutes. Scrape the ham mixture into a bowl.

2. Place the eggs in the skillet and, if you wish, combine them with ground hot red pepper. Cook over medium heat, stirring, until the eggs are scrambled but still very runny. Remove the skillet from the heat. Fold in the ham mixture. Spoon the combined mixture into a greased 13 x 9 x 2-inch baking pan.

3. Melt the remaining 3 tablespoons of butter in a medium-size saucepan over medium heat. Stir in the flour until it is blended, and cook for 1 minute. Slowly stir in the milk until it is blended. Cook, stirring, until the sauce is thick and bubbly, for about 3 minutes. Stir in the Cheddar cheese until it is melted and smooth; do not boil. Pour the sauce over the mixture in the pan.

4. Sprinkle the bread crumbs over the sauce. Cover the pan tightly and refrigerate the casserole overnight.

5. Next morning, preheat the oven to slow (325°).

6. Uncover the baking pan. Bake the casserole in the preheated slow oven (325°) for 40 minutes, or until the casserole is bubbly, and the top is set and lightly browned. Sprinkle the casserole with the herbs.

RHUBARB CITRUS COFFEE CAKE

For a "change of taste," you can use cut-up strawberries in place of the rhubarb in this recipe.

Bake at 350° for 30 minutes.
Makes 8 servings.

Nutrient Value Per Serving: 233 calories, 3 g protein, 7 g fat, 41 g carbohydrate, 165 mg sodium, 50 mg cholesterol.

1⅓ cups all-purpose flour
1½ teaspoons baking powder
   Pinch salt
3 teaspoons grated orange zest (orange part of rind only)
¼ cup (½ stick) butter, softened
¾ cup sugar
½ cup orange juice

1 egg, slightly beaten
1⅓ cups 1-inch chunks fresh rhubarb OR: frozen rhubarb (12 ounces), thawed and well drained

Topping:
2 tablespoons sugar
½ teaspoon ground cinnamon

1. Preheat the oven to moderate (350°). Grease a 9-inch tart pan with a removable bottom, or a 9 x 9 x 2-inch square baking pan.
2. Combine the flour, baking powder, salt and orange zest in a small bowl.
3. Beat together the butter and the ¾ cup of sugar in a medium-size bowl until well combined, for 5 minutes. Stir in the orange juice and the egg until well mixed; the mixture may look curdled.
4. Stir the flour mixture into the orange juice mixture just until the flour mixture is evenly moistened. Fold in the rhubarb. Pour the batter into the prepared pan.
5. Prepare the Topping: Combine the sugar with the cinnamon. Sprinkle the topping over the batter.
6. Bake the coffee cake in the preheated moderate oven (350°) for 30 minutes, or until a wooden pick inserted in the center comes out clean. If using the tart pan, remove the sides. Serve the coffee cake warm. Or cool the coffee cake, wrap it tightly and store it at room temperature.

Hot and Hearty

Don't overlook hot cereals—they're a wonderful first course for a cold-weather brunch. Spoon hot cereal into country bowls, and top with fruit, granola, honey or syrup.

Good Morning, Sunshine

■ Say "good morning" with a wonderful centerpiece. Place flowers in antique vases. Or, for a less formal touch, put blooms in anything but a vase: an enameled coffee pot, a ceramic pitcher, a glass canister. We also love a breakfast table decorated with plants—pots of herbs tied with ribbon and placed on a tray.

■ Present food in attractive containers, and leave cartons, butter tubs and so on in the kitchen. Pour juice, milk and other cold liquids into glass or ceramic pitchers; put jams, jellies and butter in small crocks, bowls or pretty jars; display muffins in an old fluted cake tin.

■ Do something dressy with napkins. Tuck them into napkin rings, wrap them with twine or raffia, or roll them up and place them in a basket.

Muffin Magic

To make light, even-textured muffins every time:

■ Add the beaten liquid ingredients to the combined dry ingredients with a few, quick stirring strokes just to moisten the dry ingredients.

■ The batter should be lumpy; if it pours smoothly from the spoon, you have overbeaten it. Overbeating causes coarse texture and tunneling throughout the muffins.

■ Fill greased muffin-pan cups only two thirds full.

❖ ❖ ❖

> *"O do you know the muffin man, that lives in Drury Lane."*
> —*Anonymous*

BLUEBERRY MUFFINS

LOW-FAT

Bake at 400° for 25 minutes.
Makes 12 muffins.

Nutrient Value Per Muffin: 203 calories, 3 g protein, 9 g fat, 28 g carbohydrate, 274 mg sodium, 44 mg cholesterol.

2 cups all-purpose flour	6 tablespoons butter, melted
½ cup sugar	1 teaspoon grated lemon zest (yellow part of rind only)
1 tablespoon baking powder	
½ teaspoon salt	
½ cup dairy sour cream	2 teaspoons lemon juice
1 egg, slightly beaten	1½ cups fresh or thawed frozen blueberries
½ cup milk	

1. Preheat the oven to hot (400°). Lightly grease twelve 2½-inch muffin-pan cups.
2. Sift together the flour, sugar, baking powder and salt onto wax paper. Reserve 2 tablespoons of the flour mixture.
3. Whisk the sour cream in a large bowl until it is smooth. Stir in the egg, milk, butter, lemon zest and lemon juice.
4. Add the flour mixture to the egg mixture and stir just until the flour mixture is moistened; the batter will not be smooth. Toss the blueberries with the reserved 2 tablespoons of flour mixture. Gently fold the blueberries into the batter.
5. Spoon the batter into the prepared muffin-pan cups, using a level ⅓-cup measure for each.
6. Bake the muffins in the preheated hot oven (400°) for 25 minutes, or until a wooden pick inserted in the centers comes out clean. Cool the muffins in the pans for 5 minutes. Remove the muffins from the pans to a wire rack. Serve the muffins warm.

Blueberry Muffins will rouse even the most determined sleepy-heads.

POPPY SEED BREAD WITH ORANGE GLAZE

Tangy-sweet orange glaze adds the perfect note to this breakfast bread. If you have any left over, you can pack it with lunches for a weekday treat.

Bake at 350° for 1 hour.
Makes 2 loaves (14 slices each).

Nutrient Value Per Slice: 251 calories, 3 g protein, 13 g fat,
31 g carbohydrate, 155 mg sodium, 31 mg cholesterol.

3 **eggs, slightly beaten**	**Orange Glaze:**
2¼ **cups granulated sugar**	¼ **cup orange juice**
1½ **cups vegetable oil**	**concentrate, thawed**
1½ **cups milk**	¾ **cup 10X (confectioners'**
3 **cups all-purpose flour**	**powdered) sugar**
1½ **teaspoons baking powder**	½ **teaspoon vanilla**
1½ **teaspoons salt**	1 **teaspoon almond extract**
1½ **tablespoons poppy seeds**	
2 **teaspoons almond extract**	

1. Preheat the oven to moderate (350°). Grease and flour two
8½ x 4½ x 2½-inch loaf pans.

2. Beat together the eggs, granulated sugar, oil and milk in a large bowl.

3. Combine the flour, baking powder and salt on wax paper. Beat the flour mixture into the egg mixture. Stir in the poppy seeds and the 2 teaspoons of almond extract. Divide the batter between the prepared pans.

4. Bake the bread in the preheated moderate oven (350°) for 1 hour, or until a wooden pick inserted in the centers comes out clean.

5. Meanwhile, prepare the Orange Glaze: Combine the orange juice concentrate, 10X (confectioners' powdered) sugar, vanilla and almond extract in a small bowl until the glaze is a good spreading consistency. Set aside the glaze.

6. Cool the loaves in the pans for 10 minutes. Run a thin knife around the edges of the pans, and remove the loaves from the pans to wire racks. Place wax paper under the wire racks. Spread the loaves with the glaze while they are still warm. Let the loaves cool. The bread is better if eaten the next day; wrap the loaves in plastic wrap or aluminum foil, and store them at room temperature.

Spilling the Beans on Coffee

Although there are some wonderful commercial coffees on the market, we think the flavor of freshly-ground coffee can't be beat. If you're a big fan of java, you might want to invest in a coffee grinder — it's relatively inexpensive for the fabulous flavor you'll get.

■ Light coffee beans, also called cinnamon roast, have a mild, delicate taste that's nice for breakfast; this coffee mixes well with milk.

■ Medium beans usually are a blend of light and dark beans. An ideal coffee for people who like a mellow, not heavy, taste.

■ Dark coffee beans often are called French roast; the beans are cooked longer to bring out their dark, smokey flavor.

■ Espresso coffee beans are roasted until they become charred, producing a strong coffee with a bitter kick. Try serving espresso with a thin slice of lemon peel. When enjoying espresso after dinner, add a splash of anisette or red wine. A mixture of one-half espresso coffee and one-half steamed milk is called cappuccino. Sprinkle cinnamon or shaved chocolate over cappuccino for a delicious treat.

■ For a deliciously different taste, flavor your regular brand of coffee (regular or decaffeinated) with spices. Add the spices to the coffee before it is brewed. We especially enjoy using cinnamon, nutmeg and/or cardamom in our coffee.

Oat Bran: A Soluble Solution for Your Heart

Oat bran is a very rich source of soluble fiber and can be easily incorporated into your everyday diet.

■ Use oat bran along with, or instead of, flour in muffin and quick bread recipes. (To help keep the cholesterol content down, minimize the use of egg yolks and substitute vegetable oil for butter.) Use oat bran in pancake and waffle batters.

■ Add oat bran to meat loaf mixtures and to bread and cookie doughs. Stir it into juice or applesauce. Thicken soups, stews and sauces with it.

■ Toast oat bran and sprinkle it on vegetables and salads to add a pleasant crunch.

■ Stuff chicken, turkey or Cornish game hens with oat bran mixtures. Coat fish or chicken pieces with oat bran before baking them.

■ Top baked fruit desserts with a sprinkling of oat bran. Add it to sweet and savory pie crusts. Or make sandwiches with oat bran bread.

❖   ❖   ❖

These breads are so delicious, you'll want to make them all: Poppy Seed Bread with Orange Glaze (recipe, page 54), Apple Pecan Bread (recipe, page 56) and Banana Bread.

BANANA BREAD

Bake at 350° for 1 hour and 20 minutes.
Makes 1 loaf (14 slices).

Nutrient Value Per Slice: 270 calories, 4 g protein, 13 g fat, 36 g carbohydrate, 328 mg sodium, 58 mg cholesterol.

2	**cups all-purpose flour**	2	**eggs**
1	**teaspoon baking soda**	1	**teaspoon vanilla**
1	**teaspoon baking powder**	3	**medium-size bananas,**
1	**teaspoon salt**		**mashed (about 1½ cups)**
½	**cup (1 stick) butter or**	½	**cup milk**
	margarine, softened	1	**cup chopped pecans**
1	**cup sugar**		**OR: walnuts**

1. Preheat the oven to moderate (350°). Grease and flour a 9 x 5 x 3-inch loaf pan.

2. Combine the flour, baking soda, baking powder and salt in a large bowl.

3. Beat the butter or margarine with the sugar in a medium-size bowl until light colored. Beat in the eggs, one at a time. Stir in the vanilla. Stir in the flour mixture alternately with the banana and the milk. Stir in ¾ cup of the pecans or walnuts. Pour the batter into the prepared pan. Sprinkle the remaining nuts over the batter.

4. Bake the bread in the preheated moderate oven (350°) for 1 hour and 20 minutes, or until a wooden pick inserted in the center comes out clean. Cool the bread in the pan on a wire rack for 10 minutes. Run a thin knife around the edges of the pan. Remove the bread from the pan to the wire rack to cool. The bread is better if eaten the next day; wrap the loaf tightly and store it at room temperature.

APPLE PECAN BREAD

Pecans and apples and cinnamon — some of our favorite flavors in one loaf. This hearty bread is delicious from the oven, but it's even better if you serve it the day after you bake it.

LOW-SODIUM

Bake at 325° for 1 hour and 10 minutes.
Makes 2 loaves (14 slices each).

Nutrient Value Per Slice: 221 calories, 2 g protein, 11 g fat, 29 g carbohydrate, 37 mg sodium, 29 mg cholesterol.

3   eggs, slightly beaten
2   cups sugar
1   cup vegetable oil
1   tablespoon vanilla
3   cups all-purpose flour
1   teaspoon baking soda
1   teaspoon ground
     cinnamon

4   cups chopped, peeled
     and cored apples
     (3 to 4 apples)
1   cup chopped pecans

Topping:
2   tablespoons sugar
½   teaspoon ground
     cinnamon

1. Preheat the oven to slow (325°). Grease and flour two 8½ x 5½ x 2½-inch loaf pans.

2. Stir together the eggs, the 2 cups of sugar, the oil and vanilla in a medium-size bowl until the ingredients are well mixed.

3. Combine the flour, baking soda and the 1 teaspoon of cinnamon on wax paper. Stir the flour mixture into the egg mixture just until they are evenly mixed. Stir in the apples and the pecans. Divide the batter between the two prepared pans.

4. Prepare the Topping: Combine the sugar with the cinnamon in a small cup. Sprinkle the topping over the batter.

5. Bake the breads in the preheated slow oven (325°) for 1 hour and 10 minutes, or until a wooden pick inserted in the centers comes out clean. Let the loaves cool in the pans on wire racks for 10 minutes. Run a thin knife around the edges of the pans. Remove the loaves from the pans to the wire racks to cool. The bread is better if eaten the next day; wrap the loaves tightly in plastic wrap or aluminum foil, and store them at room temperature.

Butter It Up!

Don't forget the little touches for a pretty brunch table: make butter or margarine curls (older kids can do these), or molded butter pats (younger ones can help here). Smaller pieces of butter soften quickly and spread easily.

❖ ❖ ❖

All-Purpose Flour Facts

All-purpose flour is a combination of soft and hard wheats. It is available bleached or unbleached, and is suitable for most baking purposes. Unbleached flour is off-white in color, bleached flour is chemically whitened.

Bleached and unbleached flours can be used interchangeably in recipes, but unbleached flour has a higher nutritional value. Both flours are enriched with iron and B-complex vitamins, the nutrients lost with the removal of the bran and germ.

❖ ❖ ❖

PIZZA PARTY

Know anyone who doesn't love pizza? Brighten up a weekend with your own pizza party! Invite everyone to pitch in. Assign tasks— some twirl the dough, some prepare the topping ingredients and others set the table. And everyone sits down to eat!

Menu

Julienned Fennel Salad*
Bacon, Tomato and Muenster Pizza (recipe, page 58)
Lemon Walnut Cake (recipe, page 237)
Orange-Zested Strawberries (recipe, page 254)

Parties with Pizzazz!

Make hosting a party easy on yourself by planning a menu of nibbles, salads and side dishes that can be made ahead and served cold, or heated quickly in the microwave. Concentrate your time on one splendid main dish that will fill your home with tempting aromas. Or create a stunning dessert to wow your guests. Then relax and enjoy!

For an easy and elegant centerpiece, arrange candlesticks with candles of varying diameters and heights in a large glass bowl. Surround the candlesticks with smooth black stones or glass floral marbles.

JULIENNED FENNEL SALAD

LOW-CHOLESTEROL

Makes 8 servings.

Nutrient Value Per Serving: 130 calories, 2 g protein, 9 g fat, 11 g carbohydrate, 337 mg sodium, 0 mg cholesterol.

Salad:
2	**medium-size fennel bulbs (about 22 ounces)**
4	**medium-size carrots, peeled**
2	**small sweet red peppers**
1	**small leek (3 ounces), split lengthwise and rinsed well**

Dressing:
3	**tablespoons fresh lemon juice**
2	**tablespoons Dijon-style mustard**
1	**tablespoon red wine vinegar**
1½	**teaspoons dried dillweed**
1	**teaspoon sugar**
½	**teaspoon salt**
⅛	**teaspoon freshly ground pepper**
⅓	**cup light olive oil**
1	**shallot, finely chopped**
8	**small Boston lettuce leaves**
	Fennel sprigs, for garnish (optional)

1. Prepare the Salad: Trim the tops from the fennel. Separate the bulbs into stalks. Cut the stalks into ⅛-inch-wide strips and set them aside.
2. Cut the carrots into 2-inch pieces. Lay them horizontally in the container of a food processor fitted with a shredding disk. Whirl until the carrot is shredded into strips. Cut the red peppers into 2 x ¼ x ¼-inch strips. Cut the green top off the leek, and slice the remainder into 2-inch-long slivers. Mix together the carrot, red pepper and leek in a bowl.
3. Prepare the Dressing: Mix together the lemon juice, mustard, vinegar, dillweed, sugar, salt and pepper in a small bowl. Set aside the dressing.
4. Heat the oil in a large skillet over medium heat. Add the shallot and cook for 3 minutes. Add the fennel. Cover the skillet and cook, stirring occasionally, for 3 minutes, or until the fennel begins to soften. Add the remaining vegetables and the dressing. Cover the skillet and cook, stirring occasionally, for 2 minutes, or until the vegetables are heated through. Remove the skillet from the heat. Cool the salad completely. (The salad can be prepared up to 48 hours in advance and refrigerated.)
5. To serve, arrange the lettuce on a serving platter. Stir the salad and spoon it onto the leaves. Garnish with fennel sprigs, if you wish.

BACON, TOMATO AND MUENSTER PIZZA

LOW-CALORIE • LOW-CHOLESTEROL

Bake at 425° for 15 to 18 minutes.
Makes 8 appetizer servings (24 pieces).

Nutrient Value Per Serving: 251 calories, 10 g protein, 13 g fat, 24 g carbohydrate, 474 mg sodium, 32 mg cholesterol.

Oatmeal Crust:
- 1 teaspoon active dry yeast
- ½ teaspoon sugar
- ½ cup plus 1 tablespoon warm water (105° to 115°)*
- 1⅓ cups bread flour
- ¼ cup plus 1 tablespoon old-fashioned rolled oats
- 1½ teaspoons safflower oil
- ½ teaspoon salt

Topping:
- 2 large onions, sliced
- 2 tablespoons (¼ stick) unsalted butter or margarine
- ½ teaspoon salt
- 5 slices bacon
- 1 medium-size tomato (about 6 ounces)
- 6 ounces sliced Muenster cheese
- 3 tablespoons sliced fresh basil leaves

A Hot Tip

A very hot oven is needed to produce a pizza crust that is crisp outside and chewy inside. A pizza stone (available at some gourmet cooking stores) is a great investment. Heated in the oven for at least 30 minutes before baking the pizza, it helps to distribute the heat evenly so the crust will not scorch.

❖　❖　❖

Julienned Fennel Salad (recipe, page 57) and Bacon, Tomato and Muenster Pizza provide the pizzazz for a party buffet.

Tip Top Toppings

To make the perfect pizza, use the finest ingredients available, including best-grade virgin olive oil and fresh herbs.

■ If you substitute dried herbs, use just a little more than half the amount of fresh herbs called for in the recipe.

■ Select fresh mozzarella, Fontina or goat cheese. Avoid hard, salty cheeses.

■ To add a fiery taste to pizza, steep chili flakes in olive oil and add them to the dough.

■ Try sun-dried tomatoes on pizza. They are available in stores, but you can make them at home, too. Halve tomatoes and squeeze them to draw out the juice. Lightly salt the halves and arrange them on a parchment paper-lined baking sheet. Dry the tomatoes in a very low oven (100° to 180°) overnight.

❖ ❖ ❖

Stuffed Mushrooms

Remove the stems from about 24 fresh mushrooms; reserve the stems for another use. Gently rinse the mushroom caps to remove any dirt; pat them dry with paper toweling. Mound a small amount of sweet Italian sausage into each mushroom cap (about ½ to 1 teaspoon per mushroom). Sprinkle the stuffed mushrooms with bread crumbs. Bake the mushrooms in a preheated hot oven (425°) for 30 minutes. Serve hot.

❖ ❖ ❖

1. Prepare the Oatmeal Crust: Combine the yeast, sugar and water in a 1-cup measure. Let the mixture stand for 5 minutes until it is foamy.
2. Combine the flour, ¼ cup of the oats, the oil and salt in the container of a food processor. With the machine running, add the yeast mixture through the feed tube. Stop the processor and check the texture of the dough. If the dough is too dry, add more water; if it is too wet, add more flour. When the texture is correct, process the dough for 30 seconds, or until it is uniformly moist and elastic. (To prepare the crust by hand, combine the flour, ¼ cup of the oats, the oil and salt in a large bowl. Stir in the yeast mixture until smooth. Knead the dough on a lightly floured surface until it is smooth and elastic, for 6 to 8 minutes.)
3. Transfer the dough to a large self-sealing plastic bag and seal the bag. Let the dough rise in a warm place until it is doubled in bulk, for 45 to 60 minutes. Punch down the dough. (At this point, the dough can be refrigerated overnight.)
4. Meanwhile, prepare the Topping: Sauté the onion in the butter or margarine in a medium-size skillet over medium heat for 8 to 10 minutes, or until the onion is soft. Increase the heat to high and sauté for 2 to 3 minutes, or until the onion is golden brown. Stir in the salt. Turn the mixture into a bowl and set it aside.
5. Wipe out the skillet. Add the bacon and cook over medium-low heat until it is crisp, for 6 to 8 minutes. Crumble the bacon coarsely when it is cool enough to handle and set it aside.
6. Preheat the oven to hot (425°).
7. Core the tomato and cut it in half horizontally. Squeeze it gently to remove the seeds and the juice. Cut the flesh into ¼-inch dice. Cut the Muenster cheese into ½-inch strips. Set aside the tomato and the cheese.
8. Roll out the dough on a lightly floured surface to about a 15 x 11-inch rectangle. Sprinkle a large baking sheet, preferably made of black steel, with the remaining tablespoon of oats. Place the dough on the sheet. Evenly arrange the onion and then the Muenster cheese over the crust. Sprinkle with the tomato and the bacon.
9. Bake the pizza in the preheated hot oven (425°) for 15 to 18 minutes, or until the bottom of the crust is golden brown. Transfer the pizza to a wire rack and sprinkle the basil on top. Cut the pizza in half lengthwise and then cut it crosswise into 2-inch widths. Slice each rectangle diagonally to make a total of 24 triangles.

*Note 1: Warm water should feel tepid when dropped on your wrist.
Note 2: The pizza can be prepared up to 6 hours in advance. Reheat it in a preheated moderate oven (350°) for 6 to 8 minutes.

A TASTE OF TAPAS

Tapas, classic Spanish appetizer dishes, are the perfect choice for weekend entertaining. You don't slave all day in the kitchen; most of the food is prepared in advance and refrigerated.

CAPONATA

LOW-CHOLESTEROL

Makes 20 servings.

Nutrient Value Per Serving: 239 calories, 2 g protein, 21 g fat, 14 g carbohydrate, 928 mg sodium, 0 mg cholesterol.

1	large eggplant (about 1¾ pounds)
2	to 3 tablespoons coarse (kosher) salt OR: 1 to 1½ tablespoons table salt
2	cups tomato paste (about three 6-ounce cans)
2½	cups red wine vinegar, or to taste
12	juniper berries, crushed
¼	teaspoon ground cloves
8	sprigs fresh thyme OR: ½ teaspoon dried thyme, crumbled
2	teaspoons sugar
4	cups olive oil

1	large onion, cut into ¾-inch chunks
2	sweet red peppers, cut into ¾-inch chunks
2	sweet green peppers, cut into ¾-inch chunks
8	stalks celery, cut diagonally into 1-inch pieces
2	yellow squash (8 ounces each), halved lengthwise and cut into ½-inch slices
1	jar (8 ounces) Greek olives, drained and pitted Chopped fresh parsley or thyme, for garnish (optional)

1. Quarter the eggplant lengthwise and cut it crosswise into ¾-inch-thick slices. Toss the eggplant with 2 tablespoons of the salt in a colander placed over a bowl. Let the eggplant stand at room temperature for at least 1 hour, or refrigerate it overnight. Squeeze out the excess liquid and blot the eggplant with paper toweling.
2. Combine the tomato paste, vinegar, juniper berries, cloves, thyme and sugar in a large saucepan. Bring the mixture to boiling. Lower the heat and simmer, uncovered, stirring often, for about 30 minutes, or until the sauce is thick (if it spatters, partially cover the saucepan). Set aside the sauce.
3. Heat the oil in a very large skillet until it is hot. Add the eggplant and cook over medium-high heat until it is golden, for about 8 minutes. Do not crowd the skillet; work in batches, if necessary. Remove the eggplant to paper toweling to drain. Add the onion and cook until it is translucent, for about 2 minutes. Remove the onion to paper toweling. Combine the onion with the eggplant in a large bowl. Add the red and green peppers to the skillet and cook until they are crisply tender, for 2 minutes. Drain the peppers and add them to the bowl. Cook the celery until it is crisply tender, for 3 minutes. Drain the celery and add it to the bowl. Cook the squash until it is crisply tender, for 4 minutes. Drain the squash and add it to the bowl. Stir the sauce and the olives into the eggplant mixture. Garnish with fresh parsley or thyme, if you wish. Serve hot, cold, or at room temperature.

Menu

Caponata*
Fusilli in Romesco Sauce*
Tortilla de Papas
(recipe, page 62)
Moroccan Eggplant
(recipe, page 63)
Vegetables in Jerez Sauce
(recipe, page 64)
Shrimp à la Gallega
(recipe, page 64)
Flan (recipe, page 65)

Quick-and-Spicy Dip

Mix ¼ cup of jalapeño jelly, 8 ounces of cream cheese and 2 chopped green onions until they are well blended. Serve the dip with crudités and tortilla chips.

❖ ❖ ❖

"Be not forgetful to entertain strangers: for thereby some have entertained angels unawares."
— *The Bible*

FUSILLI IN ROMESCO SAUCE

This dish is sweet, spicy and delicious. The classic Romesco sauce also goes well with poultry, pork or fish.

LOW-CHOLESTEROL

Bake sweet red peppers at 450° for 30 minutes.
Makes 8 servings.

Nutrient Value Per Serving: 485 calories, 11 g protein, 26 g fat, 55 g carbohydrate, 835 mg sodium, 0 mg cholesterol.

1	package (16 ounces) fusilli (corkscrew pasta)	4	to 8 dried hot red chili peppers
3	tablespoons coarse (kosher) salt OR: 1½ tablespoons table salt	2	cloves garlic, peeled
		¼	cup red wine vinegar
2	bay leaves	3	ounces toasted, blanched almonds (about ½ cup)*
¾	cup (12 tablespoons) olive oil	½	Granny Smith apple, peeled, cored and chopped
2½	pounds sweet red peppers		

1. Preheat the oven to very hot (450°).
2. Cook the fusilli in boiling water along with 2 tablespoons of the salt and the bay leaves, following the package directions. Drain the pasta, rinse it with cold water and drain it again. Discard the bay leaves. Toss the pasta with 1 tablespoon of the oil.
3. Meanwhile, rub the sweet red peppers with 1 tablespoon of the oil. Place them on the rack in the broiler pan.
4. Bake the sweet red peppers in the preheated very hot oven (450°), turning them occasionally, for 30 minutes, or until the sweet peppers are charred all over. Transfer them to a brown paper bag. Close the bag and set it aside for 15 minutes to let the steam loosen the skins. Remove the skins, stems and seeds, and discard these. Set aside the sweet peppers.
5. Quickly "toast" the hot red chili peppers in 1 tablespoon of the remaining oil in a small skillet for 30 seconds. Let the chili peppers cool.
6. Combine the sweet peppers, garlic, vinegar and the remaining 9 tablespoons of oil in the container of an electric blender or food processor. Whirl until the mixture is puréed. With the motor running, add the chili peppers, almonds, apple and the remaining tablespoon of salt. Whirl until the mixture is smooth. You should have about 4 cups of sauce.
7. Combine the cooked fusilli with the sauce in a large serving bowl and gently toss to mix them. Serve the fusilli at room temperature.

Note: To toast the almonds, place them on a baking sheet and toast them in a preheated moderate oven (350°), turning them occasionally, for 10 to 15 minutes, or until the almonds are golden.

TORTILLA DE PAPAS

This savory potato pie actually is baked on the stovetop in a skillet. It is wonderful party fare, and can be served hot or cold.

Makes 12 servings.

Nutrient Value Per Serving: 237 calories, 6 g protein, 15 g fat, 20 g carbohydrate, 420 mg sodium, 183 mg cholesterol.

½ **cup plus 2 tablespoons olive oil**
3½ **pounds all-purpose potatoes, peeled, quartered and thinly sliced**
1 **tablespoon coarse (kosher) salt OR: 1½ teaspoons table salt**
1 **onion (8 ounces), thinly sliced**
8 **eggs, slightly beaten**

1. Heat ½ cup of the oil in a large skillet over medium-high heat. Add the potatoes and cook, covered, for about 10 minutes, or until the potatoes are partially cooked. Stir in the salt and the onion. Cook, covered, over medium heat until the onion is wilted, and the potatoes are tender but not falling apart. Transfer the mixture to a bowl to cool. (Don't scrape any dark mixture stuck to the skillet into the bowl.) Stir the eggs into the potato mixture and mix well.

2. Heat 1 tablespoon of the remaining oil in a medium-size, heavy-bottomed skillet over high heat until the oil is almost smoking. Brush a little of the oil over the skillet bottom and sides. Pour the potato mixture into the skillet. Place the skillet over high heat for 1 to 2 minutes, or until the mixture starts to set around the edges. Turn the heat to the lowest setting. Cook until the mixture is set enough to turn over, for about 15 to 20 minutes.

3. Loosen the edges of the tortilla. Place a pot lid or plate over the skillet and invert the tortilla onto the lid. Clean the skillet. Return the skillet to high heat and brush it with the remaining tablespoon of oil.

4. Carefully slide the tortilla into the skillet. Cook for 1 minute. Lower the heat to the lowest setting. Cook until the tortilla top is firm to the touch, for about 15 minutes. Loosen the tortilla with a metal spatula. Place a large plate over the skillet and gently invert the tortilla onto the plate. Place a round, warmed serving plate over the tortilla and invert it. Cut the tortilla into 12 wedges and serve.

1

2

3

4

Nature's Beauty

Pots of fresh herbs can make marvelous natural centerpieces. Place the pots in pretty baskets or decorative pottery. Or snip bunches of fresh herbs and arrange them in a glass vase or brandy snifter in place of flowers. To further the natural theme, twist and tie small bunches of herbs together with raffia, and decorate each individual place setting.

❖ ❖ ❖

Eggplant Expertise

At one time, eggplant was about the size and shape of an egg—thus the name. Today, eggplant comes in a range of sizes from 2 to 12 inches, and varies in color from purple to yellowish-white.

■ Eggplants are really the fruit (technically the berry) of a plant once native to southern Asian and now grown in many countries. Soaking eggplant before cooking it is not necessary, although salt is sometimes used to draw out excess moisture before cooking eggplant.

■ To pick the perfect eggplant, look for one that is firm and heavy in relation to its size, with a uniformly rich, dark purple color. Use it as soon as possible after purchasing. To store eggplant, refrigerate it in a plastic bag for a day or two.

❖ ❖ ❖

MOROCCAN EGGPLANT

Fresh cilantro, gingerroot, garlic, cumin and lemon juice create a unique, flavorful sauce for baked eggplant.

LOW-CHOLESTEROL
Bake at 450° for 50 minutes.
Makes 12 servings.

Nutrient Value Per Serving: 131 calories, 2 g protein, 12 g fat, 8 g carbohydrate, 253 mg sodium, 0 mg cholesterol.

3 eggplants (about 1 pound each)	7 cups tightly packed fresh cilantro leaves OR: parsley leaves*
10 tablespoons olive oil	2 teaspoons ground cumin
1 teaspoon finely chopped garlic	2 tablespoons fresh lemon juice
1 teaspoon finely chopped, peeled fresh gingerroot	2 teaspoons coarse (kosher) salt OR: 1 teaspoon table salt
1 teaspoon finely chopped, seeded fresh hot chili pepper (wear rubber gloves)	Lemon slices, for garnish (optional)

1. Preheat the oven to very hot (450°).
2. Prick the eggplants several times with a fork and rub them with 1 tablespoon of the oil. Place the eggplants on a rack in a baking pan.
3. Bake the eggplants in the preheated very hot oven (450°) until they are soft, for about 50 minutes.
4. Meanwhile, combine 4 tablespoons of the remaining oil with the garlic, ginger and chili pepper in the container of a food processor or electric blender. Work in batches, if necessary. Cover and whirl until the mixture is smooth. With the motor running, start adding the cilantro or parsley leaves. When half the leaves have been used, add the cumin, lemon juice, salt and the remaining 5 tablespoons of oil. Add the remaining cilantro and whirl until the sauce is very smooth. Season with additional salt, if you wish.
5. When the eggplants are cool enough to handle, peel the skin from them with a paring knife, starting at the stem end but leaving the stem attached. Cut each eggplant lengthwise into 3 equal sections, starting just below the stem. Carefully remove the seeds with a teaspoon. Place the eggplants on a large serving platter and fan them slightly. Fill the slits in the eggplants with the cilantro sauce, using a teaspoon or pastry bag.
6. To serve, cut each eggplant crosswise into quarters. Garnish with the lemon slices, if you wish.

Note: If you are using parsley, add ground coriander to taste, if you wish, to approximate the taste of the cilantro sauce.

VEGETABLES IN JEREZ SAUCE

LOW-CALORIE • LOW-CHOLESTEROL

Makes 12 servings.

Nutrient Value Per Serving: 99 calories, 1 g protein, 9 g fat,
4 g carbohydrate, 152 mg sodium, 0 mg cholesterol.

4	ounces broccoli flowerets (about ½ head)
4	ounces cauliflower flowerets (about ½ head)
3	ounces green beans, trimmed and halved (about ¾ cup)
1	carrot, peeled and cut diagonally into ¼-inch-thick slices
2	fennel bulbs (12 ounces), tops trimmed and bulbs quartered
1	sweet red pepper (8 ounces), cut into 1-inch squares

3   **ounces small mushrooms, trimmed**

Jerez Sauce:
½   **cup olive oil**
2   **tablespoons sherry wine vinegar**
¼   **cup thinly sliced green onion, white part only**
1   **tablespoon chopped fresh thyme OR: ¼ teaspoon dried thyme, crumbled**
1   **teaspoon coarse (kosher) salt OR: ½ teaspoon table salt**

1. Place the broccoli, cauliflower, green beans, carrot and fennel in a small colander. Place the colander in a large pot of boiling water. Cook for 5 minutes, or until the vegetables are tender but still crunchy. Immerse the colander with the vegetables in ice water. Drain. Combine the cooked vegetables with the red pepper and the mushrooms in a large bowl.
2. Prepare the Jerez Sauce: Combine the oil, vinegar, green onion, thyme and salt in a small bowl. Mix the sauce with the vegetables. Transfer the vegetables to a serving platter.

SHRIMP À LA GALLEGA

Makes 6 servings.

Nutrient Value Per Serving: 379 calories, 18 g protein, 31 g fat,
10 g carbohydrate, 784 mg sodium, 115 mg cholesterol.

3	cloves garlic, peeled
¾	cup olive oil
¼	cup all-purpose flour
5	tablespoons paprika
¼	teaspoon ground hot red pepper
4	cups fish broth OR: chicken broth

1   **pound shelled and deveined shrimp (1¼ pounds with shells)**
   Salt and freshly ground white pepper, to taste
2   **tablespoons chopped parsley, for garnish**

1. Cook the garlic in the oil in a large skillet over medium-low heat until the garlic is lightly golden, for about 4 minutes. Stir in the flour, paprika and ground hot red pepper until the mixture is smooth. Stir in the fish or chicken broth until it is well mixed. Bring the mixture to boiling, stirring constantly, and cook, stirring, for 2 minutes.

Fennel

The name for both an anise-flavored herb and a bulb-like vegetable, fennel is more commonly used in Europe than in America.

■ The herb fennel, native to the Mediterranean, has feathery green foliage and stalks. The leaves are used primarily in seafood dishes, but also are added to salads and vegetables. The seeds of the herb are used to flavor salami, candy and liqueur.

■ The vegetable fennel has a large bulbous base and celery-like stalks with feathery green tops. Also known as sweet fennel or, in Italian, finocchio, the tender stalks can be eaten like celery. Sweet fennel is available from October to April.

❖ ❖ ❖

Selecting Shrimp

Raw shrimp is sold unshelled (fresh), shelled (fresh or frozen), or breaded and uncooked (frozen). Jumbo or extra large shrimp have up to 20 shrimp per pound; large shrimp have 21 to 30 per pound; medium have 31 to 40 per pound; small shrimp have over 40 per pound. One pound of unshelled shrimp yields ½ pound of cooked, shelled meat, or about 2 servings. One pound of shelled shrimp yields about 3 servings.

❖ ❖ ❖

2. Add the shrimp. Lower the heat and simmer, covered, for 3 minutes. Remove the shrimp with a slotted spoon to a medium-size bowl. Increase the heat to high, and cook the sauce until it is thickened and reduced to 3 cups, for about 5 minutes. Season with the salt and white pepper.
3. Combine 1 cup of the sauce with the shrimp in the bowl. Garnish with the parsley. Serve at room temperature. Refrigerate or freeze the remaining sauce.

FLAN

A delightfully cool and creamy ending to any spicy meal.

Bake at 350° for 35 minutes.
Makes 8 servings.

Nutrient Value Per Serving: 296 calories, 8 g protein, 13 g fat, 37 g carbohydrate, 174 mg sodium, 236 mg cholesterol.

1¼ **cups sugar**	¼ **teaspoon salt**
2 **cups milk**	¼ **to ½ teaspoon almond**
2 **cups half-and-half**	**extract**
6 **eggs**	

1. Preheat the oven to moderate (350°). Half fill a shallow 1½-quart round baking dish with hot water.
2. Heat ¾ cup of the sugar in a heavy, nonaluminum skillet over low heat until an amber-colored syrup forms, for about 5 minutes. Empty the water from the baking dish, and dry the dish thoroughly. Pour the hot syrup into the dish and quickly rotate the dish to coat the bottom and sides.
3. Heat together the milk and the half-and-half in a medium-size saucepan over medium heat until bubbles appear around the edges.
4. Beat together the eggs, the remaining ½ cup of sugar, the salt and almond extract in a medium-size bowl. Gradually stir in the hot milk. Strain the custard mixture into the coated dish. Place the dish in a larger pan filled with enough hot water to come half way up the side of the dish.
5. Bake the flan in the preheated moderate oven (350°) for 35 minutes, or until a knife inserted 1 inch from the edge comes out clean. Remove the dish to a wire rack to cool. Refrigerate the flan for 4 hours, or overnight.
6. To serve, run a metal spatula around the edge of the baking dish to loosen the flan. Place a large serving platter with a rim over the dish, and carefully invert the two. Remove the dish. The sauce will run down the sides of the flan.

What is Flan?

The word flan actually applies to three types of desserts: a pastry shell filled with fruit, custard or cream; an egg custard baked in a mold, usually with a caramel sauce; and a sponge cake baked in a shallow round pan, filled with fruit and/or custard. The recipe at right is an example of the second type of flan.

❖ ❖ ❖

Designs on Desserts

■ Keep tweezers handy for detailed decorating on cakes, cookies and hors d'oeuvres.
■ To make perfect ice cream balls, have ice cream at 40°F. A few hours before serving time, scoop the ice cream into balls, place the balls on a tray and freeze them.
■ To give a plain cake pizzazz, place a stencil pattern or doily over the top and dust the cake with 10X (confectioners' powdered) sugar or cocoa powder.

❖ ❖ ❖

SUMMER GRILL

A hot summer weekend means moving the dining room outdoors, and inviting friends over. Sizzling food whets your appetite, and the days seem to last forever. Ah, the luxury of summertime!

BRUSCHETTA

Grill the bread for these garlic toasts when your guests arrive, then top them with goat cheese and slices of ripe summer tomatoes.

LOW-CHOLESTEROL

Makes 12 servings.

Nutrient Value Per Serving: 158 calories, 5 g protein, 7 g fat, 18 g carbohydrate, 309 mg sodium, 0 mg cholesterol.

12 slices Italian bread (loaf halved lengthwise and cut crosswise)	6 ounces goat cheese
3 garlic cloves, peeled	4 ripe tomatoes, cut crosswise into 6 slices
3 tablespoons extra-virgin olive oil	Fresh mint or basil, for garnish

Menu

Bruschetta*
Grilled Vegetable Salad with
Pasta Aglio-Olio
(recipes, page 67 and 68)
Lemon and Rosemary Marinated
Mixed Grill (recipe, page 68)
Raspberry Pouffs with
Chocolate Sauce
(recipe, page 240)

Bruschetta combines grilled slices of Italian bread with tomatoes and goat cheese.

1. Prepare a hot charcoal fire.
2. Place the bread on the grill and toast it for about 1 minute on each side.
3. Remove the toasted bread to a warmed serving platter. Quickly rub both sides of each slice with the garlic. Drizzle with the oil. Spread each cut side with the goat cheese and top with 2 tomato slices, slightly overlapping. Garnish with the mint or basil and serve immediately.

GRILLED VEGETABLE SALAD WITH PASTA AGLIO-OLIO

LOW-CHOLESTEROL • LOW-FAT

Makes 10 servings.

Nutrient Value Per Serving (without Pasta Aglio-Olio):
154 calories, 5 g protein, 5 g fat, 25 g carbohydrate, 118 mg sodium, 0 mg cholesterol.

	Virgin olive oil	12	green onions, root ends removed and green tops trimmed
3	sweet red peppers, halved lengthwise, cored and seeded	12	small beets
3	sweet yellow peppers, halved lengthwise, cored and seeded	6	ears fresh corn, with husks
		1	head Boston lettuce
3	small yellow squash, halved lengthwise	1	head romaine lettuce
3	small zucchini, halved lengthwise		Pasta Aglio-Olio (recipe, page 68)
			Balsamic vinegar (see Tip, at left), to taste
			Coarse (kosher) salt, to taste

1. Prepare a hot charcoal fire.
2. Brush the oil on the cut surfaces of the red and yellow peppers. Brush all sides of the squash, zucchini and green onion with the oil.
3. Place the beets directly on the embers and check them from time to time. When the beets are tender, after about 20 minutes, remove them.
4. When the fire is medium-hot, place the red and yellow peppers on the grill rack, cut side down. Grill the peppers, turning once, for about 8 minutes, or just until they are tender. Remove the peppers and set them aside.
5. Grill the squash and the zucchini for about 3 to 4 minutes per side, or just until they are tender. Grill the green onion for about 1 to 2 minutes per side. Set aside the squash, zucchini and green onion.
6. Grill the corn in their husks, turning them several times, for about 10 minutes, or just until they are tender. When the corn are cool enough to handle, remove the husks. Cut the kernels from the cobs with a small knife. Set aside the corn kernels.
7. Peel the beets and slice them thinly. Slice the red and yellow peppers lengthwise into thin strips. Thinly slice the squash and zucchini crosswise. Set the vegetables aside.
8. To serve, line large serving platters with the Boston and romaine lettuces. Arrange the grilled vegetables in separate rows along one side of each platter. Place the Pasta Aglio-Olio along the other side of each platter. Drizzle with additional olive oil and with the vinegar. Sprinkle with the salt.

PASTA AGLIO-OLIO

LOW-SODIUM

Makes 10 servings.

Nutrient Value Per Serving: 275 calories, 6 g protein, 13 g fat, 34 g carbohydrate, 2 mg sodium, 43 mg cholesterol.

½	cup virgin olive oil	¼	cup balsamic vinegar (see Tip, page 67)
1	cup water		
2	cloves garlic, finely chopped	3	tablespoons freshly squeezed orange juice
	Crushed red pepper flakes, to taste		Coarse (kosher) salt, to taste
1	pound fresh thin Chinese egg noodles OR: capelli OR: vermicelli		

1. Heat the oil, water and garlic in a medium-size, heavy saucepan over medium-high heat. Bring the mixture to a gentle boil. Cook, uncovered, until the mixture is reduced to ⅔ cup, for about 12 minutes. Add the red pepper flakes. Set aside the aglio-olio to cool.

2. Cook the egg noodles in a large pot of boiling salted water for 2 minutes. Or cook the capelli or vermicelli until they are al dente, firm but tender to the bite. Drain the pasta and rinse it under cold running water to stop the cooking. Drain the pasta again.

3. Combine the pasta with the aglio-olio, vinegar and orange juice in a large bowl. Add the salt. Marinate the pasta at room temperature for about 30 minutes, tossing it frequently.

LEMON AND ROSEMARY MARINATED MIXED GRILL

Makes 10 servings.

Nutrient Value Per Serving: 659 calories, 35 g protein, 56 g fat, 2 g carbohydrate, 426 mg sodium, 143 mg cholesterol.

¾	cup virgin olive oil	6	rib lamb chops, 1½ inches thick (1¾ pounds)
½	cup freshly squeezed lemon juice (2 lemons)	2	racks baby-back spareribs (about 2 pounds)
2	cloves garlic, finely chopped		Coarse (kosher) salt, to taste
3	sprigs fresh rosemary		Additional rosemary sprigs, for garnish
6	chicken drumsticks (1¼ pounds)		Lemon wedges, for garnish
6	hot or sweet Italian sausages (about 1 pound)		

1. Combine the oil, lemon juice, garlic and 2 of the rosemary sprigs in a pan just large enough to hold the meats. Add the chicken, sausage and lamb chops. Marinate the meats at room temperature for 30 minutes.

2. Prepare a medium-hot charcoal fire.

3. Meanwhile, bring a large kettle of water to boiling. Add the spareribs and the remaining sprig of rosemary. Simmer the ribs over low heat for 10 minutes. Remove the ribs from the water and add them to the marinade.

Grilling Tips

A clean grill is a must. Always use a wire brush to clean the grill rack before using it. Grill residue can impart a sharp, bitter taste to the food you're cooking.

■ To start the fire, spread a layer of hardwood charcoal on the charcoal grate. Top with small bits of kindling and another two or three pieces of charcoal. Light the kindling.

■ The fire is hot when you can hold your hand at grill height for only 2 seconds; medium-hot, for 3 seconds.

■ Be patient! The biggest problem in grilling comes from trying to rush the process. Rushing risks burning the food with flames. Wait for the charcoal to burn down to create the flameless, intense heat necessary for proper cooking.

■ Avoid flare-ups; they burn or "brutalize" the food. Good preventive measures include trimming off the excess fat from meat, banking hot coals to one side of the grill, and leaving an open space on the grill rack to which you can transfer food if there is a flare-up.

❖ ❀ ❖

More Grilling Tips

■ Lightly oil the food to prevent it from sticking to the grill rack. But be careful! Using too much oil will cause flare-ups.

■ Always use tongs to maneuver food on the grill rack; a fork will pierce foods, releasing and losing the juices.

■ Need to start a fire quickly? Place one or two solid-fuel starter cubes on the charcoal grate. Light them, and place a metal chimney starter over the starter cubes. Fill the chimney with pieces of hardwood charcoal. In about 10 minutes, the charcoal will be hot enough to pour out (carefully!) onto the charcoal grate. This starting method is especially effective for urban grillers who need to avoid excess smoke.

❖   ❖   ❖

Summer evenings are made of cool drinks, warm friends and a great barbecue. Lemon and Rosemary Marinated Mixed Grill is a main course with something for everyone.

4. Place the grill rack about 10 inches above the hot coals.* Sprinkle the salt on the ribs and chicken.

5. Grill the ribs, chicken and sausage for 18 to 20 minutes, or until they are cooked through. Turn the meats often and move them around the grill rack to prevent charring. Remove the cooked meats to a heated serving platter.

6. Lower the grill rack to about 3 inches above the coals. Season the lamb chops with the salt. Grill the chops for 3 to 4 minutes per side, or until they are the desired doneness.

7. Serve the mixed grill garnished with the additional rosemary sprigs and the lemon wedges.

*__*Note:__ If you have a covered grill with a fixed rack, about 6 inches above the heat, follow this procedure: Grill the spareribs, sausage and chicken with the grill covered for 10 minutes, turning twice. Add the lamb chops to the rack over the hottest part of the fire. Grill all the meats, covered, for 3 minutes then turn them all. Grill for 3 minutes more, or until the meats are cooked through. As they finish, move the meats to the side of the rack to keep warm.*

AUTUMN HARVEST DINNER

Celebrate the fall foliage with a candelit dinner for special friends. Use your best china, tablecloth and napkins. Include an arrangement of flowers in crimson, gold and russet hues.

ROAST DUCK WITH PAN GRAVY

Roasting the duck for a long time at a low temperature removes much of the fat, and crisps the skin.

Roast at 325° for about 2 hours and 15 minutes.
Makes 12 servings (enough to feed 6 to 8 people).
Nutrient Value Per Serving: 931 calories, 52 g protein, 77 g fat, 4 g carbohydrate, 361 mg sodium, 227 mg cholesterol.

3	fresh ducks (5 to 6 pounds each)*	2	carrots, cut into 1-inch pieces
¼	teaspoon salt	2	cloves garlic, crushed and peeled
⅛	teaspoon freshly ground pepper	1¾	cups homemade chicken stock OR: chicken broth
3	medium-size onions, peeled and quartered	1	tablespoon cornstarch
2	celery stalks, cut into 1-inch pieces	1	tablespoon water

1. Preheat the oven to slow (325°).
2. Remove the excess fat from the duck cavities. Season the insides with the salt and the pepper. Truss the ducks and place them on racks in two roasting pans.
3. Roast the ducks in the lower third of the preheated slow oven (325°) for 1 hour.
4. Remove the ducks from the oven. Prick the skins all over with a 2-tined fork to let the fat run out. Carefully transfer the ducks to a cutting board that has a well around the edges. Remove the racks from the roasting pans and carefully pour off the contents of the pans into a 2-cup glass measure. Pour off as much fat as possible from the liquid in the glass measure. Place the measure briefly in the freezer to solidify the remaining fat. Remove and discard the fat. Set aside the defatted pan drippings; you should have about ¼ cup of drippings.
5. Add the onion, celery, carrot and garlic to the roasting pans. Return the ducks to the racks in the pans. Roast the ducks for approximately 1 hour and 15 minutes more. The ducks are done when the juices run clear from a pierced thigh, and an instant-reading meat thermometer registers 180° when inserted into the thigh and the breast without touching the bone.
6. Carefully drain the cavities of the ducks into the pans. Set aside the ducks on the cutting board. Remove the racks from the pans. Strain the contents of the pans into a 4-cup glass measure, pressing against the solids with a wooden spoon to extract the excess liquid. Discard the solids. Pour off as much fat as possible from the liquid in the glass measure. Place the

Menu

Champagne
Harvest Salad with Tarragon Vinaigrette (recipe, page 72)
Roast Duck with Pan Gravy*
Haricots Verts (see Tip, page 72)
Creamed Sauerkraut (recipe, page 72)
Potato Dumplings (recipe, page 73)
Pumpkin Soufflé with Calvados Crème Anglaise (recipes, page 236)
French Apple Tarte (recipe, page 235)

Champagne

Traditionally, only sparkling wines from Champagne, France were called champagne. Recently, however, many countries have begun to label their sparkling wines as champagne.

■ Most champagnes are white, a few are pink, but none are red. The best champagne is made by a special process in which the wine ferments for a second time in the bottle. This process is labor-intensive which is largely responsible for the high price.

■ Brut champagne is very dry, "Extra dry" is not quite as dry as Brut, Demi-sec is fairly sweet and Sec is sweet.

More About Champagne

- The best known champagnes are French, but California also produces some excellent champagnes that usually are less costly. Champagne is a blended wine, so a vintage on the label only means the champagne was made from various wines produced during that year. Vintage champagne is more expensive, but it has a special appeal to connoisseurs.

- As a general rule, plan on one bottle of champagne for every three guests. The new 750 milliliter bottle is a little larger than the former fifth size and should provide about four to six 4-ounce servings.

- Champagne can be served as a before-dinner drink, with meals or with dessert. It should be chilled, but not icy.

- If the cork pops noisily and flies across the room, and the champagne gushes out, you have opened the bottle incorrectly. Hold the bottle with one hand and remove the wire muzzle with the other hand. Tilt the bottle away from you slightly and hold the cork firmly. Rotate the bottle and slowly pull it away from the cork. The cork should come out in your hand.

❖ ❖ ❖

Celebrate the advent of the fall with an elegant dinner (from top to bottom): Harvest Salad with Tarragon Vinaigrette (recipe, page 72); Roast Duck with Pan Gravy; Creamed Sauerkraut (recipe, page 72); Haricots Verts (see Tip, page 72); and Potato Dumplings (recipe, page 73).

measure briefly in the freezer to solidify the remaining fat. Remove and discard the fat. Combine the pan drippings to make a total of about 1 cup; if necessary, add water to make 1 cup of liquid.

7. Combine the chicken stock or broth with the pan drippings in a saucepan, and simmer for 10 minutes. Dissolve the cornstarch in the water in a small cup. Stir the cornstarch mixture into the broth mixture. Cook until the gravy has thickened, for about 2 minutes. Keep the gravy warm.

8. Carve the ducks into serving portions. Serve them with the pan gravy.

__Note:__ If using frozen ducks, thaw them before roasting. Roast the thawed ducks at 350° for 30 minutes per pound.

HARVEST SALAD

LOW-CALORIE • LOW-CHOLESTEROL • LOW-SODIUM • LOW-FAT

Makes 6 servings.

Nutrient Value Per Serving (without Tarragon Vinaigrette):
34 calories, 2 g protein, 0 g fat, 7 g carbohydrate, 19 mg sodium,
0 mg cholesterol.

1	head Bibb lettuce	3	or 4 leaves curly endive (optional)
1	head red leaf lettuce	1	pear, halved, cored and cut into 1½ x ¼ x ¼-inch strips
1	Belgian endive, cut lengthwise into long ¼-inch-wide strips		Tarragon Vinaigrette (recipe follows)
1	bunch watercress, stemmed		

1. Wash the Bibb and red leaf lettuces, Belgian endive, watercress and, if you wish, curly endive. Dry them well.
2. Tear the Bibb and red leaf lettuces and, if using, curly endive into bite-size pieces. Place them in a large bowl along with the watercress, Belgian endive and pear strips. Toss with the Tarragon Vinaigrette and serve.

TARRAGON VINAIGRETTE

LOW-CHOLESTEROL • LOW-SODIUM

Makes ¾ cup.

Nutrient Value Per Tablespoon: 81 calories, 0 g protein, 9 g fat,
0 g carbohydrate, 3 mg sodium, 0 mg cholesterol.

1	tablespoon coarsely chopped fresh tarragon OR: ¼ teaspoon dried tarragon, crumbled	¼	teaspoon Dijon-style mustard
2	tablespoons tarragon vinegar	½	cup olive oil Pinch freshly ground pepper Pinch sugar

1. Whisk together the tarragon, vinegar, mustard, oil, pepper and sugar in a small bowl.
2. Refrigerate the dressing for at least 2 hours to allow the flavors to blend.

CREAMED SAUERKRAUT

Makes 6 servings.

Nutrient Value Per Serving: 307 calories, 4 g protein, 27 g fat,
16 g carbohydrate, 1,132 mg sodium, 85 mg cholesterol.

2	medium-size onions, finely chopped	1	can (32 ounces) sauerkraut
6	tablespoons unsalted butter	2	teaspoons white wine vinegar
1½	teaspoons caraway seeds	1	cup heavy cream
6	tablespoons all-purpose flour	¼	teaspoon freshly ground white pepper

"Come, ye thankful people, come, Raise the song of Harvest-home; All is safely gathered in, Ere the winter storms begin."
—Henry Alford

Haricots Verts

Place 1½ pounds of "haricots verts" (very thin green beans) flat in a large saucepan or skillet. Add 1 cup of water and bring to boiling. Lower the heat, cover the saucepan and simmer the green beans for 10 minutes, or just until they are tender. Drain the green beans. Toss them with a little unsalted butter, if you wish, and serve.

Dumpling

Almost every cuisine in the world has its version of the dumpling. Dumplings probably originated in China. Marco Polo returned to Italy from his travels in China with noodles (which developed into pasta), and with meat-filled dumplings that became ravioli. Dumplings can be inexpensive meal-stretchers when cooked in soup or stews, or they can be made into delicious desserts.

■ Americans think of dumplings as small spoonfuls of dough dropped into boiling soup or stew, or baked apple dumplings. Some dumplings, such as the elegant French quenelles (light-as-a-feather fish dumplings in a rich sauce), can be served as a main course or appetizer. The Italian gnocchi is made from potatoes, semolina or a spinach-and-ricotta mixture, and usually is served as a separate course in place of pasta. Chinese dumplings are savory or sweet. Savory dumplings are filled with pork, shrimp, or egg and vegetables. Sweet Chinese dumplings are filled with dried fruits, nuts, or bean pastes. Czechoslovakian dumplings include liver- and fruit-stuffed dumplings, and some flavored with poppy seeds.

■ The word "dumpling" may have originated from "dumpf," a German word meaning damp and moist, or a thick, misshapen lump.

❖   ❖   ❖

1. Sauté the onion in the butter in a large skillet over medium-high heat until the onion is translucent, for about 2 minutes. Add the caraway seeds. Reduce the heat to low, and cook for 2 minutes without letting the onion brown. Stir in the flour until it is well combined. Cook the onion mixture for 5 minutes.

2. Wash the sauerkraut in cold water and squeeze it dry. Add the sauerkraut, vinegar, cream and white pepper to the skillet. Heat the sauerkraut through, for about 1 minute, and serve.

POTATO DUMPLINGS

LOW-FAT

Dry potatoes at 200° for 10 minutes.
Makes 6 servings (14 dumplings).

Nutrient Value Per Serving: 180 calories, 5 g protein, 2 g fat, 34 g carbohydrate, 282 mg sodium, 91 mg cholesterol.

1 **pound baking potatoes, quartered**	1½ **cups all-purpose flour**
2 **egg yolks**	4 **tablespoons (½ stick) butter**
2 **teaspoons snipped fresh chives**	2 **tablespoons vegetable oil**
1 **teaspoon chopped parsley**	**Garnish (optional):**
1 **teaspoon chopped fresh dill**	1 **cup white bread crumbs (2 slices)**
1¾ **teaspoons salt**	¼ **cup chopped parsley**
⅛ **teaspoon freshly ground white pepper**	2 **tablespoons butter**

1. Place the potatoes in a medium-size saucepan with enough water to cover them. Bring the water to boiling and cook until the potatoes are fork-tender, for about 15 minutes. Drain the potatoes well. When cool enough to handle, peel them. Place the potatoes on a baking sheet and dry them in a preheated very slow oven (200°) for 10 minutes.

2. Pass the potatoes through a ricer, or mash them with a potato masher in a bowl. Add the egg yolks, chives, parsley, dill, ¾ teaspoon of the salt and the white pepper. Mix the ingredients well. Add the flour. Stir with a wooden spoon until the flour is blended and a stiff dough forms.

3. Bring a saucepan of water and the remaining 1 teaspoon of salt to simmering. Place the dough on a lightly floured cutting board and knead lightly for 1 minute. Roll the dough into a 14-inch long log. Mark off 1 inch of dough per dumpling and cut. Roll each piece of dough into a ball and drop it into the simmering water. Cook until the dumplings rise to the top, for about 6 minutes, then cook for 2 minutes more. Remove the dumplings with a slotted spoon to paper toweling to drain. The dumplings can be prepared earlier in the day up to this point.

4. To reheat the dumplings for serving, heat the butter and the oil in a large skillet over medium heat. Add the dumplings and brown them on all sides for about 6 minutes. Remove the dumplings and keep them warm.

5. To prepare the garnish, if you wish, combine the bread crumbs with the parsley in a small bowl. Sauté the mixture in the butter in a skillet for 30 seconds, stirring.

6. Serve the dumplings, sprinkled with garnish, if you wish.

MEXICAN FIESTA

South-of-the-border cuisine is easier to make than you may think. While some of the cooking techniques are unusual, with practice you'll be peeling jalapeño peppers as easily as you chop garlic!

CHORIZO-STUFFED BURRITOS

Makes 6 servings.

Nutrient Value Per Serving (without Roasted Tomatillo Salsa): 548 calories, 25 g protein, 24 g fat, 58 g carbohydrate, 420 mg sodium, 50 mg cholesterol.

½   **pound chorizo OR: Italian sausages, casings removed**
1   **tablespoon vegetable oil**
½   **cup chopped onion (1 medium-size onion)**
1   **clove garlic, chopped**
3   **cups cooked, drained pinto beans, liquid reserved**
    Salt, to taste

12   **flour tortillas**
1½   **cups shredded Monterey Jack OR: mild Cheddar cheese**
    Roasted Tomatillo Salsa (recipe, page 75)
    Dairy sour cream, for garnish (optional)
    Additional shredded cheese, for garnish (optional)

Menu

Chorizo-Stuffed Burritos*
Roasted Tomatillo Salsa*
Spiced Sesame Chicken Breasts
(recipe, page 76)
Mexican Chocolate Flan
(recipe, page 242)
Coconut Cream Pie
(recipe, page 244)

Chorizo-Stuffed Burritos are full of spicy flavor.

Fiesta Centerpiece

If you're giving a dinner party with a Mexican theme, create a sandscape centerpiece. Pour clean, dry sand onto a bright enameled tray and decorate with painted Mexican pottery or baskets, with or without flowers. Mark each guest's place with a miniature cactus.

✧ ✧ ✧

Mexican Cooking Tips

Follow these tips when you're preparing our Mexican Fiesta, or any Mexican cuisine.

■ You'll need four basic pieces of equipment to create authentic-tasting Mexican food: a blender or food processor; a spice grinder or mortar and pestle; a large, heavy skillet or griddle; and a strainer.

■ Beans should be soaked before cooking to reduce the cooking time and remove some of their gas. Cook them over low heat, no higher than a simmer. This way, the beans will retain their shape and develop a good texture.

■ To achieve a smooth purée, be sure to finely chop any dense foods, such as garlic cloves. Stir a mixture of ingredients well before placing it in the container of the blender or food processor. To purée, first pulse-chop the mixture. Then, with the blender or processor on low speed, blend until the mixture is a smooth purée. Blending should take about 20 seconds.

✧ ✧ ✧

1. Cook the chorizo or Italian sausage in the oil in a skillet over medium heat, stirring to break up the meat, for 10 minutes, or until the meat no longer is pink. Remove the chorizo from the skillet with a slotted spoon to paper toweling to drain.
2. Reduce the heat to medium-low. Add the onion to the skillet and sauté for 6 minutes, or until the onion is golden. Add the garlic and sauté for 2 minutes. Return the chorizo to the skillet.
3. Add about 1 cup of the pinto beans to the skillet and mash them to a thick purée with a potato masher or the back of a spoon. Repeat twice more with the remaining beans. Simmer the chorizo mixture until it is thick, for about 3 minutes, adding some of the reserved bean liquid if the mixture thickens too much. Season with the salt.
4. Heat a clean, dry skillet over medium heat. Place a tortilla in the skillet and heat it for several seconds on each side. Transfer the tortilla to a plate.
5. Spoon a scant ¼ cup of the chorizo filling down the center of the tortilla. Sprinkle on about 2 tablespoons of the Monterey Jack or Cheddar cheese. Roll up the tortilla, place it on a warmed serving platter and cover it with aluminum foil. Repeat with the remaining tortillas, filling and cheese. If necessary, the burritos may be kept warm in a preheated slow oven (300°) for up to 15 minutes.
6. Serve the burritos with the Roasted Tomatillo Salsa. If you wish, garnish with sour cream and additional shredded cheese.

ROASTED TOMATILLO SALSA

Fresh tomatillos — plum-size, light green, tart-tasting fruit in papery husks — are available where Mexican or Spanish cooking ingredients are sold.

LOW-CALORIE • LOW-CHOLESTEROL • LOW-SODIUM • LOW-FAT

Broil tomatillos for 10 minutes.
Makes ¾ cup sauce.

Nutrient Value Per Tablespoon: 6 calories, 0 g protein, 0 g fat, 1 g carbohydrate, 45 mg sodium, 0 mg cholesterol.

½ pound fresh tomatillos, husked and rinsed OR: 1 can (13 ounces) tomatillos, drained and rinsed	1 tablespoon chopped fresh cilantro
4 fresh serrano chili peppers OR: 2 fresh jalapeño peppers, stemmed, seeded and chopped (wear rubber gloves)	¼ cup finely chopped onion ¼ teaspoon salt ¼ cup water

1. Place the tomatillos on a baking sheet with sides.
2. Broil the tomatillos 5 inches from the heat source, turning once, for 10 minutes, or until the skins darken and blister. Cool the tomatillos completely.
3. Place the tomatillos, and any juices from the pan, in the container of a food processor or electric blender, along with the chili or jalapeño peppers. Whirl until the mixture is a coarse purée. Place the purée in a small bowl. Stir in the cilantro, onion and salt.
4. Thin the sauce with the water. Let the sauce stand for 30 minutes to 1 hour to blend the flavors.

SPICED SESAME CHICKEN BREASTS

These chicken breasts, fragrant with sesame sauce, are poached in the oven.

LOW-CALORIE • LOW-CHOLESTEROL

Bake at 350° for 30 minutes.
Makes 6 servings.

Nutrient Value Per Serving: 294 calories, 27 g protein, 18 g fat, 6 g carbohydrate, 381 mg sodium, 73 mg cholesterol.

⅓	cup plus 1 tablespoon sesame seeds	2	cups water
12	ounces fresh tomatillos, husked and rinsed OR: 1 can (13 ounces) tomatillos, drained and rinsed	2	tablespoons fresh cilantro leaves
		¼	teaspoon aniseed, ground
		1	tablespoon vegetable oil
3	fresh serrano chili peppers OR: 1 to 2 fresh jalapeño peppers, stemmed	¾	cup chicken broth
		½	teaspoon salt
		6	boned chicken breasts (about 1½ pounds)
½	cup chopped onion		Fresh cilantro sprigs, for garnish (optional)
2	cloves garlic, peeled		

1. Heat a skillet over medium heat. Add the sesame seeds and toast, stirring frequently, for 6 minutes, or until the seeds are golden brown. Transfer the toasted seeds to a plate to cool. Reserve 1 tablespoon of the toasted seeds for garnish. Place the remaining seeds in the container of a food processor and whirl until the seeds are finely ground. Set aside.
2. Combine the tomatillos, chili or jalapeño peppers, onion, garlic and water in a saucepan. Bring the mixture to boiling. Reduce the heat to medium-low and simmer for 10 minutes. Drain the tomatillo mixture.
3. Combine the tomatillo mixture, cilantro leaves and aniseed in the container of a food processor or electric blender. Whirl until the tomatillo mixture is a smooth purée. Strain the purée into a small bowl.
4. Heat the oil in a saucepan over medium heat. Add the ground sesame seeds and cook, stirring, for 3 minutes, or until the mixture masses and turns golden brown. Add the tomatillo purée, broth and salt, and stir until all the ingredients are combined. Bring the sauce to boiling. Reduce the heat to medium-low, cover the saucepan and cook for 45 minutes.
5. If a smoother texture for the sauce is desired, return it to the electric blender or food processor. Whirl until the sauce is smooth. If necessary, thin the sauce with additional broth to the consistency of cream. You should have about 1½ cups of sauce. (The sauce may be refrigerated, covered, for up to 2 days.)
6. Preheat the oven to moderate (350°). Reheat the sauce, if necessary.
7. Spoon about one third of the sauce into a 13 x 9 x 2-inch nonaluminum baking dish. Arrange the chicken in a single layer in the dish. Spoon on the remaining sauce.
8. Bake the chicken in the preheated moderate oven (350°) for 30 minutes, or until the juices run clear when the chicken is pierced with a knife.
9. Transfer the chicken to a serving platter. Spoon the sauce over the chicken. Garnish with the reserved toasted sesame seeds and, if you wish, sprigs of fresh cilantro.

More Mexican Cooking Tips

■ To keep poultry juicy, gently poach it, then allow the poultry to cool in the poaching liquid.

■ Sear meat in a very hot pan. This will give the meat a nice crust and help retain its flavor.

■ When pan-frying meat coated with a flavoring paste, use a nonstick pan and keep the heat medium-high.

■ When grilling green onions, place a piece of aluminum foil over part of the rack and lay the green tops of the onions on the foil. This prevents the tops from burning while the onion bulbs are cooking.

■ Do not overbake a flan. If the surface of the flan is pitted, like Swiss cheese, and the interior is curded and watery, it has been overcooked. When you make the flan again, reduce the baking time. If the mold has been properly caramelized, the caramel will melt into a delicious liquid lining that will allow the custard to slip out easily from the mold.

Good friends and good food make any weekend special.

Clean Greens

*To clean greens well, discard
any bruised, discolored or
tough outer leaves. Remove
the remaining leaves from the
head, trim any tough core or
rib, and wash the leaves
gently in a sink or large bowl
filled with water. Drain the
leaves and rinse. If the leaves
are very sandy, wash them in
several changes of water.*

*To dry the greens, place them
in a salad spinner, or blot
them dry gently with paper
toweling.*

Watercress and Endive with
Basil Vinaigrette adds a colorful
focal point to your table. It's
almost a centerpiece in itself!

WATERCRESS AND ENDIVE WITH BASIL VINAIGRETTE

LOW-CHOLESTEROL

Makes 4 servings.

Nutrient Value Per Serving: 138 calories, 2 g protein, 14 g fat,
3 g carbohydrate, 130 mg sodium, 0 mg cholesterol.

Basil Vinaigrette:
¼ cup olive oil
¼ cup vegetable oil
2 tablespoons balsamic
vinegar
2 tablespoons chopped
fresh basil
2 teaspoons coarse-grained
Dijon-style mustard
1 clove garlic, crushed

¼ teaspoon salt
⅛ teaspoon freshly ground
black pepper

2 large bunches watercress
2 large Belgian endive,
cored and separated
into leaves
2 large sweet red peppers,
cut into rings

1. Prepare the Basil Vinaigrette: Combine the olive and vegetable oils with
the vinegar, basil, mustard, garlic, salt and black pepper in a screw-top jar.
Cover the jar and shake well to blend all the ingredients. Chill the dressing
until about 1 hour before serving.

2. Arrange the watercress on a large serving platter. Top with the endive
leaves and the red pepper rings.

3. Sprinkle the salad with some vinaigrette; serve the rest on the side.

CHEESE AND CASHEW-STUFFED CUCUMBERS

An appetizer full of creamy flavor. You can substitute zucchini for the cucumber in this recipe.

LOW-CALORIE • LOW-CHOLESTEROL

Makes 34 appetizer servings.

Nutrient Value Per Serving: 32 calories, 2 g protein, 2 g fat, 1 g carbohydrate, 94 mg sodium, 5 mg cholesterol.

2	long, thin English cucumbers (about 15 ounces each), unpeeled and cut into ¾-inch-thick rounds	½	pound blue cheese, softened
		¼	cup unsalted cashew nuts, chopped
			Pimiento strips, for garnish (optional)

1. Scoop out about half the center of each cucumber round, using a ¾-inch melon baller or a standard, round measuring spoon.
2. Combine the blue cheese with the cashews in a medium-size bowl. Fill each round with about 1 slightly rounded teaspoonful of the cheese mixture. Cover the rounds and refrigerate them until ready to serve.
3. At serving time, if you wish, garnish each round with pimiento strips.

BUTTERMILK CORNBREAD STICKS

LOW-FAT • LOW-CALORIE

Bake at 425° for 15 minutes.
Makes 28 cornbread sticks.

Nutrient Value Per Stick: 94 calories, 2 g protein, 3 g fat, 14 g carbohydrate, 187 mg sodium, 27 mg cholesterol.

2	cups yellow cornmeal	½	teaspoon baking soda
1	cup all-purpose flour	2	eggs, slightly beaten
¼	cup sugar	2	cups buttermilk
1	tablespoon baking powder	6	tablespoons butter, melted
1	teaspoon salt		

1. Preheat the oven to hot (425°). Lightly grease a cornstick pan. Place it in the oven to warm while preparing the batter.
2. Combine the cornmeal, flour, sugar, baking powder, salt and baking soda in a large bowl. Add the eggs, buttermilk and butter to the cornmeal mixture, and stir just to moisten the cornmeal mixture.
3. Pour the batter into the cornstick molds, filling each about three quarters full.
4. Bake the cornsticks in the preheated hot oven (425°) for about 15 minutes, or until the tops are lightly browned. Cool the cornsticks in the pan on a wire rack for 5 minutes. Using a thin metal spatula, carefully remove the sticks from the pan. Repeat until all the batter is used.

The Dining Society

A great way to keep in touch with a group of people, especially those with busy schedules (which includes practically everyone), is to form a "dining society."

■ First determine the group size — 10 to 18 members is a workable number — and invite those interested to a pow-wow to plan ahead. Figure out frequency of dinners, dates, times and hosts; discuss different cuisine themes, such as "Mexicali Night," "Sensational Seafood" or a "Finger-Food Feast."

■ Decide how the dinners will be coordinated. One workable idea is to have a "host or hostess of the month." The host or hostess supplies the house, tableware, linens, ice and mixers. A small rotating group helps with set-up and clean-up, and the rest of the group supplies the various dishes.

■ It's wise to have some rules about costs. People's incomes vary considerably, so decide on a standard, approximate cost per evening and per member to avoid inequalities. Have an appointed "treasurer" to whom group members submit receipts for food or supplies purchased for the club. The treasurer calculates the total cost per event and divides it on a per member basis. It's also a good idea to decide ahead of time on a maximum budget per meal to help keep costs down.

❖   ❖   ❖

More About The Dining Society

- Establish a bring-your-own-bottle policy, to provide for different tastes and consumption. Select a person to tend bar for each evening; this helps avoid congestion and confusion.
- Decide on a "leftovers policy." Are leftovers up for grabs? Does each person take the leftover portions of the dish he or she contributed? Do the leftovers stay with the host/hostess? Or do they go to a local food bank?
- Try to plan meals around your members' schedules. If someone is going through a particularly busy time, assign him or her a dish that takes a minimum of preparation time, or is make-ahead.
- For each dinner, have each member bring xeroxed copies of the recipe for the dish he or she contributed that evening. Then, as the members are leaving, pass out the recipes — fine mementos of a lovely evening spent with friends.

❖   ❖   ❖

SPLIT PEA SOUP

LOW-CHOLESTEROL • LOW-FAT

Makes 8 servings.

Nutrient Value Per Serving: 273 calories, 18 g protein, 6 g fat, 38 g carbohydrate, 836 mg sodium, 13 mg cholesterol.

5	strips bacon	1	large, meaty smoked ham hock (about 10 ounces)
2	small onions, chopped (½ cup)	7	cups water
2	medium-size carrots, chopped (⅔ cup)	2	bay leaves
2	celery stalks, chopped (1 cup)	2	teaspoons salt
1	pound dried green split peas, picked over and rinsed	¼	teaspoon freshly ground black pepper
			Toasted Croutons (optional; recipe follows)

1. Cook the bacon in a 5-quart Dutch oven or a pot until the bacon is crisp. Remove the bacon with a slotted spoon to paper toweling to drain. Discard all but 1½ tablespoons of the fat. Add the onion, carrot and celery, and cook over medium heat just until the vegetables are tender, for about 3 minutes.
2. Add the peas, ham hock, water, bay leaves, salt and black pepper to the pot. Bring the mixture to boiling, lower the heat and simmer, covered, for about 1½ hours.
3. Remove the ham hock and cut off the meat. Return the meat to the soup. Crumble the cooked bacon. Garnish the soup with the bacon and, if you wish, Toasted Croutons.

Toasted Croutons:

Using small 1- to 1½-inch decorative cutters, cut out 32 shapes from 4 slices of whole wheat bread. Melt 2 tablespoons of butter or margarine in a large skillet over medium heat. Add the bread cutouts and sauté, tossing constantly, until they are golden brown.

Hearty Split Pea Soup is delicious with homemade Buttermilk Cornbread Sticks (recipe, page 78).

FRUIT-STUFFED PORK ROAST

Moist and full of flavor, this pork roast is stuffed with a delectable combination of dried fruit, garlic and fresh tarragon, then basted to perfection with a sherry-butter mixture.

Roast at 350° for 1 hour and 15 minutes.
Makes 10 servings.

Nutrient Value Per Serving: 496 calories, 34 g protein, 30 g fat, 22 g carbohydrate, 553 mg sodium, 123 mg cholesterol.

4 **pounds boneless pork loin roast**	½ **teaspoon freshly ground black pepper**
1 **box (11 ounces) dried mixed fruit***	½ **cup dry sherry**
1 **clove garlic, thinly sliced**	2 **tablespoons butter, melted**
1 **tablespoon dried tarragon, crumbled**	**Celery leaves, for garnish (optional)**
2 **teaspoons salt**	**Red and green apple wedges, for garnish (optional)**

1. Preheat the oven to moderate (350°).

2. If the roast is tied, remove the strings. Make a deep slice lengthwise down the roast without cutting through it. Layer the dried fruit, alternating the colors, down the slice. Fold the top of the roast over the fruit, and tie the roast securely in several places.

3. Make several shallow slits in the roast with a small knife. Push the garlic slices into the slits. Rub the roast with the tarragon, salt and black pepper. Place the roast on a rack in a roasting pan.

4. Combine the sherry with the butter in a measuring cup. Brush the mixture over the roast.

5. Roast in the preheated moderate oven (350°), basting frequently, for about 1 hour and 15 minutes, or until a meat thermometer registers 170°.

6. Remove the roast to a cutting board. Let the roast stand for 15 minutes before slicing it.

7. Garnish the roast with celery leaves and with red and green apple wedges, if you wish. Serve the roast with the defatted pan juices.

*Note: *Remove the pits from the prunes, if necessary.*

Buffet Savvy

One of the easiest ways to give a party is to make it "serve yourself." Follow these guidelines for a beautiful buffet:

■ Leave an uncluttered route between the kitchen and the serving table, so you can bring out food without detours.

■ The buffet table should have plenty of space for guests to move around it freely.

■ Set the table to facilitate ease in serving and carrying: first the plates, then the food, then the tableware and napkins. If space is limited on the main table, use side tables for cutlery, drinks, dessert, coffee and tea.

■ Wrap each set of tableware in a napkin for easy pick-up.

■ Place the proper serving utensils next to each dish.

■ Provide adequate seating and table space.

■ If you and your guests will be eating at a dining table, set the table beforehand with beverage glasses, napkins and tableware so the guests won't have to pick up these items from the buffet area.

❖ ❖ ❖

Parsnips

A root vegetable harvested after the first frost, parsnips look like ivory-colored carrots. Parsnips are a member of the Umbelliferae, or umbel family, which also includes carrots, celery, parsley and other herbs. Parsnips are native to the eastern Mediterranean.

■ Parsnips can be served as a cooked vegetable, or added to soups and stews.

■ The peak growing season is September through May. Buy small to medium-size roots, because large roots tend to be woody. Plan on buying about ¼ to ⅓ pound per serving.

■ Store parsnips in plastic bags in the refrigerator; they will keep for several weeks.

■ Trim, peel and wash the parsnips. Cut them into slices, sticks or cubes. Cook the pieces in an inch of boiling water for 5 to 10 minutes. Drain the parsnips and season them with butter, salt and pepper. Or drain and mash the parsnips. Parsnips also can be braised in broth or wine, or deep-fat fried.

❖　❖　❖

> " *There is a southern proverb— fine words butter no parsnips.* "
> —*Sir Walter Scott*

CREAMY SCALLOPED PARSNIPS

A luscious side dish that complements the Fruit-Stuffed Pork Roast, or any roasted meat, perfectly.

Bake at 325° for 50 minutes.
Makes 8 servings.

Nutrient Value Per Serving: 275 calories, 5 g protein, 15 g fat, 32 g carbohydrate, 655 mg sodium, 45 mg cholesterol.

2 pounds parsnips, peeled and cut into ¼-inch-thick slices	1½ teaspoons salt
2 cups half-and-half	¼ teaspoon freshly ground pepper
3 tablespoons all-purpose flour	1 large onion, coarsely chopped (1 cup)
3 tablespoons chopped parsley	3 tablespoons butter or margarine

1. Preheat the oven to slow (325°). Lightly butter an 8 x 8-inch square or other 2-quart baking dish.
2. Bring 1 inch of water to boiling in a medium-size saucepan over medium heat. Add the parsnips. Return to boiling. Cover the saucepan and cook the parsnips for 5 minutes, or until they are barely tender. Drain the parsnips.
3. Meanwhile, stir together the half-and-half and the flour in a small saucepan until they are well blended. Cook the mixture over low heat until it is thickened, for 3 to 4 minutes. Add the parsley, salt and pepper.
4. Layer half the parsnips and half the onion in the prepared dish. Pour on half the cream mixture. Dot with half the butter or margarine. Repeat the layering. Pour on the remaining cream mixture. Dot with the remaining butter. Cover the dish.
5. Bake the parsnips in the preheated slow oven (325°) for 40 minutes. Remove the cover. Bake for another 10 minutes, or until the parsnips are tender and the top is lightly golden.

This beautiful buffet is shown on our cover. It's perfect for warm-weather dining, when light and tasty food is the order of the day.

CHILLED CREAMY PEA SOUP

Makes 6 servings.

Nutrient Value Per Serving: 226 calories, 9 g protein, 11 g fat, 25 g carbohydrate, 307 mg sodium, 33 mg cholesterol.

3 cups fresh peas	6 medium-sized sweet red peppers
1 pint water	Whipped cream, for garnish
½ cup chopped onion	Chopped fresh mint OR: chives, for garnish
3 tablespoons butter	Dash ground nutmeg, for garnish
3 tablespoons flour	
½ teaspoon salt	
⅛ teaspoon freshly ground pepper	
3 cups milk	

1. Cook the peas in the water in a large saucepan until they are very soft.
2. Place the onion, peas and cooking liquid in the container of an electric blender or food processor. Whirl until the mixture is puréed. Refrigerate the pea purée until it is chilled.
3. Melt the butter in the top of a double boiler. Add the flour, salt and pepper. Cook the flour mixture until it is bubbly. Add the milk and cook over hot water, stirring constantly, until the mixture is smooth.
4. Add the pea purée to the flour mixture and heat the combined mixture. Refrigerate the soup. Cut off the top third of the red peppers and remove the membranes and seeds. Pour the chilled soup into the peppers unil they are three quarters full. Garnish with the whipped cream, the mint or chives and the nutmeg.

STUFFED SNOW PEAS

LOW-CALORIE • LOW-SODIUM

Makes 25 canapés.

Nutrient Value Per Serving: 62 calories, 4 g protein, 4 g fat, 1 g carbohydrate, 51 mg sodium, 15 mg cholesterol.

2 cups chicken broth	Grated orange zest (orange part of rind only)
2 cups white wine	¼ cup finely chopped celery
1 pound boned, skinless chicken breasts	⅛ cup finely chopped cashews, unsalted
½ cup fresh mayonnaise	½ pound snow peas, stemmed
1 tablespoon curry powder	

Menu

Chilled Creamy Pea Soup*
Stuffed Snow Peas*
Baked Ham in Cider*
Best-Ever Biscuits*
Fresh Berries in Tuiles with
Caramel Sauce (recipe, page 226)

Billowy Whipped Cream

For the lightest whipped cream, chill the beaters and bowl in the refrigerator for about an hour before whipping the cream. Begin beating the cream at low speed, and increase the mixer speed as the cream gains in volume. Beat the cream until stiff peaks form. Remember that ultra-pasteurized heavy cream doesn't whip up as well as plain pasteurized heavy cream.

Cloves

The cloves we use in cooking actually are the dried, unopened buds of the clove tree. They are known for their aromatic scent and strong flavor. Sometimes the head of the clove is removed to make a milder seasoning. This milder form of the spice is used to make ground cloves. When using whole cloves in cooking, be sure to remove them before serving, or remind your guests not to eat them. Oil of clove can be used sparingly for lighter-colored dishes; be wary of its overwhelming flavor.

❖ ❖ ❖

1. Combine the broth with the wine in a medium-size saucepan and bring the mixture to boiling. Add the chicken. Lower the heat and simmer until the chicken is white and firm. Remove the chicken from the saucepan and chop it very finely. Place the chopped chicken in a large bowl. Add the mayonnaise, curry powder, orange zest, celery and cashews and mix well.
2. Slice open one side of each snow pea and fill it with a small amount of the chicken mixture. Arrange the stuffed snow peas on a serving tray.

BAKED HAM IN CIDER

LOW-CALORIE

Bake at 325° for about 3 hours.
Makes 16 to 18 servings.

Nutrient Value Per Serving: 177 calories, 19 g protein, 8 g fat, 7 g carbohydrate, 1,278 mg sodium, 50 mg cholesterol.

10- to 12-pound fully-cooked bone-in ham **Whole cloves**	**¼ cup firmly packed light brown sugar** **2 cups cider**

1. Preheat the oven to slow (325°).
2. Score the fat side of the ham in a diamond pattern, cutting ¼ inch deep and 1¼ inches apart; do not cut into the meat. Place a clove in the center of each diamond. Place the ham in a roasting pan, sprinkle it with brown sugar and pour the cider into the pan. Cover the pan tightly with aluminum foil.
3. Bake the ham in the preheated slow oven (325°), basting with the pan juices every 30 minutes, for about 3 hours, or until a meat thermometer registers 140°. Remove the ham from the pan. Let the ham stand for 20 minutes before slicing it.

BEST-EVER BISCUITS

LOW-CHOLESTEROL

Bake at 425° for 12 minutes.
Makes 12 biscuits.

Nutrient Value Per Serving: 120 calories, 3 g protein, 5 g fat, 17 g carbohydrate, 214 mg sodium, 1 mg cholesterol.

2 cups unsifted flour **1 tablespoon baking powder** **½ teaspoon salt**	**¼ cup vegetable shortening** **¾ cup buttermilk** **¾ cup water**

1. Preheat the oven to hot (425°).
2. Combine the flour, baking powder, buttermilk and salt in a bowl.
3. Cut the shortening into the flour mixture with a pastry blender until the mixture is crumbly. Add the buttermilk and the water, and stir the mixture with a fork just until a soft, puffy dough forms.
4. Turn out the dough onto a floured pastry cloth. Lightly knead the dough 8 times. For tender biscuits, handle the dough as little as possible.
5. Roll or pat the dough into a ½-inch thickness. Cut out the dough with a floured 2-inch biscuit cutter, working from the rim to the center of the dough. Place the rounds, 1 inch apart, on an ungreased baking sheet.
6. Bake the biscuits in the preheated hot oven (425°) for 12 minutes, or until the biscuits are golden brown.

From the Garden

3

Most of us grew up thinking of vegetables as something you ate along with the main dish, generally at your parent's repeated urging. Today we're trying to boost the fiber in our diets, and cut back on excess sodium, cholesterol and fat. That makes vegetables and greens invaluable allies to good health. And health issues aside, the dishes you can create using Mother Nature's bounty will delight your family and friends.

As entrées, dishes needn't be "vegetarian" for a vegetable to have star billing. Case in point: Spaghetti Squash with Italian Sausage Marinara (recipe, page 113). Other main dish wonders include creamy Asparagus Lasagna (recipe, page 87) and south-of-the-border inspired Asparagus and Chicken Enchiladas (recipe, page 89).

Vegetables also get pizzazz with new flavor combinations. Sesame Broccoli and Yellow Peppers (recipe, page 91) is as colorful as it is delicious. Tangy citrus juices enliven Braised Leeks in Tomato Orange Sauce (recipe, page 103). And mashed potatoes get a makeover with our Apple and Potato Mash (recipe, page 106) or Fluffy Yogurt Potatoes (recipe, page 109).

Having a party? Wow your guests with our Curried Mushroom Turnovers (recipe, page 94) or Oyster Mushrooms Rockefeller (recipe, page 96).

We've even got your salad bowl covered! Starting with a Classic Vinaigrette (recipe, page 117), we give you a terrific variety of salads, from our simple Rainbow Salad with Mustard Lemon Dressing (recipe, page 118) to the exotic Arugula and Red Leaf Lettuce with Raspberry Vinaigrette (recipe, page 122). With these recipes, salads in your house never will be the same again!

Spaghetti Squash with Italian Sausage Marinara (recipe, page 113) is a great alternative to the pasta-based original.

FRUITS & VEGETABLES

From the garden or from the store, fruits and vegetables are crucial to a healthy diet — and they're deliciously versatile.

AUTUMN FRUIT SALAD

LOW-CHOLESTEROL

Makes 6 servings.

Nutrient Value Per Serving: 208 calories, 1 g protein, 14 g fat, 22 g carbohydrate, 191 mg sodium, 0 mg cholesterol.

6	tablespoons olive oil	¼	teaspoon ground pepper
3	tablespoons fresh lemon juice	2	medium-size Red Delicious apples (about 12 ounces)
1	tablespoon honey	2	medium-size Bosc or Anjou pears, firm but ripe (about 12 ounces)
2	teaspoons chopped fresh tarragon OR: ½ teaspoon dried tarragon, crumbled	½	cup chopped red onion
½	teaspoon salt	2	quarts mixed salad greens

1. Whisk together the oil, lemon juice, honey, tarragon, salt and pepper in a large bowl.
2. Quarter and core the apples and the pears, and cut them into wedges: do not peel them. Toss the fruits and the onion with the dressing.
3. Line a shallow salad bowl or individual salad plates with the greens. Mound the fruit mixture in the center of the greens and serve.

The Salad Bowl

A clear glass bowl displays a colorful salad to the best advantage. A ceramic or wooden salad bowl adds an earthy, country-style touch to the dinner table. A brightly colored plastic bowl is an attractive choice for a picnic or patio meal.

Apples Galore

A is for apple . . . always appetizing and always available. This most popular of fruits also is amazingly adaptable, equally at home in main dishes, sauces, desserts and more.

Autumn Fruit Salad combines the bounty of tree and field — ripe apples and pears, red onions and tasty mixed greens.

ASPARAGUS LASAGNA

A meatless alternative to the Italian favorite, this lasagna can be made early in the day, or the day before, and reheated.

LOW-CALORIE • LOW-CHOLESTEROL

Bake at 325° for 30 minutes, then bake at 350° for 15 minutes.
Makes 12 servings.

Nutrient Value Per Serving: 311 calories, 19 g protein, 16 g fat, 23 g carbohydrate, 638 mg sodium, 48 mg cholesterol.

5 **tablespoons butter or margarine**	2 **pounds asparagus, trimmed, cooked and cooled (see Tip, page 89)**
2 **green onions, thinly sliced**	
1 **pound mushrooms, trimmed and coarsely chopped**	1 **container (16 ounces) cottage cheese**
¼ **cup all-purpose flour**	1 **package (8 ounces) Monterey Jack cheese, shredded**
1 **teaspoon salt**	
⅛ **teaspoon freshly ground pepper**	1 **cup grated Parmesan cheese**
2½ **cups milk**	
9 **lasagna noodles, cooked according to package directions and drained**	

1. Melt 3 tablespoons of the butter or margarine in a large saucepan over medium heat. Add the green onion and the mushrooms. Cover the saucepan and cook until the mushrooms are tender, for about 4 minutes. Stir in the flour, salt and pepper. Gradually add the milk and cook, stirring, until the mushroom sauce is thickened, for about 8 minutes.

2. Preheat the oven to slow (325°). Grease a 13 x 9 x 2-inch baking pan.

3. Spread a little mushroom sauce in the prepared pan. Place 3 noodles on top, slightly overlapping them. Lay half the asparagus, half the cottage cheese, half the Monterey Jack cheese, a third of the Parmesan cheese and a third of the mushroom sauce on top. Repeat with another layer of noodles, the remaining asparagus, cottage cheese and Monterey Jack cheese, a third of the Parmesan cheese and a third of the mushroom sauce. Top with a final layer of noodles and the remaining mushroom sauce. Sprinkle with the remaining Parmesan cheese. Dot with the remaining 2 tablespoons of butter. Cover the pan with aluminum foil.

4. Bake the lasagna in the preheated slow oven (325°) for 30 minutes. Uncover the pan and increase the oven temperature to moderate (350°). Bake for about 15 minutes more, or until the lasagna is golden brown and bubbly. Let the lasagna stand for 15 minutes before cutting it.

Stalking Asparagus

The Egyptians offered it as a gift to their gods. The Greeks prized it as an aphrodisiac. Monet immortalized it on canvas. Louis XIV made a nobleman of the gardener who discovered how to grow it year-round. Such is the legacy of the asparagus, whose delicate yet distinctive flavor has been savored by artists and emperors throughout time.

■ Asparagus is an excellent source of vitamins A, B-complex, C and E, and the minerals potassium, zinc and phosphorus.

■ When shopping for asparagus, look for bright green spears with smooth skins and compact tips; these are the freshest, most flavorful asparagus. Angular or flat stalks will be tough, stringy and bland-tasting. White asparagus is grown without light, which inhibits the normally deep green color. Usually imported and sold in jars as a gourmet item, the flavor of white asparagus often is quite bland.

■ To store, wrap the ends of raw asparagus in moist paper toweling or stand them in 2 inches of water, loosely covered, and refrigerate for up to 3 days. Cover and refrigerate cooked asparagus for up to 2 days.

FUSILLI WITH ASPARAGUS

LOW-CHOLESTEROL

Makes 6 servings.

Nutrient Value Per Serving: 441 calories, 12 g protein, 16 g fat, 64 g carbohydrate, 585 mg sodium, 0 mg cholesterol.

⅓ cup olive oil
¾ pound asparagus, trimmed and cut into 1-inch pieces
4 large green onions (white part only), sliced diagonally
4 cloves garlic, finely chopped
4 ounces mushrooms, sliced
1 large tomato (8 ounces), diced
1 teaspoon dried basil, crumbled
½ teaspoon dried oregano, crumbled

½ cup dry white wine
¾ cup chicken broth
½ cup pitted black olives, cut into wedges
1 teaspoon salt
½ teaspoon freshly ground black pepper
1 tablespoon cornstarch
1 pound fusilli, cooked according to package directions
Grated Parmesan cheese (optional)

1. Heat the oil in a large, heavy skillet. Add the asparagus, green onion and garlic, and stir-fry over high heat for 2 minutes. Add the mushrooms and

Fusilli with Asparagus is a wonderful blend of pasta, asparagus, olives, mushrooms, olive oil and a hint of herbs.

To Cook Asparagus

(Two pounds of fresh asparagus of uniform diameter)

On the Stove Top:

■ Snap off and discard any tough stem ends; thick spear ends may be peeled. Remove the scales with a knife and wash the spears to remove any sand from the tips.

■ Fill a large skillet with enough water to cover the asparagus. Add ½ teaspoon of salt and bring to boiling. Add the asparagus to the skillet and return to boiling. Cook, uncovered, for 3 to 6 minutes for medium-thick spears, 6 to 9 minutes for thick spears, or until the tip of a knife can be inserted easily into the thick ends of the asparagus. Remove to paper toweling to drain.

■ You also can cook asparagus in a large kettle by standing the spears upright in about 3 inches of boiling water and cooking them, covered, for 6 minutes.

To Microwave Asparagus:

Prepare the asparagus as above. Place the spears in a microwave-safe 12 x 8-inch shallow dish, with the tips pointing toward the center of the dish. Add ¼ cup of water. Cover the dish with microwave-safe plastic wrap turned back at one corner to vent slightly. Microwave at full power for 9 to 11 minutes for 2 pounds of asparagus, 6 to 9 minutes for 1 pound of asparagus, or until the asparagus is tender but firm. Immediately uncover the dish to stop the cooking. One pound yields about 4 servings.

stir-fry for 2 minutes more. Add the tomato, basil and oregano, and stir-fry for 2 minutes. Stir in the wine, ½ cup of the broth, the olives, salt and black pepper, and bring the mixture to boiling.

2. Mix together the cornstarch and the remaining ¼ cup of broth in a small cup until the mixture is smooth. Pour the cornstarch mixture into the skillet. Cook, stirring constantly, until the sauce thickens and boils.

3. To serve, place the fusilli in a shallow serving bowl. Pour the asparagus sauce over the pasta and toss gently to mix well. Serve with grated Parmesan cheese, if you wish.

ASPARAGUS AND CHICKEN ENCHILADAS

A south-of-the-border-style treat with a deliciously different twist.

Bake at 425° for 25 minutes.
Makes 12 servings.

Nutrient Value Per Serving: 457 calories, 24 g protein, 25 g fat, 35 g carbohydrate, 865 mg sodium, 83 mg cholesterol.

½ **cup (1 stick) butter or margarine**	3 **cups cooked, shredded chicken (1 pound uncooked)**
½ **cup all-purpose flour**	½ **cup finely chopped onion (1 medium-size onion)**
3 **cups chicken broth**	
1 **container (8 ounces) dairy sour cream**	2½ **pounds asparagus, trimmed and cooked (see Tip, at left)**
½ **cup green taco sauce**	
1 **dozen 7-inch flour tortillas**	½ **cup grated Parmesan cheese**
3 **cups grated Monterey Jack cheese (12 ounces)**	

1. Melt the butter or margarine in a medium-size saucepan over medium heat. Stir in the flour and cook, stirring, for 1 minute. Gradually add the broth and cook, stirring occasionally, until the mixture is thick, for about 5 minutes. Remove the saucepan from the heat. Stir in the sour cream and the taco sauce, and set aside.

2. Preheat the oven to hot (425°). Lightly butter two 9 x 9 x 2-inch glass baking dishes.

3. Work with 1 tortilla at a time. On the first tortilla, place about 2 tablespoons of the Monterey Jack cheese, ¼ cup of the chicken, some of the onion and enough asparagus to extend to both ends of the tortilla. Spoon 3 tablespoons of the sauce down the center of the tortilla. Roll up the tortilla and place it, seam side down, in one of the prepared dishes. Repeat with the remaining tortillas. Sprinkle the tortillas with any remaining Monterey Jack cheese and sauce, and the Parmesan cheese.

4. Bake the enchiladas in the preheated hot oven (425°) for 25 minutes, or until they are bubbly and lightly golden. Serve.

❖ ❀ ❖

GREEN BEAN PASTA SALAD

LOW-CHOLESTEROL

Makes 6 generous servings.

Nutrient Value Per Serving: 373 calories, 8 g protein, 23 g fat, 35 g carbohydrate, 815 mg sodium, 3 mg cholesterol.

8	ounces penne OR: any other tubular-shape pasta
1	pound green beans, stems removed and cut into 2-inch lengths
½	cup olive oil
¼	cup red wine vinegar
1	teaspoon salt
1	teaspoon Dijon-style mustard
¼	teaspoon freshly ground pepper

½	cup pitted and chopped black olives, preferably Mediterranean
½	cup sliced pimiento-stuffed green olives
4	green onions, cut into 2-inch lengths and cut lengthwise into thin strips
¼	cup grated Parmesan cheese

1. Cook the pasta following the package directions. Add the green beans during the last 5 minutes of cooking time. Drain the pasta-bean mixture well. Rinse the pasta-bean mixture with cold water and drain again.
2. Combine the oil, vinegar, salt, mustard and pepper in a large bowl. Whisk until the ingredients are well blended. Add the pasta-green bean mixture and mix well. Stir in the black olives, green olives and green onion. Toss with the Parmesan cheese just before serving.

WARM BEETS PIQUANT

Makes 4 servings.

Nutrient Value Per Serving: 242 calories, 5 g protein, 17 g fat, 20 g carbohydrate, 579 mg sodium, 19 mg cholesterol.

2	pounds fresh beets (about 2 bunches), scrubbed and stems removed
¼	pound thickly-sliced bacon, cut crosswise into ¼-inch strips
1	medium-size onion, halved and thinly sliced

6	tablespoons cider vinegar
1½	teaspoons sugar
½	teaspoon salt
¼	teaspoon freshly ground pepper
¼	cup finely chopped parsley

1. Place the beets in a 3-quart saucepan and cover them with water. Bring to boiling, cover the saucepan and simmer until the beets are tender, for about 45 to 50 minutes. Drain the beets and cool them to room temperature. Peel the beets and slice them ¼ inch thick.
2. Cook the bacon in the same saucepan until it is crisp. Remove the bacon with a slotted spoon and set it aside. Add the onion to the bacon fat and sauté, stirring occasionally, for 3 minutes. Add the vinegar, sugar, salt and pepper. Bring the mixture to boiling and cook, stirring constantly, for 2 minutes more, or until the dressing is slightly thickened. Remove the dressing from the heat.
3. Stir the beets into the dressing and heat briefly. Just before serving, sprinkle with the bacon and the parsley. Serve the beets warm.

Pick of the Crop

■ **Beets:** Look for small, round beets with smooth, firm flesh and fresh green tops. Cut off 1 inch from the tops, and store beets in plastic bags in the refrigerator for up to 2 weeks.

■ **Corn:** Be sure the ears are worm- and decay-free. Peel back the tip of the corn husk and test a kernel with your fingernail: It should be firm and spurt a milky fluid. Use fresh corn immediately, or refrigerate it with the husk intact for 1 day.

■ **Green Beans:** Look for smooth, blemish-free pods; beans should be so crisp that they "snap" easily. Refrigerate beans, unwashed, in a plastic bag. Use green beans within 2 or 3 days.

■ **Spinach:** Use only crisp, dark green leaves. Refrigerate spinach, unwashed, in a plastic bag; use as soon as possible.

■ **Sweet Peppers:** Choose firm, well-shaped, glossy peppers. Store peppers, unwashed, in the refrigerator and use them within 1 week.

■ **Tomatoes:** Select firm fruit with smooth skins and an even color. Never refrigerate tomatoes; they become mushy. Store them in a cool, dark place until they are ripe.

■ **Yellow Squash and Zucchini:** Look for small, firm, blemish-free squash. Store them, unwashed, in a plastic bag in the refrigerator for no longer than 4 days.

❖   ❖   ❖

BROCCOLI WITH GARLIC

When sautéing the garlic, be careful not to overbrown it, as this will make the dish bitter.

LOW-CALORIE ● LOW-CHOLESTEROL

Makes 4 servings.

Nutrient Value Per Serving: 94 calories, 5 g protein, 6 g fat, 9 g carbohydrate, 115 mg sodium, 0 mg cholesterol.

1　head broccoli (about 1½ pounds)	⅛　teaspoon salt
1½ tablespoons olive oil	⅛　teaspoon freshly ground pepper
1　clove garlic, finely chopped	

1. Bring a large pot of water to boiling over high heat.
2. Peel the broccoli stems. Cut the stems lengthwise into long, thin strips so each has a floweret or two at the top. Drop them into the boiling water. Cook for 3 minutes, or just until the broccoli is tender. Drain the broccoli.
3. Heat the oil in a large, heavy skillet over medium heat. Add the garlic and cook for 1 minute, or until the garlic is lightly golden. Add the broccoli and toss until it is coated and hot. Sprinkle with the salt and the pepper.

SESAME BROCCOLI AND YELLOW PEPPERS

LOW-CALORIE ● LOW-CHOLESTEROL

Makes 4 servings.

Nutrient Value Per Serving: 88 calories, 5 g protein, 5 g fat, 10 g carbohydrate, 259 mg sodium, 8 mg cholesterol.

1　tablespoon sesame seeds	1　tablespoon butter
4　cups broccoli flowerets	1　teaspoon vinegar
1　small sweet yellow pepper OR: red pepper, cut into ¾-inch slices	1　teaspoon cornstarch
	½　teaspoon finely chopped, peeled fresh gingerroot
¼　cup chicken broth	¼　teaspoon salt
1　tablespoon dry sherry (optional)	

1. Heat a medium-size saucepan over medium heat. Add the sesame seeds and toast them, shaking the pan, for 2 to 3 minutes, or until the seeds are golden brown. Transfer the sesame seeds to a plate and set them aside.
2. Fill the saucepan with water and bring it to boiling. Add the broccoli and cook for 3 to 5 minutes, or until the broccoli is crisply tender. Add the yellow or red pepper and stir for 30 seconds. Drain the vegetables in a colander. Place the drained vegetables in a serving bowl and cover the bowl to keep the vegetables warm.
3. Meanwhile, whisk together the broth, sherry if you wish, butter, vinegar, cornstarch, ginger and salt in the saucepan. Bring the mixture to boiling, whisking constantly, and cook for 1 minute. Add the cooked vegetables, and toss to coat them. Return the vegetables to the serving bowl. Sprinkle the vegetables with the toasted sesame seeds.

CREAMY CORN CASSEROLE

Bake at 350° for 35 to 40 minutes.
Makes 8 servings.

Nutrient Value Per Serving: 291 calories, 13 g protein, 22 g fat,
12 g carbohydrate, 623 mg sodium, 120 mg cholesterol.

2 **eggs**	1 **teaspoon finely chopped**
1½ **cups dairy sour cream**	**canned or pickled**
2 **cups fresh corn kernels**	**jalapeño peppers**
(from 3 to 4 ears)	1 **teaspoon salt**
OR: 1 package (10	¼ **teaspoon freshly ground**
ounces) frozen corn	**pepper**
kernels, thawed	8 **ounces Monterey Jack**
½ **cup fresh white bread**	**cheese, cut into**
crumbs (from 1 slice	**¾-inch cubes**
bread)	½ **cup (2 ounces) shredded**
1 **can (4 ounces) chopped**	**Cheddar cheese**
green chili peppers	

1. Preheat the oven to moderate (350°). Grease a 10-inch quiche dish or
6-cup shallow baking dish.
2. Combine the eggs with the sour cream in a large bowl. Mix in the corn,
bread crumbs, chili peppers, jalapeño peppers, salt and pepper. Mix the
ingredients well. Stir in the Monterey Jack cheese. Pour the mixture into
the prepared dish.
3. Bake the casserole in the preheated moderate oven (350°) for 35 to
40 minutes, or until a knife inserted in the center comes out clean. Sprinkle
the casserole with the Cheddar cheese for the last 5 minutes of baking.
4. Let the dish stand on a wire rack for 10 minutes. Then cut the casserole
into wedges to serve.

THYMED CARROTS AND CELERY

LOW-CALORIE • LOW-CHOLESTEROL

Makes 4 servings.

Nutrient Value Per Serving: 56 calories, 1 g protein, 3 g fat,
7 g carbohydrate, 198 mg sodium, 8 mg cholesterol.

4 **medium-size carrots,**	¼ **teaspoon dried thyme,**
peeled and sliced	**crumbled**
(about 8 ounces)	¼ **teaspoon salt**
½ **cup sliced celery**	⅛ **teaspoon freshly ground**
¼ **cup chopped onion**	**pepper**
(1 small onion)	½ **teaspoon lemon juice**
1 **tablespoon butter**	

1. Cook the carrots and the celery in a small amount of lightly salted boiling
water in a medium-size saucepan, covered, just until the carrots and celery
are tender, for about 5 minutes. Drain the carrot mixture.
2. Sauté the onion in the butter in the same saucepan over medium heat,
stirring occasionally, until the onion is tender. Stir in the carrot mixture,
thyme, salt, pepper and lemon juice. Heat to serving temperature.

Kernel Know-How

The sooner you cook corn on the cob after picking it, the better. If the corn is freshly picked, the stem on the cob will be pale green and moist. After about a day, the stem turns chalky white; eventually it turns brown. One ear of cooked corn contains about 80 calories.

❖ ❖ ❖

Carrots

A produce counter staple, carrots are a thrifty and versatile vegetable. The predecessor of today's large, fleshy, orange-rooted plant probably was a plant with a pale yellow root that grew some 2,000 years ago in south central Asia and the Near East. Europeans found carrots easy to cultivate and nourishing to eat. One carrot has only 20 calories and is an excellent source of vitamin A.

❖ ❖ ❖

SAUTÉED CORN AND SWEET PEPPERS

MICROWAVE

Makes 4 generous servings.

Nutrient Value Per Serving: 249 calories, 5 g protein, 14 g fat, 31 g carbohydrate, 663 mg sodium, 23 mg cholesterol.

3	tablespoons butter	½	sweet red pepper, cut into ¼-inch dice (about ¾ cup)
1	tablespoon vegetable oil		
4	cups fresh corn kernels (from 4 large or 6 medium-size ears)	2	tablespoons finely chopped fresh cilantro OR: fresh dill
2	tablespoons water	1	teaspoon salt
½	sweet green pepper, cut into ¼-inch dice (about ¾ cup)	¼	teaspoon freshly ground pepper

1. Heat the butter and the oil in a large skillet over medium-high heat. Add the corn and the water, and sauté for 5 to 8 minutes, or until the corn is tender. Add the green and red peppers, and sauté for 2 minutes more.
2. Add the cilantro or dill, the salt and pepper. Toss to mix the ingredients well, and serve.

Microwave Instructions
(for a 650-watt variable power microwave oven)

Ingredient Changes: Reduce the butter to 2 tablespoons. Eliminate the oil and the water.
Directions: Combine the corn with the butter in a microwave-safe 2-quart casserole dish. Cover and microwave at full power for 4 minutes. Stir in the green and red peppers. Cover and microwave at full power for 7 minutes. Stir in the cilantro or dill, the salt and pepper. Serve.

SWEET AND SOUR CABBAGE AND CARROTS

LOW-CHOLESTEROL

Makes 4 servings.

Nutrient Value Per Serving: 134 calories, 3 g protein, 7 g fat, 17 g carbohydrate, 340 mg sodium, 0 mg cholesterol.

2	tablespoons vegetable oil	1	medium-size onion, chopped
1	pound green cabbage, cut into ¾-inch squares	1	tablespoon sugar
3	medium-size carrots, peeled and sliced ⅛ inch thick	2	tablespoons reduced-sodium soy sauce
		1	teaspoon vinegar

1. Heat the oil in a large, heavy pot or Dutch oven over medium-high heat. Add the cabbage, carrots, onion and sugar. Cook, stirring, until the vegetables are very well browned and softened, for 10 to 12 minutes; the vegetables should scorch a little. Remove the pot from the heat.
2. Stir the soy sauce and the vinegar into the vegetables. Serve hot.

CURRIED MUSHROOM TURNOVERS

*These tasty little turnovers make excellent hors d'oeuvres for a party.
They can be made ahead, frozen, and baked just before serving. Serve the
warm turnovers with cool plain yogurt for dipping, if you wish.*

LOW-CALORIE

Bake at 400° for 17 to 20 minutes.
Makes 3½ dozen small turnovers.

Nutrient Value Per Turnover: 62 calories, 1 g protein, 3 g fat,
7 g carbohydrate, 96 mg sodium, 8 mg cholesterol.

Cream Cheese Pastry:
2 cups all-purpose flour
½ teaspoon salt
½ stick (¼ cup) unsalted
    butter, thinly sliced
1 package (3 ounces) cream
    cheese, chilled
3 to 4 tablespoons ice water

Filling:
8 ounces red-skinned
    potatoes, peeled and
    cut into ¼-inch dice
    (1½ cups)
4 teaspoons vegetable oil
¾ cup finely chopped onion
1 clove garlic, finely
    chopped

2 teaspoons curry powder
1 teaspoon ground cumin
1 teaspoon salt
¼ teaspoon ground
    cinnamon
⅓ cup plain nonfat yogurt
1 pound white mushrooms,
    trimmed and finely
    chopped, or cut into
    ¼-inch dice (4⅓ cups)
¼ cup tomato sauce

Glaze:
1 egg beaten with
    ½ teaspoon water

Additional plain nonfat
    yogurt, chilled (optional)

1. Prepare the Cream Cheese Pastry: To prepare the pastry by hand,
place the flour and the salt in a large bowl and stir to combine. Add the
butter and the cream cheese cut into small pieces. With a pastry blender or
2 knives, cut in the butter and cream cheese until the mixture resembles
coarse crumbs. Gradually add the ice water just until the mixture comes
together. To prepare the pastry with a food processor, combine the flour
with the salt in the container of the processor. Add the butter and the
cream cheese cut into small pieces. Pulse on and off until the mixture
resembles coarse crumbs. Gradually add the ice water, pulsing on and off,
just until the mixture comes together.
2. Pat the dough into a 5 x 7-inch rectangle and cut the rectangle in half.
Wrap each half in plastic wrap. Refrigerate both dough halves for 2 to
3 hours, or overnight.
3. Prepare the Filling: Cook the potatoes in 3 teaspoons of the oil in a
large, heavy skillet over medium-high heat, stirring occasionally, until the
potatoes are well browned, for about 5 minutes. Add the remaining
teaspoon of oil and the onion. Reduce the heat to medium and cook until the
onion is softened, for 3 to 4 minutes.
4. Add the garlic and cook for 1 minute. Add the curry powder, cumin, salt
and cinnamon, and cook, stirring, for 30 seconds. Stir in the yogurt and
cook until the mixture is dry, for 2 to 3 minutes. Add the mushrooms and
sauté until they are softened, for about 3 minutes. Stir in the tomato sauce
and cook until the mixture is almost dry, for 2 to 3 minutes more. Cool the
filling to room temperature. If making the filling ahead, cover and

Much Ado About Mushrooms

- Tree-Ear or Wood-Ear:
Valued for its chewy texture
rather than its faint flavor. Sold
fresh and dried.
- Chanterelle: Trumpet-
shaped with reddish-yellow
color and apricot-like flavor.
Sold fresh or dried.
- Morel: Hollow, spongy cap
with aromatic, nutty flavor.
Size can vary tremendously.
Usually sold dried.
- Enoki: Tiny-capped and long-
stemmed; grows in clusters.
Mild flavor suited to salads or
sautés; should be cooked only
for 30 seconds to 1 minute.
- Cremini Brown: Related to
White Button mushrooms, with
a woodier, beefy flavor. Can be
substituted for button
mushrooms in most recipes.
- Shiitake: Oriental variety
with a smoky taste, dark brown
cap and creamy white
underside. Can grow as large
as 8 inches in diameter. Sold
fresh or dried.
- Oyster: Creamy or white
with smooth, soft texture, fan
shape and mild flavor. Size
varies from tiny to large.
- White Button: The all-
purpose mushroom with a
meaty taste and firm texture.
- Porcini (Italy) or Cèpes
(France): Fresh mushrooms of
this variety have a silken flesh
and meaty flavor. When dried,
they have a stronger flavor.

refrigerate it until needed. Return the filling to room temperature before using it to fill the pastry.

5. Using a lightly floured rolling pin, roll out half the dough on a lightly floured surface to a 10 x 8-inch rectangle. Fold the rectangle in thirds like a business letter. Roll out the dough once again to a 15 x 12-inch rectangle. Using a 3-inch round biscuit cutter, cut out as many circles as possible. Gather the scraps of dough and chill them. Then reroll and cut out the remaining dough. Repeat with the other half.

6. Preheat the oven to hot (400°). Prepare the Glaze.

7. Working with one circle of dough at a time, place a scant tablespoon of the cooled filling in the center of the circle. Using a small pastry brush or your fingertip, paint a line of the Glaze along the edge of half the circle. Gather up the 2 sides, taco-style, pinch them in the center to hold (the turnover will be full), and pinch the seam shut. Starting at one point of the crescent, pinch and pleat the edge to hold it tightly, or crimp it with a fork. Place the turnover on an ungreased baking sheet. Repeat with the remaining circles and filling. Brush the tops of the turnovers with the Glaze. Prick each turnover once in the center with a fork.

8. Bake the turnovers in the preheated hot oven (400°) until they are golden brown, for 17 to 20 minutes. Serve the hot turnovers with chilled additional plain yogurt, if you wish.

A medley of mushrooms (from top left, clockwise): Tree-Ear or Wood-Ear, Cremini Brown, Shiitake, Oyster, White Button, Porcini or Cèpes, Enoki, Morel, Chanterelle.

95

OYSTER MUSHROOMS ROCKEFELLER

A wonderful twist on classic Oysters Rockefeller. Serve these delicacies in little ramekins or au gratin dishes. They can be assembled a few hours ahead, and broiled just before serving.

Broil for 3 to 5 minutes.
Makes 4 servings.

Nutrient Value Per Serving: 178 calories, 6 g protein, 13 g fat, 12 g carbohydrate, 699 mg sodium, 40 mg cholesterol.

1 **pound fresh spinach, well washed, large stems removed**	1 **tablespoon butter**
½ **pound oyster mushrooms**	¼ **cup plain dry bread crumbs**
1 **cup chicken broth**	6 **tablespoons heavy cream**
¼ **cup finely chopped onion**	½ **teaspoon salt**
1 **small clove garlic, finely chopped**	⅛ **teaspoon freshly ground pepper**
½ **teaspoon fennel seeds OR: aniseed, crushed**	⅛ **teaspoon grated nutmeg**
	1 **tablespoon grated Parmesan cheese**

1. Place the spinach leaves, with water clinging to them, in a large, heavy pot. Cover the pot and place it over high heat. Cook, stirring once or twice, until the spinach is wilted. Drain the spinach in a strainer, pressing to remove the excess moisture. Cool the spinach slightly and chop it coarsely; you should have about 1 cup.

2. Preheat the broiler.

3. Remove the toughest end of each mushroom (about ¼ inch). Cut each mushroom in half or thirds.

4. Combine the broth, onion, garlic, fennel seeds or aniseed and the butter in a medium-size saucepan over medium heat. Bring the mixture to boiling. Add the mushrooms, reduce the heat to simmer and gently cook the mushrooms, stirring occasionally, just until they are tender, for 2 to 3 minutes. Remove the mushrooms with a slotted spoon and distribute them evenly among 4 flameproof au gratin dishes or ramekins. Place the dishes on a baking sheet. Discard the cooking liquid.

5. Combine the bread crumbs, 4 tablespoons of the cream, the salt, pepper and nutmeg in a small bowl. Transfer the mixture to the container of a food processor along with the spinach. Cover and whirl until the mixture is puréed; you should have about 1 cup of sauce.

6. Top each dish of mushrooms with ¼ cup of the sauce. Drizzle each with 1½ teaspoons of the remaining cream and top with ¾ teaspoon of the Parmesan cheese. Place the dishes 4 inches from the heat source and broil until the tops are bubbly and brown, for 3 to 5 minutes. Serve hot.

Mushroom Magic

- For the freshest mushrooms, select those with firm, heavy caps and no visible, open gills on the undersides. Avoid very wet, sticky mushrooms.
- Dry moist mushrooms before storing them.
- Never clean mushrooms before refrigerating them.
- Do not store mushrooms in a cardboard carton, under plastic wrap or in a plastic bag; refrigerate them in a brown paper bag. (Enoki mushrooms should remain in their vacuum-sealed plastic packaging, and be used within 2 days.)
- Mushrooms can remain in wooden baskets with wooden lids. Add a piece of damp paper toweling if they dry out.
- Mushrooms (except Enoki, see above) can be stored for up to 3 days, but they should be used as soon as possible.
- Do not wash or soak mushrooms; they'll become waterlogged. Clean them with a pastry or mushroom brush, or wipe them with damp paper toweling. Give very dirty mushrooms a quick rinse.
- Trim off about ¼ inch of the mushroom stem.
- Soak dried mushrooms in warm tap water for 1 hour, or until they are softened, before using them.
- Strain and reserve dried mushroom soaking liquid as a flavor enhancer for soups, sauces and stews. The liquid will keep for up to 2 days in the refrigerator.

In the Know About Mushrooms

A simple plant with no roots, stems or leaves, mushrooms rely on non-living organic matter for food because they cannot produce their own.

■ There are thousands of wild mushrooms, but only a few are cultivated. Mushrooms are grown commercially in natural caves, or in specially designed buildings where the humidity, temperature, ventilation and light can be controlled.

■ One cup of mushrooms contains only 18 calories and a trace of fat. It also provides 1 gram of protein, 3 grams of carbohydrates and 3 milligrams of sodium.

SAUTÉ OF THREE MUSHROOMS

Makes 4 servings.

Nutrient Value Per Serving: 131 calories, 3 g protein, 12 g fat, 6 g carbohydrate, 397 mg sodium, 31 mg cholesterol.

¼ cup (½ stick) butter
8 ounces white mushrooms, quartered through stems
4 ounces shiitake mushrooms, stems removed and caps thinly sliced
4 ounces brown cremini mushrooms OR: 4 more ounces white mushrooms, stems sliced ⅛ inch thick
½ cup dry white wine
½ teaspoon salt
⅛ teaspoon freshly ground pepper

Melt the butter in a large, heavy skillet over medium heat. Add the white, shiitake and cremini or additional white mushrooms. Increase the heat to high and cook the mushrooms, tossing, until they are well browned, for about 3 minutes. Add the wine and boil until it is reduced to a glaze, for 5 to 7 minutes. Toss the mushrooms with the salt and the pepper, and serve them hot.

ENOKI MUSHROOM SALAD

LOW-CHOLESTEROL

Makes 4 servings.

Nutrient Value Per Serving: 168 calories, 7 g protein, 12 g fat, 9 g carbohydrate, 563 mg sodium, 13 mg cholesterol.

2 large sweet red peppers
2 packages (3½ ounces each) enoki mushrooms
3 tablespoons olive oil
4 ounces smoked ham, cut into 2 x ¼-inch strips
⅔ cup 1 x ¼-inch strips of celery heart
2 tablespoons fresh lemon juice
¼ teaspoon salt
⅛ teaspoon freshly ground pepper

1. Preheat the broiler.
2. Place the red peppers on the broiler pan. Broil the red peppers 4 inches from the heat source, turning them frequently, until they are blackened all over, for about 10 minutes.
3. Transfer the red peppers with tongs to a plastic or paper bag. Seal the bag and let the red peppers steam for 10 minutes. Remove the red peppers from the bag. Remove their blackened skins with a sharp knife. Core and seed the red peppers, and cut them into ¼-inch-wide strips. Pat the strips dry on paper toweling and transfer them to a large bowl.
4. Separate the enoki mushrooms and cut off any tough or discolored stem ends (about 2 inches). Add the mushrooms to the bowl with the roasted pepper strips.
5. Heat 1 tablespoon of the oil in a small skillet over medium heat. Add the ham and toss for 1 minute to warm it slightly. Transfer the ham to the bowl with the mushrooms.
6. Add the remaining oil, the celery strips, lemon juice, salt and pepper to the mushroom mixture. Toss to coat the vegetables, and serve.

MUSHROOM BREAD

This bread makes a tasty accompaniment to soup, and also is delicious when used for grilled cheese sandwiches.

LOW-FAT

Bake at 350° for 45 minutes.
Makes 1 large loaf (14 servings).

Nutrient Value Per Slice: 219 calories, 9 g protein, 5 g fat, 34 g carbohydrate, 145 mg sodium, 31 mg cholesterol.

2	tablespoons butter	¼	cup warm water (105° to 115°)*
8	ounces white mushrooms, finely chopped	1	package (¼ ounce) active dry yeast
½	teaspoon dried thyme, crumbled	1	egg, at room temperature
¼	teaspoon freshly ground black pepper	4	to 4½ cups bread flour OR: all-purpose flour
1	cup milk	¾	cup grated Parmesan cheese (3 ounces)
1	tablespoon sugar		

1. Melt the butter in a large skillet over medium heat. Add the mushrooms, thyme and black pepper, and cook, stirring frequently, until the mixture is dry, for about 5 minutes. Transfer the mushroom mixture to a bowl and cool it to room temperature.

Mushroom Bread, fragrant with thyme and tangy Parmesan cheese, puts mushrooms to an unexpected but delicious use. The recipe calls for white mushrooms, but you may substitute brown mushrooms, or use a combination of each.

Avoid the Draft!

For a warm, draft-free place to let dough rise, use your oven. If it is electric, warm the oven to 200°, turn it off and let it cool for 5 minutes, keeping the oven door closed. If the oven is gas, leave the oven door slightly ajar and the pilot light will provide enough warmth for the dough to rise.

❖ ❖ ❖

" Here is bread, which strengthens man's heart, and therefore called the staff of life. "
—Matthew Henry

2. Heat the milk in a small saucepan over low heat just until bubbles begin to appear on the surface. Stir together the sugar and the warm water in a small bowl to dissolve the sugar. Sprinkle the yeast on top, stir and let the yeast mixture stand until it is creamy, for about 5 minutes.

3. Whisk the egg in a large bowl. Reserve 1 teaspoon of the egg, covered. Add the yeast mixture, 1 cup of the flour and the milk to the egg. Whisk until the mixture is smooth. Add 1 cup more flour and beat with an electric mixer for 2 minutes. Reserve 1 tablespoon of the Parmesan cheese. Beat the remainder of the cheese into the bread batter.

4. Beat in the mushroom mixture. With a wooden spoon, stir in enough of the remaining flour to make a soft dough. Transfer the dough to a lightly floured surface and knead until the dough is smooth and elastic, for about 10 minutes. Place the dough in a lightly greased bowl and turn the greased side up. Cover the bowl with plastic wrap and let the dough rise in a warm place, away from drafts, until it is doubled in size, for about 1 hour.

5. Punch down the dough. Let it rest for 5 minutes.

6. Generously grease a 9 x 5 x 3-inch loaf pan. Pat out the dough on a lightly floured surface into a 12 x 9-inch rectangle. Starting from one short end, roll up the dough jelly-roll style. Place the dough, seam side down, in the prepared pan. Cover the pan with plastic wrap. Let the dough rise in a warm place, away from drafts, until it is almost doubled in size, for about 50 minutes.

7. Preheat the oven to moderate (350°).

8. Brush the top of the loaf with the reserved egg and sprinkle it with the reserved Parmesan cheese.

9. Bake the loaf in the preheated moderate oven (350°) until it is golden brown and sounds hollow when tapped on the top, for about 45 minutes. Check the loaf after 30 minutes; if it is browning too fast, tent it with aluminum foil. When the loaf is done, remove it from the oven and turn off the oven. Run a metal spatula around the sides of the pan and turn out the loaf. Place the loaf back on the rack in the turned off oven for 5 minutes. Remove the loaf from the oven again, and cool it completely on a wire rack.

Note: Warm water should feel tepid when dropped on your wrist.

ROASTED WHITE ONIONS

Roasting makes these onions succulent. You can toss them with butter, chives and parsley, as we do here, or keep them on hand to enhance a stew.

LOW-CALORIE • LOW-CHOLESTEROL • LOW-SODIUM • LOW-FAT

Roast at 375° for 40 to 45 minutes.
Makes 4 servings.

Nutrient Value Per Serving: 52 calories, 1 g protein, 3 g fat, 6 g carbohydrate, 71 mg sodium, 8 mg cholesterol.

12 ounces small (1½-inch) white onions, peeled (about 20 onions)	1 tablespoon chives, cut at random lengths
1 tablespoon unsalted butter	1½ teaspoons finely chopped flat-leaf Italian parsley
	⅛ teaspoon salt

1. Preheat the oven to moderate (375°).
2. Place the onions, 5 or 6 at a time, in a single line on a sheet of aluminum foil. Roll up the foil so the onions remain in a single line, and wrap the foil tightly. Place the foil roll on a baking sheet.
3. Bake the onions in the preheated moderate oven (375°) for 40 to 45 minutes, or until the onions are tender when pierced with a knife. When they are cool enough to handle, unwrap the onions.
4. Melt the butter in a medium-size skillet over low heat. Add the onions, chives, parsley and salt. Cook until the onions are heated through.

SHALLOT GARLIC BUTTER

Sweet shallots and garlic blend beautifully in this butter. Use it on grilled fish, chicken or beef, and on vegetables, rice or potatoes.

LOW-SODIUM

Makes about 36 teaspoons.

Nutrient Value Per Teaspoon: 36 calories, 0 g protein, 4 g fat, 1 g carbohydrate, 10 mg sodium, 10 mg cholesterol.

2 tablespoons plus ½ cup (1 stick) unsalted butter, softened	3 tablespoons dry white wine
7 tablespoons finely chopped shallots (about 5 shallots)	1 tablespoon thinly sliced chives
1 tablespoon finely chopped garlic	1 teaspoon lemon juice
	⅛ teaspoon salt
	Pinch freshly ground white pepper

1. Melt 2 tablespoons of the butter in a small skillet over low heat. Add the shallots and the garlic, and cook until the shallots are softened, for about 7 minutes. Add the wine, increase the heat to high and cook until the wine has evaporated, for about 2 minutes. Refrigerate the mixture until it is cold.
2. Combine the remaining ½ cup of butter with the chives, lemon juice, salt and white pepper in a medium-size bowl. Stir in the cooled shallot mixture. Spoon the butter mixture onto a piece of plastic wrap. Roll the butter mixture into a 7-inch log, twisting the ends to seal. Refrigerate the shallot garlic butter for up to 1 week, or overwrap it in aluminum foil, label, date and freeze it for up to 6 months. Slice off pats of the butter as needed.

The Cholesterol Lowdown on Onions

Onions not only add wonderful flavor to cooking, they help lower cholesterol levels in the blood. Just half a raw onion a day can boost your HDL level dramatically ("high density lipoproteins" help sweep excess cholesterol out of the bloodstream). A tablespoon of cooked onions can reverse the blood's clotting tendency after a high-fat meal, and onions help regulate blood sugar levels. Yellow and white onions are more effective in these ways than the milder red onion.

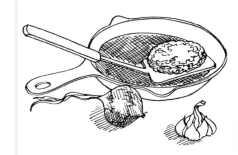

Onions: From Store to Stove to Storage

	FLAVOR	USES	BEST TO BUY	STORAGE
YELLOW ONIONS	Strongest in flavor and pungency of all onion varieties.	Good all-purpose onions for soups, stews, stocks, sauces, alone as side dish, and so on.	Firm, tight skin; dry, with no sprouts or decay at neck.	Cool, dry place. Keeps well for months.
SPANISH ONIONS (Includes Imperial Valley, Vidalia, Walla Walla, Maui, Texas and Bermuda onions)	Sweet. Vidalia are especially sweet.	Onion marmalade; onion rings; omelets; pizza topping; sautéed; stuffed and baked. Vidalia are excellent eaten raw.	Firm, tight skin; dry, with no sprouts or decay at neck.	Cool, dry place. Will keep for months; if temperature is below 70°, it is not necessary to refrigerate them.
RED ITALIAN ONIONS	Mild and sweet; less pungent flavor than Spanish or yellow onions.	Raw in salads and sandwiches; sautéed with red cabbage and apples; stir-fried with other ingredients.	Firm, dry skin, with no sprouts or decay at neck.	Cool, dry place. Will keep for weeks.
WHITE, OR "BOILING" ONIONS	Mild.	Whole in stews; creamed.	Firm, tight skin; no sprouts. Smaller size (1" to 2" diameter) keeps better than larger size.	Refrigerate or keep in cool, dry, airy place. Lasts for weeks.
LEEKS	Mellow, earthy.	Popular in French dishes such as vichyssoise; stews; by themselves; braised as side dish; appetizers. Usually the bottom white part is used.	Fresh, green tops; avoid dry or slimy leeks. Stalks should be pliable; rigid stalks indicate woody, tasteless leeks. Note: Young leeks are especially tender.	Trim stalks and some of green part. Refrigerate, unwashed, in plastic bag with air space. Will keep for several weeks.
RAMPS	Strong, onion-garlic.	An alternative to chives or scallions, but in smaller amount; use both tops and bottoms. Good in soups, sautéed dishes, or blanched as side dish.	Firm, dry green tops. Note: Grow wild in mountainous areas; available in specialty stores or farmer's markets in spring.	Store, unwashed, wrapped in damp paper toweling in a plastic bag; use within a few days.
SHALLOTS	Oniony, with hint of garlic.	In butter sauce for fish, meats, rice, vegetables, and so on; roasted whole as side dish; with lamb chops; raw in vinaigrette dressing.	Firm, tight skins; not shriveled. They grow in clusters like garlic.	Refrigerate or keep in cool, dry, airy place. Will keep for weeks.
CHIVES	Mild, oniony.	Seasoning for dips, soups, salads or fish; chopped as garnish. The pretty purple flowers are good in salads.	Bright green; dry, not slimy.	Store, unwashed, wrapped in damp paper toweling, then in plastic; refrigerate. Will keep about 1 week.
SCALLIONS, OR GREEN ONIONS	Somewhat stronger than chives.	Garnishes; Tex-Mex dishes; fried rice; stir-frying; can substitute for chives.	Bright green, with dry tops and firm bulbs.	Store, unwashed, in a plastic bag; use within 1 week.
PEARL ONIONS	All mild; the biggest difference is their colors: red, white, yellow.	Braised; pickled; caramelized; with peas; in stews, such as coq au vin, boeuf bourguignonne.	Firm, tight-fitting skins. They usually are sold in pint baskets.	Refrigerate them in a basket; they keep for a month. Periodically check for rotting onions; remove bad onions from the basket.

VIDALIA ONION RINGS

While you can eat Vidalia onions out of hand as you would an apple, we prefer them this way — light, sweet and crispy.

LOW-CHOLESTEROL

Makes 6 servings.

Nutrient Value Per Serving: 149 calories, 3 g protein, 7 g fat, 19 g carbohydrate, 183 mg sodium, 0 mg cholesterol.

¾　**cup all-purpose flour**
½　**teaspoon salt**
¾　**cup cold water**
2　**Vidalia OR: 1 Spanish onion (8 ounces total), sliced into ⅛-inch-thick rings**

Vegetable oil for deep frying
Coarse (kosher) salt (optional)

Onion Ideas

- Cooking whole onions? Pierce each one with a fork and it will keep its shape.
- Slip your hand inside a food-storage bag while you grate an onion. When you've grated enough, turn the bag inside out, leaving the onion inside, ready to store in the fridge.
- To slice an onion perfectly, cut it in half lengthwise. Stick a fork in the rounded side of each half and cut between the tines.

No-Tears Chopping

Cry no more . . . . Try one of these suggestions with your next onion: Freeze the onion, peel it under cold water before chopping it, and put a small piece of bread in your mouth. To chop quickly and neatly, cut the onion in half through the root end, and peel. Lay one half flat, hold it at the root end, and make two horizontal cuts from the wider end of the onion. (Cut up to— not into—the root end.) Make several lengthwise vertical cuts, turn the onion; and make more cuts across the width. Discard the root end. Repeat with the remaining half of the onion.

✧ ✧ ✧

Leek-ing Information

More subtle in flavor and more digestible than other members of the onion family, leeks are very versatile vegetables. They can be boiled, braised, blanched or steamed (they're even worn on hats in Wales on St. David's Day). One cooked leek contains about 38 calories, and is rich in vitamin A and potassium.

✧ ✧ ✧

1. Combine the flour with the salt in a medium-size bowl. Pour in the cold water, whisking until the batter is blended and the consistency of heavy cream. Separate the onion slices into rings.
2. Heat 1 inch of the oil in a Dutch oven or large, deep skillet over medium-high heat until a deep-frying thermometer registers 375°.
3. Drop 6 to 10 onion rings into the batter, tossing with a fork to coat them. Drop the rings individually into the oil in a single layer. Cook the rings, turning them once, for 2 to 3 minutes, or until the rings are golden brown. Drain the rings on paper toweling. Sprinkle them with coarse salt, if you wish. Repeat with the remaining onion rings. Serve the onion rings hot or warm.

BRAISED LEEKS IN TOMATO ORANGE SAUCE

Often used to enliven and round out the flavor of soups and stews, leeks also are delicious on their own.

LOW-CHOLESTEROL

Makes 6 appetizer servings.

Nutrient Value Per Serving: 138 calories, 2 g protein, 5 g fat, 23 g carbohydrate, 207 mg sodium, 0 mg cholesterol.

6 leeks (8 ounces each), trimmed of all but 2 inches of green, and root ends trimmed	1⅓ cups fresh orange juice (from 5 oranges)
½ teaspoon salt	2 tablespoons olive oil
2 tablespoons fresh lemon juice	2 medium-size tomatoes (6 ounces each), peeled, seeded and chopped, with their juice
2 bay leaves	½ teaspoon fennel seeds

1. Cut the leeks in half lengthwise to within 1½ inches of the root ends. Rinse the leeks well, being certain to clean between each layer of leaves.
2. Combine the leeks with ¼ teaspoon of the salt, 1 tablespoon of the lemon juice and 1 bay leaf in a shallow skillet with cold water to cover. Bring the mixture to boiling. Lower the heat and simmer, partially covered, turning over the leeks once, for about 15 to 20 minutes, or until the leeks are tender when pierced with a knife. Drain the leeks and transfer them to a serving bowl.
3. Combine the orange juice, oil, tomatoes, fennel seeds and remaining bay leaf in a medium-size, heavy-bottom saucepan. Boil the mixture until it is reduced to 1¼ cups, for about 7 minutes. Remove the saucepan from the heat. Discard the bay leaf. Stir in the remaining ¼ teaspoon of salt and the remaining tablespoon of lemon juice. Pour the sauce over the leeks and cool the mixture to room temperature. Cover the bowl and refrigerate the mixture for 4 hours, or overnight. Bring the leeks and sauce to room temperature, and serve.

ZUCCHINI ANTIPASTO

Although this dish is called an antipasto, it also can be served as a side dish to a pasta entrée, such as our Ravioli Marinara (recipe, page 45).

LOW-CALORIE • LOW-CHOLESTEROL

Makes 4 servings.

Nutrient Value Per Serving: 85 calories, 2 g protein, 7 g fat, 5 g carbohydrate, 141 mg sodium, 0 mg cholesterol.

3	large zucchini (1½ pounds), trimmed and sliced diagonally ¼ inch thick	¼	teaspoon salt
2	tablespoons olive oil	⅛	teaspoon freshly ground pepper
1½	tablespoons lemon juice	1	lemon, thinly sliced and seeds removed, for garnish (optional)
2	green onions, thinly sliced (3 tablespoons)		

1. Bring a large pot of lightly salted water to boiling. (If you wish to serve this dish with ravioli, choose a fairly large pot so the water can be used again to cook the ravioli.) Working in 3 batches, drop in the zucchini slices. Return the water to boiling and cook for 1 to 2 minutes, or until the zucchini is crisply tender. Transfer the zucchini with a slotted spoon to a bowl of cold water to stop the cooking. Transfer the zucchini with a slotted spoon to paper toweling to dry.
2. Transfer the zucchini to a large bowl. Add the oil, lemon juice, green onion, salt and pepper, and toss to coat the zucchini. Arrange the zucchini slices, alternating with lemon slices if you wish, on 4 individual salad plates. Serve the zucchini hot or at room temperature.

FRIED ZUCCHINI SPEARS

LOW-CALORIE • LOW-CHOLESTEROL

Makes 4 servings.

Nutrient Value Per Serving: 63 calories, 2 g protein, 5 g fat, 5 g carbohydrate, 289 mg sodium, 0 mg cholesterol.

3	medium-size zucchini (1 pound)	1	clove garlic, finely chopped
1	tablespoon plus 1 teaspoon olive oil	1	tablespoon dry bread crumbs
½	teaspoon grated lemon zest (yellow part of rind only)	½	teaspoon salt
		¼	teaspoon freshly ground pepper

1. Halve the zucchini lengthwise. Cut each half in half crosswise, then cut each piece lengthwise into 4 wedge-shaped sticks.
2. Sauté the zucchini in 1 tablespoon of the oil in a large skillet just until the zucchini is crisply tender, for 3 to 4 minutes. Remove the zucchini.
3. Add the remaining teaspoon of oil to the skillet. Add the lemon zest and the garlic to the skillet and sauté, stirring, for 30 seconds. Stir in the bread crumbs and the zucchini, and sauté for 15 seconds to heat through. Transfer the zucchini mixture to a serving platter. Season with the salt and the pepper.

Zucchini

Zucchini, a green-skinned, Italian squash, looks somewhat like a cucumber and ranges in length from 6 to 8 inches. The skin may be evenly dark and green or striped with white. Its flesh is creamy white, its texture is tender and it has a mild flavor.

■ Originally developed in Italy, zucchini is a variety of summer squash. However, it is available year-round, with the peak season during the summer months. Purchase 1 pound for 2 to 3 servings. A 3½-ounce raw serving contains 17 calories.

■ Zucchini does not need to be peeled. Just wash it, cut off the ends, and cut the zucchini into slices or strips, or dice it. Serve zucchini raw, cook it briefly in a small amount of water, or sauté it in butter or olive oil.

ZUCCHINI, CORN AND PEPPER SAUTÉ

LOW-CHOLESTEROL • MICROWAVE

Makes 4 servings.

Nutrient Value Per Serving: 120 calories, 3 g protein, 6 g fat, 18 g carbohydrate, 293 mg sodium, 4 mg cholesterol.

1 large sweet red pepper, cut into ½-inch cubes	¼ cup water
1 tablespoon vegetable oil	1½ teaspoons butter
1 large zucchini, cut into 1½ x ½-inch sticks	¼ teaspoon ground cumin
	½ teaspoon salt
1 package (10 ounces) frozen corn kernels	⅛ teaspoon freshly ground pepper

1. Sauté the red pepper in the oil in a saucepan over medium heat for 3 minutes, or until the red pepper is softened. Add the zucchini and cook for 1 to 2 minutes. Stir in the corn and the water. Cover the saucepan and cook the mixture for 3 minutes.

2. Stir in the butter, cumin, salt and pepper. Serve hot.

Microwave Instructions
(for a 650-watt variable power microwave oven)

Ingredient Changes: Eliminate the water and the butter.
Directions: Combine the red pepper, zucchini and oil in a microwave-safe ½-quart casserole dish. Microwave, uncovered, at full power for 3 minutes. Stir in the corn, cumin, salt and pepper. Cover and microwave at full power for 4 minutes, stirring once. Let stand for 1 minute before serving.

MINT MARINATED ZUCCHINI

LOW-CALORIE • LOW-CHOLESTEROL • LOW-FAT

Makes 6 servings.

Nutrient Value Per Serving: 30 calories, 2 g protein, 0 g fat, 6 g carbohydrate, 372 mg sodium, 0 mg cholesterol.

2 pounds zucchini OR: yellow squash, scrubbed and cut into 1-inch pieces	¼ teaspoon freshly ground pepper
½ cup olive oil	2 tablespoons finely chopped fresh mint OR: 1 tablespoon dried mint, crumbled
½ cup red wine vinegar	
1½ teaspoons sugar	
1 teaspoon salt	2 cloves garlic, finely chopped

1. Lightly brown the zucchini in the oil in a large skillet for about 5 minutes. Remove the zucchini to a shallow 1-quart serving dish.

2. Add the vinegar, sugar, salt and pepper to the skillet. Bring the mixture to boiling. Lower the heat and simmer, uncovered, for 3 minutes, stirring. Pour the mixture over the zucchini. Add the mint and the garlic, and toss to combine the ingredients.

3. Cover the dish and refrigerate the zucchini for several hours, or overnight, stirring gently several times. Serve at room temperature.

SEASONED SCALLION TURNOVERS

Quick and fairly easy to prepare, these crisp turnovers are good to serve when you're entertaining. They can be assembled hours in advance and panfried at the last minute, or cooked in advance and reheated in a 350° oven. The scallion flavor is sweet and mellow, and the yogurt provides a cooling note.

LOW-CHOLESTEROL

Makes 8 appetizer servings.

Nutrient Value Per Serving: 214 calories, 4 g protein, 12 g fat, 22 g carbohydrate, 286 mg sodium, 1 mg cholesterol.

1¾ cups all-purpose flour	7 to 8 tablespoons cold water
1 teaspoon salt	6 tablespoons olive oil
½ teaspoon sugar	5 large scallions (green
½ teaspoon ground cumin	onions), thinly sliced
½ teaspoon ground coriander	(both white and green
1 tablespoon solid vegetable	parts)
shortening	½ cup plain nonfat yogurt

1. Combine the flour, ½ teaspoon of the salt, the sugar, cumin and coriander in a medium-size bowl. Rub in the shortening with your fingers or a fork until it is blended. Stir in enough of the cold water until the dough masses together. Turn out the dough and knead until the dough is smooth. The dough can be refrigerated, wrapped, for up to 2 days.

2. Roll out the dough on a lightly floured surface to a ⅛-inch thickness. Cut out 18 to 20 circles using a 3-inch round biscuit cutter. Using 1 tablespoon of the oil, brush oil on the circles, leaving a ⅛-inch border on each. Sprinkle the circles evenly with the remaining ½ teaspoon of salt.

3. Spoon about 1 rounded teaspoon of the scallions in the center of each circle. Fold each circle in half, and crimp the edges to seal; if necessary, brush the edges with water to seal.

4. Heat the remaining 5 tablespoons of oil in a large skillet over medium heat. Add the turnovers and panfry, turning them once, for 3 minutes, or until they are crisp and golden. Place the yogurt in a small dish, and serve it as a dip with the turnovers.

APPLE AND POTATO MASH

This flavorful dish is known in Germany as Himmel und Erde, for the sky (apples) and earth (potatoes).

Makes 4 servings.

Nutrient Value Per Serving: 286 calories, 4 g protein, 12 g fat, 42 g carbohydrate, 150 mg sodium, 31 mg cholesterol.

1¾ pounds russet or baking potatoes, peeled and cut into 1-inch cubes (about 4 cups)	2 large cooking apples, such as Rome, Granny Smith OR: Golden Delicious, peeled, cored and cut into 1-inch cubes (about 2½ cups)
4 tablespoons unsalted butter or margarine	¼ teaspoon salt

The Perfect Potato

As a powerhouse of nutrition, potatoes can't be beat!

■ A 5-ounce potato supplies 6% of the day's recommended protein, 8% of magnesium, folacin and phosphorus, 10% of copper, niacin and iron, 15% of iodine, 20% of vitamin B_6, and 35% of vitamin C. Potatoes also are naturally low in sodium, are virtually fat-free and contain no cholesterol.

■ Eat the whole potato, skin and all (washed, of course) — the skin is full of dietary fiber. At the least, cook a potato in its skin, or peel it very thinly, to preserve the nutrients.

■ A medium-size, baked potato, undressed, contains about 100 calories — less than a cup of lowfat fruit yogurt!

❖ ❀ ❖

"What small potatoes we all are, compared to what we might be!"
—*Charles Dudley Warner*

Potato Pointers

- Buy firm, unblemished potatoes. Avoid any that are soft, bruised, cracked, wrinkled, sprouted or have a green tinge.

- Potatoes can be bought in bulk, which generally is more cost effective, and stored for weeks in a cool (40° to 50°), dark place.

- Do not refrigerate potatoes. Refrigeration will affect both their taste and consistency.

- Do not soak potatoes in water for more than 10 minutes. Excessive soaking results in vitamin loss.

- Some handy potato equivalencies: 1 pound of potatoes equals 3 medium-size potatoes, or about 3 cups of peeled and sliced potatoes, or about 2 cups of French fries.

❖ ❖ ❖

1. Cook the potatoes in enough boiling salted water to cover them in a large saucepan over medium-high heat for about 15 minutes, or until the potatoes are fork-tender.

2. Meanwhile, when the potatoes are almost tender, melt 2 tablespoons of the butter or margarine in a medium-size skillet over low heat. Add the apples and sauté, stirring occasionally, for about 10 minutes, or until the apples are tender and golden; do not brown them. Ladle about ½ cup of the potato cooking liquid into the skillet with the apples. Bring the mixture to boiling and boil for 2 minutes.

3. Drain the potatoes and add them to the apples along with the remaining 2 tablespoons of butter. Remove the skillet from the heat. Crush the potato-apple mixture with a potato masher until it is blended and coarsely mashed. Season with the salt. Serve at once.

POTATOES PRIMAVERA

Makes 6 servings.

Nutrient Value Per Serving: 207 calories, 7 g protein, 11 g fat, 23 g carbohydrate, 133 mg sodium, 25 mg cholesterol.

1½ **pounds russet OR: baking potatoes, peeled and cut into 1-inch cubes**	1 **cup cherry tomatoes, cut in half**
¼ **cup (½ stick) unsalted butter or margarine**	1 **green onion, thinly sliced**
1 **medium-size carrot, peeled and thinly sliced**	6 **tablespoons grated Parmesan cheese**
1 **small clove garlic, crushed**	2 **tablespoons fresh lemon juice**
1 **cup frozen green peas, slightly thawed**	¼ **teaspoon freshly ground black pepper**
1 **medium-size zucchini (about 4 ounces), trimmed and coarsely shredded (about 1¼ cups)**	2 **tablespoons pine nuts (pignoli), lightly toasted**

1. Cover the potatoes with cold water in a large saucepan. Bring to boiling and cook for 10 to 15 minutes, or until the potatoes are fork-tender. Drain the potatoes in a colander.

2. Meanwhile, melt the butter or margarine in a large skillet over low heat. Add the carrot and the garlic, and sauté, stirring occasionally, for 2 minutes. Add the green peas and the zucchini, and cook, stirring occasionally, for 1 to 2 minutes, or until the vegetables are tender. Remove the garlic from the skillet.

3. Stir the potatoes, tomatoes, green onion and 4 tablespoons of the Parmesan cheese into the skillet. Cook the mixture, covered, over low heat for about 2 minutes, or until the tomatoes are heated through. Stir in the lemon juice and the black pepper.

4. To serve, sprinkle with the remaining 2 tablespoons of Parmesan cheese and the pine nuts.

ROASTED POTATOES, PEPPERS AND ONIONS WITH ROSEMARY

This simple side dish is perfect with roasted pork or chicken.

LOW-CHOLESTEROL

Bake at 400° for 45 minutes.
Makes 4 servings.

Nutrient Value Per Serving: 245 calories, 4 g protein, 11 g fat, 34 g carbohydrate, 700 mg sodium, 0 mg cholesterol.

1½ **pounds russet OR: baking potatoes, peeled and quartered lengthwise**	4 **cloves garlic**
	3 **tablespoons olive oil**
1 **large sweet red pepper, halved, stemmed, seeded and cut into 8 wedges**	1 **tablespoon fresh rosemary OR: 1 teaspoon dried rosemary, crumbled**
1 **large sweet green pepper, halved, stemmed, seeded and cut into 8 wedges**	1¼ **teaspoons salt**
4 **small onions, halved and quartered lengthwise**	¼ **teaspoon freshly ground black pepper**
	Fresh rosemary sprigs, for garnish (optional)

1. Preheat the oven to hot (400°).
2. Arrange the potatoes and the red and green peppers alternately in a spoke pattern in a large, shallow 12-inch round baking dish. Pile the onions in the center. Scatter the garlic over the top. Drizzle with the oil, and sprinkle with the rosemary, salt and black pepper.
3. Bake in the preheated hot oven (400°) until the vegetables are lightly golden and tender, for about 45 minutes. Garnish with the fresh rosemary sprigs, if you wish.

NEW POTATO AND GREEN ONION FRITTATA

We love this dish, prepared with tiny, tender, newly harvested round red potatoes; leave the skins on for extra color and texture.

LOW-CALORIE

Broil for 3 to 4 minutes.
Makes 6 servings.

Nutrient Value Per Serving: 251 calories, 14 g protein, 14 g fat, 16 g carbohydrate, 567 mg sodium, 381 mg cholesterol.

4 **to 5 thin green onions, trimmed**	8 **eggs**
	½ **cup water**
1 **pound small round red (new) potatoes, cut into ½-inch cubes (about 2 cups)**	1 **cup shredded mozzarella cheese (4 ounces)**
	2 **tablespoons grated Parmesan cheese**
1 **tablespoon vegetable oil**	¼ **teaspoon freshly ground black pepper**
1 **small clove garlic, crushed**	
1 **teaspoon salt**	

One Potato, Two Potato

All potatoes are not created equal. Some are tiny, some are huge, some are tender, and others are meaty. But each is delicious—if you use it in the right dish.

■ Russet Burbank: Large, oblong shape with rough dark skin. Produces the fluffy texture people love best in mashed, baked and French-fried potatoes. The Idaho, a baking potato, is a popular variety.

■ Round Red: Excellent for boiling or steaming and, thus, perfect for salads or alone. Always leave the rosy-red skin intact. Round reds (or whites) sold right after harvest without being stored are called "new potatoes."

■ All-Purpose: Long, oblong shape with thin, smooth, beige skin. Ideal for roasting, boiling, steaming and panfrying. Varieties are California and White Rose.

■ Round White: Plump with relatively thin, smooth, beige skin. Use as you would the All-Purpose group (above), and for soups and stews. Varieties include All-Purpose, Eastern and Maine.

❖ ❖ ❖

Here's Looking at Yogurt

Yogurt is made by adding certain bacterial cultures to milk. Per cup, whole milk yogurt has 155 calories and 8 grams of fat; lowfat yogurt, 143 calories and 3 grams of fat; nonfat yogurt, 127 calories and just a trace of fat. A cup of nonfat yogurt provides half of your daily calcium requirement.

- Use plain nonfat yogurt to top baked potatoes, and garnish them with snipped fresh herbs.
- Use yogurt blended with, or instead of, mayonnaise to cut fat, cholesterol and calories in dressings for tuna, chicken and potato salads and coleslaw.
- Top bean or vegetable soups, chilis and stews with a dollop of plain yogurt.
- Substitute yogurt for sour cream in dips.
- Yogurt provides the same tanginess and tender crumbs to coffee cakes, muffins and other baked goods that sour cream does, at only a fraction of the calories.

1. Cut the white part of the green onion into thin slices (you should have a scant ¼ cup), and set aside. Cut the dark green tops into thin slices (you should have about ⅓ cup), and reserve.
2. Sauté the potatoes in the oil in a medium-size, nonstick, heavy skillet over medium heat, tossing occasionally, until the potatoes are browned and tender when pierced with the tip of a fork, for about 10 minutes. Reduce the heat to low. Stir in the white part of the green onion, the garlic and salt, and sauté for 2 minutes.
3. Preheat the broiler.
4. Meanwhile, beat together the eggs and the water in a medium-size bowl until the mixture is frothy. Add ½ cup of the mozzarella cheese, 1 tablespoon of the Parmesan cheese and the black pepper. Pour the egg mixture into the skillet, stirring to distribute the potatoes evenly. Cover the pan and cook the frittata over medium heat until the edges are set, for about 4 minutes. Uncover and tilt the pan slightly while lifting the edge of the frittata so the uncooked egg in the center flows underneath. Cover the pan and cook until the frittata is thoroughly set, for about 4 minutes.
5. Combine the reserved green onion tops with the remaining ½ cup of mozzarella cheese and the remaining tablespoon of Parmesan cheese in a small bowl. Sprinkle the cheese mixture over the top of the frittata.
6. Broil the frittata 4 inches from the heat source until the top is lightly golden and the cheese melts, for about 3 to 4 minutes.
7. Carefully slide the frittata onto a serving platter, cut it into wedges and serve it hot.

FLUFFY YOGURT POTATOES

Yogurt adds a special tang to mashed potatoes.

LOW-FAT

Broil for 3 to 6 minutes, if you wish.
Makes 4 servings.

Nutrient Value Per Serving: 252 calories, 7 g protein, 7 g fat, 41 g carbohydrate, 1,430 mg sodium, 19 mg cholesterol.

2 pounds russet OR: baking potatoes, peeled and cut into 1-inch cubes (about 5 cups) Cold water	2½ teaspoons salt 1 cup plain nonfat yogurt OR: skim milk 2 tablespoons unsalted butter, melted

1. Cover the potatoes in a large saucepan with the cold water. Add the salt and bring to boiling. Cook the potatoes for 10 to 15 minutes, or until they are fork-tender. Drain the potatoes and return them to the saucepan.
2. Meanwhile, preheat the oven to broil if you wish to brown the potatoes.
3. Mash the potatoes with a potato masher; a hand-held electric mixer can be used, but the texture will be a little different. Add the yogurt or skim milk to the potatoes.
4. Using a pastry bag fitted with a decorative tip, pipe the potato mixture into a flameproof 9-inch round pie plate or similar shallow baking dish. Or spread the potato mixture in the dish, and form a decorative design on top with a fork. Drizzle with the butter.
5. If you wish, broil the potato mixture for 3 to 6 minutes, or until the top is lightly browned.

BUTTERNUT SQUASH AND POTATOES ANNA

This classic French dish usually is made with potatoes alone, first browned on top of the stove, then baked and unmolded. Here, thin slices of butternut squash are layered with the potatoes for a special taste.

Bake at 425° for 30 minutes.
Makes 8 servings.

Nutrient Value Per Serving: 217 calories, 3 g protein, 12 g fat, 27 g carbohydrate, 407 mg sodium, 31 mg cholesterol.

½ **cup (1 stick) butter**	½ **teaspoon freshly ground pepper**
2½ **pounds red-skinned potatoes (about 11 medium-size potatoes), peeled and cut into ⅛-inch slices***	1 **small butternut squash (about 2 pounds), cut in half lengthwise, seeded, peeled and cut into ⅛-inch slices***
4 **tablespoons chopped parsley**	**Fresh parsley sprigs, for garnish (optional)**
1 **teaspoon salt**	

1. Preheat the oven to hot (425°).
2. Melt the butter, without stirring, in a small, heavy saucepan over very low heat. Spoon off and discard the white foam from the top. You should have about 7 tablespoons of clarified butter.

The Great American Vegetable

Squash in all its forms has been an American staple since the buffalo roamed free. Below are some fast facts to help you enjoy it more.

- Choose squash that is firm and heavy for its size; this indicates a meatier interior.
- Since the hard shells of winter squashes give them a longer life than the summer varieties, you can keep them for 3 months or more in a cool, dark, well-ventilated place.
- Don't discard the seeds! They're edible and good sources of protein. Roast and lightly salt squash seeds for a healthful snack, or sprinkle them over a salad as a garnish.
- The pulp of a squash will soak up the juices of whatever dish you cook with it, making squash the perfect side dish for flavorful meat roasts.

❖   ❖   ❖

Butternut Squash and Potatoes Anna is a delectable variation of the classic French dish.

3. Trace the bottom of a medium-size, cast iron skillet onto a piece of aluminum foil, and cut out the tracing. Brush the skillet with some of the clarified butter and place the foil circle in the skillet bottom. Spoon in 2 tablespoons of the clarified butter. Place a potato slice in the center of the foil and surround the slice with a circle of overlapping potato slices; overlap the slices by half. Then edge with another circle of potato slices, overlapping them in the opposite direction and completely covering the bottom of the skillet. Drizzle with 1 tablespoon of the clarified butter and sprinkle with 1 tablespoon of the parsley, ¼ teaspoon of the salt and ⅛ teaspoon of the pepper. Repeat, using the squash slices. Repeat the 2 layers once more, then end with a layer of potato. (Three layers of potato will sandwich 2 layers of squash.) Drizzle any remaining butter over the top. Press down firmly on the vegetable layers.

4. Place the skillet over medium-high heat and brown the vegetables for 5 minutes. Cut another piece of aluminum foil to fit the top of the skillet, and butter the foil circle in the center. Cover the vegetables with the foil circle, buttered side down. Top with an ovenproof, heavy saucepan just large enough to weight down the vegetables.

5. Bake the vegetables in the preheated hot oven (425°) for 30 minutes.

6. Peel off the top foil. Run a knife around the edge of the skillet to loosen the vegetables from the pan. Invert a serving platter over the skillet. Carefully invert the skillet and platter to unmold the potato-squash cake. Carefully peel back the foil circle, using a knife blade to hold the potatoes in place as you peel. Garnish with the fresh parsley sprigs, if you wish. Cut the potato-squash cake into wedges to serve.

*Note: The potatoes and squash can be sliced with a food processor fitted with the thin blade slicer.

YELLOW SQUASH WITH ROSEMARY

LOW-CALORIE • LOW-CHOLESTEROL

Makes 4 servings.

Nutrient Value Per Serving: 92 calories, 2 g protein, 7 g fat, 8 g carbohydrate, 446 mg sodium, 8 mg cholesterol.

1½	pounds yellow squash	1	tablespoon butter
2	cloves garlic, finely chopped	2	tablespoons finely chopped parsley
½	teaspoon dried rosemary, crumbled OR: 1 teaspoon chopped fresh rosemary	1	tablespoon lemon juice
		¾	teaspoon salt
1	tablespoon olive oil	¼	teaspoon freshly ground pepper

1. Cut the squash lengthwise into ¼-inch slices, and then cut it crosswise into ¼-inch strips.

2. Sauté the garlic and the rosemary in the oil and the butter in a large skillet for 5 seconds. Add the squash and cook, stirring constantly, until the squash is crisply tender, for about 4 minutes.

3. Add the parsley, lemon juice, salt and pepper, and toss to combine the ingredients. Transfer the squash to a serving platter and serve.

BUTTERNUT SQUASH CAKES WITH RASPBERRY SAUCE

Although these moist and tender little pancakes are wonderful for breakfast, brunch or dessert, they also are a good accompaniment to roasted pork or pork chops. Try them with other toppings, such as applesauce, blueberry sauce, honey or maple syrup.

LOW-FAT

Makes 7 servings (about twenty-one 3-inch pancakes).

Nutrient Value Per Serving: 288 calories, 8 g protein, 8 g fat, 48 g carbohydrate, 362 mg sodium, 94 mg cholesterol.

2 eggs	2 cups shredded, peeled butternut OR: other winter squash or pumpkin (9 to 10 ounces), well-drained and squeezed dry through several layers of cheesecloth
1 container (8 ounces) large curd cottage cheese	
⅓ cup all-purpose flour	
2 tablespoons sugar	
½ teaspoon salt	
¼ teaspoon baking powder	1 tart cooking apple, peeled and shredded
¼ teaspoon ground nutmeg	Vegetable oil
¼ cup milk	Raspberry Sauce (recipe follows)
2 tablespoons butter or margarine, melted	Dairy sour cream (optional)
½ teaspoon vanilla	

1. Beat together the eggs and the cottage cheese in a large bowl. Add the flour, sugar, salt, baking powder and nutmeg, and beat until the ingredients are well blended. Beat in the milk, butter or margarine and the vanilla. Stir in the squash and the apple.

2. Heat an oiled large griddle over medium heat. (If using an electric griddle, heat to 325°.) Or heat a nonstick skillet brushed with vegetable oil over medium heat.

3. Using 2 level measuring tablespoonfuls of batter for each pancake, spoon the batter onto the griddle, spreading each pancake to a 3-inch round. Cook the pancakes on the first side for about 3 minutes, or until the batter bubbles, and the pancakes become slightly dry around the edges and medium golden brown on the bottom. Flip the pancakes with a spatula (flip very carefully, as these pancakes are very fragile), and cook for about 2 to 3 minutes more, or until the pancakes are done. Serve the pancakes hot with the Raspberry Sauce and, if you wish, sour cream.

Raspberry Sauce:

Combine 1 package (12 ounces) of frozen dry-pack raspberries, or 3 cups of fresh raspberries, with ¾ cup of sugar in a medium-size saucepan, and set aside. Dissolve 2 tablespoons of cornstarch in 2 tablespoons of raspberry-flavored liqueur in a small bowl, stirring until the ingredients are well combined. Stir the cornstarch mixture into the raspberry mixture in the saucepan. Cook the sauce over medium heat, stirring occasionally, until it thickens and bubbles, for about 5 minutes. Remove the saucepan from the heat and press the sauce through a fine sieve with the back of a spoon. Discard the seeds. Cool the sauce to room temperature.

Pick Your Squash

■ Acorn squash, so named for its nut-like shape, has a moist, nutty taste. Golden acorn squash is slightly sweeter than green acorn squash; both varieties are widely available. Green acorn squash should be dark gray-green with orange spots. Golden acorn is golden-orange in color. Both are high in vitamins A and C, and niacin.

■ Buttercup squash is dark green in color with grayish flecks, and has a hat-like stem. Buy the squash with the stem intact to prolong its freshness. It has a sweet flavor and smooth texture, but is slightly drier than other squashes. It is high in vitamins A and C, iron, potassium and fiber.

■ Butternut squash has a creamy, "butter-nutty" flavor; the smaller the squash, the sweeter the taste. Look for squash with pale, golden-beige coloring. It contains vitamin A, niacin, calcium, potassium, phosphorus and iron.

■ Golden Nugget is the size of an apple, and is ideal for individual servings. When ripe, this squash is bright orange and wonderfully sweet. Its nutritional values are similar to buttercup squash.

■ Hubbard squash is quite large and economical, often weighing 20 pounds or more. The rind can be gray-green, blue-green or orange in color. This squash has a firm texture and a sweet, nutty taste. It contains vitamins A, B$_1$ and B$_2$, niacin, phosphorous, protein and potassium.

Also called vegetable spaghetti, this squash is aptly named. When cooked, its interior fluffs up into long strands, which absorb the flavor of any accompanying sauce; the larger the squash, the thicker the strands. Until recently, spaghetti squash was purely a home-grown novelty; now it is available in most supermarkets.

■ Select unblemished, smooth-skinned squash. Spaghetti squash can range from bright to whitish-yellow in color. It is marketed from late summer through winter. Spaghetti squash can be stored for many months in a cool, dry place.

■ Spaghetti squash is low in calories and high in potassium, fiber, vitamin A and niacin.

■ Although you can serve spaghetti squash with a sauce like the pasta version, it also is wonderful just tossed with butter and grated Parmesan cheese. Or you can chill cooked spaghetti squash and toss it with a vinaigrette dressing.

❖　❖　❖

SPAGHETTI SQUASH WITH ITALIAN SAUSAGE MARINARA

A taste-tempting alternative to its higher-calorie pasta counterpart.

LOW-CHOLESTEROL

Bake squash at 375° for 45 to 60 minutes.
Makes 6 servings.

Nutrient Value Per Serving: 390 calories, 20 g protein, 25 g fat, 23 g carbohydrate, 1,121 mg sodium, 70 mg cholesterol.

1　**large spaghetti squash (about 3 pounds)**

Italian Sausage Marinara:
1½　**pounds sweet Italian sausage (8 to 10 sausages)**
2　**large onions, chopped**
2　**large cloves garlic, finely chopped or put through a garlic press**
1　**can (28 ounces) whole Italian tomatoes, undrained and cut up**
1　**bay leaf**
1　**tablespoon dried basil, crumbled**

½　**teaspoon dried oregano, crumbled**
½　**teaspoon dried rosemary crumbled**
¼　**teaspoon salt**
¼　**teaspoon freshly ground black pepper**
⅛　**teaspoon crushed red pepper flakes**
½　**cup chopped parsley**

1　**tablespoon butter
Fresh parsley sprigs, for garnish (optional)
Freshly grated Parmesan cheese (optional)**

1. Preheat the oven to moderate (375°).
2. Prick the squash with a long fork in a dozen places all over. Place the squash on a glass pie plate or in a shallow baking pan.
3. Bake the squash in the preheated moderate oven (375°) until it is tender when pierced with a fork, for 45 to 60 minutes. Cut the squash in half and cool it briefly.
4. Meanwhile, prepare the Italian Sausage Marinara: Remove and discard the sausage casings. Crumble the meat into large clumps into a medium-size, heavy skillet. Sauté the meat over medium heat until it is lightly browned, for about 10 minutes. Drain off the fat from the meat and return the meat to the skillet.
5. Add the onion to the meat and sauté over medium heat for 3 to 5 minutes, or until the onion is tender. Stir in the garlic and cook for 1 minute. Add the tomatoes with their liquid, the bay leaf, basil, oregano, rosemary, salt, black pepper and red pepper flakes. Bring the mixture to boiling. Reduce the heat to low and simmer until the sauce is thickened and reduced to about 5 cups, for about 1 hour and 10 minutes. Remove the skillet from the heat. Discard the bay leaf. Stir in the chopped parsley.
6. With a spoon, scoop out and discard the center portion of seeds from the squash. Working around the edge toward the center, scoop out the strands of spaghetti squash onto a warmed serving platter. Add the butter, and toss with a fork to melt the butter and fluff the squash. Top with the hot sauce. If you wish, garnish with the fresh parsley sprigs and serve with freshly grated Parmesan cheese.

TOMATOES WITH MARINATED CREAM CHEESE

This is great as a salad, but we love it with Italian bread as a first course.

Makes 4 generous servings.

Nutrient Value Per Serving: 430 calories, 6 g protein, 42 g fat,
11 g carbohydrate, 798 mg sodium, 62 mg cholesterol.

1 package (8 ounces) cream cheese, chilled	¼ cup sliced pimiento-stuffed green olives
6 tablespoons vegetable oil	2 teaspoons finely chopped pickled jalapeño peppers (optional)
¼ cup red wine vinegar	
1 tablespoon finely chopped fresh dill OR: fresh cilantro	4 ripe tomatoes (1½ pounds)
¾ teaspoon salt	6 green onions, cut into 6-inch lengths and cut lengthwise into thin julienne strips
¼ teaspoon freshly ground pepper	
1 clove garlic, finely chopped	

1. Cut the cream cheese into ½-inch cubes. Return the cream cheese to the refrigerator while preparing the dressing.
2. Whisk together the oil, vinegar, dill or cilantro, salt, pepper and garlic in a large bowl. Stir in the olives and, if you wish, jalapeño peppers. Add the cream cheese and toss gently to coat the cheese evenly. Cover the bowl and chill the mixture, stirring occasionally, for at least 1 hour.
3. Core the tomatoes and cut them into ½-inch wedges. Sprinkle half the green onion over a serving platter. Arrange the tomatoes on top. Sprinkle the remaining green onion over the tomatoes. Spoon the cream cheese over the top. Pour the dressing over all.

PANFRIED PLUM TOMATOES

LOW-CALORIE • LOW-CHOLESTEROL

Makes 4 servings.

Nutrient Value Per Serving: 42 calories, 1 g protein, 3 g fat,
3 g carbohydrate, 140 mg sodium, 0 mg cholesterol.

4 plum tomatoes (about 10 ounces)	¼ teaspoon dried oregano, crumbled
1 tablespoon olive oil	¼ teaspoon salt
2 tablespoons chopped parsley	⅛ teaspoon freshly ground pepper
½ teaspoon dried basil, crumbled	

1. Halve the tomatoes lengthwise. Heat a heavy skillet over medium-high heat. Add the oil and heat for 1 minute.
2. Add the tomatoes, cut side down, and cook for 2 to 3 minutes, or until the tomatoes are slightly browned. Turn over the tomatoes. Sprinkle with the parsley, basil, oregano, salt and pepper. Cook for 1 minute. Serve the tomatoes hot.

Terrific Tomatoes

Red, yellow, green, cherry, plum and regular round: these are only some of the many varieties of tomato.
■ Native to Peru, this popular fruit was grown there by the Incas. The Aztecs in Mexico also grew tomatoes and called them "tomatl." In the 1500's, tomatoes were introduced by explorers to Europe, where they were dismissed as both a curiosity and probably poisonous. It wasn't until the 1800's that the tomato finally gained acceptance. Now, tomatoes are second only to potatoes in popularity.
■ The tomato is the fruit of a plant of the nightshade family and is related to potato, pepper, eggplant and tobacco.

Tomato Toss

For an easy-on-you side dish, halve 4 plum tomatoes and drizzle them with 1 tablespoon of olive oil. Sprinkle the tomatoes with salt and pepper to taste, and with fresh or dried herbs. Good herb choices include basil, parsley, oregano, dill and cilantro.

❖ ❖ ❖

Tomato Tidbits

- One medium-size tomato delivers nearly half the RDA of vitamins A and C, some niacin and fiber, and only 30 calories.
- If you cook tomato sauce in a non-enameled cast iron pot, you'll give yourself an iron boost — the acid in tomatoes draws out the iron from the cast iron.
- Fresh tomatoes are available year-round, but their peak growth period is from May to October. Select tomatoes that are firm and unblemished, and preferably ripened on the vine.
- Small tomatoes are good for sauces and casseroles. Medium-size or large tomatoes are preferred for slicing or stuffing. Allow ½ pound, 1 large, or 1 medium-size tomato for serving as a vegetable.

SAUTÉED TOMATOES WITH BLUE CHEESE SAUCE

A creamy accompaniment to crisp grilled chops or baked chicken.

Makes 6 servings.

Nutrient Value Per Serving: 210 calories, 8 g protein, 17 g fat, 8 g carbohydrate, 673 mg sodium, 46 mg cholesterol.

6	medium-size tomatoes (about 2 pounds)	¼	cup half-and-half
¼	cup (½ stick) butter	2	tablespoons finely chopped parsley
6	ounces blue cheese, crumbled (about 1½ cups)	½	teaspoon salt
		¼	teaspoon freshly ground pepper

1. Preheat the oven to slow (250°). Halve the tomatoes crosswise.
2. Melt the butter in a medium-size skillet over medium-high heat. Add the tomatoes, cut side down, and cook for 3 minutes. Turn over the tomatoes and cook for 2 to 3 minutes more. Remove the tomatoes to a serving platter and keep them warm in the slow (250°) oven.
3. Stir the blue cheese, half-and-half, parsley, salt and pepper into the skillet. Cook the mixture over medium heat, whisking constantly, until the sauce is smooth and bubbling slightly. Pour the sauce over the tomatoes and serve hot.

STEWED TOMATOES AND CORN

LOW-CALORIE • LOW-CHOLESTEROL

Makes 4 servings.

Nutrient Value Per Serving: 100 calories, 3 g protein, 4 g fat, 16 g carbohydrate, 200 mg sodium, 0 mg cholesterol.

½	cup thinly sliced celery	¼	teaspoon paprika
1	medium-size onion, coarsely chopped	¼	teaspoon dried thyme, crumbled
2	tablespoons chopped sweet green pepper	⅛	teaspoon freshly ground pepper
1	tablespoon vegetable oil	1	cup frozen whole kernel corn
1	can (16 ounces) tomatoes, undrained and broken up with a fork		

1. Sauté the celery, onion and green pepper in the oil in a medium-size saucepan until the vegetables are tender, for about 3 minutes.
2. Stir in the tomatoes with their liquid, the paprika, thyme and pepper. Bring the mixture to boiling. Lower the heat, cover the saucepan and simmer for 10 minutes. Add the corn. Simmer, uncovered, for 3 minutes. Serve the vegetables hot.

Oil You Need to Know

Use this chart to compare the flavor and fat content of several polyunsaturated and monounsaturated vegetable oils commonly used for sautéing and salad dressing.

Oil	Saturated Fat	Sautéing Quality and Taste	Dressing Taste
peanut	17 percent	Acceptable; no taste	No taste
avocado	15 to 20 percent	Acceptable; no taste	No taste
soy	14 percent	Acceptable; no taste	No taste
roasted sesame	14 percent	Smokes; use with other oil	Use sparingly for flavor
olive	14 percent	Depending on brand, adds excellent flavor	Superb
extra-light olive	14 percent	Imparts no flavor	Fair
corn	13 percent	Acceptable; no taste	No taste
sunflower	10 percent	Acceptable; no taste	No taste
safflower	9 percent	Acceptable; no taste	No taste
walnut	9 percent	Smokes; inappropriate	Excellent nutty taste
hazelnut	7 percent	Smokes; inappropriate	Lovely nutty taste
canola	6 percent	Acceptable; no taste	No taste

The sautéing quality and flavor of each variety of oil was tested on a piece of boneless, skinless chicken breast. Each oil's flavor in salad dressing also was tested by mixing the oil with vinegar and dipping lettuce into it.

With few exceptions, oils have been chemically stripped of their flavors, so most taste neutral. Extra-virgin olive oil is often more flavorful than 100 percent pure olive oil, but not necessarily. Brands vary. Extra virgin, however, is always more expensive.

It is important to reduce total fat intake, not just saturated fat intake.

Saturated Fats

These fats remain solid at room temperature, come mainly from animals, and are linked to heart disease because they can raise blood cholesterol levels. Saturated fats include butterfat, suet and lard; coconut oil and palm kernel oil also are highly saturated.

Polyunsaturated Fats

These fats remain liquid at room temperature and come mainly from plants. They help lower the undesirable low-density lipoprotein (LDL) cholesterol in your blood, thereby offering protection against heart disease. The polyunsaturates include soy, peanut, corn, sesame, sunflower, safflower, walnut, hazelnut and cottonseed oils.

Monounsaturated Fats

These fats also remain liquid at room temperature, but are thicker than the polys. They lower the bad LDL cholesterol, without affecting the good high-density lipoprotein (HDL) cholesterol. The monounsaturates are olive, almond, avocado and canola oils.

Silent Partners: All About Oil

As a silent partner diligently working behind the scenes, the right oil will help you achieve the perfect balance of flavor and texture.

■ Though oils used in cooking generally are taken for granted, it is their presence in recipes that helps to meld various ingredients together, and also brings out wonderful subtleties of flavor in foods.

■ Oils deliver health benefits too. They help provide energy, prolong digestion and act as carriers for vitamins A, D, E and K. But all vegetable oils are not the same. Those with a high ratio of mono- and polyunsaturated fats to saturated fatty acids are considered more healthful; others, with a high saturated-fat content, are thought to raise cholesterol levels. The bad guys include coconut oil (87% saturated fat), palm kernel oil (81%) and palm oil (49%), and should be avoided. These oils are widely used in processed foods, so check all product labels before you buy. Luckily, monounsaturated and polyunsaturated oils — the good guys — are plentiful, tasty and versatile!

❖ ❖ ❖

CLASSIC VINAIGRETTE

Whether you whisk by hand, use a food processor or simply drizzle on the oil and vinegar separately, vinaigrette is an easy, elegant way to dress a salad. This version uses garlic and Dijon-style mustard for extra flavor.

LOW-CHOLESTEROL

Makes about 1 cup (use ½ cup to dress 12 cups of greens; refrigerate remainder for up to 6 days).

Nutrient Value Per Tablespoon: 91 calories, 0 g protein, 10 g fat, 0 g carbohydrate, 87 mg sodium, 0 mg cholesterol.

4	tablespoons vinegar	¼	teaspoon freshly ground pepper
2	teaspoons Dijon-style mustard	1	clove garlic, unpeeled
½	teaspoon salt	6	tablespoons vegetable oil
		6	tablespoons olive oil

1. To make the Vinaigrette by hand: Whisk together the vinegar, mustard, salt and pepper in a small bowl until the ingredients are well blended and the salt is dissolved.
2. Add the garlic, using one of the following methods: Peel the clove. Cut horizontal and vertical parallel lines toward the root end. Then cut the slices crosswise into tiny pieces. Add the chopped garlic to the vinegar mixture.
3. Or place the unpeeled clove in a garlic press and squeeze. Scrape the garlic from the press with a small knife into the vinegar mixture.
4. Or lightly crush the peeled clove with the side of a knife and rub the salad bowl with the clove.
5. Gradually whisk the vegetable and olive oils into the vinegar mixture until the vinaigrette is well blended and smooth. Use the vinaigrette immediately, or refrigerate it for a day or two. Whisk the vinaigrette just before using it.
6. To make the Vinaigrette in a jar: Place all the ingredients in a screw-top jar, screw the top on tightly, and shake until the ingredients are well blended and smooth.
7. To make the Vinaigrette in a food processor or electric blender: Drop the garlic into the container while the machine is running. Stop the machine. Scrape the sides of the container with a spatula. Add the vinegar, mustard, salt and pepper. Whirl for 2 to 3 seconds.
8. Gradually add the vegetable and olive oils through the feed tube of the processor or the blender top while the machine is running, and blend for another second or two.
9. To add fresh herbs: With scissors, snip enough fresh herbs (tarragon, oregano, dill) to equal 1 to 2 tablespoons. Add the herbs to the vinaigrette just before serving it.
10. To add dried herbs: Add about 1 teaspoon of crumbled dried herbs to the vinegar, and let the herbs steep for 5 to 10 minutes before mixing the vinaigrette.
11. For table presentation, pour some of the vinaigrette into the salad bowl. Cross the serving utensils across the bottom. Place the greens on top of the utensils. Gently toss the greens. Pass the extra vinaigrette.

Oils to try: extra-virgin or virgin olive oil, safflower, peanut, corn, sesame or walnut oil.
Vinegars to try: red or white wine, cider, distilled white, balsamic or fruit vinegar.

ORIENTAL RADISH SALAD

LOW-CALORIE • LOW-CHOLESTEROL

Makes 4 servings.

Nutrient Value Per Serving: 68 calories, 1 g protein, 4 g fat, 9 g carbohydrate, 236 mg sodium, 0 mg cholesterol.

2 **cups coarsely shredded radishes (about 32 medium-size radishes)**	1 **tablespoon sugar**
1 **cucumber, halved lengthwise and sliced ¼ inch thick**	1 **tablespoon Oriental sesame oil**
2 **green onions, sliced**	1 **tablespoon reduced-sodium soy sauce**
2 **tablespoons lemon juice**	⅛ **teaspoon salt**
	Lettuce (optional)

1. Combine the radish, cucumber and green onion in a small bowl, and toss to mix them.
2. Whisk together the lemon juice, sugar, sesame oil, soy sauce and salt in a small bowl. Pour the dressing over the vegetables and toss to mix. Serve the salad immediately, on a bed of lettuce if you wish.

RAINBOW SALAD WITH MUSTARD LEMON DRESSING

LOW-CALORIE • LOW-CHOLESTEROL

Makes 4 servings.

Nutrient Value Per Serving: 67 calories, 1 g protein, 4 g fat, 8 g carbohydrate, 461 mg sodium, 0 mg cholesterol.

2 **cups shredded romaine lettuce**	6 **radishes, thinly sliced**
1 **large sweet red pepper, diced**	**Mustard Lemon Dressing (recipe follows)**
2 **ribs celery, thinly sliced**	6 **cherry tomatoes, halved, for garnish**
2 **medium-size carrots, peeled and thinly sliced**	1 **tablespoon vegetable oil**

1. Toss the lettuce with the red pepper, celery, carrot and radish in a medium-size bowl.
2. Drizzle with the Mustard Lemon Dressing. Garnish with the cherry tomatoes. Drizzle with the oil. Serve the salad immediately.

Mustard Lemon Dressing:

Mix 2 tablespoons of lemon juice, 1 teaspoon of prepared yellow mustard, ½ teaspoon of salt and ¼ teaspoon each of crumbled dried oregano, ground cumin and freshly ground pepper in a small bowl until they are well blended.

Sesame Oil

A polyunsaturate (14% saturated fat), sesame oil appears mainly in Oriental, Middle Eastern and Indian cooking. Excellent for shallow- and deep-frying, it lends a nutlike taste to food. A thicker, darker version is used in Chinese dishes.

Romaine

Romaine lettuce has a long head of loose leaves with large cross ribs. The darker green outer leaves can be tough; the lighter green inner leaves are more tender and have a white core. The standard green used to make Caesar salad, romaine has a nutty flavor and crisp texture.

Corn Oil

Corn oil, a polyunsaturate (13% saturated fat), is one of the most common oils used in America. Its neutral flavor allows the true taste of food to shine through. It is great for all types of frying—and for mixing with herbs and vinegars to create sumptuous salad dressings.

ANTIPASTO SALAD

Makes 4 servings.

Nutrient Value Per Serving: 175 calories, 7 g protein, 14 g fat, 5 g carbohydrate, 538 mg sodium, 30 mg cholesterol.

	Parsley Garlic Mayonnaise (recipe follows)	1	**carrot, cut into sticks**
4	**slices Genoa salami (2 ounces)**	1	**stalk celery, cut into sticks**
2	**ounces Provolone, cut into sticks**	½	**sweet green pepper, thinly sliced**
4	**leaves romaine lettuce**	¼	**sweet red pepper, thinly sliced**

1. Prepare the Parsley Garlic Mayonnaise.
2. Form the salami into cornucopias and fasten them with wooden picks. Fill the salami cornucopias with the Provolone.
3. Place 1 lettuce leaf on each of 4 individual salad plates. Top each leaf with a salami cornucopia and with some of the carrot sticks, celery sticks, green pepper and red pepper. Add a dollop of the mayonnaise.

Parsley Garlic Mayonnaise:
Using a garlic press, crush 1 small clove of garlic into a small bowl. Stir in ⅓ cup of reduced-calorie mayonnaise, ¼ cup of chopped parsley and 1 teaspoon of lemon juice.

CONFETTI SLAW

LOW-CHOLESTEROL

Makes 6 servings.

Nutrient Value Per Serving: 126 calories, 2 g protein, 9 g fat, 11 g carbohydrate, 207 mg sodium, 0 mg cholesterol.

1½	**pounds cabbage, shredded (about 2 quarts)**	3	**tablespoons distilled white vinegar**
1	**medium-size onion, finely chopped (½ cup)**	1	**tablespoon sugar**
1	**carrot, coarsely grated**	½	**teaspoon salt**
¼	**sweet red pepper, finely chopped (about ¼ cup)**	¼	**teaspoon freshly ground pepper**
¼	**cup vegetable oil**	¼	**teaspoon dried dillweed**
		¼	**teaspoon dry mustard**

1. Combine the cabbage, onion, carrot and red pepper in a large bowl.
2. Combine the oil, vinegar, sugar, salt, pepper, dillweed and mustard in a small bowl. Pour the dressing over the vegetable mixture and mix well. Cover the bowl and refrigerate the slaw until serving time.

WATERCRESS, ENDIVE AND BLUE CHEESE SALAD WITH TOASTED WALNUTS

LOW-CHOLESTEROL

Toast walnuts at 350° for 6 to 8 minutes.
Makes 4 servings.

Nutrient Value Per Serving: 240 calories, 4 g protein, 24 g fat, 4 g carbohydrate, 265 mg sodium, 5 mg cholesterol.

5	tablespoons walnut oil	¼	cup walnuts, chopped
1½	tablespoons red wine vinegar	3	heads Belgian endive
¼	teaspoon salt	1	bunch watercress, rinsed
⅛	teaspoon freshly ground black pepper	¼	cup crumbled blue cheese

1. Preheat the oven to moderate (350°).
2. Meanwhile, mix together the oil, vinegar, salt and black pepper in a small bowl. Set aside the dressing.
3. Toast the walnuts in a shallow baking pan in the preheated moderate oven (350°) for 6 to 8 minutes, or until the walnuts are lightly browned. Cool the walnuts.
4. Wipe the endive with damp paper toweling. Cut a thin slice from the bottom of each. Break off the leaves at the base. Arrange the endive leaves on a serving platter or 4 individual salad plates. Trim the stems from the watercress and arrange the watercress over the endive. Scatter the walnuts and the blue cheese evenly over all. Drizzle with the dressing.

WARM SPINACH WITH CIDER VINAIGRETTE

LOW-CALORIE • LOW-CHOLESTEROL

Makes 4 servings.

Nutrient Value Per Serving: 62 calories, 3 g protein, 5 g fat, 4 g carbohydrate, 194 mg sodium, 12 mg cholesterol.

2	packages (10 ounces each) fresh spinach	⅛	teaspoon ground nutmeg
2	tablespoons cider vinegar	⅛	teaspoon salt
1½	tablespoons butter	⅛	teaspoon freshly ground pepper

1. Rinse the spinach in a big bowl or sink full of cool water. Pull off only the largest and toughest stems, and discard them.
2. Place the spinach, with water clinging to the leaves, in a large, heavy pot or Dutch oven. Place the pot over high heat. Cook, stirring and turning the leaves several times, just until the spinach is wilted, for about 2 minutes.
3. Stir in the vinegar, butter, nutmeg, salt and pepper. Turn the spinach into a serving dish. Serve the spinach hot.

Endive

There are two varieties of endive available. One is a bitter salad green, which also is called curly endive or chicory. It often is mistaken for escarole. The other is Belgian endive, the sprout of the witloof chicory root, which can be steamed or braised as a vegetable, or used raw in salads.

■ Curly endive grows in a loose head with delicate, narrow, jagged-edged leaves that curl at the ends. Curly endive is available year-round, but the peak season is from June to October. Allow 1 head, which should weigh about 1 pound, for 3 to 4 servings.

■ Belgian endive grows in a compact 4- to 6-inch pale yellow head. This vegetable was discovered accidentally when coffee chicory roots that had been left covered began to sprout white leaves. A Belgian horticulturist grew the first Belgian endive in a cellar. Most endive of this variety still is imported from Belgium to our markets. It is available from September to May, but is best from November to April.

■ Cook the tiny Belgian Endive heads and serve them as a vegetable, or separate the leaves and use them in salads or in a raw vegetable platter with dip. Six heads of Belgian endive weigh about 1 pound and yield 3 to 4 servings.

Preparing a Salad

- Most large greens should be torn—not cut—into bite-size pieces. However, romaine and Belgian endive can be cut crosswise into thin slices.
- For a well-dressed salad, toss the greens in a large bowl with a small amount of the dressing so the leaves are lightly coated. Add more dressing, if you wish, but not so much that an excess gathers in the bottom of the bowl.
- If the salad already is arranged, drizzle it with a little dressing, toss it, and pass the remaining dressing for each person to add.
- To keep salad from getting soggy, add the dressing just before serving.
- Heavier ingredients, such as radishes and cucumbers, can sink to the bottom of the bowl. Dress them separately and arrange them on top of the salad greens.

❖ ✿ ❖

> " *My salad days,*
> *When I was*
> *green*
> *in judgement.* "
> —*William Shakespeare*

SALAD WITH HEARTY RUSSIAN DRESSING

LOW-CALORIE • LOW-CHOLESTEROL

Makes 4 servings.

Nutrient Value Per Serving: 94 calories, 3 g protein, 6 g fat, 8 g carbohydrate, 102 mg sodium, 5 mg cholesterol.

Hearty Russian Dressing:
½ cup plain nonfat yogurt
¼ cup mayonnaise
2 tablespoons catsup
  Salt and freshly ground pepper, to taste

  Heart of large head romaine lettuce

8 cherry tomatoes, halved
2 thin slices purple onion, separated into rings
4 radishes, sliced
½ cup leftover vegetables OR: thawed frozen green peas

1. Prepare the Hearty Russian Dressing: Whisk together the yogurt, mayonnaise and catsup in a small bowl. Stir in the salt and pepper.
2. Tear the lettuce into bite-size pieces; you should have 4 to 5 cups. Divide the lettuce among 4 individual salad bowls. Add equal amounts of the cherry tomatoes, onion rings and radish to each bowl. Using half the dressing, spoon it over each salad. Reserve the remaining dressing, refrigerated, for another use. Sprinkle each salad with some of the leftover vegetables or thawed green peas.

ROMAINE SALAD WITH CREAMY AVOCADO DRESSING

LOW-CHOLESTEROL

Makes 4 servings.

Nutrient Value Per Serving: 118 calories, 4 g protein, 8 g fat, 9 g carbohydrate, 169 mg sodium, 2 mg cholesterol.

1 ripe California avocado
½ cup plain nonfat yogurt OR: dairy sour cream
2 tablespoons lemon juice
1 small clove garlic, peeled
½ teaspoon ground cumin
¼ teaspoon salt

⅛ teaspoon freshly ground pepper
16 small romaine lettuce leaves, washed and dried
8 radishes, sliced (½ cup)
1 medium-size red onion, peeled and cut into rings

1. Halve the avocado lengthwise. Remove and reserve the pit. Scoop out the pulp with a spoon and place it in the container of a food processor or electric blender. Add the yogurt or sour cream, the lemon juice, garlic, cumin, salt and pepper. Whirl the mixture until it is puréed. If using the dressing later, transfer it to a bowl and bury the reserved avocado pit inside it. Cover the bowl with plastic wrap and refrigerate the dressing.
2. Arrange 4 lettuce leaves on each of 4 individual dinner plates. Divide the radish and the onion rings equally among the plates. Using half the dressing, spoon it equally over the salads. Reserve the remaining dressing, stored in a bowl with the avocado pit and refrigerated, for another use.

ARUGULA AND RED LEAF LETTUCE WITH RASPBERRY VINAIGRETTE

The bright green arugula leaves and the red leaf lettuce make this salad as colorful as it is delicious.

LOW-CHOLESTEROL

Makes 4 servings.

Nutrient Value Per Serving: 194 calories, 6 g protein, 14 g fat, 14 g carbohydrate, 202 mg sodium, 0 mg cholesterol.

2 **bunches arugula**	¼ **cup vegetable oil**
1 **small head red leaf lettuce**	¼ **teaspoon salt**
1 **head Bibb lettuce**	⅛ **teaspoon freshly ground pepper**
1 **medium-size sweet red pepper**	1 **cup frozen lima beans, cooked according to package directions**

Raspberry Vinaigrette:
¼ **cup raspberry vinegar**

1. Tear the tender green arugula leaves from the stems. Wash the leaves very carefully in several changes of cold water, because arugula is very sandy. Dry the leaves in a salad spinner, or blot them dry with paper toweling (you should have about 5 cups of leaves), and set them aside.
2. Remove and discard any discolored leaves from the red leaf lettuce. Remove the remaining leaves from the head and wash them in several changes of cold water. Dry the leaves in a salad spinner, or blot them dry with paper toweling (you should have about 3 cups), and set them aside.
3. Remove the leaves from the Bibb lettuce head and wash them in several changes of cold water. Dry the leaves in a salad spinner, or blot them dry with paper toweling (you should have about 4 cups), and set them aside.
4. Halve the red pepper lengthwise, core and seed it. Cut each red pepper half crosswise into halves. Cut each piece into thin slivers and set aside.
5. Prepare the Raspberry Vinaigrette: Combine the vinegar, oil, salt and pepper in a screw-top jar. Cover the jar and shake until the vinaigrette is well blended.
6. Tear the greens into bite-size pieces and place them in a large salad bowl. Drizzle the greens with ¼ cup of the vinaigrette, and toss to coat the greens. Arrange the red pepper slivers and the lima beans over the top. Pass the remaining vinaigrette with the salad.

Main Dish Salad with Pork:

Cut 12 to 16 ounces of cooked pork (broiled thin pork loin chops work well) into thin ¾ x ¼-inch pieces. Marinate the pork in the Raspberry Vinaigrette for about 30 minutes. Drain the pork, reserving the vinaigrette. Dress the salad as in Step 6 above. Arrange the meat on top of the salad.
Makes 4 servings.
Nutrient Value Per Serving: 424 calories, 38 g protein, 25 g fat, 14 g carbohydrate, 279 mg sodium, 97 mg cholesterol.

Arugula

Also known as "rocket" and "rugula," arugula has spicy, bright green leaves that resemble watercress. Snip the stems and use the leaves in salads with an oil and vinegar dressing, or try arugula with an herb butter on bread. It's also wonderful with brie as a sandwich filling.

Red Leaf Lettuce

This colorful lettuce comes in large heads of loose, green leaves tipped in red or bronze, with frilly edges. Red leaf lettuce has a delicate flavor that works best served with a subtle dressing.

Measure for Measure

A dressed salad doesn't keep very well, so it's better to prepare just enough for your guests than to have dressed leftovers. Estimate about 1 cup of green salad per person, if the salad will be served with other dishes. Dress the salad one part at a time, and refrigerate the leftover, undressed greens in plastic bags to use the next day. Remove tomatoes from a salad before storing it, to avoid wilting the lettuce.

Watercress

A member of the mustard family, watercress has succulent, crisp, peppery-tasting leaves. It is cultivated in large ponds, and grows wild in springs and along streams. Watercress is a good source of vitamins A and C.

■ Believed to be native to the eastern Mediterranean region, watercress is available year-round, sold in small bunches. Purchase 1 bunch per 3 or 4 individual salad servings.

■ To prepare watercress for use, untie each bunch and discard any wilted or yellowing leaves. Wash the leaves in a bowl of very cold water. Drain the watercress well and blot the leaves dry with paper toweling or dry them in a salad spinner. Refrigerate watercress with the stems in water and the leaves wrapped in damp paper toweling. Use watercress within a few days of purchasing it.

■ Combine watercress with other greens in salads, or use it as a sandwich filling with herb butter. Watercress also is good tossed with orange and red onion slices.

❖ ❖ ❖

WATERCRESS AND ENDIVE WITH GINGER VINAIGRETTE

This peppery salad is the perfect accompaniment to any stir-fried main dish.

LOW-CHOLESTEROL
Makes 4 servings.

Nutrient Value Per Serving: 249 calories, 2 g protein, 24 g fat, 9 g carbohydrate, 231 mg sodium, 0 mg cholesterol.

Ginger Vinaigrette:
2 tablespoons rice vinegar
2 tablespoons lemon juice
2 teaspoons Dijon-style mustard
1 teaspoon ground ginger
¼ teaspoon salt
¼ teaspoon freshly ground pepper
5 tablespoons vegetable oil
2 tablespoons olive oil
1 large bunch watercress
½ cucumber (halved crosswise)
1 navel orange
1 head Belgian endive OR: 2 bunches arugula
4 to 5 slices red onion, separated into rings

1. Prepare the Ginger Vinaigrette: Combine the vinegar, lemon juice, mustard, ginger, salt, pepper and the vegetable and olive oils in a screw-top jar. Cover the jar and shake until the ingredients are well mixed. Set aside.
2. Remove and discard any blemished or yellow leaves and tough stems from the watercress. Rinse the watercress leaves in cold water. Dry the leaves in a salad spinner, or blot them dry with paper toweling (you should have about 6 cups of leaves), and set aside.
3. Peel the half cucumber, halve it lengthwise and remove the seeds. Cut the cucumber quarters crosswise into thin slices and set aside.
4. Cut the peel, including the white pith, from the orange. Cut the orange crosswise into thin slices and cut each slice in half. Set aside.
5. If using the endive, cut off the core and cut the endive diagonally into thin slices (you should have about 2 cups). If using the arugula, tear the green leaves from the stems and wash them very carefully in several changes of cold water. Dry the leaves in a salad spinner, or blot them dry with paper toweling, and set aside.
6. Place the watercress on 4 individual salad plates. Arrange the orange and cucumber slices over the watercress. Scatter the onion rings over the top, and arrange the endive or arugula around the edge of each salad. Drizzle the vinaigrette over the salads and serve.

Main Dish Salad with Shrimp:
Arrange 12 to 16 ounces of cold, cooked, shelled and deveined medium- to large-size shrimp over or around the salads. *Makes 4 servings.*
Nutrient Value Per Serving: 347 calories, 23 g protein, 25 g fat, 9 g carbohydrate, 453 mg sodium, 193 mg cholesterol.

Holiday Wingdings

4

They say there's no place like home for the holidays. These special occasions give us time to celebrate the important things in life: family, home and friends. And what better way to do it than with a feast!

Our Happy Holidays Dinner would be a great choice for Thanksgiving, but it's also perfect any time you want an old-fashioned dinner with all the trimmings. Our feast, shown at left, will have everyone shouting for more!

Christmas and children are a natural combination. What better way to enjoy this magical season than with a kid-style cookie bake? Your whole family will enjoy making pretty Stained Glass Cookies (recipe, page 138), Chocolate Mint Thins (recipe, page 140), Toffee Toppers and Butterscotch Nut Bells (recipes, page 142).

When the weather turns warm, we think of serving delicious, light food. Our 900-Calorie Fest features Mushroom-Stuffed Pork Loin (recipe, page 144) with creamy pan gravy, but it's still a waist-watcher's delight! To top off this feast, Strawberry Layer Cake with Fluffy Frosting (recipe, page 150), is a heavenly indulgence.

We didn't forget fun celebrations like St. Patrick's Day: Our traditional Kilkenny Corned Beef with Killybegs Horseradish Sauce, Bantry Brown Bread and Shamrock Sugar Cookies, (recipes start on page 152), will get you into the spirit of the day. And for the graduate in your family, our raise-the-rafters Graduation Buffet (recipes start on page 156) gives you lots of make-ahead dishes so you can enjoy the party as much as your guests.

Whatever the occasion, we wish you a wonderful time!

Sour Cherry Cranberry Sauce (recipe, page 132), Steamed Vegetables with Cheddar Cheese Sauce (recipe, page 131), Bread Stuffing with Currants and Almonds (recipe, page 130), Avocado and Grapefruit Salad with Poppy Seed Dressing (recipes, page 134), Loin of Pork with Prunes (recipe, page 132), Pecan Wild Rice Stuffing (recipe, page 135) and Black-Eyed Peas and Lima Beans (recipe, page 136).

ROAST TURKEY WITH PECAN WILD RICE STUFFING

Roast at 400° for 15 minutes, then at 325° for 3 hours and 15 minutes. Makes 10 servings, with leftovers.

Nutrient Value Per Serving (6 ounces turkey with stuffing and gravy): 644 calories, 62 g protein, 28 g fat, 35 g carbohydrate, 1,176 mg sodium, 218 mg cholesterol.

Pecan Wild Rice Stuffing
(recipe, page 135)

Roast Turkey:
1   turkey (about 12 pounds), thawed if frozen (see Tip, page 128)
¾   teaspoon salt
½   teaspoon freshly ground pepper
2   cups water
2   carrots, peeled and cut into 1-inch pieces
2   stalks celery, cut into 1-inch pieces
2   medium-size onions, peeled and quartered
4   parsley sprigs

Giblet Gravy:
     Turkey giblets
1   can (13¾ ounces) chicken broth
1   bay leaf
2   cups defatted pan drippings
2   tablespoons butter or margarine
¼   cup all-purpose flour
     Salt and freshly ground pepper, to taste

Garnish (optional):
     Cranberries, sautéed green and red apple wedges, and sprigs of fresh sage

1. Prepare the Pecan Wild Rice Stuffing. The stuffing can be prepared one day in advance and refrigerated. The stuffing, whether made in advance or not, should be brought to room temperature before stuffing the turkey.
2. Prepare the Roast Turkey: Preheat the oven to hot (400°). Remove the neck and giblets from the turkey and reserve them. Rinse the turkey well inside and out with cold water, and pat it dry with paper toweling. Sprinkle the body and neck cavities with ½ teaspoon of the salt and ¼ teaspoon of the pepper. Spoon the stuffing loosely into both cavities. Transfer any remaining stuffing to a baking pan and cover it. Place the pan in the oven with the turkey for the last 30 minutes of roasting time, to heat the stuffing through. Tie the turkey legs to the tail with string, and skewer the neck skin to the back. Place the turkey, breast side up, on a rack in a roasting pan with a tight-fitting cover. (If no cover is available, make a cover of aluminum foil to be sealed tightly around the pan.) Add the water, carrot, celery, onion and parsley to the pan. Sprinkle the turkey with the remaining ¼ teaspoon each of salt and pepper.
3. Roast the turkey, uncovered, in the preheated hot oven (400°) for 15 minutes. Reduce the temperature to slow (325°). Cover the pan with the tight-fitting lid or aluminum foil. Roast for 2½ hours. Uncover the pan

"*O come, let us sing unto the Lord:*
let us make a joyful noise to the rock of our salvation.
Let us come before his presence with thanksgiving, and make a joyful noise unto him with psalms."
—The Bible

and roast for 45 minutes more, or until a meat thermometer inserted in the thickest part of the thigh, without touching the bone, registers 180° to 185° and the center of the stuffing registers 160° to 165°, or the drumstick moves up and down freely, or the thick part of the thigh feels soft when pressed, or the juices are yellow or almost colorless when the inner thigh is pierced with a fork tine. Remove the turkey from the oven. Let it stand for 15 to 30 minutes before carving. Reserve the drippings in the roasting pan.

4. Meanwhile, prepare the Giblet Gravy: Combine the reserved neck and giblets (except the liver) with the broth and the bay leaf in a medium-size saucepan. Bring the mixture to boiling. Lower the heat, cover and simmer for 1 hour, or until the giblets are tender. Add the liver and simmer for 15 minutes more. Drain the mixture, reserving the broth. Discard the bay leaf and the neck. Finely chop the giblets and reserve them.

5. When the turkey is done, strain the drippings from the roasting pan into a 4-cup glass measure. Skim off the fat and discard it. You should have at least 2 cups of drippings without fat. Add enough of the giblet broth to make a total of 3¾ cups. Melt the butter or margarine in a small saucepan. Stir in the flour and cook for 2 minutes. Gradually whisk in the broth mixture. Cook over medium heat, whisking constantly, until the mixture thickens and boils. Skim the foam from the top of the gravy. Lower the heat, add the reserved giblets and simmer for 5 minutes. Add the salt and pepper. Pour the gravy into a gravy boat.

6. If you wish, garnish the turkey with cranberries, sautéed green and red apple wedges, and sprigs of fresh sage. To store, remove the stuffing from the turkey. Refrigerate the turkey and the stuffing separately.

Our favorite Roast Turkey is perfectly partnered with Pecan Wild Rice Stuffing (recipe, page 135). For a delicious and colorful garnish, edge your serving platter with red and green apple wedges, sprigs of fresh sage and whole cranberries.

MICROWAVE COOKING DIRECTIONS FOR TURKEY
(625- to 700-watt microwave ovens)

If frozen, thaw the turkey as directed in the Tip, at right. Thawing a turkey in the microwave is not recommended.

Preparation:

1. Free the legs from the tucked position. Do not cut the band of skin.
2. Remove the neck and giblets from the neck and body cavities. To microwave these, place 3 cups of water, ½ teaspoon of salt, the neck, gizzard and heart in a microwave-safe 2-quart casserole dish. Cover and microwave at half power for 35 minutes. Add the liver, cover and microwave for 10 minutes more. The cooked neck, giblets and stock can be used to make the turkey gravy, or be mixed together with the stuffing.
3. Rinse the turkey and drain it well.
4. If you wish, loosely stuff the neck and body cavities. Cover any exposed stuffing with plastic wrap.
5. Turn back the wings to hold the neck skin in place. Return the legs to the tucked position. No trussing is necessary.
6. Make the Browning Sauce: Microwave ½ stick of butter in a microwave-safe bowl at full power for 30 to 40 seconds, or until the butter is melted. Blend in ¼ teaspoon of paprika and ⅛ teaspoon of browning and seasoning sauce. Stir the Browning Sauce well before using it.

MICROWAVE OVEN
Cooking Schedule

For stuffed or unstuffed turkey
Approximate cooking time in 625- to 700-watt microwave ovens

WEIGHT (pounds)	4	5	6	7	8	9	10	11	12
PART I: Breast side down at full power									
*Time 1:	8	10	12	14	16	18	20	22	24
Time 2:	8	10	12	14	16	18	20	22	24
PART II: Breast side up at half power (50%)									
Time 3:	8	10	12	14	16	18	20	22	24
Time 4:	8	10	12	14	16	18	20	22	24
Time 5:	8	10	12	14	16	18	20	22	24
Time 6:	8	10	12	14	16	18	20	22	24
TOTAL COOKING TIME:	48	60	72	84	96	108	120	132	144

*All times are in minutes.

Talking Turkey: Storing and Thawing

Storing:

- Fresh turkey should be refrigerated at all times. Cook it within 1 to 2 days of purchase.
- Frozen whole turkey should be stored in its original wrapper for up to 12 months at 0° or lower.

Thawing:

Never thaw a frozen turkey at room temperature. The National Turkey Federation recommends thawing frozen turkey by one of the following two methods.

Conventional (long) Method; thawing time — 3 to 4 days, or about 24 hours for each 5 pounds of whole frozen turkey.

- Leave the frozen turkey in its original wrapper.
- Place the turkey on a tray in the refrigerator and thaw the turkey slowly. Once it is thawed, cook or refrigerate the turkey immediately.

Cold Water (short) Method; thawing time — about 30 minutes per pound of whole frozen turkey.

- Leave the frozen turkey in its original wrapper.
- Place the turkey in the sink or a large pan.
- Completely cover the wrapped turkey with cold tap water.
- Change the water in the sink or pan every 30 minutes.
- Keep the turkey immersed in the cold water at all times. Once it is thawed, cook or refrigerate the turkey immediately.

Carving a Turkey

Here's a simple step-by-step guide to perfect carving.

■ Remove the turkey from the roasting pan. (To make the turkey easier to move, place a strip of folded, heavy-duty aluminum foil across the width of the pan before placing the uncooked turkey in the pan.) Let the bird rest for 15 to 30 minutes. Remove the stuffing. Carve one side of the turkey at a time.

■ Place the turkey, breast side up, on a cutting board. Steady the bird with the back of the carving fork to avoid sticking the tines into the meat. Cut through the skin between the breast and thigh. Move the leg to find the joint. Cut through the joint to remove the leg.

■ Slightly stretch apart the drumstick and the thigh to find the joint. With a firm downward movement of the knife, cut through the joint.

■ Working parallel to the bone, cut slices from the thigh. To remove the wing, cut through the skin at the corner of the breast around the wing. Move the wing to find the joint. Cut through the joint to remove the wing with a piece of the breast.

■ Starting on the outside of the breast, cut down diagonally to produce thin slices. Use the back of the carving fork to avoid sticking the tines into the meat. Carve the other side of the turkey as needed to refill the serving platter.

❖   ❖   ❖

Cooking:

1. Place the turkey, breast side down, in a microwave-safe dish. If the turkey tips, level it with a microwave-safe item so it will cook evenly.
2. Brush the back of the turkey with 1 tablespoon of the Browning Sauce.
3. See the Microwave Oven Cooking Schedule, page 128, for the cooking time. Use the schedule closest to the weight of the turkey. Follow the Part I and Part II Cooking Times without any interruptions.
4. Microwave at full power for Time 1. Rotate the turkey one half turn. Microwave for Time 2. Remove and discard the pan drippings.
5. Turn the turkey breast side up. If the turkey is stuffed, remove the plastic wrap. Brush with the Browning Sauce. If the turkey tips, level it.
6. Microwave at half power for Times 3, 4 and 5. At the end of each Time, rotate the turkey one quarter turn, discard the pan drippings and brush the turkey with the Browning Sauce. If overbrowning occurs, shield the turkey with small pieces of aluminum foil. After Time 5, check for doneness. A meat thermometer inserted in the thickest part of the thigh, without touching the bone, should register 180° to 185°; in the thickest part of the breast, 170°; in the center of the stuffing, 160° to 165°. If any of these temperatures have not been reached, cook for Time 6. Recheck the temperature and cook longer, if necessary.
7. Cover the turkey with aluminum foil. Let the turkey stand for 20 minutes before carving it.

CONVENTIONAL OVEN
Timetable for Roasting Turkey (325°)

WEIGHT (pounds)	STUFFED (hours)	UNSTUFFED (hours)
6 to 8	3 to 3½	2½ to 3½
8 to 12	3½ to 4½	3 to 4
12 to 16	4 to 5	3½ to 4½
16 to 20	4½ to 5½	4 to 5
20 to 24	5 to 6½	4½ to 5½

Do not roast turkey overnight at very low oven temperatures.

TESTING FOR DONENESS
The turkey is done when:
■ A meat thermometer inserted in the meatiest part of the thigh, without touching the bone, reads 180° to 185°; in the center of the stuffing, 160° to 165°.
■ The turkey juices run clear.
■ The drumsticks move up and down easily.

RESTING PERIOD
■ Let the roasted turkey stand at room temperature for 15 to 30 minutes. This allows the juices to settle and the meat to firm up for easier carving.

BREAD STUFFING WITH CURRANTS AND ALMONDS

LOW-CHOLESTEROL
Makes 10 cups (enough to stuff a 14-pound turkey).
Nutrient Value Per ½ Cup: 166 calories, 4 g protein, 8 g fat, 20 g carbohydrate, 273 mg sodium, 13 mg cholesterol.

1	large onion, chopped (1 cup)
1	cup finely chopped celery (3 to 4 stalks)
½	cup (1 stick) butter
1	loaf (16 ounces) bread, preferably homemade, cut into ½- to ¾-inch cubes (about 12 cups)
½	teaspoon dried thyme, crumbled
½	teaspoon dried rosemary, crumbled
	Pinch dried sage
½	teaspoon salt
¼	teaspoon freshly ground pepper
1	cup chicken broth OR: giblet stock, as needed
1	cup currants
1	cup slivered almonds (4 ounces), toasted
1	tart apple, peeled, cored and chopped (1½ cups)

1. Sauté the onion and the celery in the butter in a large skillet over medium heat until the vegetables are softened, for about 10 minutes.
2. Combine the onion mixture with the bread cubes in a large bowl. Add the thyme, rosemary, sage, salt, pepper and broth or stock. Toss the ingredients together until the bread cubes are evenly moistened. Add the currants, almonds and apple, and toss until the ingredients are well mixed.
3. Stuff the turkey. Or place the stuffing in a 13 x 9 x 2-inch baking pan and bake in a preheated moderate oven (350°) for about 45 minutes, or until the stuffing is crispy and browned on top, and moist underneath.

Almond Joy

Did you know that almonds are classified botanically as a fruit? Almonds are rich in magnesium and phosphorus, and have a good amount of riboflavin as well. One ounce, or about 20 to 25 nuts, has about 170 calories.

■ To oven roast almonds, spread the nuts in a shallow baking pan or baking sheet coated with butter or oil. Bake the almonds in a preheated moderate oven (350°) for 10 minutes, or until the almonds are golden in color, shaking the pan occasionally to redistribute the nuts.

■ To skillet roast almonds, sauté them in butter or oil until the almonds are golden in color; keep shaking the skillet to redistribute the nuts.

■ To toast almonds in the oven or skillet, follow the same procedures above, but omit the butter or oil.

■ To blanch almonds, place whole shelled almonds in a saucepan. Cover the almonds with water and bring to boiling. Drain the nuts, return them to the saucepan and cover them with cold water. Drain the almonds again, and press each almond between your fingers to slip off the skin.

❖   ✿   ❖

Steamed Vegetables with Cheddar Cheese Sauce (recipe, page 131), Sour Cherry Cranberry Sauce (recipe, page 132) and Bread Stuffing with Currants and Almonds.

Cheddar is Better

More Cheddar cheese is consumed annually in this country than any other type of cheese. Cheddar is named after a small village in Somerset, England, where the cheese first was made in the 17th century. The best Cheddars were farm-made, aged from 2 to 5 years to develop a firm, sharp taste with a natural, pale gold color.

■ Cheddar cheese is not always orange-colored. A true Cheddar may be off-white in color. Most Cheddar is tinted with annatto, a natural yellow-red vegetable dye made from the seeds of a tropical tree. In olden days, marigold petals or coloring from carrots were used to tint cheese curds.

■ Today Cheddar cheese is made in many parts of the world, including Canada, Australia, New Zealand and France. American-made Cheddars usually are named for the state or county of origin. Vermont, New York and Wisconsin are major Cheddar cheese producers.

■ Colby, named after a Wisconsin town, is a type of Cheddar that contains less salt and is marketed within four weeks after manufacturing.

■ Longhorn is a mild Cheddar named after the breed of cow from whose milk the cheese was made originally.

■ Tillamook is made in the Oregon county of that name.

STEAMED VEGETABLES WITH CHEDDAR CHEESE SAUCE

Bake at 325° for 20 to 25 minutes.
Makes 8 servings.

Nutrient Value Per Serving: 313 calories, 15 g protein, 21 g fat, 20 g carbohydrate, 400 mg sodium, 63 mg cholesterol.

1	small head cauliflower, stems trimmed and head cut into flowerets (about 4 cups)
1	small head broccoli, stems trimmed and head cut into flowerets (about 4 cups)
6	large carrots, trimmed, peeled, halved and cut lengthwise into thick sticks (about 2½ cups)

Cheddar Cheese Sauce:

¼	cup (½ stick) butter
¼	cup all-purpose flour
2½	cups milk
½	cup white wine
2	teaspoons Dijon-style mustard
¼	teaspoon freshly ground white pepper
1	package (10 ounces) yellow sharp Cheddar cheese, grated
⅛	teaspoon ground hot red pepper

1. Steam the cauliflower in a large pot just until it is tender, for about 4 minutes. Remove the cauliflower with a slotted spoon to a bowl of ice water to stop the cooking. Then remove the cauliflower with a slotted spoon to paper toweling. Repeat with the broccoli, steaming for about 4 minutes, and with the carrots, for about 4 minutes.

2. Prepare the Cheddar Cheese Sauce: Melt the butter in a medium-size saucepan over medium heat. Whisk in the flour until it is well mixed. Cook, whisking, for 1 minute. Slowly whisk in the milk until it is well mixed. Whisk in the wine. Bring the mixture to boiling. Lower the heat to medium and cook, whisking occasionally, until the mixture is smooth and thick, for 3 to 4 minutes. Whisk in the mustard and the white pepper. Reduce the heat to low. Gradually whisk in the Cheddar cheese and the ground hot red pepper until they are well mixed and the cheese has melted. Do not let the sauce boil. (The vegetables and the cheese sauce can be prepared ahead up to this point and refrigerated.)

3. When ready to bake, preheat the oven to slow (325°).

4. Arrange the vegetables in a 13 x 9 x 2-inch baking dish. Pour the sauce over the vegetables to cover them.

5. Bake in the preheated slow oven (325°) until the sauce and vegetables are heated through, for 20 to 25 minutes. (If the vegetables and the sauce have been refrigerated, add 10 to 15 minutes to the heating time.)

SOUR CHERRY CRANBERRY SAUCE

This sauce is more tart than traditional cranberry sauce. It also is a bit more liquid than some, so you may wish to serve it in small bowls.

LOW-CHOLESTEROL • LOW-SODIUM • LOW-FAT

Makes about 5 cups.

Nutrient Value Per ¼ Cup: 71 calories, 0 g protein, 0 g fat, 18 g carbohydrate, 0 mg sodium, 0 mg cholesterol.

¼ **pound dried sour cherries, pitted* OR: 1 can (1 pound) sour cherries in water, drained Warm water**	1 **pound whole cranberries** 2 **cups water** 1½ **cups sugar** **Fresh mint sprigs, for garnish (optional)**

1. If using the dried cherries, place them in a small bowl with just enough warm water to cover them. Let the cherries stand until they are plump, for about 10 minutes. Drain the cherries.
2. Rinse the cranberries and drain them. Pick over the cranberries, discarding any stones or grit.
3. Combine the 2 cups of water with the sour cherries, cranberries and sugar in a medium-size, nonaluminum saucepan. Bring the mixture to boiling, stirring to mix the ingredients thoroughly. Cook until the cranberry skins pop, for about 5 minutes. Remove the saucepan from the heat. Skim and discard any froth from the top of the sauce. Cool the sauce and refrigerate it, covered. Serve the sauce cold. Garnish with fresh mint sprigs, if you wish.

*Note: *Dried sour cherries usually are available in health food stores. If you substitute canned cherries, the yield of cranberry sauce will increase to about 6 cups.*

LOIN OF PORK WITH PRUNES

The meat is simmered on top of the stove, so the oven is free for other tasks. If there is meat left over, slice it thinly to make delicious sandwiches.

LOW-CALORIE

Makes 12 servings.

Nutrient Value Per Serving: 288 calories, 30 g protein, 10 g fat, 18 g carbohydrate, 648 mg sodium, 85 mg cholesterol.

1 **boneless pork loin (4 to 4½ pounds)** 1 **tablespoon salt** ¾ **teaspoon freshly ground white pepper** ½ **teaspoon ground ginger** 20 **or more pitted prunes**	½ **cup finely chopped onion** 1 **tablespoon butter** 1½ **cups prune juice** 3 **tablespoons all-purpose flour** 3 **tablespoons water**

1. If the loin is tied, untie it. Trim the excess fat from the meat. Wipe the meat clean with paper toweling. Make a deep slice lengthwise down the meat, without cutting through it.

Cranberry

A sour-tasting berry, cranberries grow on low vines in bogs. Although the American Indians used cranberries long before the Pilgrims arrived, it was the Pilgrims who called these berries "craneberries" because the blossoms resembled the heads of cranes. The word later developed into the present-day "cranberry."

■ The primary cranberry producers are Massachusetts, New Jersey, Wisconsin, Washington and Oregon.

■ Cranberries are used to make canned jellied or whole berry sauces, relishes and juice, all of which are an excellent source of vitamin C.

■ Cranberries mature in the fall and are sold fresh from October through December. Look for firm, unblemished berries with a bright luster. Avoid soft and dull-looking berries. Cranberries also are available frozen.

❖　❖　❖

2. Combine the salt, white pepper and ginger in a small bowl. Rub the mixture all over the meat. Insert the prunes down the center cut in the meat, leaving no spaces between them. Roll up the meat tightly and tie it at 2-inch intervals with kitchen twine.
3. Sauté the onion in the butter in a large Dutch oven until it is soft, for 5 to 10 minutes. Remove the onion. If the pork doesn't fit into the pot, cut it in half. Brown the meat on all sides, including the ends. Return the onion to the pot.
4. Add ½ cup of the prune juice. Cover the pot and simmer for 45 minutes, basting the meat occasionally.
5. Add the remaining 1 cup of prune juice. Turn over the meat. Continue simmering, covered, basting occasionally, for 20 to 30 minutes, or until the meat is tender and an instant-reading meat thermometer inserted in the center registers 160°.
6. When the meat is done, remove it to a serving platter and keep it warm.
7. Skim any fat from the cooking liquid. Stir together the flour and the water in a small cup until the mixture is smooth. Stir in 4 to 5 tablespoons of the cooking liquid until it is well blended. Stir the flour mixture into the cooking liquid in the pot. Cook over medium-high heat, stirring occasionally, until the gravy is reduced and thickened to the desired consistency, for 2 to 3 minutes; you should have about 1½ cups of gravy.
8. Remove the strings from the meat, and thinly slice the pork. Serve the loin of pork with the gravy.

CORNMEAL MUFFINS

Bake at 425° for 20 to 22 minutes.
Makes 10 muffins.

Nutrient Value Per Muffin: 160 calories, 3 g protein, 6 g fat, 23 g carbohydrate, 202 mg sodium, 17 mg cholesterol.

1 cup yellow cornmeal	¼ teaspoon salt
1 cup all-purpose flour	1¼ cups milk
1 tablespoon sugar	¼ cup (½ stick) butter or
2 teaspoons baking powder	margarine, melted

1. Preheat the oven to hot (425°). Grease ten 2½-inch muffin-pan cups.
2. Combine the cornmeal, flour, sugar, baking powder and salt in a medium-size bowl and stir to mix the ingredients well. Add the milk and butter or margarine, and stir just until the dry ingredients are moistened. Pour the batter into the prepared muffin-pan cups, dividing it evenly.
3. Bake the muffins in the preheated hot oven (425°) for 20 to 22 minutes, or until the centers spring back when lightly touched with your fingertip and the tops are rounded and lightly golden. Cool the muffins in the pan on a wire rack.

AVOCADO AND GRAPEFRUIT SALAD

The smooth texture of avocado and the tangy taste of fresh grapefruit complement each other perfectly in this salad.

LOW-CHOLESTEROL

Makes 8 servings.

Nutrient Value Per Serving: 336 calories, 3 g protein, 26 g fat, 28 g carbohydrate, 148 mg sodium, 0 mg cholesterol.

4 large grapefruits, preferably ruby red	1 head green leafy lettuce
4 small ripe avocados	1 cup Poppy Seed Dressing (recipe, below)

1. Remove the rind, including the white pith, from the grapefruit. Cut the flesh into sections, removing the membrane and the seeds. Place the grapefruit sections in a bowl.
2. Peel and pit the avocados. Cut the flesh into about ½ inch wide strips. Add the avocado strips to the grapefruit. Toss well to coat the avocado with the grapefruit juice to prevent discoloration. Cover the bowl with plastic wrap and refrigerate the fruit until serving time.
3. To serve, arrange the lettuce on a serving platter. Arrange the grapefruit and avocado over the top. Drizzle with a little of the Poppy Seed Dressing. Serve the remaining dressing on the side.

POPPY SEED DRESSING

Refrigerate extra dressing and serve it over berries or other fruit. Make sure the poppy seeds are fresh.

LOW-CHOLESTEROL

Makes 2 cups.

Nutrient Value Per Tablespoon: 82 calories, 0 g protein, 7 g fat, 5 g carbohydrate, 69 mg sodium, 0 mg cholesterol.

¾ cup sugar	2 tablespoons onion juice*
1 teaspoon dry mustard	1 cup vegetable oil
1 teaspoon salt	2 tablespoons poppy seeds
⅓ cup distilled white vinegar	

1. Mix together the sugar, mustard, salt and vinegar in a small bowl. Add the onion juice and stir it in thoroughly.
2. Add the oil slowly, beating with an electric mixer at medium speed until the oil is well mixed; the dressing should be very thick. Beat in the poppy seeds. Refrigerate the dressing until you are ready to use it.

*Note: To make the onion juice, grate a medium-size onion on the fine side of a grater, or chop the onion in an electric blender or small food processor until the onion is liquid. Strain the grated or chopped onion over a small bowl, and reserve the juice.

Avocado

The avocado, or alligator pear, was found originally in Mexico and Central America. The fruit has a buttery-textured, nutty-tasting flesh. Although avocados do have a high fat content, most of it is unsaturated fat. Half an 8-ounce avocado has 150 calories and provides vitamin C, riboflavin, magnesium and potassium.

■ The California Fuerte avocado, available from October to May, is green, thin-skinned and weighs 8 to 16 ounces. The Hass variety, sold from May to October, has a dark, pebbly skin. Florida avocados generally are larger than those from California. Sold from July to January, they are smooth and light green.

■ To select an avocado, hold it in your hand and press the ends gently. If the fruit yields to gentle pressure, it's ripe and ready. Most avocados are not allowed to mature on the tree, and will be hard. Let underripe avocados stand at room temperature to ripen. To hasten the ripening, keep avocados in a brown paper bag at room temperature.

■ The flesh of the avocado discolors when the avocado is cut. Brush the cut surfaces with citrus juice, diluted vinegar or an ascorbic-acid mixture to reduce the discoloration. If you use only half an avocado, keep the remaining half unpeeled, with the pit still in, wrapped in aluminum foil and refrigerated.

The Right Stuff-ing

■ Just before roasting the turkey is the time to stuff it. If you stuff the turkey any earlier, you run the risk of getting food poisoning.

■ Allow ¾ cup of stuffing per pound for turkeys weighing more than 10 pounds, ½ cup of stuffing per pound for smaller turkeys.

■ Never freeze stuffing that is inside a cooked or uncooked turkey. Remove all the stuffing from a cooked turkey, wrap the stuffing separately and refrigerate it.

❖ ❖ ❖

Wild Rice

"Wild rice" is not a rice at all, but the seed of a water grass native to some of our northern states. It is harvested by hand by people working out of small boats, which accounts for the high price of wild rice.

■ ❖ ■

Wild rice varies in length. The longer the grain, the longer the cooking time and the higher the price. When cooked, the long, slender, brownish grains have a sweet, nutty flavor. Wild rice is available by itself, or mixed with long-grain white rice.

❖ ❖ ❖

PECAN WILD RICE STUFFING

We love this combination of wild rice, sweet pecans and tart apples with a faint taste of orange liqueur.

Makes 10 servings.

Nutrient Value Per Serving: 293 calories, 6 g protein, 18 g fat, 29 g carbohydrate, 613 mg sodium, 29 mg cholesterol.

¾ cup wild rice	¼ teaspoon ground cinnamon
3 cups chicken broth, preferably homemade	2 tablespoons orange-flavored liqueur
1 cup white wine	½ teaspoon salt
8 tablespoons (1 stick) butter	¼ teaspoon freshly ground pepper
1 cup pecans, chopped	¾ cup pecan rice* OR: white rice
½ cup finely chopped cooked ham	
2 Granny Smith apples, cored, seeded and chopped	

1. Pick over the wild rice and remove any stones or grit. Rinse the rice in a bowl of cold water. Drain the rice in a fine-mesh sieve and rinse it again.

2. Combine the wild rice, broth, wine and 2 tablespoons of the butter in a large saucepan. Bring the mixture to boiling. Lower the heat and simmer, covered, for 40 minutes.

3. While the wild rice is cooking, melt the remaining 6 tablespoons of butter in a large skillet over medium heat. Add the pecans and sauté until they are lightly browned, for 3 to 4 minutes. Add the ham, apples and cinnamon, and sauté until the apples are almost cooked, for about 5 minutes. Add the liqueur, salt and pepper, and cook for 3 minutes more. Set aside the ham mixture.

4. Add the pecan rice or white rice to the wild rice. Simmer, covered, for 20 minutes more, or until the rice is done.

5. Drain the remaining liquid from the rice. Return the rice to the saucepan. Stir in the ham mixture. Heat over medium-low heat, stirring, until the stuffing is heated through. The stuffing can be prepared 1 day in advance and refrigerated. Bring the stuffing to room temperature before stuffing the turkey.

*Note: Pecan rice is a long-grain rice with a pecan-like flavor, grown in Louisiana. It can be found in the rice section of some supermarkets or in specialty food stores. If it is unavailable, substitute white rice.

BLACK-EYED PEAS AND LIMA BEANS

LOW-CHOLESTEROL

Makes 8 servings.

Nutrient Value Per Serving: 211 calories, 11 g protein, 9 g fat, 17 g carbohydrate, 307 mg sodium, 10 mg cholesterol.

1   **package (8 ounces) bacon, cut into ⅛-inch pieces**
1   **small sweet red pepper, cored, seeded and finely chopped (½ cup)**
2   **stalks celery, finely chopped (½ cup)**
1   **large onion, finely chopped (1 cup)**
1   **package (10 ounces) frozen lima beans**

2   **packages (10 ounces each) frozen black-eyed peas, cooked according to package directions OR: 2½ cups cooked black-eyed peas (about 7 ounces dried)**
2   **teaspoons red wine vinegar**
1   **cup chicken broth**
1   **cup water**
¼   **teaspoon crushed red pepper flakes**
½   **teaspoon freshly ground black pepper**

1. Sauté the bacon in a large, heavy saucepan or Dutch oven over medium-high heat until the bacon is browned, for about 6 minutes. Remove the bacon with a slotted spoon to paper toweling to drain. Remove all but 3 tablespoons of the bacon fat from the saucepan.
2. Add the red pepper, celery and onion to the saucepan and sauté until the vegetables are softened, for about 10 minutes.
3. Add the lima beans, black-eyed peas, vinegar, broth, water, red pepper flakes and black pepper. Stir to mix the ingredients. Bring the mixture to boiling. Lower the heat and simmer, covered, for 30 minutes to allow the flavors to blend thoroughly.
4. Just before serving, stir the bacon into the bean mixture. Serve hot.

PUMPKIN PIE

Bake at 425° for 15 minutes, then at 350° for 45 to 50 minutes.
Makes 8 servings.

Nutrient Value Per Serving: 274 calories, 6 g protein, 12 g fat, 36 g carbohydrate, 201 mg sodium, 81 mg cholesterol.

1¾   **cups pumpkin purée, fresh (see Tip, at right) OR: 1 can (16 ounces) solid-pack pumpkin**
1   **can (12 ounces) evaporated milk**
¾   **cup sugar**
2   **eggs, slightly beaten**
1   **teaspoon ground cinnamon**

½   **to 1 teaspoon ground ginger**
¼   **teaspoon ground cloves Pinch ground nutmeg**
1   **unbaked 9-inch homemade pie shell OR: unbaked 9-inch store-bought deep-dish pie shell Whipped cream, for garnish (optional)**

Pumpkin Purée

To make pumpkin purée for pie filling, cut a pumpkin in half crosswise, and remove the seeds and stringy material. Cover the cut side of each pumpkin half with a piece of aluminum foil. Place the pumpkin halves on a baking sheet and bake, foil side up, in a preheated moderate oven (350°) for about 1½ hours, or until the flesh is very tender when a fork is stuck into it. When the pumpkin is cool enough to handle, scoop out the flesh and mash it in a food processor, or force it through a sieve. If the purée is watery, drain it in a colander lined with cheesecloth. A 2- to 3-pound pumpkin yields about 2 to 3 cups of purée.

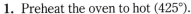

> *"What calls back the past, like the rich pumpkin pie?"*
> —*John Greenleaf Whittier*

A delectable taste of tradition: Pumpkin Pie, topped with cream.

1. Preheat the oven to hot (425°).
2. Combine the pumpkin, evaporated milk, sugar, eggs, cinnamon, ginger, cloves and nutmeg in a large bowl, and stir until all the ingredients are mixed thoroughly.
3. Place a baking sheet on the oven rack. Place the pie shell on the baking sheet. Carefully pour the pumpkin filling into the shell.
4. Bake the pie in the preheated hot oven (425°) for 15 minutes. Reduce the oven temperature to moderate (350°). Bake for 45 to 50 minutes more, or until the pie is almost set in the center. Cool the pie on a wire rack. If you wish, garnish the top of the pie with whipped cream or spoon a dollop alongside each individual serving.

137

PEANUT BRITTLE TRIANGLES

Bake at 375° for 20 minutes.
Makes about 3 dozen triangles.

Nutrient Value Per Serving: 169 calories, 4 g protein, 10 g fat, 18 g carbohydrate, 176 mg sodium, 26 mg cholesterol.

2¼ **cups all-purpose flour**	½ **cup granulated sugar**
1 **teaspoon baking soda**	½ **cup firmly packed brown**
1 **teaspoon salt**	**sugar**
1 **package (8 ounces) peanut**	1 **teaspoon vanilla**
brittle	2 **eggs**
1 **cup (2 sticks) butter or**	**Canned vanilla frosting**
margarine	**Whole peanuts**
1 **cup peanut butter**	

1. Preheat the oven to moderate (375°). Grease a 15 x 10 x 1-inch jelly-roll pan.
2. Sift together the flour, baking soda and salt. Crush the peanut brittle.
3. Beat together the butter or margarine and the peanut butter in a large bowl with an electric mixer at high speed until they are well blended. Beat in the granulated and brown sugars, the vanilla and eggs. Gradually add the flour mixture to the butter mixture. Stir in 1¼ cups of the peanut brittle.
4. Spread the batter in the prepared pan. Sprinkle the remaining peanut brittle on top of the batter.
5. Bake in the preheated moderate oven (375°) for 20 minutes. Cool on a wire rack. Cut into 2-inch triangles, and decorate with frosting and peanuts.

STAINED GLASS COOKIES

Bake at 350° for 10 minutes.
Makes about 5 dozen cookies.

Nutrient Value Per Serving: 123 calories, 1 g protein, 3 g fat, 22 g carbohydrate, 80 mg sodium, 15 mg cholesterol.

5 **cups all-purpose flour**	2 **eggs**
1 **teaspoon baking powder**	2 **teaspoons vanilla**
1 **teaspoon salt**	1 **teaspoon lemon extract**
1 **cup (2 sticks) butter or**	**Vegetable oil**
margarine	1 **pound assorted sour ball**
2 **cups sugar**	**candies**

1. Sift together the flour, baking powder and salt onto the wax paper.
2. Beat together the butter or margarine and the sugar in a large bowl with an electric mixer at high speed until the mixture is fluffy. Beat in the eggs, one at a time, the vanilla and the lemon extract until they are well blended.

Cooking with Kids

To youngsters, baking can seem like magic—especially when they get to sample the results. Baking cookies with your kids is one of the best ways we know to introduce your children to the fun of cooking. Set aside a good chunk of time—this is an experience that shouldn't be rushed. Explain each stage of the baking process as you work. And though you should emphasize safety at all times, try to do so without unduly alarming your children.

3. Stir the flour mixture into the butter mixture to make a stiff dough. Wrap the dough in wax paper and refrigerate it for 3 hours, or overnight.

4. Preheat the oven to moderate (350°).

5. Brush baking sheets generously with the oil; this makes the cookies easier to remove from the sheets after baking.

6. Roll out the dough, one quarter at a time, on a lightly floured pastry cloth or board to a ¼-inch thickness. Cut the dough into hearts, flowers or other shapes with 3-inch cookie cutters. Cut out the centers with 1 to 1½-inch cookie cutters.

7. Place no more than 4 or 5 cookies at a time on each prepared baking sheet. Place a sour ball in the center hole of each cookie.

8. Bake the cookies in the preheated moderate oven (350°) for 10 minutes, or until the candy melts and the cookies are golden. Cool the cookies on the baking sheets on wire racks for 2 minutes. Gently loosen the edges around each cookie with a long, sharp knife, and transfer the cookies with a metal spatula to the wire racks to cool completely.

Note: If the candy centers become too firm, return the cookies to the oven for 2 minutes, or until the candy melts slightly. Then remove the cookies from the baking sheets at once.

Stained Glass Cookies, Peanut Brittle Triangles, Chocolate Mint Thins (recipe, page 140), Chocolate Caramel Squares (recipe, page 141), Toffee Toppers (recipe, page 142).

CHOCOLATE MINT THINS

Chocolate and mint—a dynamic combination. For a change of taste, substitute peanut brittle pieces for the mint patties in this recipe.

Bake at 375° for 10 minutes.
Makes about 2 dozen cookies.

Nutrient Value Per Serving: 120 calories, 1 g protein, 5 g fat, 18 g carbohydrate, 81 mg sodium, 19 mg cholesterol.

1½ cups all-purpose flour	1 teaspoon vanilla
¼ cup cocoa powder (not a mix)	1 egg
½ teaspoon baking soda	1 package (6 ounces) chocolate-covered mint patties
¼ teaspoon salt	Canned frosting
¾ cup sugar	Green food coloring
½ cup (1 stick) butter or margarine, at room temperature	Tube of green decorator icing

1. Sift together the flour, cocoa, baking soda and salt onto wax paper.

2. Beat together the sugar and the butter or margarine in a medium-size bowl with an electric mixer at high speed until the mixture is well blended. Beat in the vanilla and the egg. Reduce the mixer speed to low.

3. Gradually beat the flour mixture into the butter mixture until all the ingredients are well blended. If the dough is very soft, chill it in the refrigerator for 30 minutes.

4. Preheat the oven to moderate (375°).

5. Divide the dough into thirds. Combine 2 of the thirds, and shape this larger portion of the dough into mounds equal in number to the number of mint patties. Top each mound with a mint patty, then with a piece of the remaining third of the dough. Carefully shape the dough around each mint patty so that the patty is covered completely by the dough. If the dough becomes too soft while you are working with it, refrigerate it until it is stiff. Place the cookies, 2 inches apart, on greased baking sheets. Score the cookies with a fork to flatten them slightly.

6. Bake the cookies in the preheated moderate oven (375°) for 10 minutes, or until the cookies are firm on top. Cool the cookies on the baking sheets on wire racks for 3 minutes. Then carefully remove the cookies to the wire racks to cool completely.

7. Tint the frosting green. Top the cookies with the tinted frosting, and then decorate with swirls of the green decorator icing. Let the frosting set completely before storing them. Store the cookies between layers of wax paper in a tightly covered container.

Age Appropriate

Work with one age group at a time to avoid disparities of attention spans and skills.

Preschoolers:

■ The 2- to 5-year-old group is the most challenging to work with; excitement runs very high, and attention spans are very short.

■ Cooking tasks should be simple and similar to play activities: Measuring flour is like playing with sand, kneading and rolling dough is similar to working with clay, decorating cookies is like arts and crafts.

■ Needless to say, you should supervise closely all activities of this age group.

Grade-Schoolers:

■ The 6- to 10-year-old set really enjoys the cooking process, and tends to be more attentive than preschoolers.

■ Step-by-step recipes involving assembly-line tasks particularly appeal to this age group.

■ By this age, kids want to know why things are being done, how and why they work. Let the kids do most of the baking; you provide advice and information.

Teen-agers:

■ This group wants to do it themselves. For the most part, this is fine. Just keep an eye on the oven activity, and let them know the ground rules before they start.

❖ ❖ ❖

The Kids' Party Line

- A special invitation adds to a child's sense of anticipation.
- Plan the party with your child. It will make him or her feel involved, and provide you with "private" time together.
- For a quick cleanup, use festive paper plates and cups. Stick to serving finger foods; no knives or forks are needed.
- Keep the napkins handy! Kids often wind up with more food on them than in them.
- Serve fun foods, such as hero sandwiches or pizza. Cut food into fun shapes with holiday cookie cutters, and use edible garnishes on serving platters. Don't use toothpicks; it's too easy to swallow them accidentally.
- If you're having a cookie baking party, let each child choose his or her favorite few cookies to take home — a delicious party favor.
- Take Polaroids throughout the party, and be sure to get at least one shot of each child. As the kids leave, present each one with his or her own personal party picture.
- Balloons and streamers are fairly inexpensive, and can help put kids in a party mood.
- Keep the number of kids reasonable. An overly large group is overwhelming for the kids, and for you.
- Have enough adult helpers — two adults for every six children.

CHOCOLATE CARAMEL SQUARES

Oh, do we love these cookies! Melted chocolate candy bars are folded into a brownie batter for a truly delectable treat.

Bake at 350° for 37 minutes.
Makes about 2½ dozen squares.

Nutrient Value Per Serving: 120 calories, 2 g protein, 6 g fat, 15 g carbohydrate, 53 mg sodium, 22 mg cholesterol.

1 cup plus two tablespoons all-purpose flour	2 eggs, slightly beaten
½ cup firmly packed light brown sugar	1 teaspoon vanilla
⅓ cup (about ¾ stick) butter or margarine, at room temperature	½ teaspoon baking powder
5 bars (2.1 ounces each) chocolate-coated caramel and marshmallow bars	1 can (3½ ounces) blanched sliced almonds
¼ cup milk	Canned frosting (optional) Candied cherries (optional)

1. Preheat the oven to moderate (350°). Grease a 13 x 9 x 2-inch baking pan.
2. Combine 1 cup of the flour with the brown sugar in a small bowl. Cut in the butter or margarine until the mixture becomes a crumbly dough. Press the mixture into the prepared pan.
3. Bake in the preheated moderate oven (350°) for 12 minutes, or until the crust is a light golden brown. Cool the crust in the pan on a wire rack while preparing the filling.
4. Melt the candy bars with the milk in a small saucepan over medium-low heat. Cool the mixture slightly. Then very slowly beat the candy mixture into the eggs in a small bowl, beating constantly to prevent curdling. Beat in the vanilla, then the remaining 2 tablespoons of flour mixed with the baking powder. Pour the filling over the crust. Sprinkle the almonds over the top.
5. Bake the cake in the preheated moderate oven (350°) for 25 minutes, or until the top is firm. Cool the cake in the pan on a wire rack. Cut the cake into squares or bars with a sharp knife. Decorate the squares with frosting and candied cherries, if you wish.

TOFFEE TOPPERS

Bake at 350° for 10 minutes.
Makes about 4 dozen cookies.

Nutrient Value Per Serving: 172 calories, 2 g protein, 9 g fat,
21 g carbohydrate, 119 mg sodium, 19 mg cholesterol.

5 cups all-purpose flour	12 soft chocolate-covered
1 teaspoon baking powder	toffee bars
1 teaspoon salt	(1⅛ ounces each),
1 cup (2 sticks) butter or	crushed*
margarine	Canned frosting (optional)
2 cups sugar	Sugar decorations, such as
2 eggs	nonpareils or confetti
2 teaspoons vanilla	(optional)

1. Sift together the flour, baking powder and salt onto wax paper.
2. Beat together the butter or margarine and the sugar in a large bowl with an electric mixer at high speed until the mixture is fluffy. Beat in the eggs, one at a time, then the vanilla until the mixture is well blended.
3. Stir in the flour mixture to make a stiff dough. Remove 1⅓ cups of the dough to a small bowl, and stir the toffee into this dough. Wrap the plain and toffee doughs in wax paper and chill them for 3 hours, or overnight.
4. Preheat the oven to moderate (350°).
5. Roll out the plain dough, one quarter at a time, on a lightly floured surface to a ¼-inch thickness. Cut out the dough with 3-inch cookie cutters. Place the cookies on baking sheets, and top each plain cookie with a dollop of the toffee dough.
6. Bake the cookies in the preheated moderate oven (350°) for 10 minutes, or until they are golden. Remove the cookies to wire racks to cool completely. Store them in a tightly covered metal container.
7. If you wish, decorate the cookies by dipping their tops in frosting, then in sugar decorations. Let the frosting set before storing the cookies.

*Note: Toffee can be crushed in a food processor. It may form a paste; this is fine for the recipe.

BUTTERSCOTCH NUT BELLS

Bake at 400° for 10 minutes.
Makes 4 dozen cookies.

Nutrient Value Per Serving: 105 calories, 2 g protein, 4 g fat,
16 g carbohyrate, 89 mg sodium, 17 mg cholesterol.

3¼ cups unsifted all-purpose	2 cups firmly packed light
flour	brown sugar
1 teaspoon salt	2 eggs
½ teaspoon baking soda	1 cup ground almonds
¾ cup (1½ sticks) butter	1 teaspoon vanilla
or margarine	Pink frosting from
	a 4-ounce tube

Baking with Kids: Getting Started

After you and your kids have decided upon the number, variety and types of cookies you want to make, sit down and read through the recipes. Make sure your children understand all the cooking and baking terms used.

■ Check to see that you have all the ingredients you'll need. If you need to buy some things, make a shopping list that notes the exact amounts required.

■ Make sure you have all the utensils called for in the recipe.

■ Cooking will be easier if you have enough work space, so start by clearing your counter of any clutter.

■ Remind your children that they always must wash and dry their hands before they work with food and set them an example yourself.

Safety First

A few important rules to teach your children about working in the kitchen:

■ Never pick up a knife by the blade, only by the handle. When you cut, make sure the sharp edge is facing down, away from your fingers. When finished, always put the knife down on its side. Never leave a knife in the sink.

■ If there is a pot cooking on the stove, always turn the handle toward the side or back of the stove so no one will bump into the handle.

■ Always keep oven mitts and potholders near the stove. Use a potholder to lift a hot pan or pot from the stove, and put on oven mitts before putting a pan into a hot oven or removing it.

■ To check a pan in the oven, first pull out the oven rack partially. Do not reach your hands all the way into the oven. Have a wire rack ready for cooling baked goods on the counter nearest to the oven.

■ When you use an electric appliance, be sure your hands are clean and dry before you plug it in or unplug it.

■ If you are using an electric mixer, never put your fingers or a metal utensil in the bowl while the machine is running.

■ If you have long hair, always tie it back before cooking to keep it away from the stove, and out of food.

■ If you're wearing a long-sleeved shirt or blouse, roll up the sleeves while cooking.

■ Wear an apron to protect your clothing when you cook.

1. Sift together the flour, salt and baking soda onto wax paper.
2. Beat together the butter or margarine and the brown sugar in a large bowl with an electric mixer at high speed until the mixture is fluffy. Beat in the eggs, one at a time, until they are well combined, then the ground almonds and the vanilla.
3. Stir in the flour mixture to make a stiff dough. Wrap the dough in wax paper and refrigerate it for 3 hours, or overnight.
4. Preheat the oven to hot (400°).
5. Roll out the dough, a quarter at a time, on a lightly floured pastry cloth or board to a ¼-inch thickness. Cut out the dough with 3-inch bell-shaped cookie cutters. Place the bells, 1 inch apart, on baking sheets.
6. Bake the cookies in the preheated hot oven (400°) for 10 minutes, or until the cookies are golden. Remove the cookies with a spatula to wire racks. Cool the cookies completely before decorating them.
7. Place a star tip on the frosting tube and pipe lines to decorate the bells. Let the frosting set before storing the cookies.

HOLIDAY SUGAR COOKIES

A crisp, roll-out cookie flavored with a hint of lemon.

Bake at 375° for 10 minutes.
Makes 5 dozen cookies.

Nutrient Value Per Serving: 97 calories, 1 g protein, 3 g fat, 15 g carbohydrate, 77 mg sodium, 15 mg cholesterol.

5 cups unsifted all-purpose flour	2¼ cups sugar
1 teaspoon baking powder	2 eggs
1 teaspoon salt	2 teaspoons vanilla
1 cup (2 sticks) butter or margarine	1 teaspoon lemon extract
	Assorted frostings and decorations (optional)

1. Sift together the flour, baking powder and salt onto wax paper.
2. Beat together the butter or margarine and the sugar in a large bowl with an electric mixer at high speed until the mixture is fluffy. Beat in the eggs, one at a time, beating well after each addition. Beat in the vanilla and the lemon extract until all the ingredients are well blended.
3. Stir in the flour mixture to make a stiff dough. Wrap the dough in wax paper and refrigerate it for 3 hours, or overnight.
4. Preheat the oven to moderate (375°).
5. Roll out the dough, a quarter at a time, on a lightly floured pastry cloth or board to ¼-inch thickness. Cut the dough into assorted shapes, with your favorite 3-inch cookie cutters. Place the cookies, 2 inches apart, on lightly greased baking sheets.
6. Bake the cookies in the preheated moderate oven (375°) for 10 minutes, or until the cookies are lightly brown. Remove the cookies with a metal spatula to wire racks to cool. Store the cookies in a metal tin.
7. If you wish, decorate the cookies with canned frosting or icing in a tube; place cinnamon red hots or colored sprinkles on top.

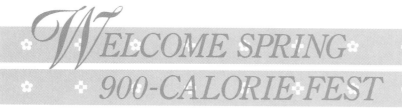

MUSHROOM-STUFFED PORK LOIN

LOW-CALORIE • LOW-CHOLESTEROL

Roast at 400° for 30 minutes, then at 350° for 30 to 40 minutes.
Makes 16 servings.

Nutrient Value Per Serving: 208 calories, 27 g protein, 8 g fat,
6 g carbohydrate, 218 mg sodium, 72 mg cholesterol.

½ cup very finely chopped shallots (3½ ounces)
2½ pounds mushrooms, very finely chopped
¼ teaspoon reduced-calorie margarine
2 tablespoons Madeira OR: dry white wine
1 tablespoon lemon juice
1 teaspoon dried thyme, crumbled
1 teaspoon salt

½ teaspoon freshly ground pepper
1 trimmed boneless center-cut pork loin, untied (4 pounds)
2 ounces jarred red pimientos, drained and sliced into ⅛-inch-wide strips (scant ½ cup)
1½ cups plus 2 tablespoons water
2 tablespoons cornstarch OR: all-purpose flour

1. Sauté the shallots, and as much of the mushrooms as will fit, in the margarine in a large, nonstick skillet. As the mixture cooks down, add the remaining mushrooms. Cook, stirring, for 20 minutes. Stir in the Madeira or white wine, the lemon juice, thyme, ½ teaspoon of the salt and the pepper. Cook, stirring, for 10 to 20 minutes, or until the liquid has evaporated. Watch carefully toward the end; the mushroom mixture should be almost dry.
2. Preheat the oven to hot (400°).
3. Place the loin, boned side up, fat-trimmed side down, on a work surface. Place a knife to one side on the top of the loin and cut down two thirds of the way through the meat. With the knife still in the meat, turn the side of the knife parallel to the work surface and cut across, but not all the way through, the meat to form a pocket. Open up the pocket.
4. Season the pocket with the remaining ½ teaspoon of salt. Pat the mushroom stuffing evenly over the bottom part of the pocket. Arrange the pimiento strips, slightly overlapping, on the stuffing in 3 long rows down the length of the roast.
5. Roll up the pork from the long side to enclose the stuffing. Turn the stuffed roast seam side up and tie it at 1½-inch intervals with kitchen twine. Insert 3 wooden picks through each end to hold in the stuffing. Place the roast, seam side down, on a rack in a large roasting pan. Add 1½ cups of the water to the pan.

Welcome Spring 900-Calorie Fest

Mushroom-Stuffed Pork Loin*
Zucchini Chicken Soup (recipe, page 146)
Roasted Yellow Peppers (recipe, page 146)
Winter Greens and Grapefruit Salad with Warm Citrus Dressing (recipe, page 147)
Cranberry Coulis (recipe, page 147)
Maple Lime Sweet Potatoes (recipe, page 148)
Cardamom Wreaths (recipe, page 148)
Spiced Coffee Vienna (recipe, page 149)
Choice of One Dessert:
Strawberry Layer Cake with Fluffy Frosting (recipe, page 150)
OR: Pumpkin Cheesecake (recipe, page 151)

"Sweet spring, full of sweet days and roses, A box where sweets compacted lie."
—George Herbert

6. Roast the pork loin in the preheated hot oven (400°) for 30 minutes. Reduce the heat to moderate (350°). Roast for 30 to 40 minutes more, or until a meat thermometer inserted in the thickest portion of the meat, without touching the stuffing, registers 160°.

7. Remove the pork from the pan; let it stand for 10 minutes before slicing.

8. Transfer the pan juices to a saucepan; you should have about 2 cups. Stir the cornstarch or flour into the remaining 2 tablespoons of water in a small cup until the mixture is smooth. Add the cornstarch mixture to the saucepan, and bring the combined mixture to boiling. Lower the heat and simmer, stirring, for 1 minute, or until the gravy has thickened slightly. Serve the gravy with the pork.

Mushroom-Stuffed Pork Loin, Roasted Yellow Peppers (recipe, page 146), Cranberry Coulis (recipe, page 147) and Maple Lime Sweet Potatoes (recipe, page 148).

ZUCCHINI CHICKEN SOUP

A light and delicious way to begin a meal. We also love this soup served with crusty French bread and cheese.

LOW-CALORIE • LOW-CHOLESTEROL • LOW-FAT

Makes 8 servings (6 cups).

Nutrient Value Per Serving: 40 calories, 2 g protein, 1 g fat, 6 g carbohydrate, 647 mg sodium, 0 mg cholesterol.

1½ **pounds zucchini, sliced into ⅛-inch-thick rounds**	½ **cup chopped seeded tomatoes**
½ **teaspoon salt**	2 **teaspoons lemon juice**
2 **medium-size onions, coarsely chopped**	½ **teaspoon dried tarragon, crumbled**
½ **to 1 teaspoon reduced-calorie margarine**	¼ **teaspoon dried basil, crumbled**
1 **quart defatted homemade chicken stock OR: canned chicken broth**	

1. Place the zucchini in a colander in the sink. Sprinkle the zucchini with the salt, and toss the zucchini. Let the zucchini stand for 20 minutes. Dry the zucchini with paper toweling.

2. Sauté the zucchini and the onion in ½ teaspoon of the margarine in a large, nonstick saucepan over medium-high heat for 5 minutes. If necessary, add the remaining ½ teaspoon of margarine to prevent sticking.

3. Add the stock and the tomatoes. Bring the mixture to boiling. Lower the heat and simmer for 10 to 15 minutes, or until the vegetables soften.

4. Season with the lemon juice, tarragon and basil. Serve the soup hot.

ROASTED YELLOW PEPPERS

This is a very simple side dish, but it adds a wonderful touch of color to your dinner plate.

LOW-CALORIE • LOW-CHOLESTEROL • LOW-SODIUM • LOW-FAT

Makes 8 servings.

Nutrient Value Per Serving: 7 calories, 0 g protein, 0 g fat, 1 g carbohydrate, 1 mg sodium, 0 mg cholesterol.

4 **medium-size sweet yellow peppers (about 1¼ pounds)**	**Olive oil (optional)**

1. Preheat the broiler. Lay the yellow peppers in a single layer on the broiler pan.

2. Broil the yellow peppers 2 inches from the heat source, turning them frequently, until they are blackened, for 15 minutes. Cool the peppers under cold water. Remove the blackened skin with a knife, but leave the stems intact. Slice the peppers in half through the stems, and core and seed the peppers. Blot the peppers dry with paper toweling. Serve the roasted peppers immediately, or refrigerate them until serving time. Bring the roasted peppers to room temperature before serving them.

3. At serving time, drizzle the roasted peppers with olive oil, if you wish.

A Light Alternative to Heavy Soups

If you're trying to cut down on extra fat, or just are in the mood for a light-style feast, don't serve creamed soups such as oyster stew, New England clam chowder, or cream of broccoli, potato or pumpkin. Instead, explore soups made with defatted beef or poultry stock, or with a puréed vegetable base. These include Manhattan clam chowder (tomato based), escarole, Greek-style lemon, vegetable and quick-to-fix egg drop soup. If you simply must have a creamy soup, you can cut the fat content by preparing a cream soup without using cream. Use whole or lowfat milk plus several tablespoons of flour, if necessary, to thicken the soup. To thin a thick, vegetable purée soup, add skim milk, a little at a time, until the desired consistency is reached. Garnish soups with slivered green onions, julienned vegetables, fruit slices or fresh herbs.

Grapefruit

The fact that this citrus fruit grows in clusters like grapes was probably the inspiration for its name. The ancestor of today's grapefruit was the pomelo, native to China and India, which was imported to the West Indies. Trees were transplanted to this country by Spanish settlers from the West Indies. A pomelo resembles an elongated grapefruit with a thick yellow rind. It is not grown commercially.

■ Grapefruit trees flourish in warm climates. Florida and Texas are the major producing states from September to June, while Arizona and southern California supply grapefruit from January to October.

■ There are many varieties of grapefruit, but all can be divided into two types. White grapefruit has pale yellow flesh with a bright yellow rind. Pink grapefruit has pink flesh with a pinkish blush on its yellow rind. Grapefruit is an excellent source of vitamin C.

■ Select firm, smooth fruit that is heavy for its size. Grapefruit is about three-quarters liquid, so heaviness is an excellent indication of the juiciness of the fruit. Grapefruit also is available canned as segments or as juice.

■ Fresh grapefruit will keep at room temperature for up to 2 weeks. You also can store grapefruit in the fruit bin of the refrigerator for about 3 weeks.

❖ ❖ ❖

WINTER GREENS AND GRAPEFRUIT SALAD WITH WARM CITRUS DRESSING

A salad of mixed greens tossed with a tangy citrus dressing—a perfect choice to help celebrate the end of winter.

LOW-CALORIE • LOW-CHOLESTEROL • LOW-SODIUM

Makes 8 servings.

Nutrient Value Per Serving: 76 calories, 2 g protein, 4 g fat, 10 g carbohydrate, 78 mg sodium, 0 mg cholesterol.

16	cups torn assorted lettuce leaves, including red leaf and romaine	**Warm Citrus Dressing:**	
1	to 2 Belgian endive, ends trimmed and leaves separated	½	cup pink grapefruit juice
		2	tablespoons balsamic vinegar
		¼	teaspoon salt
2	medium-size pink grapefruits, sectioned	2	cloves garlic, pressed or crushed
		2	tablespoons olive oil

1. Arrange the lettuce and the endive in a large bowl. Set aside the grapefruit sections.
2. Prepare the Warm Citrus Dressing: Combine the grapefruit juice, vinegar and salt in a 2-cup measure.
3. Sauté the garlic in the oil in a small skillet for 1 to 2 minutes, or until the garlic is golden. Let the oil cool to lukewarm.
4. Strain the oil into the grapefruit juice mixture and discard the garlic.
5. Arrange the grapefruit sections over the greens. Pour the dressing over, toss the salad and serve.

CRANBERRY COULIS

LOW-CHOLESTEROL • LOW-SODIUM • LOW-FAT

Makes 2½ cups.

Nutrient Value Per 2 Tablespoons: 32 calories, 0 g protein, 0 g fat, 8 g carbohydrate, 0 mg sodium, 0 mg cholesterol.

1	cup water	1	bag (12 ounces) fresh or thawed frozen cranberries
½	cup plus 2 tablespoons sugar		

1. Combine the water, sugar and cranberries in a medium-size saucepan. Bring the mixture to boiling. Boil, uncovered, stirring occasionally, for 5 minutes, or until the berries pop and the mixture thickens slightly.
2. Transfer the mixture to a small serving bowl and cool the mixture slightly. Cover the bowl with plastic wrap and refrigerate the coulis for several hours, or until it is cold.

MAPLE LIME SWEET POTATOES

The flavor of baked sweet potatoes is complemented beautifully by the tart-sweet syrup poured over them before serving.

LOW-CHOLESTEROL • LOW-SODIUM • LOW-FAT

Bake at 350° for about 50 minutes.
Makes 8 servings.

Nutrient Value Per Serving: 159 calories, 2 g protein, 0 g fat, 37 g carbohydrate, 16 mg sodium, 0 mg cholesterol.

3 **pounds sweet potatoes, scrubbed**	½ **cup reduced-calorie imitation maple syrup** 4 **teaspoons fresh lime juice**

1. Preheat the oven to moderate (350°).
2. Bake the sweet potatoes in the preheated moderate oven (350°) for about 45 minutes, or until the potatoes are tender.
3. Meanwhile, stir together the maple syrup and the lime juice in a 1-cup glass measure. Set aside the syrup mixture, but do not refrigerate it.
4. Do not turn off the oven. When the potatoes are cool enough to handle, peel them. Cut the potatoes in half lengthwise. Slice each half lengthwise into ½-inch-wide slices. Layer the slices in an ovenproof 2-quart dish. Pour about three quarters of the syrup mixture over the potatoes.
5. Bake the potatoes at 350° until they are warm, for about 5 minutes. Pour the remaining syrup over the potatoes, and serve.

CARDAMOM WREATHS

Freshly baked bread adds a homey touch to any dinner.

LOW-SODIUM • LOW-FAT

Bake at 350° for 25 minutes.
Makes 2 wreaths (14 servings each).

Nutrient Value Per Serving: 110 calories, 4 g protein, 1 g fat, 20 g carbohydrate, 75 mg sodium, 20 mg cholesterol.

¼ **cup warm water (105° to 115°)***	1 **cup plus 2 tablespoons canned evaporated skim milk**
¼ **cup sugar**	½ **teaspoon salt**
1 **envelope active dry yeast**	½ **teaspoon ground cardamom**
2 **eggs, slightly beaten**	4½ **to 5½ cups all-purpose flour**
¼ **cup reduced-calorie margarine**	1 **egg white**

1. Combine the water, 1 tablespoon of the sugar and the yeast in a large bowl. Stir until the yeast is dissolved. Let the yeast mixture stand until it is bubbly, for about 10 minutes.

Lighter Side Dishes

Try some of these innovative ways to skim extra fat and calories off a meal and still produce a flavorful feast.

■ For a change from candied yams, oven-bake yams without butter or the traditional marshmallows. Instead, cube the yams, drizzle them with maple syrup, top them with a small spoonful of brown sugar or naturally sweet crushed pineapple, and bake them just until they are heated through.

■ Acorn squash is a wonderful choice for a calorie-conscious side dish. Cut acorn squash into rings and place the rings in a shallow baking dish. Add a little water, cover the dish and bake until the squash is just tender. Garnish the squash rings with chunky cranberry relish or fruit chutney.

■ When preparing cheesy onions, use reduced-calorie margarine instead of butter, lowfat milk (with a little flour stirred in rather than cream as thickener), and reduced-fat cheese such as Swiss or Jarlsberg. For a change of seasoning, add a pinch of crumbled sage.

Cardamom

The aromatic seed pods of the cardamom plant first were used in India to season curries. Cardamom is a perennial plant with wide leaves. The pods develop on the flower stalks that grow at the base of the leaf stems, close to the ground.

. ❖ .

Cardamom is available ground or as whole pods. The three-sided pods are creamy-white in color, and are used to flavor hot fruit or wine punch, and coffee. Ground cardamom can be used in coffee cakes, rolls, pastries or cookies.

❖ ❖ ❖

Spring Flowers

For a special welcome to each guest at your springtime dinner, set a miniature crystal vase with a nosegay of fresh flowers at each table setting. Or, for a more informal look, use glass tumblers and mixed bouquets of wild flowers and sprigs of fresh herbs. Either way, your table will be transformed into an indoor garden announcing the arrival of spring.

❖ ❖ ❖

2. Beat in the remaining sugar, the eggs, margarine, 1 cup of the evaporated skim milk, the salt and cardamom. Beat in 3 cups of the flour until the mixture is smooth. Gradually add enough of the remaining flour to form a soft dough. Let the dough stand, covered, for 30 minutes.

3. Turn out the dough onto a heavily floured surface. Knead until the dough is smooth and elastic, for about 8 to 10 minutes. Press the dough into a greased large bowl and turn the greased side up. Cover the bowl and let the dough rise in a warm place, away from drafts, until it is doubled in size, for about 1 hour.

4. Divide the dough in half, and work with one half at a time. Divide the half into thirds. Roll each third between your palms and a lightly oiled surface into a 22-inch-long rope. Braid the 3 ropes together, starting from the center and working to the ends. Trim the ends to be even.

5. Place a 3½- to 4-inch-diameter soufflé dish or metal bowl in the center of a baking sheet. Grease the outside of the dish. Wrap the braid around the dish to form a wreath. Bring the ends together and trim the excess dough. Pinch the ends to seal them.

6. Roll the dough trimmings into an 11-inch-long rope. Shape the rope into a bow without knotting, keeping the trailing ends of the dough parallel to each other. Place the bow over the sealed portion of the wreath. Repeat with the remaining half of the dough to make a second wreath.

7. Beat the remaining 2 tablespoons of milk with the egg white in a small cup. Brush the wreaths with the egg wash. Lightly cover the wreaths with plastic wrap and let them rise in a warm place, away from drafts, until they are doubled in size, for 45 minutes to 1 hour. Brush the wreaths again with the egg wash.

8. Meanwhile, preheat the oven to moderate (350°).

9. Bake the wreaths, one at a time, in the middle of the preheated moderate oven (350°) for 25 minutes, or until each is golden brown and hollow-sounding when tapped. Cool the wreaths on wire racks.

*Note: Warm water should feel tepid when dropped on your wrist.

Spiced Coffee Vienna

LOW-CHOLESTEROL • LOW-FAT

Makes 6 servings.

Nutrient Value Per Serving: 2 calories, trace protein, 0 g fat, trace carbohydrate, 1 mg sodium, 0 mg cholesterol.

3	cups extra-strong hot coffee	4	whole cloves
2	3-inch cinnamon sticks	4	whole allspice
			Softly whipped cream
			Ground nutmeg
			Sugar

1. Pour the coffee into a chafing dish with a flame underneath. Add the cinnamon, cloves and allspice. Steep the mixture over very low heat for 10 to 15 minutes. Strain the mixture.

2. Pour the coffee into heatproof wine glasses or cups. Top with the whipped cream and the nutmeg. Serve the coffee with sugar.

STRAWBERRY LAYER CAKE WITH FLUFFY FROSTING

Feathery light and delicious, this cake is a bit tricky to make, so let the experienced baker in the house try it first.

LOW-FAT

Bake cake layers at 400° for 5 minutes.
Makes 8 servings.

Nutrient Value Per Serving: 190 calories, 5 g protein, 4 g fat, 32 g carbohydrate, 181 mg sodium, 137 mg cholesterol.

Layer Cake:
- ⅔ cup sifted cake flour (not self-rising)
- 1½ teaspoons baking powder
- ¼ cup sugar
- 1 teaspoon grated orange zest OR: lemon zest (orange or yellow part of rind only)
- 4 eggs, separated
- ⅛ teaspoon salt

Strawberry Filling:
- 1 envelope whipped topping mix
- ½ cup cold skim milk
- ¼ cup reduced-sugar strawberry spread

Fluffy Frosting:
- ⅓ cup sugar
- 2 tablespoons dark corn syrup
- 3 tablespoons water
- 2 egg whites

1. Preheat the oven to hot (400°). Grease three 8 x 1½-inch round nonstick layer cake pans. Line the bottoms with aluminum foil and grease the foil.

2. Prepare the Layer Cake: Sift together the flour and the baking powder onto a piece of wax paper. Combine the sugar with the orange or lemon zest on a second piece of wax paper. Beat together the sugar mixture and the egg yolks in a small bowl with an electric mixer at high speed for 7 minutes. Beat in the flour mixture; the combined mixture will be very thick and sticky.

3. Beat the egg whites and the salt in a clean bowl with clean beaters until soft peaks form. Stir one third of the whites into the yolk mixture. Fold in the remaining whites. Divide the batter evenly among the prepared pans.

4. Bake the cake layers in the preheated hot oven (400°) for 5 minutes, or until the layers pull away from the sides of the pans and spring back when lightly touched with your fingertip. Loosen the layers around the edges with a thin knife. Invert the layers onto wire racks. Peel off the aluminum foil. Cool the layers completely.

5. Prepare the Strawberry Filling: Prepare the whipped topping mix following the package directions, using the skim milk instead of whole milk. Fold in the strawberry spread. Refrigerate the filling for 10 minutes to firm it up, if necessary.

6. Set one cake layer on a cake plate. Spread the layer with half the filling and top with the second layer. Spread with the remaining filling and top with the third layer. Refrigerate the cake for 1 hour before frosting it.

7. Prepare the Fluffy Frosting: Combine the sugar, corn syrup and water in a very small, heavy saucepan.

8. Beat the egg whites in a small bowl until firm peaks form. Bring the corn syrup mixture to boiling. Continue boiling, without stirring, until the mixture registers 242° on a candy thermometer. With the electric mixer running, very slowly pour the hot syrup mixture in a thin stream into the whites, beating constantly. Continue beating at high speed until stiff, glossy peaks form. Frost the cake, and serve it.

Guilt-Free Goodies

For delectable desserts without guilt, skip heavy fruitcake in favor of a rolled sponge cake with a real whipped cream filling. Replace a double-crust apple pie with an open-faced apple tart glazed with strained apricot preserves. And pass up the fudge cake for cream puffs filled with lowfat frozen yogurt, ice milk or low-calorie pudding, and dusted with 10X (confectioners' powdered) sugar.

❖ ✿ ❖

*"Is it so small a thing
To have enjoyed the sun,
To have lived light in the spring,
To have loved, to have thought, to have done."*
—*Matthew Arnold*

Cheesecake

Just about every country that produces cheese has a sweet cheese dessert similar to cheesecake. Some are made like custard pies, some are chilled and molded in a special shape. Italy's "Torta di Ricotta" and "Cassata alla Siciliana" are popular cheese desserts. Greece has "melopita," a honey-sweetened cheese mixture in pastry. No matter where a cheesecake is made, its basis is usually a fresh, soft, unripened cheese such as cream cheese, ricotta, cottage or pot cheese. Today you can find everything from tofu cheesecake to "no cheese" cheesecake.

❖ ❖ ❖

PUMPKIN CHEESECAKE

Once you try our creamy pumpkin cheesecake, you may want to substitute it on the menu any time pumpkin pie is called for.

LOW-CALORIE • LOW-FAT

Bake at 350° for 45 minutes.
Makes 10 servings.

Nutrient Value Per Serving: 133 calories, 7 g protein, 2 g fat, 23 g carbohydrate, 276 mg sodium, 57 mg cholesterol.

Nonstick vegetable cooking spray	3 tablespoons all-purpose flour
3 tablespoons finely crushed zwieback biscuit crumbs	2 eggs, slightly beaten
1½ cups lowfat cottage cheese	¾ cup skim milk
1½ cups canned pumpkin purée (not pie filling)	2 teaspoons fresh lemon juice
½ cup granulated sugar	1 teaspoon ground cinnamon
¼ cup firmly packed dark brown sugar	½ teaspoon ground ginger
	½ teaspoon salt
	⅛ teaspoon ground nutmeg

1. Preheat the oven to moderate (350°). Spray nonstick vegetable cooking spray on the inside of an 8-inch springform pan with a tight-fitting bottom. Sprinkle the pan with the biscuit crumbs.

2. Place the cottage cheese in the container of a food processor. Whirl until the cheese is very smooth (there should be no lumps), scraping down the side of the container.

3. Add the pumpkin purée, granulated and brown sugars, flour, eggs, milk, lemon juice, cinnamon, ginger, salt and nutmeg to the processor. Whirl until the cheese mixture is smooth. Let the cheese mixture stand in the processor for 5 minutes. Ladle the cheese mixture into the prepared pan.

4. Bake the cheesecake in the preheated moderate oven (350°) for 45 minutes; the outer edge will be set but the center still will be soft. Turn off the oven. Let the cake stay in the oven for 30 minutes.

5. Cool the cake slightly in the pan on a wire rack. Refrigerate the cheesecake in the pan, lightly covered, overnight, or until the cake is well chilled. To serve, run a sharp knife around the outer edge of the cake, and remove the pan side.

ST. PATRICK'S DAY

This hearty meal of corned beef, soda bread, fresh vegetables and sweets will have you singing "When Irish Eyes Are Smilin'" in no time at all!

SHANNON VEGETABLE PLATTER

Makes 12 servings.

Nutrient Value Per Serving: 212 calories, 5 g protein, 8 g fat, 33 g carbohydrate, 141 mg sodium, 21 mg cholesterol.

12	medium-size boiling potatoes (about 4 pounds)	1	large head green cabbage
2	packages (1 pound each) baby carrots	½	cup (1 stick) butter or margarine
		¼	cup chopped parsley

1. Peel the potatoes and the carrots. (This can be done 1 day in advance. Cover the vegetables with cold water in a bowl, and refrigerate them.)
2. Cook the potatoes and the carrots, separately, in 2 saucepans of boiling salted water for 15 minutes, or until the vegetables are fork-tender. Drain the vegetables. Return the saucepans to low heat, add the vegetables and toss them over heat to dry them. Place the vegetables on a warmed serving platter and keep them warm.
3. Cut the cabbage into 12 wedges. Soak the wedges in warm, salted water in a large bowl for 1 minute. Drain the wedges and arrange them, overlapping, in a large skillet. Pour in enough boiling water to cover the wedges. Cover the skillet and return the water to boiling. Lower the heat and simmer for 3 minutes. Remove the cabbage and drain it on paper toweling. Arrange the cabbage on the platter with the potatoes and carrots.
4. Heat together the butter or margarine and the chopped parsley in a small saucepan until the butter mixture is bubbly. Pour the butter mixture over the vegetables to coat them well.

KILKENNY CORNED BEEF

Bake at 325° for 3 hours.
Makes 12 servings.

Nutrient Value Per Serving: 459 calories, 28 g protein, 33 g fat, 11 g carbohydrate, 1,833 mg sodium, 155 mg cholesterol.

1	piece corned beef brisket (about 5 pounds)	½	cup firmly packed light brown sugar
	Boiling water	⅓	cup prepared mustard
1	tablespoon mixed pickling spices		Orange wedges, for garnish
	Killybegs Horseradish Sauce (recipe follows)		Watercress sprigs, for garnish

St. Patrick's Day

Kilkenny Corned Beef with Killybegs Horseradish Sauce*
Shannon Vegetable Platter*
Bantry Brown Bread (recipe, page 154)
Irish Stout
Shamrock Sugar Cookies (recipe, page 155)
Blarney Castle Parfaits (recipe, page 155)
Dublin Irish Coffee (recipe, page 154)

"Oh Ireland, isn't it grand you look— Like a bride in her rich adornin'? And with all the pent-up love of my heart I bid you the top o' the mornin'!"

—*John Locke*

1. Preheat the oven to slow (325°).
2. Wash the corned beef brisket. Place the meat in a large roasting pan on the oven rack. Cover the meat with the boiling water and add the pickling spices. Cover the pan with aluminum foil.
3. Bake the corned beef in the preheated slow oven (325°) for 2 hours, or until the meat is tender when pierced with a two-tined fork. Allow the corned beef to cool in the cooking liquid. The corned beef can be prepared one day in advance up to this point and refrigerated.
4. Prepare the Killybegs Horseradish Sauce.
5. About 1 hour before serving, drain the cooked corned beef and place it in a roasting pan.
6. Bake the corned beef in the preheated slow oven (325°) for 30 minutes.
7. Combine the brown sugar with the mustard in a small bowl, and spread the mixture over the corned beef. Bake for 30 minutes more, or until the corned beef is well glazed. Place the corned beef on a serving platter. Garnish with the orange wedges and the watercress sprigs. Cut the corned beef into thin slices, and serve the corned beef with the sauce.

Killybegs Horseradish Sauce:

Combine 1 container (8 ounces) of dairy sour cream with 2 tablespoons of prepared mustard and 2 tablespoons of prepared horseradish in a glass or ceramic bowl. Cover the bowl with plastic wrap and refrigerate the sauce for at least 2 hours to blend the flavors.

Kilkenny Corned Beef, Bantry Brown Bread (recipe, page 154), Shannon Vegetable Platter (recipe, page 152). The proper beverage to drink is, of course, a frothy mug of Irish stout!

BANTRY BROWN BREAD

South of Cork lies Bantry Bay, a land of seafaring men who keep warm with large mugs of strong tea and wedges of hearty bread.

LOW-CHOLESTEROL • LOW-FAT

Bake at 375° for 45 minutes.

Makes one 7-inch round loaf (12 generous slices).

Nutrient Value Per Slice: 186 calories, 5 g protein, 5 g fat, 32 g carbohydrate, 351 mg sodium, 1 mg cholesterol.

1	cup all-purpose flour	¼	cup currants
¼	cup plus 2 tablespoons sugar	¼	cup vegetable shortening
2	teaspoons baking powder	1¼	cups buttermilk
1	teaspoon baking soda	1	tablespoon water
1	teaspoon salt		
2	cups whole wheat flour		

1. Preheat the oven to moderate (375°).
2. Sift together the all-purpose flour, ¼ cup of the sugar, the baking powder, baking soda and salt into a medium-size bowl. Stir in the whole wheat flour and the currants. Cut in the shortening with a pastry blender or fork until the mixture resembles small peas. Stir in the buttermilk.
3. Turn out the dough onto a lightly floured pastry cloth or board. Knead the dough 10 times, and shape it into a 7-inch round loaf. Place the loaf on a baking sheet. Cut a cross in the top of the loaf.
4. Bake the bread in the preheated moderate oven (375°) for 40 minutes. Remove the loaf from the oven.
5. Combine the remaining 2 tablespoons of sugar with the water in a saucepan. Bring the mixture to boiling. Brush the hot glaze over the hot loaf. Bake for 5 minutes more, or until the loaf is golden. Serve.

DUBLIN IRISH COFFEE

LOW-SODIUM

Makes 1 serving.

Nutrient Value Per Serving: 133 calories, 1 g protein, 5 g fat, 6 g carbohydrate, 10 mg sodium, 17 mg cholesterol.

	Boiling water		Hot coffee
1	teaspoon sugar		Softly whipped cream
1	ounce (2 tablespoons) Irish whiskey		(about 2 tablespoons)

Heat a heavy stemmed glass with the boiling water and pour out the water. Combine the sugar with the whiskey in the glass. Stir in the coffee to within 1 inch of the rim. Pour the whipped cream over the back of the stirring spoon onto the coffee. Serve the coffee without further stirring.

Baking Soda

Baking soda works only when combined with an acid substance, such as in baking powder mixtures, or when an acidic liquid—buttermilk, sour milk, chocolate, honey, corn syrup, molasses or yogurt—is used.

❖   ❖   ❖

Irish Foods

Simple, hearty and allowing the flavors of a dish to come through without masking them with a sauce: these are the principle rules governing Irish cooking. This homey cuisine relies on fresh ingredients, seasonal vegetables and fruits for its purity of taste. Plain boiled or roasted meats, soda bread and stew are among the many specialties of Ireland, not forgetting that delectable finish to a feast known as Irish coffee.

❖   ❖   ❖

Vanilla

A fragrant flavoring, vanilla extract is extracted or percolated from the vanilla bean with alcohol and water. The vanilla bean is the fruit of an exquisite, pale yellow orchid that is native to Mexico and grows in clusters of 12 or more blossoms on a vine.

■ When the fruit is harvested, it resembles a green bean. It is dried and covered to induce fermentation. The process is repeated until the bean turns dark brown. The process of curing and drying takes 6 months, which accounts for the high price of a single bean.

■ Vanilla beans may be stored in a tightly sealed jar of sugar. To use the beans, simmer them in milk, and use the flavored milk to make desserts. After the milk has been flavored, remove the beans, rinse them and dry them well. Return the dried beans to the jar of sugar to store. The sugar in which the beans are kept may be used as flavored sugar. Vanilla beans stored in sugar will last almost indefinitely, but gradually will lose their flavor. The 6- to 8-inch-long vanilla beans are available in specialty food stores.

■ If a vanilla bean is split lengthwise, the minute black seeds in the center can be scraped out to use as a flavoring.

SHAMROCK SUGAR COOKIES

LOW-CHOLESTEROL • LOW-SODIUM

Bake at 375° for 7 minutes.
Makes 4 dozen cookies.

Nutrient Value Per Cookie: 77 calories, 1 g protein, 4 g fat, 9 g carbohydrate, 22 mg sodium, 4 mg cholesterol.

1 cup butter-flavored vegetable shortening	2¼ cups all-purpose flour
1 cup granulated sugar	1 teaspoon baking powder
1 egg	¼ teaspoon ground ginger
½ teaspoon vanilla	¼ teaspoon salt
	Green decorating sugar

1. Beat together the shortening, granulated sugar, egg and vanilla in a large bowl with an electric mixer at high speed until the mixture is fluffy.
2. Combine the flour, baking powder, ginger and salt in a small bowl. Stir the flour mixture into the shortening mixture to make a stiff dough. Divide the dough in half and shape it into two balls. Wrap the balls of dough in wax paper and chill them for at least 2 hours.
3. Preheat the oven to moderate (375°).
4. Roll out the dough on a lightly floured board to a ¼-inch thickness. Cut out the dough with a 2½- or 3-inch shamrock-shaped cookie cutter. Place the cookies, 1 inch apart, on ungreased baking sheets. Sprinkle the cookies with the green decorating sugar.
5. Bake the cookies in the preheated moderate oven (375°) for 7 minutes, or until the cookies are light brown around the edges. Remove the cookies to wire racks to cool. Store the cookies in a tightly covered metal tin.

BLARNEY CASTLE PARFAITS

Makes 12 servings.

Nutrient Value Per Serving: 304 calories, 3 g protein, 10 g fat, 35 g carbohydrate, 79 mg sodium, 40 mg cholesterol.

½   gallon vanilla ice cream
1   bottle (12 ounces) green
      crème de menthe OR:
      1½ cups light corn syrup
      combined with a few
      drops green food coloring
      and 2 teaspoons
      peppermint extract

Scoop the ice cream into 12 parfait or sherbet glasses. Top with the crème de menthe or the corn syrup mixture.

GRADUATION BUFFET

CRISPY PARMESAN CHICKEN

LOW-CALORIE

Bake at 400° for 45 to 55 minutes.
Makes 12 servings.

Nutrient Value Per Serving: 332 calories, 32 g protein, 20 g fat, 4 g carbohydrate, 602 mg sodium, 175 mg cholesterol.

	Nonstick vegetable cooking spray	1	teaspoon salt
2	cups freshly grated Parmesan cheese (about 10 ounces)	3	eggs
		2	tablespoons water
1½	cups prepared bread crumbs	3	broiler chickens (about 2 pounds each), skin removed, and each cut into 8 pieces
1½	teaspoons freshly ground white pepper	½	cup (1 stick) unsalted butter, melted

Graduation Buffet

Crispy Parmesan Chicken*
Herbed Meat Loaf with Tangy Chili Sauce*
Marinated Cucumbers (recipe, page 158)
Mediterranean Potato Salad (recipe, page 158)
Zucchini Blondies (recipe, page 159)
Lemon Limeade (recipe, page 159)
Peach Muffins (recipe, page 160)
The Best Chocolate Cake (recipe, page 161)

Good eating: Crispy Parmesan Chicken and Marinated Cucumbers (recipe, page 158).

Graduation: A Time for Memories

For a reception that's easy on you — loaded with laughter, school spirit and visions of bright futures — all it takes is some prep work and a little bit of imagination.

■ To cut costs and work load, consider going in with other parents or family members for a group effort.

■ Make the great outdoors a part of your party — and weatherproof the festivities with rented tents. Everyone will appreciate the extra breathing space and will feel more free to circulate.

■ Combine the pretty with the practical in your outdoor lighting. Edge the patio with citronella candles, and string tiny white lights through the trees and bushes.

■ Make as many dishes as possible ahead of time and freeze them. Put frozen dishes in the refrigerator to thaw the day before the party. If your freezer space is limited, ask your neighbors if they have space to lend.

■ Make or buy extra ice.

■ Stimulate conversation (and a chuckle or two) with a photo collage of your graduate's life and times: the first day of kindergarten, a visit to Santa, heading off to summer camp, school plays and sporting events — even the prom. Just make sure there's nothing too embarrassing in the photos!

❖ ❖ ❖

1. Preheat the oven to hot (400°). Spray jelly-roll pans or baking pans with nonstick vegetable cooking spray. Do not line the pans with aluminum foil.
2. Combine the cheese, bread crumbs, pepper and salt in a large bowl.
3. Whisk together the eggs and the water in a large bowl.
4. Using a fork, dip the chicken pieces first into the egg mixture, tapping the pieces against the bowl to remove the excess liquid, then into the cheese mixture to coat the pieces. Place the chicken in the prepared pans, skinned side up.
5. Bake the chicken in the preheated hot oven (400°) for 25 minutes. Brush the chicken with the butter. Bake for 20 to 30 minutes more, or until the juices run clear when the chicken is pierced with a knife. If the chicken browns too quickly, cover it loosely with aluminum foil. Transfer the chicken to a serving platter. Serve the chicken at room temperature.

HERBED MEAT LOAF WITH TANGY CHILI SAUCE

LOW-CALORIE

Bake at 350° for 50 minutes.
Makes 12 servings.

Nutrient Value Per Serving: 209 calories, 16 g protein, 12 g fat, 10 g carbohydrate, 806 mg sodium, 90 mg cholesterol.

Nonstick vegetable cooking spray	½ **teaspoon dried sage, crumbled**
2 **pounds ground chuck**	½ **teaspoon dried rosemary, crumbled**
2 **eggs, slightly beaten**	1 **cup thinly sliced green onion, white and green parts**
10 **tablespoons fresh bread crumbs**	
2 **teaspoons salt**	3 **tablespoons chopped parsley**
1 **teaspoon freshly ground pepper**	⅓ **cup milk**
1 **teaspoon ground cumin**	**Tangy Chili Sauce (recipe follows)**
1 **teaspoon dried thyme, crumbled**	

1. Preheat the oven to moderate (350°). Spray a 9 x 5 x 3-inch loaf pan with nonstick vegetable cooking spray.
2. Combine the chuck with the eggs in a large bowl. Add the bread crumbs, salt, pepper, cumin, thyme, sage and rosemary. Mix the ingredients together. Add the green onion, parsley and milk, and work them into the meat. Pack the meat mixture into the prepared pan.
3. Bake the meat loaf in the preheated moderate oven (350°) for 50 minutes, or until the juices run clear. During the baking, carefully drain off the excess liquid once or twice. If the meat loaf is browning too quickly, cover it loosely with aluminum foil. When the meat loaf is done, drain off the remaining liquid. Cool the meat loaf on a wire rack. Refrigerate the meat loaf until it is chilled.
4. Cut the meat loaf into ½-inch-thick slices, and halve the slices. Serve with the Tangy Chili Sauce.

Tangy Chili Sauce:
Combine a 12-ounce bottle of chili sauce with ¼ cup of lime juice and 1 tablespoon of prepared horseradish in a small bowl. Refrigerate the sauce until serving time.

MARINATED CUCUMBERS

LOW-CALORIE • LOW-CHOLESTEROL • LOW-SODIUM • LOW-FAT

Makes 12 servings.

Nutrient Value Per Serving: 33 calories, 1 g protein, 0 g fat, 8 g carbohydrate, 11 mg sodium, 0 mg cholesterol.

1¼	cups rice wine vinegar OR: white wine vinegar	6	large cucumbers (3½ pounds), peeled, halved lengthwise, seeded and cut into ½-inch slices
1	cup water		
3	tablespoons sugar		
1	tablespoon crushed dillweed		

1. Combine the vinegar, water, sugar and dillweed in a medium-size saucepan. Bring the marinade to boiling. Lower the heat and simmer for 5 minutes. Combine the marinade with the cucumbers in a noncorrosive bowl and marinate the cucumbers, refrigerated, overnight.

2. To serve, drain the cucumbers and discard half the marinade. Combine the cucumbers with the remaining marinade in a serving bowl.

MEDITERRANEAN POTATO SALAD

LOW-CHOLESTEROL

Makes 12 servings.

Nutrient Value Per Serving: 233 calories, 3 g protein, 15 g fat, 24 g carbohydrate, 314 mg sodium, 0 mg cholesterol.

2	cans (6 ounces each, drained weight) ripe pitted olives	3	medium-size sweet green peppers OR: sweet red peppers OR: a combination, diced
½	cup olive oil	½	cup sliced green onions
1	tablespoon dried oregano, crumbled	3	tablespoons chopped parsley
3	pounds red new potatoes	½	cup fresh lemon juice
		½	teaspoon salt

1. Drain and rinse the olives, and place them in a medium-size bowl. Add ¼ cup of the oil and the oregano, and stir to coat the olives. Cover the bowl and refrigerate the olives.

2. Cook the potatoes in a large pot of boiling salted water just until they are tender. Drain the potatoes. When the potatoes are cool enough to handle, remove the skin. Cut the potatoes into ½-inch cubes.

3. Combine the potatoes with the green or red peppers, the green onion, parsley and olives with their marinade in a large bowl.

4. Whisk the remaining ¼ cup of oil with the lemon juice and the salt in a medium-size bowl. Pour the dressing over the potatoes, and mix to coat the vegetables. Refrigerate the potato salad, covered. Mix the potato salad again just before serving.

Graduation Daze

Nothing's greater for recent graduates than a rock-and-rollicking party. Since it's their big day, sit down and have a planning pow-wow: what they want to eat, who they want to invite, whether afternoon or evening is better, and what kind of music they want—even if you'll have to hold your ears!

❖   ❖   ❖

Setting the Scene

For a graduation bash, it's a fun idea to use decorations in the school's colors — such as vivid blues and yellows — and use the colors to pull together all the elements of the party.

■ Roll up white napkins and tie them with ribbons in the school colors to look like diplomas.

■ When choosing serving pieces, just about anything goes: silver, wood, ceramic, glass. Or go with brightly colored plastic for a more casual atmosphere.

■ Rent a helium tank and buy balloons in the school's colors. As each guest arrives, give him or her a filled balloon and a marking pen. The guest writes whatever he or she wants on their balloon. Keep the balloons in one big bunch for decoration. Then, at the end of the party, let them go.

❖   ❖   ❖

ZUCCHINI BLONDIES

Bake at 350° for 40 minutes.
Makes 16 servings.
Nutrient Value Per Blondie: 206 calories, 3 g protein, 10 g fat, 29 g carbohydrate, 155 mg sodium, 44 mg cholesterol.

	Nonstick vegetable cooking spray	2	eggs, slightly beaten
1	cup unbleached all-purpose flour	1	teaspoon vanilla
1	teaspoon baking powder	1	cup shredded, unpeeled zucchini (6 ounces), squeezed dry
½	teaspoon salt	½	cup walnuts (2 ounces), coarsely chopped
⅛	teaspoon baking soda	¾	cup semisweet chocolate pieces
⅓	cup butter or margarine, softened		
1¼	cups firmly packed light brown sugar		

1. Preheat the oven to moderate (350°). Spray an 8 x 8 x 2-inch baking pan with nonstick vegetable cooking spray. Line the bottom of the pan with wax paper and spray the paper.
2. Sift together the flour, baking powder, salt and baking soda into a bowl.
3. Beat together the butter or magarine and the brown sugar in a medium-size bowl until the mixture is light colored and fluffy. Add the eggs and the vanilla, and beat lightly. Stir in the flour mixture. Fold in the zucchini, walnuts and half the chocolate pieces. Pour the batter into the prepared pan. Sprinkle the remaining chocolate pieces on top of the batter.
4. Bake the blondies in the preheated moderate oven (350°) for 40 minutes, or until a cake tester inserted in the center comes out clean. Check the blondies after 30 minutes; if they are darkening too quickly, cover them loosely with aluminum foil. Cool the blondies in the pan on a wire rack. When the cake is completely cool, loosen the edges with a knife and invert it onto the wire rack. Remove the wax paper. Invert the cake again onto a serving plate, and cut the cake into 16 squares.

LEMON LIMEADE

LOW-CHOLESTEROL • LOW-SODIUM • LOW-FAT

Makes 12 servings.
Nutrient Value Per Serving: 76 calories, 0 g protein, 0 g fat, 21 g carbohydrate, 1 mg sodium, 0 mg cholesterol.

1½	cups freshly squeezed lemon juice (from 6 to 8 lemons)*	¾	cup freshly squeezed lime juice (from 6 to 10 limes)*
		8	cups water
		1	cup superfine sugar

Combine the lemon and lime juices in a 3- to 4-quart container. Stir in the water and the sugar. Chill the mixture. Stir it once again before serving.

__Note:__ To get the maximum juice from lemons and limes, soak them in hot water for 10 minutes. Then roll the fruit on a countertop, pressing down on them with your palms. You also can microwave the lemons at full power for 1½ minutes, and the limes for 1 minute before rolling them. Then cut and juice the lemons and limes.

PEACH MUFFINS

LOW-CHOLESTEROL

Bake at 400° for 20 minutes.
Makes 1 dozen muffins.

Nutrient Value Per Muffin: 152 calories, 3 g protein, 7 g fat,
20 g carbohydrate, 407 mg sodium, 24 mg cholesterol.

	Nonstick vegetable cooking spray	1	egg, slightly beaten
1¾	cups sifted unbleached all-purpose flour	⅓	cup corn oil
2	tablespoons sugar	⅓	cup milk
2	teaspoons baking powder	½	cup puréed fresh OR: well-drained canned peaches
1	teaspoon salt	½	cup finely diced peaches, fresh or canned
½	teaspoon ground cinnamon		
½	teaspoon ground ginger		**Cinnamon Sugar Topping:**
½	teaspoon ground nutmeg	2	tablespoons sugar
2	teaspoons grated lemon zest (yellow part of rind only)	1	teaspoon ground cinnamon

1. Preheat the oven to hot (400°). Spray twelve 2½-inch muffin-pan cups with nonstick vegetable cooking spray.

2. Combine the flour, sugar, baking powder, salt, cinnamon, ginger, nutmeg and lemon zest in a medium-size bowl.

3. Whisk together the egg, oil and milk in a small bowl. Stir in the peach purée until it is well blended.

160

Happy occasions call for happy endings. Golden Peach Muffins, served with thick peach jam on the side, are a moist and delicious dessert treat. And everyone loves blondies, so try our chocolate-studded Zucchini Blondies (recipe, page 159).

Chocolate

Unsweetened chocolate is the base from which all other chocolate products are made. Roasted cocoa beans are pressed until the cocoa butter liquefies; the resulting liquor is poured into molds to harden into 1-ounce cakes of chocolate. Semisweet chocolate is a blend of sugar, cocoa butter and unsweetened chocolate.

✧ ✧ ✧

*" **T** he setting sun, and music at the close, As the last taste of sweets, is sweetest last, Writ in remembrance more than things long past. "*
— *William Shakespeare*

4. Make a well in the center of the dry ingredients. Pour in the liquid mixture all at once. Stir just until the dry ingredients are evenly moistened. Fold in the diced peaches. Fill the prepared muffin-pan cups about two thirds full of batter.
5. Prepare the Cinnamon Sugar Topping: Combine the sugar with the cinnamon in a small bowl. Sprinkle the topping over the batter.
6. Bake the muffins in the preheated hot oven (400°) for 20 minutes, or until a cake tester inserted in the centers comes out clean. Check the muffins after 15 minutes; if they are browning too quickly, cover them loosely with aluminum foil. Run a knife around each muffin to loosen it, and turn out the muffins onto a wire rack to cool.

THE BEST CHOCOLATE CAKE

Bake at 350° for 20 to 30 minutes.
Makes 12 servings (one 9-inch three-layer cake).

Nutrient Value Per Serving: 795 calories, 9 g protein, 53 g fat, 82 g carbohydrate, 531 mg sodium, 187 mg cholesterol.

1½ cups boiling water	1½ teaspoons salt
¾ cup Dutch-processed unsweetened cocoa powder	1 cup (2 sticks) unsalted butter, softened
4 eggs, at room temperature	**Fudge Frosting:**
1½ teaspoons vanilla	1 pound semisweet chocolate
3¼ cups sifted cake flour	2 cups heavy cream
2 cups sugar	1 cup coarsely chopped walnuts
2 tablespoons baking powder	

1. Preheat the oven to moderate (350°). Grease three 9-inch round layer cake pans and line them with wax paper rounds. Grease and flour the paper.
2. Whisk together the boiling water and the cocoa in a small bowl until the mixture is smooth. Cool the mixture to room temperature.
3. Combine the eggs with the vanilla in a small bowl. Lightly whisk in one quarter of the cooled cocoa mixture.
4. Combine the flour, sugar, baking powder and salt in a large bowl. Beat with an electric mixer at low speed for 1 minute, or until it is blended.
5. Add the remaining cocoa mixture and the butter to the flour mixture. Raise the speed to medium-high; beat for 1½ minutes, scraping down the sides of the bowl. Add the egg mixture in thirds, beating on medium-high for 20 seconds after each addition. Pour the batter into the prepared pans.
6. Bake the layers in the preheated moderate oven (350°) for 20 to 30 minutes, or until a cake tester inserted near the centers comes out clean. The layers should not shrink from the pan sides. Cool the layers in the pans on wire racks for 10 minutes. Loosen the sides of the layers and invert them onto lightly greased wire racks. Remove the wax paper.
7. Prepare the Fudge Frosting: Chop the chocolate very finely in the container of a food processor. Heat the cream in a saucepan until bubbles appear around the edges. With the motor running, add the hot cream to the chocolate in a steady stream. Process until the mixture is smooth. Transfer the frosting to a bowl. Let the frosting cool at room temperature until it is a good spreading consistency; do not stir the frosting.
8. Spread the frosting between the 3 layers, sprinkling each layer with ¼ cup of the chopped walnuts. Frost the top and sides of the cake. Decorate with the remaining walnuts.

On the Light Side

5

The phrase "lighten up" has taken on an entirely new meaning in today's kitchen. Now more than ever, families are paying attention to what they eat and how their diet affects their overall health. Each recipe in this book has been flagged to let you know at a glance whether it is "low-calorie," "low-cholesterol," and so on. This chapter goes even further, with dishes specifically selected towards an eye on good health.

Soup's on! Full of flavor and full of nutrition, these soups won't overload you with excess fat, sodium or cholesterol. And we're not talking about clear chicken broth! Try our Mexican Tomato Soup (recipe, page 164), Buttermilk Tomato Soup (recipe, page 165) or Dilled Borscht (recipe, page 167) and see what we mean.

Despite rumors to the contrary, meat is not bad for you. Meat is an excellent source of protein, and red meat in particular is one of the best available sources of iron. The key is in the cooking. Poached Eye-Round Roast (recipe, page 168) is a perfect choice for a nutrient-rich main dish, as is Fruit-Stuffed Pork Tenderloin (recipe, page 173). And we haven't forgotten poultry. Mediterranean Chicken, accented with garlic, onions, tomatoes and rosemary (recipe, page 176) is a dish you'll want to serve again and again.

For taste and nutritional benefits, food from the sea can't be beat. Seasoned Salmon in Parchment (recipe, page 178) is amazingly easy to prepare. And just a taste of Angel Hair Pasta with Shrimp (recipe, 179) will have your family wanting more.

If you're trying to cut down on meat altogether, we show you how to combine various foods to insure getting a complete protein. Spicy Bean Enchiladas with Chunky Salsa (recipe, page 180) puts to rest the dated idea that good food must be bland. And Broccoli Lasagna Rolls (recipe, page 182) are a delicious low-fat alternative to the meat-based favorite.

Remember, too, a regular program of physical activity and managing stress will contribute to you and your family's general well-being. Here's to good eating!

Turkey in the Slaw (recipe, page 177) is a colorful combination of thin slices of turkey and two kinds of nutrient-rich cabbage with a low-calorie dressing.

163

*S*OUP'S ON!

Soup is a delicious way to start your meal — and help curb your appetite so you eat less of other foods. It also is a great meal in itself. Anyway you look at it, soup is super!

MEXICAN TOMATO SOUP

An old favorite, spiced up south-of-the-border style. Serve it with a tossed green salad and quesadillas made with lowfat Monterey Jack cheese for a healthful, fun meal.

LOW-CALORIE • LOW-CHOLESTEROL

Makes 8 servings.

Nutrient Value Per Serving: 100 calories, 4 g protein, 5 g fat, 16 g carbohydrate, 118 mg sodium, 0 mg cholesterol.

2	corn tortillas	1	can (17 ounces) plum tomatoes, drained (reserve liquid) and chopped
1	teaspoon corn oil		
1	medium-size onion, chopped (about 1 cup)		
1	small jalapeño pepper, halved, seeded and chopped (wear rubber gloves)	2	quarts chicken broth
		1	cup frozen corn
			Grated zest of 1 lime (green part of rind only)
5	cloves garlic, finely chopped		Juice of 2 limes
			Salt, to taste (optional)
1	tablespoon ground cumin		Additional limes (optional)
¼	teaspoon ground hot red pepper, or to taste		Chopped fresh cilantro OR: parsley, for garnish

1. Cut the tortillas into tiny strips. Sauté the tortilla strips in the oil in a large, nonstick skillet over medium heat until the strips are golden and crisp, for about 3 to 4 minutes. Remove the tortilla strips from the skillet and set them aside.

2. Add the onion, jalapeño pepper, garlic, cumin and ground hot red pepper to the skillet, and sauté for 3 to 5 minutes.

3. Add the tomatoes and cook for 3 minutes.

4. Add the tomato liquid and the broth, and bring the mixture to boiling. Lower the heat and simmer for 30 minutes.

5. Stir in the corn, lime zest and lime juice, and simmer for 5 minutes more, or until the corn is cooked. Season with salt, if you wish, and additional lime juice if necessary. Garnish the soup with the tortilla strips and the cilantro or parsley.

BUTTERMILK TOMATO SOUP

LOW-CALORIE • LOW-CHOLESTEROL • LOW-FAT

Makes 8 servings.

Nutrient Value Per Serving: 49 calories, 3 g protein, 1 g fat, 7 g carbohydrate, 217 mg sodium, 2 mg cholesterol.

1	small onion, finely chopped	1	can (15 ounces) stewed tomatoes
3	shallots, finely chopped	2	cups buttermilk
1	tablespoon diet margarine	⅛	teaspoon freshly ground white pepper

1. Sauté the onion and the shallots in the margarine in a medium-size, nonstick saucepan over medium-high heat. Add the tomatoes and heat them through. Purée the mixture in an electric blender or food processor. Return the purée to the saucepan.

2. Add the buttermilk and the white pepper. Heat the soup, but do not boil it. Serve the soup immediately. If the soup should boil and "curdle," run it through the blender in small batches to smooth it.

Creamy Buttermilk Tomato Soup can be garnished with a swirl of nonfat yogurt, if you wish.

CORN CHOWDER

LOW-CHOLESTEROL • LOW-FAT

Makes four servings (1 quart).

Nutrient Value Per Serving: 168 calories, 7 g protein, 2 g fat, 33 g carbohydrate, 397 mg sodium, 3 mg cholesterol.

¼ **cup chopped green onion**	1 **package (10 ounces) frozen corn kernels**
¼ **teaspoon vegetable oil**	2 **tablespoons instant nonfat dry milk powder**
1¼ **cups chicken broth, fat removed**	⅛ **teaspoon dry mustard**
1 **cup lowfat milk**	**Salt and freshly ground pepper, to taste**
¾ **pound potatoes, peeled and cut into ½-inch cubes (2 cups)**	

1. Sauté the green onion in the oil in a nonstick saucepan for 2 minutes. Add the broth, milk and potatoes, and simmer until the potatoes are tender, for 12 minutes. Add the corn and cook for 1 minute.
2. Purée 1 cup of the chowder in the container of a food processor. Return the purée to the saucepan. Stir in the milk powder, mustard and salt and pepper. Heat the chowder gently to serving temperature.

LA SOUPE PROVENÇALE

LOW-CHOLESTEROL • LOW-SODIUM • LOW-FAT

Makes 4 servings.

Nutrient Value Per Serving: 233 calories, 14 g protein, 2 g fat, 43 g carbohydrate, 45 mg sodium, 0 mg cholesterol.

⅔ **cup dried pea beans* (7 ounces)**	1 **carrot, sliced**
6 **cups water**	1 **can (14½ ounces) low-sodium tomatoes, undrained and broken up**
4 **cups low-sodium beef broth OR: 4 packages (1.1 ounces each) low-sodium beef broth powder plus 4 cups water**	1 **bay leaf**
	¼ **to ½ teaspoon crushed red pepper flakes**
2 **cloves garlic, chopped**	¾ **teaspoon dried oregano, crumbled**
1 **large leek, chopped**	1 **strip orange zest (about 2 x ½ inches; orange part of rind only)**
1 **stalk celery, chopped**	

1. Soak the pea beans in 4 cups of the water in a medium-size bowl, covered, at room temperature overnight. Pour off the water. Rinse the pea beans and drain them well.
2. Combine the broth, the remaining 2 cups of water and the pea beans in a medium-size saucepan. Bring the mixture to boiling over high heat. Reduce the heat and simmer the pea beans, uncovered, for 1¼ hours.
3. Add the garlic, leek, celery, carrot, tomatoes with their liquid, bay leaf, red pepper flakes, oregano and orange zest. Return the mixture to boiling over medium heat. Cook, uncovered, stirring occasionally, for 30 minutes, or until the pea beans are tender. Serve.

*Note: Pea beans are a smaller variety of Great Northern beans.

Soup Sidekicks

Make soup your main dish for dinner and round out the meal with one of these light accompaniments.

■ Brush slices of baguettes with olive oil. Place the slices on a baking sheet and bake them at 375° for about 20 minutes, or until they are golden in color. Rub the bread slices with a clove of garlic.

■ Cut toast into triangles and spread the triangles with a teaspoon or two of herbed goat cheese. Broil the triangles until the cheese bubbles. Top with chopped tomato.

■ Slice unpeeled potatoes and place the slices on a nonstick baking sheet coated with nonstick vegetable cooking spray. Sprinkle the potato slices with paprika, lemon juice and lots of freshly ground pepper. Bake the slices at 400° for 30 minutes, or until they are golden in color.

■ Rice cakes can add a crunchy texture to your meal with few calories and no sodium or fat. Top the cakes with a dollop of peanut butter and a thin slice of apple. For a quick mini-pizza, layer a rice cake with a tomato slice, a pinch of basil and a sprinkling of lowfat mozzarella. Broil the rice cake for a few seconds, and serve it warm.

■ Use reduced-calorie versions of mayonnaise and sour cream, and nonfat yogurt, to replace regular mayonnaise and sour cream in recipes. The textures are similar, but the calories and fat will be lowered significantly.

Borscht

There are as many recipes for this Russian and Polish soup as there are spellings of its name. Borscht can be thick or thin, meat or meatless, and can be served hot or cold. This soup usually is made with beets, and topped with sour cream. The most authentic recipes are made with a fermented liquid called "kvas," brewed from rye bread, water, sugar, yeast and flour.

❖   ❖   ❖

DILLED BORSCHT

LOW-CALORIE • LOW-CHOLESTEROL • LOW-FAT

Makes 4 servings.

Nutrient Value Per Serving: 93 calories, 4 g protein, 1 g fat, 18 g carbohydrate, 887 mg sodium, 0 mg cholesterol.

2 cups shredded raw beets	Freshly ground pepper, to taste
4 cups beef broth	Additional vinegar, (optional)
1 medium-size onion, sliced	Cooked and cubed potato, for garnish
¼ cup red wine vinegar	Plain yogurt, for garnish
1 tablespoon honey	Dill sprigs, for garnish
½ small cabbage, shredded (about 3 cups)	
⅓ cup chopped fresh dill	
Salt (optional)	

1. Combine the beets, broth, onion, vinegar and honey in a large saucepan. Bring the mixture to boiling over medium heat. Cover the saucepan, lower the heat and simmer for 20 minutes.

2. Add the cabbage, cover the saucepan and simmer for 10 minutes more, or until the cabbage and beets are tender. Stir in the dill. Add salt, if you wish, the pepper and, if necessary, additional vinegar.

3. Ladle the soup into 4 individual soup bowls and top each with some of the potato, a dollop of the yogurt and the dill sprigs.

Plain yogurt substitutes for the more traditional sour cream in Dilled Borscht.

*L*OW-DOWN ON LEAN

Meat and poultry both are terrific sources of protein and iron. And, with these cooking techniques and great recipes, you can enjoy meat without worrying about excess fat and cholesterol.

POACHED EYE-ROUND ROAST

Try serving this savory roast with steamed French-style green beans and pan-roasted potatoes. Reserve the poaching liquid for the Mushroom Tomato Sauce (recipe, page 170), or for use in other sauces and soups.

LOW-CALORIE • LOW-CHOLESTEROL • LOW-SODIUM • LOW-FAT

Makes 8 servings.

Nutrient Value Per Serving: 166 calories, 26 g protein, 5 g fat, 3 g carbohydrate, 68 mg sodium, 61 mg cholesterol.

1 **2-pound beef eye-round roast**	**Salt and freshly ground pepper, to taste**
1 **carrot, chopped**	**About 10 cups water**
½ **medium-size onion, chopped**	**Mushroom Tomato Sauce (recipe, page 170)**
¼ **cup celery leaves**	

1. Tie the roast at 2-inch intervals. Sear the roast, without using oil, in a nonstick saucepan just large enough to hold the meat, or in a Dutch oven lightly coated with nonstick vegetable cooking spray. (Searing the meat provides a roasted look, no messy roasting pan to clean and added flavor to the poaching liquid.)

2. Remove the roast from the saucepan. Wipe the fat from the saucepan with paper toweling. Scrape up any crusty bits from the bottom of the saucepan. Return the roast to the saucepan with the carrot, onion, celery leaves and salt and pepper. Add enough of the water to just cover the meat; the roast will float. Cover the saucepan and bring the water to boiling. Reduce the heat to a simmer.

3. Simmer the roast until its internal temperature registers 130° on an instant-reading meat thermometer inserted in the thickest part of the meat. (Use 15 minutes per pound as an estimate.) Slip the tines of a large fork under the string to remove the roast from the poaching liquid to check the temperature. Check the saucepan occasionally to make sure the poaching liquid is not boiling.

4. Remove the roast to a carving board or serving platter. Cover the meat tightly with aluminum foil. Reserve the poaching liquid. Let the roast stand until its internal temperature reaches 140° for rare, for about 10 minutes. Drain the excess juices back into the poaching liquid.

5. Prepare the Mushroom Tomato Sauce.

6. Remove the string from the roast. Carve the meat into very thin slices. Serve the roast with the sauce.

Beef Calorie and Fat Scorecard

(3-ounce cooked, trimmed portion)

CUT	CALORIES	TOTAL FAT
Eye round, roasted	155	5.5 g
Top round, broiled	162	5.3 g
Round tip, roasted	162	6.4 g
Tenderloin, broiled	174	7.9 g
Sirloin steak, broiled (wedge bone)	177	7.4 g
Bottom round, braised	189	8.2 g
LESS LEAN		
Flank, broiled	207	12.7 g
Short rib (some fat; difficult to trim), braised	251	15.4 g

Poaching is an excellent way to keep lean cuts of beef tender and moist — and do so in a third less time than roasting. Poached Eye-Round Roast is a perfect example of this technique.

MUSHROOM TOMATO SAUCE

This sauce is wonderful with Poached Eye-Round Roast (recipe, page 168), but is equally delicious with other meats.

LOW-CALORIE • LOW-CHOLESTEROL • LOW-FAT

Makes 8 servings.

Nutrient Value Per Serving: 19 calories, 1 g protein, 0 g fat, 3 g carbohydrate, 86 mg sodium, 0 mg cholesterol.

½	pound mushrooms, thinly sliced	4	teaspoons all-purpose flour
2	tablespoons thinly sliced green onion	¾	cup defatted poaching liquid from Poached Eye-Round Roast (recipe, page 168) OR: beef broth
1	teaspoon reduced-calorie margarine	½	teaspoon dried thyme, crumbled
½	cup chopped, seeded tomatoes		
3	tablespoons dry white wine		

1. Sauté the mushrooms and the green onion in the margarine in a medium-size saucepan over very low heat until the mushrooms are soft, for 8 to 10 minutes. Stir in the tomatoes and the wine.

2. Stir the flour into 2 tablespoons of the poaching liquid or broth in a small cup until the flour mixture is smooth.

3. Add the remaining poaching liquid and the thyme to the saucepan. Stir in the flour mixture. Bring the combined mixture to boiling. Lower the heat and simmer for 1 minute, or until the sauce thickens slightly. Spoon 3 to 4 tablespoons of the sauce over each serving.

HEARTY BEEF CHILI

LOW-CALORIE • LOW-CHOLESTEROL • LOW-FAT

Makes 8 servings.

Nutrient Value Per Serving: 263 calories, 29 g protein, 8 g fat, 19 g carbohydrate, 264 mg sodium, 67 mg cholesterol.

2	pounds bottom round OR: round tip roast	2	fresh jalapeño peppers, halved, seeded and chopped (wear rubber gloves)
1	large onion, finely chopped		
3	large cloves garlic, finely chopped	2	teaspoons chili powder
2½	cups no-salt-added beef broth OR: regular canned beef broth, refrigerated and fat skimmed	1	package (10 ounces) frozen corn kernels, thawed
		1	can (15¼ ounces) red kidney beans
			Cooked rice (optional)

1. Cut the meat into 1- to 1½-inch cubes. Combine the meat, onion, garlic and ½ cup of the broth in a medium-size saucepan. Cover the saucepan and bring the mixture to boiling. Lower the heat and simmer for 15 minutes. Check the mixture once and add a little water, if necessary, to prevent the mixture from drying out. Uncover the saucepan and cook over very high heat until the meat lightly browns and most of the liquid has evaporated, for about 15 to 20 minutes.

Breeding Leaner Animals

Farmers are producing healthier-to-eat beef, lamb and pork primarily by breeding leaner animals and by raising them on more nutritious feed. But other high-tech possibilities are on the horizon.

■ At Penn State University, pigs were injected with somatotropin (a growth hormone). The results: more rapid growth, more lean meat and less fat.

■ Some scientists are investigating the possibilities of stimulating or inhibiting the action of animals' growth hormones; other scientists are trying to prevent animal cells from synthesizing fat.

■ All these techniques are still in the experimental stage. So for now, shop wisely, pass up the spareribs for the pork loin, enjoy skinless chicken and turkey, and make the most of cooking techniques that add little or no fat, such as poaching and braising.

❖   ❖   ❖

Trim Tips

It's easier to judge the "trim" on a piece of meat than the marbling. Trim refers to the amount of fat left around the periphery; it also is called "separable fat." The average fat thickness on retail cuts of meat now is less than ⅛ inch.

❖   ❖   ❖

Meats that Make the Grade

Since 1926, the USDA has graded beef on a voluntary basis: Producers are not required to submit their meat for grading, and they pay a fee to the USDA for the grading process. Over time, the percentage of fat required to qualify for different grades has diminished. USDA "Prime" is the best grade, followed by USDA "Choice," then USDA "Select."

■ Marbling, the tiny streaks of fat interlaced with lean muscle tissue, is used as the main indicator for grading. The more marbled the meat, the more tender it is—and the more fat it contains. So, ironically, the fattier the cut, the more expensive it is and the less healthy it is to eat.

❖ ❖ ❖

Choosing the Cut

Beyond choosing the grade of meat, the smart shopper needs to know about cuts to make the healthiest meat decisions. The fact is that the fat content of meat varies more from cut to cut than it does from grade to grade, so the best advice is to become familiar with the cuts offered (see Beef Calorie and Fat Scorecard, page 169).

❖ ❖ ❖

2. Add the remaining 2 cups of broth, the jalapeño peppers and chili powder to the saucepan. Bring the mixture to boiling. Lower the heat and simmer, covered, for 1 to 1½ hours, or until the meat is tender. Stir in the corn and the kidney beans. Cook for 2 minutes more, or until the vegetables are heated through. Serve the chili hot, with rice if you wish.

GRILLED LAMB WITH ROSEMARY

LOW-CALORIE • LOW-CHOLESTEROL • LOW-SODIUM

Grill for 35 to 40 minutes for rare.
Makes 16 servings.

Nutrient Value Per Serving: 159 calories, 24 g protein, 6 g fat, 2 g carbohydrate, 125 mg sodium, 74 mg cholesterol.

1 leg of lamb (6 pounds), well trimmed, boned and butterflied* (about 4 pounds after trimming and boning)	2 tablespoons chopped fresh rosemary OR: 2 teaspoons dried rosemary, crumbled
½ cup fresh lemon juice	½ teaspoon salt
½ cup fresh lime juice	¼ teaspoon freshly ground pepper
3 large cloves garlic, pressed	

1. Place the lamb in a shallow, 4-quart ceramic or glass dish. Add the lemon juice, lime juice, garlic, rosemary, salt and pepper, and turn the lamb to coat it. Cover the dish and refrigerate the lamb for at least 1 hour, but no more than 2 hours.
2. Prepare a medium-hot charcoal fire, and place a drip pan in the center of the barbecue under the grill rack.
3. Grill the lamb for 35 to 40 minutes, or until an instant-reading meat thermometer inserted in the thickest part of the meat registers 135° to 140° for rare, or 145° for medium-rare.
4. Slice the meat on the diagonal. Serve the grilled lamb warm or at room temperature.

Note: Ask your butcher to prepare the lamb. Or, if you wish, you can prepare the lamb yourself. First, trim all but a very thin layer of fat from the lamb. Place the lamb, fat side down, on a cutting board. Cut through the meat along the bones. Scrape the meat from around the bones and remove the bones. Cut the thicker sections of the meat almost in half and open the leg, like a book, into a flat piece. Pound the meat, if necessary, to an even thickness.

VEAL KEBABS WITH ONION SAUCE

LOW-CALORIE

Broil for 15 to 18 minutes.
Makes 4 servings.

Nutrient Value Per Serving: 249 calories, 31 g protein, 9 g fat, 11 g carbohydrate, 474 mg sodium, 140 mg cholesterol.

¼	cup fresh orange juice
1	teaspoon grated orange zest (orange part of rind only)
⅛	teaspoon red pepper flakes
1	pound trimmed, boneless veal shoulder OR: loin, cut into 12 cubes (1½ to 2 inches)

Onion Sauce:
- 6 green onions, chopped, both white and green parts
- 1 large white onion, chopped
- 1 cup chicken broth, refrigerated and defatted

- 1 tablespoon orange juice
- ¼ teaspoon dried thyme, crumbled
- ¼ teaspoon salt
- ⅛ teaspoon freshly ground black pepper
- ¼ cup milk

Nonstick vegetable cooking spray
- 1 sweet red pepper, cored, seeded and cut into 8 squares
- 1 large zucchini, cut diagonally into 8 slices, ½ inch thick
- 4 medium-size whole mushrooms with stems
Cooked rice (optional)

1. Combine the ¼ cup of orange juice with the orange zest and the red pepper flakes in a large bowl. Add the veal cubes and stir to coat them well. Cover the bowl and refrigerate the veal for 24 hours, stirring once.

2. Prepare the Onion Sauce: Combine the green onion, white onion and broth in a small saucepan. Bring the mixture to boiling. Cover the saucepan tightly, lower the heat and simmer for 20 minutes, or until the vegetables are very soft. Stir in the 1 tablespoon of orange juice, the thyme, salt and black pepper. When the onion mixture is cool enough to handle, place it in the container of an electric blender or food processor. Cover and whirl until the mixture is a smooth purée. Stir in the milk. Transfer the sauce to a small, covered container and refrigerate the sauce until the next day.

3. To cook the kebabs, preheat the broiler. Spray the rack of the broiler pan with nonstick vegetable cooking spray.

4. Thread 3 veal cubes onto each of 4 medium-size skewers, alternating them with 2 red pepper squares and 2 zucchini slices. Thread a whole mushroom at the end of each skewer. Brush the vegetables and veal with the orange juice marinade.

5. Broil the kebabs 5 inches from the heat source for 10 minutes. Turn over the kebabs and brush them again with the marinade. Broil for 5 to 8 minutes more, or until the veal no longer is pink.

6. Meanwhile, reheat the Onion Sauce in a small saucepan. Serve the kebabs with the sauce and, if you wish, with rice.

Veal

The most delicate meat of all, veal is bland in taste, making it ideal for cooking with sauces. The best quality veal comes from young, milk-fed calves less than 3 months old, when the meat shows virtually no pink at all.

■ Veal is a fine-grained meat, with no marbling and only a thin external layer of fat. It has a large amount of connective tissue that requires cooking at low to moderate temperatures. Do not broil thin slices of veal; these are best pan-fried, braised or roasted.

■ Veal scaloppine, sometimes called veal scallops, is the most expensive cut and comes from the leg. The slices are thin and boneless, and are pounded to break some of the connective tissue. Scaloppine also may be made from the loin or shoulder.

■ Less expensive cuts of veal include breast of veal, shoulder and shanks. Cuts of veal are similar to cuts of beef, but are smaller in size.

Apricots

One of the first fruits of summer, apricots also are canned and dried for year-round eating. Apricots traveled the globe westward from China through Persia and the Mediterranean area to England, where the Arab spelling "alburquq" was changed to "abricock" and later to the present word. The Spaniards brought the fruit to Mexico, and northward to the missions in California in the early 18th century. California now is the major producer of apricots in the United States.

■ Fresh apricots appear in late May or early June, and last through early August.

■ It takes 6 pounds of fresh apricots to yield 1 pound of dried apricots. Dried apricots are costly, but their ambrosial flavor makes up for the expense. A little goes a long way toward flavoring cakes, desserts and even main dishes.

■ Keep fresh apricots at room temperature until they are fully ripe. Then refrigerate them. To ripen apricots quickly, place them in a closed paper bag in a warm room. Canned apricots should be refrigerated once they are opened. Dried apricots, sold in packages or boxes, should be placed in an airtight container and refrigerated after opening.

■ Apricots are an excellent source of vitamins A and C. A half cup of fresh apricot halves has only 36 calories.

FRUIT-STUFFED PORK TENDERLOIN

LOW-CALORIE • LOW-FAT

Bake at 400° for 40 to 50 minutes.
Makes 4 servings.

Nutrient Value Per Serving: 245 calories, 29 g protein, 6 g fat, 19 g carbohydrate, 285 mg sodium, 152 mg cholesterol.

¼ cup dried currants	¼ teaspoon salt
¼ cup finely chopped dried apricots	¼ teaspoon dried rosemary, crumbled
2 tablespoons bourbon	⅛ teaspoon dried sage, crumbled
1 tablespoon water	⅛ teaspoon freshly ground pepper
1 pound boneless pork tenderloin	1 egg, slightly beaten
1 cup fresh pumpernickel bread crumbs	

1. Preheat the oven to hot (400°). Soak the currants and the apricots in the bourbon and the water in a small bowl, and set aside.
2. Cut the pork tenderloin lengthwise down the center, but not all the way through. Pound the pork between 2 pieces of wax paper until the meat is an even ¼-inch thickness.
3. Add the bread crumbs, salt, rosemary, sage, pepper and egg to the fruit mixture, and mix the ingredients well. Spread the stuffing down the center of the pork, leaving a ½-inch border on each end. Bring up the long sides of the tenderloin to enclose the filling, overlapping the long edges slightly. Push in the short ends as you roll. Secure the roll with string every 2 inches. Place the pork on a rack in a roasting pan.
4. Bake the pork in the preheated hot oven (400°) for 40 to 50 minutes, or until an instant-reading meat thermometer registers 160° when inserted in the thickest part of the meat without touching the stuffing. Let the pork stand for 5 minutes. Remove the string. Thinly slice the pork and serve.

Pork Calorie and Fat Scorecard

(3-ounce cooked, trimmed portion)

CUT	CALORIES	TOTAL FAT
Tenderloin, roasted	141	4.1 g
Leg, roasted	187	9.1 g
Loin center cut, broiled	196	8.9 g
LESS LEAN		
Country-style ribs (some fat), braised	334	28.8 g
Spareribs (some fat; difficult to trim), braised	338	25.8 g

CHINESE SHREDDED PORK WITH CRISPY VEGETABLES

LOW-CALORIE • LOW-CHOLESTEROL

Makes 4 servings.

Nutrient Value Per Serving: 193 calories, 18 g protein, 9 g fat, 45 g carbohydrate, 377 mg sodium, 45 mg cholesterol.

10 **ounces boneless pork cutlets, from leg, loin or tenderloin**	3 **teaspoons vegetable oil**
3 **teaspoons grated, peeled fresh gingerroot**	2 **tablespoons reduced-sodium soy sauce**
3 **cloves garlic, very finely chopped**	2 **cups ½-inch-thick slices bok choy (Chinese cabbage)**
1 **dried hot red chili pepper**	2 **teaspoons cornstarch**
1 **medium-size yellow squash, halved lengthwise, each half cut crosswise into ¼-inch-thick slices (about 1¾ cups)**	1 **to 2 tablespoons balsamic vinegar (see Tip, page 67)**
2 **medium-size sweet red peppers, cut into 1-inch squares (2 cups)**	⅓ **cup canned whole water chestnuts, drained, rinsed and halved** **Cooked rice (optional)**

1. Slice the pork cutlets across the grain into ¼-inch-thick slices. Cut each slice into 3-inch-long strips. Combine the pork, 1 teaspoon of the ginger and one third of the garlic in a small bowl.

2. Sauté the remaining ginger and garlic with the chili pepper, squash and red peppers in 2 teaspoons of the oil in a large, nonstick skillet over medium heat, stirring constantly, for 5 minutes. Add water, if necessary, to prevent sticking. Add the soy sauce and cook for 1 to 2 minutes, or until the vegetables are crisply tender. Transfer the mixture to a bowl and discard the chili pepper.

3. Sauté the pork in the remaining 1 teaspoon of oil in the skillet over high heat for 3 to 4 minutes, or until the pork no longer is pink. Lower the heat and return the vegetables, along with the bok choy, to the skillet.

4. Dissolve the cornstarch in the vinegar in a cup. Stir the cornstarch mixture into the skillet. Bring the cornstarch mixture to boiling and cook, stirring, for 1 minute, or until the sauce thickens slightly. Sprinkle with the water chestnuts. Serve with hot cooked rice, if you wish.

Calorie-Cutting Cooking

There is no question that the fat in meat is what gives it flavor and tenderness, and that leaner, healthier cuts can be less tempting to eat. Certain cooking techniques, such as frying, actually can add fat to meat. But there are ways to prepare meat to maximize the flavor without a fat overload.

■ Stir-frying: Slice meat or poultry across the grain thinly, about ⅛-inch-thick. (Cutting across the grain helps to tenderize tough cuts.) Quickly panfry the meat, uncovered, using very little added fat.

■ Poaching or No-Fat Braising: Brown unfloured meat in a nonstick pan using no added fat. A regular pan can be used if it is sprayed lightly with nonstick vegetable cooking spray. Finish cooking the meat, covered, in a simmering liquid until the meat is tender. Simmering the meat breaks down its tough muscle fibers and connective tissue.

■ Roasting: Roast leaner cuts of beef and lamb on a rack in a roasting pan to an internal temperature of 135° to 140°; pork to 160°; veal to 170°; poultry (whole bird), to 180°F.

■ Broiling or Grilling: Cook meat quickly by direct heat, either in the oven broiler or over hot coals. Both methods allow the fat to drain during the cooking process.

Proper Preparation

You can help skim off calories and fat by preparing meat and poultry in a variety of styles. Certain cuts allow the meat to cook without added fat; others allow the fat in the meat to drain while cooking.

■ Cubing: Cut the meat into small, uniform-sized cubes. Braise the cubes in stews, grill them or broil them on skewers, as for kebabs.

■ Scaloppine: Slice the meat across the grain into ½-inch-thick slices. Use the scaloppine as is, or for extra tenderness, pound the slices between pieces of wax paper to a ⅛-inch-thickness. Panfry the meat in a small amount of oil.

■ Marinating: Soak the food in an acid-based solution, such as vinegar, wine or citrus juice, or a combination of these, to soften muscle fibers and add flavor with very little or no fat.

❖ ❖ ❖

Sesame Oil

Sesame oil, a polyunsaturate (14% saturated fat), appears mainly in Oriental, Middle Eastern and Indian cooking. Excellent for shallow- and deep-frying, it lends a nutlike taste to food. Oriental sesame oil is a thicker version used to add flavor to Chinese dishes, rather than for frying. It is darker in color than regular sesame oil, and can be found in the Oriental food section of many supermarkets, or in Oriental specialty food stores.

MARINATED CHICKEN SALAD WITH SESAME DRESSING

LOW-CALORIE • LOW-CHOLESTEROL • LOW-FAT

Broil chicken for 8 minutes.
Makes 4 servings.

Nutrient Value Per Serving: 248 calories, 31 g protein, 7 g fat, 15 g carbohydrate, 566 mg sodium, 66 mg cholesterol.

1 **pound boned, skinless chicken breast halves**

Marinade:
3 **tablespoons reduced-sodium soy sauce OR: tamari sauce**
3 **tablespoons dry sherry**
1 **teaspoon finely chopped garlic**
1 **teaspoon finely chopped, peeled fresh gingerroot**
1 **teaspoon honey**

Sesame Dressing:
½ **cup chopped fresh cilantro OR: parsley**
3 **tablespoons rice vinegar**

1 **tablespoon peanut oil**
2 **teaspoons Oriental sesame oil (see Tip, at left) Pinch crushed red pepper flakes**

3 **cups shredded romaine lettuce**
2½ **cups broccoli flowerets including 1 inch of stem, lightly steamed or raw**
1¼ **cups diagonally sliced carrots, $1/16$-inch thick, lightly steamed or raw Nonstick vegetable cooking spray**

1. Make 3 diagonal slices, about ¼ inch deep, across the top of each piece of chicken. Arrange the chicken in a 11¾ x 7½ x 1¾-inch glass baking dish.
2. Prepare the Marinade: Combine the soy or tamari sauce with the sherry, garlic, ginger and honey in a small bowl. Add the marinade to the chicken in the pan, and turn the chicken to coat it. Cover the pan with plastic wrap and marinate the chicken, refrigerated, for at least 3 hours.
3. Meanwhile, prepare the Sesame Dressing: Combine the cilantro or parsley with the vinegar, peanut oil, Oriental sesame oil and red pepper flakes in a small screw-top jar. Set aside.
4. Arrange the lettuce, broccoli and carrots on a large serving platter. Cover the platter with damp paper toweling while broiling the chicken.
5. Preheat the oven to broil. Spray the rack in the broiler pan with nonstick vegetable cooking spray. Remove the chicken from the marinade and discard the marinade. Arrange the chicken, sliced side up, on the prepared broiler pan rack.
6. Broil the chicken 5 inches from the heat source for 5 minutes. Turn over the chicken and broil for 3 minutes more, or until the chicken no longer is pink in the center.
7. When the chicken is cool enough to handle, slice it thinly and arrange the slices over the vegetables on the platter. Shake the dressing, drizzle it over the salad, and serve.

❖ ❖ ❖

175

MEDITERRANEAN CHICKEN

LOW-CALORIE • LOW-CHOLESTEROL • LOW-FAT

Makes 4 servings.

Nutrient Value Per Serving: 238 calories, 30 g protein, 5 g fat, 18 g carbohydrate, 290 mg sodium, 68 mg cholesterol.

1 **tablespoon all-purpose flour**	1 **sweet yellow pepper, chopped (1 cup)**
1/8 **teaspoon freshly ground black pepper**	1 **teaspoon dried rosemary, crumbled**
2 **whole chicken breasts (about 1½ pounds), skinned and cut in half**	1/4 **teaspoon crushed red pepper flakes**
	1/4 **teaspoon salt**
1 **teaspoon olive oil**	1¼ **pounds plum tomatoes, chopped**
6 **cloves garlic, finely chopped**	1/4 **cup sliced black olives**
3 **onions, chopped (2½ cups)**	**Whole wheat French bread**

1. Combine the flour with the black pepper on a large plate. Dip the chicken in the flour mixture to coat the chicken well. Pat off the excess flour.

2. Heat the oil in a large, nonstick skillet over medium heat. Add the chicken, meat side down, and cook for 6 to 8 minutes, or until the chicken is golden brown in color.

3. Turn over the chicken. Add the garlic, onion, yellow pepper, rosemary, red pepper flakes and salt. Cook for 8 minutes, or until the onion is soft.

4. Add the tomatoes and the olives. Cook, covered, over medium-low heat for 25 minutes, or until the chicken no longer is pink near the bone. Serve the chicken with the whole wheat French bread.

Sodium: Read the Labels

Although many products now claim to have reduced their sodium levels, it is important to understand the wording of the labels to make healthy choices when you're trying to reduce sodium in your diet.

■ Sodium-free: This means that the sodium content is less than 5 milligrams per serving.

■ Very low sodium: 35 milligrams or fewer per serving.

■ Low sodium: 140 milligrams or fewer per serving.

■ Reduced sodium: Sodium content is at least 75% lower than that contained in the regular version of the product.

■ Unsalted, no salt added and without added salt: No salt was used in preparing the product, which would be prepared with salt ordinarily. However, Federal rules place no ceiling on the amount of sodium the product may contain naturally.

■ Reduced salt: The amount of salt used in processing the product has been reduced, but there is no rule about how large the reduction has to be. A careful reading of the label may reveal this.

■ If you're wondering why some no-salt foods cost more than their salted counterparts, processors say that more "real ingredients" are used to make up for the absence of salt.

❖ ❖ ❖

Mediterranean Chicken, with traditional accents of garlic, onion, tomatoes, olives and rosemary, is a deliciously healthy main dish.

How to Shake the Salt Habit

A taste for salt is acquired. Newborn babies dislike salty foods. But by the time children reach school age, they clamor for salty foods because they have learned to like the flavor. The following tips can help you train your taste buds to like less salt — or none at all.

■ Always taste your food before you salt it. Many people reach for the salt shaker without thinking. Gradually reduce the amount of salt you add to foods.

■ Experiment with herbs and spices: freshly ground pepper, dry mustard, garlic, onion, flavored vinegars, lemon juice, hot peppers and grated horseradish. Fruit and fruit juices also are excellent seasonings, especially for vegetables and poultry.

■ Use low-sodium or reduced-sodium products. Canned broth, bouillon cubes, soy sauce, ham, bacon and cheese now can be found in reduced-sodium form.

■ Steam or microwave vegetables. These cooking methods add no sodium or fat, and allow the true flavors of the vegetables to come through. Serve with a sprinkling of lemon or lime juice.

■ Research substitutes thoroughly. There is no health advantage to using sea salt instead of table salt; both are sodium chloride and equally likely to elevate blood pressure levels in susceptible people.

TURKEY IN THE SLAW

LOW-CALORIE • LOW-CHOLESTEROL • LOW-FAT

Makes 4 servings.

Nutrient Value Per Serving: 270 calories, 26 g protein, 8 g fat, 24 g carbohydrate, 376 mg sodium, 60 mg cholesterol.

1 cup shredded green cabbage OR: Savoy cabbage
1 cup shredded red cabbage
1 raw carrot, coarsely grated
2 to 3 packages low-calorie sweetener (optional)
¼ cup reduced-calorie mayonnaise
¼ cup plain nonfat yogurt Light salt and freshly ground white pepper, to taste
4 teaspoons reduced-calorie Thousand Island dressing
8 slices reduced-calorie whole wheat bread*
10 ounces cooked turkey, sliced thinly

1. At least 1 hour before serving, mix the shredded cabbages in a mixing bowl with the carrot, sweetener if you wish, mayonnaise and yogurt. Add the salt and white pepper.
2. Just before serving the sandwiches, spread 1 teaspoon of the Thousand Island dressing on each of 4 slices of the bread. Top each slice with some of the turkey and the slaw, and cover with 1 of the remaining bread slices. Press down lightly and slice each sandwich diagonally.

Note: Reduced-calorie whole wheat bread, usually sliced very thinly, has 35 to 40 calories per slice.

POLLO ALLA VINAIGRETTE

A taste of Spain, made quickly and easily in one skillet. And yes, the recipe does call for an entire bulb of garlic.

LOW-CALORIE • LOW-SODIUM

Makes 4 servings.

Nutrient Value Per Serving: 251 calories, 20 g protein, 17 g fat, 4 g carbohydrate, 74 mg sodium, 77 mg cholesterol.

1 chicken (4 pounds), cut into serving pieces
1 tablespoon olive oil
1 whole bulb (not clove) garlic, finely chopped
4 large yellow onions, sliced
1 bay leaf
½ cup red wine vinegar
½ cup water

1. Brown the chicken in the oil in a large skillet over medium-high heat, working in batches, if necessary, to avoid crowding in the skillet.
2. Add the garlic, onion, bay leaf, vinegar and water to the skillet. Bring the mixture to boiling over medium-high heat. Reduce the heat and cover the skillet. Simmer over low heat, stirring occasionally, for 25 minutes, or until the chicken is cooked through. Drain the chicken and reserve the cooking liquid.
3. Place the chicken on a serving platter, and serve with the reserved cooking liquid as gravy.

SEASONED SALMON IN PARCHMENT

LOW-CALORIE • LOW-CHOLESTEROL

Bake at 325° for 12 to 15 minutes.
Makes 1 serving.

Nutrient Value Per Serving: 316 calories, 27 g protein, 19 g fat, 13 g carbohydrate, 329 mg sodium, 62 mg cholesterol.

1	salmon fillet (4 ounces)	2	large mushroom caps, sliced
2	to 3 grinds black pepper		
1	teaspoon crushed fresh rosemary	1	tablespoon finely chopped shallots
3	green onions, chopped	4	to 6 thin asparagus spears
2	tablespoons diet margarine	½	lime
			White wine, for sprinkling (optional)

More Salt-Shaking Tips

- You can help reduce the sodium level of canned foods, such as tuna, beans and vegetables, by rinsing them quickly under cold water.

- Eat more foods that are rich in potassium. A study by the U.S. Department of Agriculture has shown that people who consume a lot of high-potassium foods — such as oranges and orange juice, bananas, mangos, dried fruits, cantaloupe, dried peas and beans — excrete more sodium in their urine than the average person. Do not take potassium supplements unless your physician prescribes them; an overdose of potassium can cause nausea, vomiting and an irregular heartbeat.

- Avoid potassium-based salt substitutes. The idea is to minimize your desire for a salty taste, not to substitute one form of salt for another.

- Check all food labels for their sodium content. Compare different brands of the same product; some may have considerably less sodium than others. Keep in mind that if 2,200 milligrams of sodium is your total daily allowance, 300 milligrams in one ounce of dry breakfast cereal (360 with just ½ cup of milk) may be too much to start off the day. (See the Tip on page 176 for some useful information about reading food labels.)

❖   ❖   ❖

Seasoned Salmon in Parchment is moist and full of flavor — and it's baked with no added fat.

Nutrition from the Sea

Fish and shellfish are hard to beat for their nutritional and health benefits.

■ Most fish are low in total fat and calorie content. Lean, uncooked cod, pollock and halibut have only 100 calories per quarter pound. Even the more fatty varieties of fish, such as lake trout, king salmon and mackerel, have only twice that amount.

■ All fish and shellfish contain some amount of Omega-3 fatty acids, the unsaturated fats that are thought to help lower levels of cholesterol in the blood. But the fatty species of fish generally contain the highest levels of Omega-3's, more than twice those of the lean varieties. Even fish or shellfish that contain higher levels of cholesterol — shrimp and lobster, for example — still supply beneficial amounts of this wonder substance.

■ Fish and shellfish also supply niacin, riboflavin, vitamins B_6 and B_{12}, and at least a half dozen trace minerals, including calcium, magnesium and potassium. Saltwater seafood also is the richest natural source of iodine. Yet all fish, whether fresh or saltwater, are low in sodium.

❖   ❖   ❖

1. Season the salmon fillet with the black pepper, rosemary and one third of the green onion.
2. Preheat the oven to slow (325°). Cut out an 8-inch-diameter circle from parchment paper or aluminum foil. Spread the circle with 1 tablespoon of the margarine.
3. Lightly sauté the mushrooms, shallots and remaining green onion in the remaining 1 tablespoon of margarine.
4. Make a bed of the asparagus spears on the parchment circle.
5. Place the salmon fillet on top of the asparagus and top it with the mushroom mixture.
6. Squeeze the lime over all. Sprinkle with a little white wine, if you wish. Seal the pouch by double-folding the edges together. Place the pouch on a baking sheet.
7. Bake the salmon in the preheated slow oven (325°) for 12 to 15 minutes. Place the pouch on a warmed plate and serve. Slash open the pouch at the table to release the fragrant steam.

ANGEL HAIR PASTA WITH SHRIMP

LOW-CALORIE • LOW-SODIUM • LOW-FAT

Makes 6 servings.

Nutrient Value Per Serving: 244 calories, 24 g protein, 2 g fat, 31 g carbohydrate, 140 mg sodium, 140 mg cholesterol.

24	large shrimp (about 1½ pounds total)	½	cup sun-dried tomatoes, soaked in water, drained and chopped
½	pound angel hair pasta		Pesto Sauce (recipe follows)

1. Prepare a charcoal fire. Grill the shrimp just until they are cooked through and the shells turn pink.
2. Meanwhile, cook the angel hair pasta in 4 quarts of boiling water in a large pot, following the package directions. Drain the pasta.
3. Peel the shrimp and toss it with the pasta, tomatoes and Pesto Sauce.

PESTO SAUCE

LOW-CHOLESTEROL • LOW-SODIUM

Makes 6 servings.

Nutrient Value Per Serving: 102 calories, 2 g protein, 10 g fat, 2 g carbohydrate, 48 mg sodium, 2 mg cholesterol.

2	cups fresh basil	½	cup safflower oil
½	cup pine nuts		OR: olive oil
½	cup grated Parmesan cheese	4	cloves garlic

Purée the basil, pine nuts, Parmesan cheese, safflower or olive oil and the garlic in the container of an electric blender.

$\mathcal{H}$OW TO EAT WITHOUT MEAT

By combining a variety of foods, you can eat meatless but still have complete proteins and a full range of nutrients in your diet.

SPICY BEAN ENCHILADAS WITH CHUNKY SALSA

LOW-CALORIE • LOW-CHOLESTEROL • LOW-FAT

Bake at 375° for 2 to 3 minutes.
Makes 6 servings.

Nutrient Value Per Serving: 284 calories, 14 g protein, 6 g fat, 47 g carbohydrate, 602 mg sodium, 3 mg cholesterol.

Chunky Salsa:
1	**pound ripe tomatoes, cored, halved and coarsely chopped**
¼	**cup firmly packed, coarsely chopped fresh cilantro OR: parsley**
1	**tablespoon balsamic vinegar (see Tip, page 67) OR: red wine vinegar**
1	**fresh or canned, hot or mild chili pepper, seeded and finely chopped (optional)**

Bean Filling:
3	**cups canned red kidney beans, undrained (one and a half 19-ounce cans)**
1½	**teaspoons hot chili powder**
¼	**teaspoon ground cumin**
¼	**teaspoon ground coriander**
½	**pound small red-skinned potatoes**
12	**corn tortillas, 5 inches in diameter***
½	**cup shredded lowfat Cheddar cheese (2 ounces)**
½	**cup shredded lowfat OR: regular Monterey Jack cheese (2 ounces)**

1. Prepare the Chunky Salsa: Combine the tomatoes, cilantro or parsley, balsamic or red wine vinegar and, if you wish, chili pepper in a small bowl. Cover the bowl and refrigerate the salsa.
2. Prepare the Bean Filling: Combine the kidney beans with their liquid, chili powder, cumin and coriander in a medium-size, nonstick skillet. Cook over medium-high heat, stirring often, until the liquid evaporates slightly, for 2 to 3 minutes. Remove the skillet from the heat. Partially mash the kidney beans.
3. Boil the potatoes until they are tender. When they are cool enough to handle, peel them. Mash the potatoes in a small bowl until they are smooth. Stir in the kidney bean mixture. Wipe the skillet clean.
4. Preheat the oven to moderate (375°). Place a piece of wax paper on the countertop.

The Magic Combination

As you know, red meat, fish, poultry, eggs and milk all provide high-quality, complete protein. Most vegetables and grains are low in one or more of the EAAs (essential amino acids) and therefore supply incomplete protein.
■ By eating specific combinations of lower-quality protein foods at the same meal, you can obtain the equivalent of a complete protein without meat, fish, poultry, eggs or dairy products. In other words, you combine two protein sources in such a way that one makes up for the amino acids missing in the other, thus increasing the total protein value of the meal.

❖ ❖ ❖

Protein Quality Scale

Eggs	**100**
Milk	**90**
Fish	**87**
Cheese	**76**
Meat & Poultry	**73**
Nuts & Seeds From peanuts to cashews	**46-63**
Legumes From kidney to soybeans	**41-66**
Grains From corn to rice	**55-76**

Protein: The Untold Story

The protein in the food we eat is not used directly by the body. Food protein consists of chains of amino acids that act as building blocks for the body to manufacture its own protein. There are 22 amino acids that are linked together in different combinations to form proteins.

■ There are eight amino acids for adults (nine for infants) that the body cannot manufacture, and there are some that it cannot make fast enough to meet its needs. These are the essential amino acids (EAAs), and the only way to obtain them is through food. If one of the EAAs is not supplied in the needed amount, the total amount of protein that the body can synthesize will be limited.

■ The EAAs are present in most foods, but a few of them may be present in amounts that are too small to do their job properly. So the quality of food protein consumed is dependent on whether the food supplies all the essential amino acids, and also on whether the amount supplied is sufficient for the body's needs.

■ The egg is an excellent source of high-quality protein. Egg protein contains all the EAAs and supplies them in the necessary amounts; it's also easy to digest. So the egg has been designated as the "reference protein" and assigned a quality value of 100. The protein quality of all other protein sources can be measured against the egg.

5. Fill the cleaned skillet with water to a 1-inch depth. Bring the water just to simmering. Place 1 tortilla into the hot water for 30 to 60 seconds, or until the tortilla is soft. Remove the tortilla to the wax paper. Blot with paper toweling. Spread about ¼ cup of the filling down the center of the tortilla. Fold the unfilled sides inward to meet the filling in the center. Place the filled tortilla on an ovenproof platter.
6. Repeat with the remaining tortillas and filling. Sprinkle the enchiladas with the Cheddar and Monterey Jack cheeses.
7. Bake the enchiladas in the preheated moderate oven (375°) for 2 to 3 minutes, or just until the cheeses melt; the filling need not be piping hot. Spoon the salsa over the top of the enchiladas.

Note: Purchase tortillas that do not list lard among their ingredients.

WHITE BEAN TOMATO SOUP

LOW-FAT

Makes 4 servings (about 2 quarts).

Nutrient Value Per Serving: 332 calories, 20 g protein, 7 g fat, 49 g carbohydrate, 529 mg sodium, 16 mg cholesterol.

½ pound dried white kidney OR: white Northern beans Water	1¼ quarts water
	1 tablespoon tomato paste
	¾ teaspoon fennel seeds, crushed
1½ cups coarsely chopped onion	1 vegetable bouillon cube, crushed
1 medium-size white turnip (6 ounces), peeled and chopped into ½-inch pieces	½ cup chopped flat-leaf Italian parsley (about 1 large bunch)
2 cloves garlic, finely chopped	2½ ounces Swiss OR: Jarlsberg cheese, cut into julienne sticks
1 teaspoon olive oil	Additional flat-leaf Italian parsley, for garnish (optional)
1 can (16 ounces) whole tomatoes, undrained	

1. Pick over the white beans and rinse them under running water. Place the white beans and enough water to cover them in a medium-size saucepan. Cover the saucepan. Bring the water to boiling and boil the white beans gently for 2 minutes. Remove the saucepan from the heat and let it stand, covered, for 1 hour. Add more water, if necessary, to cover the white beans. Bring the water to boiling again, lower the heat and simmer, covered, for 1 to 1½ hours, or until the beans are tender.
2. Sauté the onion, turnip and garlic in the oil in a nonstick Dutch oven until the vegetables begin to brown lightly. Add the tomatoes with their liquid, breaking them up with a wooden spoon. Add the 1¼ quarts of water, the tomato paste, fennel seeds, bouillon cube and chopped parsley.
3. Bring the mixture to boiling. Lower the heat and simmer, uncovered, for 45 minutes, or until the turnip is tender. Add the white beans. Gently warm the soup until it is heated through.
4. Ladle the soup into 4 individual soup bowls. Garnish each serving with 2 julienne sticks of the Swiss or Jarlsberg cheese and, if you wish, with additional parsley.

BROCCOLI LASAGNA ROLLS

LOW-CHOLESTEROL • LOW-FAT

Bake at 375° for 30 minutes.
Makes 8 servings (3 pieces per serving).

Nutrient Value Per Serving: 382 calories, 23 g protein, 12 g fat,
45 g carbohydrate, 654 mg sodium, 38 mg cholesterol.

Tomato Sauce:
- ½ cup finely chopped sweet green pepper
- ¼ cup finely chopped shallots OR: onion
- 4 cloves garlic, finely chopped
- 1 teaspoon olive oil
- 1 can (35 ounces) whole plum tomatoes, undrained
- 2 tablespoons tomato paste

Filling:
- ⅓ cup finely chopped, peeled carrot
- ½ cup finely chopped onion
- 1 teaspoon olive oil

- 1 package (10 ounces) frozen broccoli stalks, thawed, drained and finely chopped
- 1 container (32 ounces) part-skim ricotta cheese
- ⅔ cup grated Parmesan cheese
- 2 egg whites, slightly beaten
- 1 teaspoon dried basil, crumbled
- ½ teaspoon salt
- ¼ teaspoon freshly ground white pepper

- 12 curly-edge lasagna noodles
- Nonstick vegetable cooking spray

1. Prepare the Tomato Sauce: Sauté the green pepper, the shallots or onion and the garlic in the oil in a medium-size saucepan for 3 to 4 minutes, or until the vegetables are softened. Add the tomatoes with their liquid and the tomato paste, breaking up the tomatoes with a spoon. Bring the sauce to boiling. Lower the heat and simmer, uncovered, for 45 minutes, or until the sauce has thickened.
2. Meanwhile, prepare the Filling: Sauté the carrot and the onion in the oil in a small skillet until the vegetables are softened, for 4 to 5 minutes. Transfer the vegetable mixture to a medium-size bowl.
3. Squeeze the broccoli between sheets of paper toweling until it is almost dry. Add the broccoli to the bowl with the vegetable mixture. Stir in the ricotta cheese, Parmesan cheese, egg whites, basil, salt and white pepper.
4. Preheat the oven to moderate (375°).
5. Cook the lasagna noodles, following the package directions, just until they are al dente, tender but firm to the bite. Drain the noodles.
6. Spread a generous ⅓ cup of the filling down the length of each noodle. Roll up the noodles jelly-roll style. Slice the rolls in half crosswise with a serrated knife, using a gentle back-and-forth action.
7. Spoon a thin layer of the sauce over the bottom of a 13 x 9 x 2-inch baking dish. Arrange the rolls, curly edges up, in the prepared pan. Spray a piece of aluminum foil with nonstick vegetable cooking spray. Tightly cover the pan with the foil, greased side down.
8. Bake the rolls in the preheated moderate oven (375°) for 30 minutes, or until the rolls are heated thoroughly. Meanwhile, reheat the remaining sauce. When the rolls are done, serve them immediately with the reheated sauce spooned over.

Side by Side

Cornmeal, legumes, rice, wheat and potatoes each are a source of incomplete protein. But when these foods are paired with other incomplete proteins and eaten at the same meal, the combination provides the amino acids needed to form a complete protein.

■ Because foods such as milk and eggs are complete proteins, they can be coupled with incomplete sources to provide the maximum complete protein benefits.

■ The following recipes are good examples of food combinations that provide maximum complete protein benefits.

1. Cornmeal and legumes: Spicy Bean Enchiladas with Chunky Salsa (recipe, page 180).

2. Rice and legumes: For example, a meatless chili served over hot cooked rice.

3. Wheat and legumes: Spicy Bulgur-Stuffed Green Peppers (recipe, page 185).

4. Legumes and dairy products: White Bean Tomato Soup (recipe, page 181).

5. Rice and dairy products: Spicy Rice, Peas and Corn with Tomato Raita (recipe, pages 184-185).

6. Potatoes and dairy products: Potato Carrot Puff (recipe, page 183).

7. Wheat and dairy products: Broccoli Lasagna Rolls (recipe, at left).

Fiber Facts

Fiber comes in two forms:

■ Insoluble fibers do not dissolve in water. They are found in whole grains, some breakfast cereals, bran, dried beans and peas, and most fruits and vegetables, especially those eaten with their skin. These fibers absorb water and swell up, providing bulk and facilitating digestion. Insoluble fiber also may reduce the risk of colon cancer and diverticulosis by moving potential carcinogens and fat out of the intestines quickly before they do any harm. In addition, some scientists believe that high-fiber foods decrease the absorption of calories and fat.

■ Water-soluble fibers are either pectin, found in apples, citrus fruits and some vegetables, or gums, found in oatmeal and beans. These fibers seem to help lower blood cholesterol levels.

■ While fiber provides no essential nutrients, it makes you more comfortable by providing the bulk needed to keep digestion running smoothly. Fiber also may help prevent obesity, heart disease and colon cancer.

❖   ❖   ❖

" A wise man should consider that health is the greatest of human blessings. "
—*Hippocrates*

POTATO CARROT PUFF

The perfect star for your next brunch—just add a green salad and some crusty French bread.

LOW-CALORIE • LOW-CHOLESTEROL • LOW-FAT

Bake at 450° for 25 to 30 minutes.
Makes 6 servings.

Nutrient Value Per Serving: 169 calories, 10 g protein, 4 g fat, 22 g carbohydrate, 402 mg sodium, 12 mg cholesterol.

Nonstick vegetable cooking spray	¼ teaspoon dried rosemary, crumbled
Flour, for dusting	¾ teaspoon salt
1 pound all-purpose potatoes, peeled and shredded	⅛ teaspoon freshly ground pepper
¾ pound carrots, peeled and shredded	¾ cup lowfat milk
1 teaspoon vegetable oil	3 tablespoons all-purpose flour
1 tablespoon chopped parsley	½ cup shredded Gruyère cheese (2 ounces)
	7 egg whites

1. Preheat the oven to very hot (450°). Spray the sides and bottom of an 11¾ x 7½ x 1¾-inch baking dish with nonstick vegetable cooking spray. Sprinkle with flour to coat the dish.

2. Combine the potatoes with the carrots in a large, deep, nonstick skillet. Add water to cover the vegetables. Simmer for 10 minutes, or until the vegetables are almost tender. Drain the potato-carrot mixture and blot it dry with paper toweling.

3. Sauté the potato-carrot mixture in the oil in the skillet over high heat for 4 to 5 minutes. Transfer the potato-carrot mixture to a large bowl. Stir in the parsley, rosemary, salt and pepper.

4. Combine the milk with the 3 tablespoons of flour in a small saucepan. Heat the milk mixture, stirring, over medium heat until it has thickened slightly, for about 1 minute. Add the milk mixture to the potato-carrot mixture in the bowl, along with the Gruyère cheese. Let the cheese mixture cool just until it is warm to the touch.

5. Beat the egg whites in a large bowl until soft peaks form. Stir one third of the whites into the cheese mixture. Fold in the remaining whites. Gently pour the cheese mixture into the prepared pan and smooth the top.

6. Bake the puff in the preheated very hot oven (450°) for 25 to 30 minutes, or until it is puffed and golden. Serve immediately.

SPICY RICE, PEAS AND CORN WITH TOMATO RAITA

LOW-CHOLESTEROL • LOW-FAT

Makes 4 servings.

Nutrient Value Per Serving: 447 calories, 15 g protein, 4 g fat, 88 g carbohydrate, 1,105 mg sodium, 7 mg cholesterol.

2	**cups chopped onion (2 large onions)**
3	**cloves garlic, finely chopped**
1	**teaspoon vegetable oil**
1½	**cups uncooked rice**
1½	**teaspoons ground coriander**
1½	**teaspoons ground cumin**
1	**teaspoon chili powder**
¼	**teaspoon ground turmeric**

2¼ to 3¼ **cups water**
     Tomato Raita (recipe follows)
1   **cup frozen peas, thawed and at room temperature**
1   **cup frozen kernel corn, thawed and at room temperature**
1   **medium-size carrot, peeled and shredded**
1½ to 2 **teaspoons salt**

1. Sauté the onion and the garlic in the oil in a large, nonstick saucepan for 3 minutes, or until the onion softens. Lower the heat. Stir in the rice, coriander, cumin, chili powder and turmeric, and toss to coat the rice.
2. Add 2 cups of the water. Simmer the rice, covered, for 20 minutes. Then add as much of the remaining 1¼ cups of water as necessary to cook the rice completely.
3. Meanwhile, prepare the Tomato Raita.

Fabulous Filling Fiber

If you fill up with fiber before the main course, you're less likely to overload on other, more fattening, foods.

■ Vegetables are loaded with fiber, are filling, and make a non-fattening foundation for snacks or hors d'oeuvres. Use the delicate leaves of Belgian endive to hold small portions of chick pea salad or lowfat, low-sodium cheese spreads. Stuff cherry tomatoes with salmon salad. Or broil mushroom caps filled with a mixture of shredded low-sodium Swiss cheese, capers and chopped parsley; serve warm.

■ Use fiber-rich carrot or zucchini bread to make hors d'oeuvres or finger sandwiches. Slice and serve the bread with slivers of smoked turkey.

❖ ❀ ❖

Great sources of dietary fiber include fruits and vegetables, as well as legumes such as kidney beans, navy beans, split peas and lentils.

Bulgur

Sometimes called parboiled wheat, bulgur is whole wheat that has been cooked, dried, partially debranned and cracked into coarse fragments.

■ The making of bulgur is our oldest recorded use of wheat. This ancient food originated in the Near East.

■ Bulgur is delicious used in salads or soups, and is a good alternative to rice or potatoes.

■ To rehydrate bulgur, soak it in twice its volume of boiling water, and let it stand until all the water has been absorbed or the bulgur particles are tender. Drain off any excess water.

■ Store bulgur in an airtight container in a cool place, and use it within 6 months.

❖　❖　❖

4. When the rice is tender, stir in the peas, corn, carrot and salt. Cook the rice mixture over low heat, stirring, for 2 to 3 minutes to heat the vegetables through.
5. Mound the rice mixture onto a serving platter. Serve with the Tomato Raita spooned over the rice, or on the side.

Tomato Raita:
Place 1 container (16 ounces) of plain nonfat yogurt in a serving bowl. Sprinkle it with 1 seeded and finely chopped tomato.

SPICY BULGUR-STUFFED GREEN PEPPERS

LOW-CALORIE • LOW-CHOLESTEROL • LOW-FAT

Makes 6 servings.

Nutrient Value Per Serving: 197 calories, 5 g protein, 4 g fat, 37 g carbohydrate, 399 mg sodium, 0 mg cholesterol.

1　cup bulgur	1　tablespoon lemon juice
1　cup canned chick peas	¾　teaspoon salt
1　tablespoon olive oil	3　medium-size sweet green
½　teaspoon ground coriander	peppers (about 1½
¼　teaspoon ground	pounds), halved, cored,
cinnamon	seeded and parboiled
¼　teaspoon ground ginger	

1. Prepare the bulgur following the package directions.
2. While the bulgur is soaking, place the chick peas in the container of a food processor and whirl until they are puréed. Or finely mash the chick peas by hand in a bowl.
3. Heat the oil in a small, nonstick saucepan. Add the chick pea purée, coriander, cinnamon and ginger, and sauté for 1 minute. Stir the mixture into the bulgur along with the lemon juice and the salt.
4. Mound the bulgur mixture into the green pepper halves. Serve the stuffed peppers warm or at room temperature.

VEGETABLE ENCHILADAS

LOW-CALORIE • LOW-CHOLESTEROL • LOW-FAT

Makes 12 servings.

Nutrient Value Per Serving: 177 calories, 8 g protein, 3 g fat, 34 g carbohydrate, 813 mg sodium, 0 mg cholesterol.

1	head broccoli, thinly sliced	2	zucchini, thinly sliced
1	head cauliflower, thinly sliced	½	cup soy sauce
1	sweet green pepper, thinly sliced	½	cup water
		1	teaspoon ground hot red pepper
1	sweet red pepper, thinly sliced	1	teaspoon ground cumin
1	red onion, thinly sliced	24	corn tortillas
2	yellow squash, thinly sliced		Tomatillo Sauce (recipe follows)

1. Mix together the broccoli, cauliflower, green and red peppers, onion, squash and zucchini in a bowl. Combine the soy sauce with the water, and pour the soy mixture over the vegetables. Toss in the ground hot red pepper and the cumin.
2. Steam the tortillas until they are soft. Place ¼ cup of the filling onto each tortilla, and roll up the tortilla. Top the enchiladas with the Tomatillo Sauce.

TOMATILLO SAUCE

LOW-CALORIE • LOW-CHOLESTEROL • LOW-SODIUM • LOW-FAT

Makes 12 servings.

Nutrient Value Per Serving: 17 calories, 1 g protein, trace fat, 3 g carbohydrate, 1 mg sodium, trace cholesterol.

8	tomatillos*, husked	3	cloves garlic, peeled
2	serrano peppers		Salt and freshly ground pepper, to taste (optional)
1	cup fresh cilantro, coarsely chopped		
½	red onion, cut into chunks		

1. Combine the tomatillos, serrano peppers, cilantro, onion and garlic in a medium-size saucepan. Add enough water to cover, and boil until the vegetables are tender. Remove the saucepan from the heat.
2. Pour the vegetables with their cooking liquid into the container of an electric blender. Whirl until the vegetables are puréed. If you wish, season the purée with salt and freshly ground pepper.
3. Serve the sauce warm or at room temperature.

*Note: Tomatillos are available in the produce section of some supermarkets and in Mexican or specialty food stores.

Nutritious Nibbles

Even the most devoted snacker doesn't confuse snacking with healthy eating. If you took a poll and asked people to name their favorite snacks, the list probably would include ice cream, candy, cookies, doughnuts, cheese and crackers, potato chips, pretzels, nuts and pizza. These typical snacks certainly are convenient and easy to eat, but they also are high in calories, fat, sodium, or all three.

■ Chances are you grew up thinking snacking was a bad habit. Basically, there's nothing wrong with snacking; the fault lies only in the choice of snack foods. Since snacking is here to stay, the solution is to select foods that are tasty and loaded with nutrients. Snacks of wholesome foods with minimal processing can contribute protein, vitamins, minerals and fiber to your diet.

■ Try to avoid soft drinks, chips, candy and the like, which provide little but excess calories to your diet. Avoid fried snacks, which add extra fat to the calories. Munch on fresh fruit and vegetables instead of goodies with a high sugar content.

■ When you have a "snack attack," try one of the guilt-free, nutritious nibbles from the list on page 187.

❖ ❖ ❖

Guilt-Free Snack Attacks

Under 25 Calories:
- 1 bell pepper, cut into strips
- ½ cup broccoli flowerets
- 3 stalks celery
- 1 small cucumber
- 1 medium-size tomato
- ¼ cup fresh blueberries
- 5 large green olives
- 1 large kosher pickle

Under 50 Calories:
- 1 large raw carrot
- 1 cup tomato juice
- 1 ounce turkey (no skin)
- 2 rye crackers
- 10 grapes
- ½ medium-size grapefruit
- 1 cup fresh strawberries
- ½ cup unsweetened applesauce
- 1 cup air-popped popcorn
- ½ medium-size banana
- 1 cup cauliflower flowerets
- 10 cherries
- 1 cup watermelon
- 1 large tangerine

Under 75 Calories:
- 5 roasted chestnuts
- 1 medium-size apple
- 1 ounce part-skim mozzarella
- ½ cup plain nonfat yogurt
- ⅓ cup ice milk
- 1 ounce lean ham
- ½ baked sweet potato
- 2 rice cakes
- 3 small, fresh apricots

Under 100 Calories:
- 1 frozen fruit bar
- ⅓ cup sherbet
- 2 fig newtons
- 1 tablespoon peanut butter
- 3½ ounces wine
- 1 frozen waffle

SPINACH WITH FETA

We love spinach in any form, but we particularly like it prepared with flavorful feta cheese.

LOW-CALORIE • LOW-CHOLESTEROL • LOW-FAT

Makes 4 servings.

Nutrient Value Per Serving: 45 calories, 4 g protein, 1 g fat, 7 g carbohydrate, 157 mg sodium, 2 mg cholesterol.

3	tablespoons chicken broth OR: water	1½	pounds fresh spinach, cleaned and trimmed
¾	cup thinly sliced red onion	¼	teaspoon freshly ground black pepper
¼	teaspoon dried thyme, crumbled	1	tablespoon crumbled feta cheese

1. Heat the broth or water in a large skillet over medium heat. Add the onion and the thyme. Cook until the onion is soft, for about 6 minutes, adding water, if necessary, to prevent sticking.
2. Add the spinach, with the rinse water still clinging to the leaves, and the black pepper. Increase the heat to high and cook, stirring, just until the spinach is wilted.
3. Add the feta cheese to the spinach mixture and cook, stirring, until heated through, for about 1 minute.

TANGY RADISH SALAD

LOW-CALORIE • LOW-CHOLESTEROL • LOW-FAT

Makes 4 servings.

Nutrient Value Per Serving: 23 calories, 1 g protein, 0 g fat, 5 g carbohydrate, 166 mg sodium, 0 mg cholesterol.

2	bunches radishes, shredded	2	tablespoons rice-wine vinegar
1	cucumber, seeded and shredded	1	tablespoon reduced-sodium soy sauce
⅓	cup shredded carrot	½	teaspoon lime juice

Squeeze the radishes and the cucumber dry in several changes of paper toweling. Combine the radishes and the cucumber with the carrot, vinegar, soy sauce and lime juice in a large serving bowl, and toss to mix the ingredients well.

Microwave Magic

6

If you have a microwave oven and use it regularly, you probably ask yourself, "How did I ever do without it?" If you don't have one yet, you're missing out on some spectacular modern-day magic. This chapter was designed as a microwave mini-cookbook to show you how versatile this appliance can be.

We begin with soups and snacks. Pita Pizzas (recipe, page 190) are so simple, even your kids can whip them up in no time at all. Eggplant cooks particularly well in the microwave, so for the more sophisticated snacker, our Eggplant Marinara (recipe, page 192) is a must to try.

Now, on to the soups! Split Pea Soup with Ham (recipe, page 195) is a hearty way to take the edge off your appetite. And our Vegetable Soup with Meatballs (recipe, page 196) is irresistible to kids and adults alike.

For the main course, you'll be amazed at the variety of dishes you can make in your microwave. Shrimp and Vegetables with Chili Beurre Blanc Sauce (recipe, page 198) is light, delicious and fast. Cornish Game Hens with Currant Couscous (recipe, page 202) is a feast to remember. And main courses such as savory Flank Steak Rolls with Herbs and Veal (recipe, page 204), or Beef Tostada Pie Con Queso (recipe, page 207) are positively soul-satisfying.

A great meal deserves a great side dish, so we offer a selection that includes creamy Scalloped Potatoes with Leeks (recipe, page 212), a Tian of Winter Vegetables (recipe, page 214) and Apple-Stuffed Acorn Squash (recipe, page 219). There's even a handy chart on page 218 to help you cook almost any vegetable in the microwave to perfection—whether you microwave the main dish or not.

We also provide you with lots of tips to help you maximize your microwave oven know-how. And don't forget to check out our section in Chapter 7 on microwave desserts. Once you've cooked your way through this chapter, you'll be hooked!

Tiny meatballs, browned to perfection in the microwave oven, add a hearty touch to homemade beef broth for Vegetable Soup with Meatballs (recipe, page 196).

SOUPS & SNACKS

You still may be discovering just how versatile your microwave can be. This chapter should further your exploration. There's no faster way to whip up "a little something" when you have a snack attack. And soups go together like magic!

PITA PIZZAS

Use a browning tray in this recipe so the pita bases remain crisp.

LOW-FAT • MICROWAVE

Makes 6 servings.

Nutrient Value Per Serving: 261 calories, 9 g protein, 7 g fat, 41 g carbohydrate, 903 mg sodium, 11 mg cholesterol.

6 **individual pita breads**	⅓ **cup chopped olives**
1 **tablespoon oil**	1 **sweet red pepper, cut**
1¼ **cups thick tomato sauce**	**into thin strips**
¾ **cup shredded mozzarella cheese**	**Crushed red pepper flakes**

Microwavable Snacks Kids Can Make

- Hot cocoa
- Prepared soups
- Scrambled eggs
- Nachos
- S'Mores
- English muffin pizzas
- Microwave brownie mix
- Hot dog in a bun
- Baked apples
- Quesadillas
- Instant hot cereal
- Hot cheese sandwich

❖ ❖ ❖

> *" 'T is not the meat, but 'tis the appetite Makes eating a delight. "*
> —*Sir John Suckling*

Pita Pizzas are perfect crowd pleasers, whether your assembled guests are kids or grown-ups.

Microwave Pizzeria

Traditional pizzas have a yeast dough, which doesn't work well in the microwave. Use pita breads or rice cakes, which don't get as soggy. Try some of the following toppings:

- California Dreamin': Brush pita bread with olive oil and top with sliced marinated artichokes and mushrooms, thyme and oregano. Sprinkle with grated Fontina cheese.
- Little Italy: Top with tomato sauce, oregano, shredded mozzarella cheese, pepperoni and hot red pepper flakes.
- Pizza Nizza: Top with a mixture of onion, tomatoes, tiny black olives, garlic and chopped fresh herbs.
- Pizza Giardiniera: Top with finely chopped marinated vegetables and sliced cheese.
- Pizza Spagnola: Top with roasted garlic and chopped chorizo sausage.
- Tex-Mex Pizza: Top with picante sauce and Cheddar cheese. Serve with sour cream and guacamole.
- Pizza Florentine: Top with ricotta cheese blended with chopped spinach and parsley.
- Triple Pepper: Top with tomato sauce, sweet pepper slices, diced pimiento and red pepper flakes.
- Pizza via Buffalo: Top with shredded Buffalo chicken wing meat and liquid red pepper seasoning. Serve with blue cheese dressing on the side.
- The Rathbone: Top with fresh basil, sliced tomatoes, fruity olive oil and shredded mozzarella cheese.

1. Preheat the microwave browning tray, following the manufacturer's directions.
2. Lightly brush the bottoms of the pita breads with the oil.
3. Spread the tops of the breads with the tomato sauce, mozzarella cheese, olives, red pepper strips and red pepper flakes, keeping the ingredients about ½ inch from the edges of the breads to avoid running over.
4. Microwave at half power for 1 to 2 minutes. Serve the pizzas whole, in halves or in quarters.

PIZZA DIP

The fabulous flavors of pizza in one melting dip. Serve it with raw vegetables, pita wedges or chunks of crusty Italian bread.

MICROWAVE

Makes 24 servings.

Nutrient Value Per Serving: 122 calories, 8 g protein, 9 g fat, 2 g carbohydrate, 235 mg sodium, 29 mg cholesterol.

1	tablespoon olive oil	1	package (8 ounces) cream cheese, cut into 1-inch cubes
1	medium-size onion, chopped		
2	cloves garlic, finely chopped	¼	cup chopped green olives OR: black olives OR: a combination
1	can (14 ounces) plum tomatoes, drained and chopped	2	green onions, chopped
		2	tablespoons chopped fresh parsley
¾	pound lowfat mozzarella cheese, cut into ½-inch cubes	1	teaspoon dried oregano, crumbled
¾	pound lowfat Muenster cheese, cut into ½-inch cubes	1	teaspoon hot red pepper flakes OR: to taste

1. Combine the oil, onion and garlic in a microwave-safe 1½-quart saucepan with a handle, or in a microwave-safe casserole dish. Microwave at full power for 3 minutes.
2. Add the tomatoes. Microwave at full power, stirring twice, for 7 minutes, or until the tomatoes have cooked down and evaporated a bit.
3. Add the mozzarella, Muenster and cream cheeses, the olives, green onion, parsley, oregano and hot red pepper flakes. Microwave at half power, stirring twice, for 5 minutes, or just until the cheeses melt.

Note: *To reheat the dip, microwave at one quarter power for 3 to 5 minutes, stirring after 1 minute.*

EGGPLANT MARINARA

Unlike many eggplant dishes, this one requires no oil. We like it best served pizza-style on a slice of toasted garlic bread.

MICROWAVE

Makes 6 servings.

Nutrient Value Per Serving: 165 calories, 11 g protein, 10 g fat, 11 g carbohydrate, 189 mg sodium, 22 mg cholesterol.

1	medium-size to large eggplant	½	pound lowfat mozzarella cheese, cut into 6 slices
1½	cups Microwave Tomato Sauce (recipe follows)		Fresh basil sprigs, for garnish

1. Peel the eggplant and cut it into six ¾-inch-thick rounds. Place the rounds in a single layer in a microwave-safe 12 x 8 x 2-inch baking dish. Cover the dish tightly.
2. Microwave at full power for 2 minutes.
3. Uncover the dish and pour off any liquid. Spread the Microwave Tomato Sauce over the eggplant, and top with the mozzarella cheese.
4. Microwave, uncovered, at half power for 1 minute, or until the mozzarella cheese just begins to melt. Garnish with the basil sprigs.

MICROWAVE TOMATO SAUCE

Make extra batches of this sauce in the summer, when fresh tomatoes are plentiful, and freeze the extra to use during the winter. You can peel and seed the tomatoes, if you wish.

LOW-CHOLESTEROL • LOW-SODIUM • MICROWAVE

Makes 8 servings (1 quart).

Nutrient Value Per Serving: 52 calories, 2 g protein, 2 g fat, 8 g carbohydrate, 14 mg sodium, 0 mg cholesterol.

1	tablespoon olive oil	¼	cup chopped fresh parsley
1	large onion, chopped	2	teaspoons freshly squeezed lemon juice
2	cloves garlic, finely chopped		Salt and freshly ground black pepper, to taste
2½	pounds ripe tomatoes		
½	small carrot, peeled and sliced		

1. Place the oil, onion and garlic in a microwave-safe 9-inch dish. Microwave at full power, stirring once, for 2 minutes.
2. Core and cut the tomatoes into eighths. Toss the tomatoes with the onion mixture. Add the carrot, parsley and lemon juice. Cover the dish with microwave-safe plastic wrap.
3. Microwave at full power for 15 minutes, rotating the dish every 3 to 4 minutes.
4. Remove the plastic wrap. Transfer the tomato mixture to the container of a food processor. Whirl the mixture until it is puréed. Return the purée to the dish. Season with the salt and black pepper.
5. Microwave, uncovered, at full power for 15 minutes more, or until the sauce thickens, stirring the sauce and rotating the dish every few minutes.

What's Your Wattage?

The microwave oven has given a new meaning to the term "fast foods." But its speed and efficiency vary according to the quantity and kind of food being cooked, and the oven's output wattage. The wattage may be printed in the manufacturer's manual or on the oven's name plate, located on the side, the back or inside the oven door. Or try the following test:
■ Combine 1 cup of water with ice in a 2-cup measure. Stir for 2 minutes, or until the ice stops melting and the water is very cold. Remove the ice. Pour 1 cup of the cold water into a microwave-safe glass measure. Microwave, uncovered, at full power until the water begins to boil. If the water boils in less than 3½ minutes, your microwave is producing 600 to 700 watts of energy on full power. If it takes 3½ to 4½ minutes to boil, the wattage output is 500 to 600 watts. If the heating time is more than 4½ minutes, the wattage output is less than 500 watts. High-power microwave ovens, which range from 600 to 700 watts, cook faster than lower-wattage models, and most microwave recipes are developed for these more powerful ovens. If your oven's output is less than this, you'll need to experiment with small increments of additional cooking time, or seek out a microwave cookbook with low-wattage recipes or adaptations.

The Mysterious Magic Box

Children are fascinated by a microwave oven; it's a slice of *Star Trek* right in their very own kitchens! But, as with any appliance, they need clear guidelines to insure proper and safe use of the microwave.

■ Supervise children carefully when they first are learning how to use the microwave. Then, based on their age and ability, let them try certain projects on their own, but be sure to be on hand for any questions or emergencies.

■ Teach them how to set the time and power levels, and to work the different oven features. Stress the fact that they never should turn on an empty oven.

■ Get kids in the habit of setting the oven to the minimum amount of time and checking for doneness. Explain about standing time.

■ Explain that, although a microwave oven doesn't get hot, what's inside it does. Demonstrate how to use a potholder, and make clear that food should be allowed to cool slightly before being tasted.

■ Show children the proper way to remove a lid or plastic wrapping after cooking: lifting the cover away from their hands and faces to avoid burns from the hot steam.

■ Make it a rule that your children must always ask permission to use the microwave.

■ Another rule: Cleaning up after cooking is mandatory.

ACORN SQUASH PURÉE

This mellow squash purée makes a good accompaniment for most meats and poultry. It also can be transformed into a vibrantly spiced soup.

MICROWAVE

Makes 4 servings purée or soup.

Nutrient Value Per Serving: 111 calories, 1 g protein, 6 g fat, 14 g carbohydrate, 281 mg sodium, 17 mg cholesterol.

1	acorn squash (1½ pounds)	¼	cup parsley sprigs
1	tablespoon chopped onion	1	tablespoon half-and-half
2	tablespoons unsalted butter	½	teaspoon salt
		⅛	teaspoon pepper

1. Prick the squash several times with a fork. Place the squash in the microwave. Microwave, uncovered, at full power for 7 minutes, turning over the squash once during the cooking. Halve and seed the squash.
2. Place the squash halves, cut side down, on a microwave-safe dinner plate. Microwave, uncovered, at full power for 3 minutes, or until the squash is soft. Let the squash stand for a few minutes.
3. Meanwhile, place the onion and the butter in a microwave-safe 4-cup measure. Microwave, uncovered, at full power for 3 minutes.
4. Scoop out the flesh from the squash into the container of a food processor. Add the onion mixture, parsley sprigs, half-and-half, salt and pepper. Whirl the mixture until it is puréed. Transfer the purée to a serving dish and serve it immediately.

Acorn Squash Soup:

Place the squash purée in a microwave-safe 8-cup measure. Stir in 1 can (13¾ ounces) of chicken broth, 1 teaspoon of chili powder, ½ teaspoon of ground cumin, ⅛ teaspoon of oregano, ⅛ teaspoon of ground ginger and 3 to 5 drops of liquid red-pepper seasoning. Cover the measure with microwave-safe plastic wrap, slightly vented in one place. Microwave at full power for 8 to 10 minutes, or until the soup comes to a full boil. Stir in ¼ cup of half-and-half. Serve the soup immediately. *Nutrient Value Per Serving:* 148 calories, 2 g protein, 9 g fat, 15 g carbohydrate, 864 mg sodium, 22 mg cholesterol.

MULLED CRANBERRY JUICE

For a spiked version of this drink, add 1 ounce of light rum or vodka just before serving.

LOW-CHOLESTEROL • LOW-SODIUM • LOW-FAT • MICROWAVE

Makes 1 serving.

Nutrient Value Per Serving: 108 calories, trace protein, trace fat, 28 g carbohydrate, 5 mg sodium, 0 mg cholesterol.

⅔	cup cranberry juice cocktail	1	orange wedge
1	cinnamon stick	1	whole clove

1. Combine all the ingredients in a microwave-safe large mug.
2. Microwave at full power for 2 minutes, or until the juice boils.

FRUIT AND NUT BREAD

This bread is a great choice for microwave baking because of its high moisture content. Toasting the walnuts really brings out their sweet goodness.

LOW-CHOLESTEROL • LOW-SODIUM • LOW-FAT • MICROWAVE

Makes 2 loaves (16 servings).

Nutrient Value Per Serving: 126 calories, 2 g protein, 3 g fat, 24 g carbohydrate, 38 mg sodium, trace cholesterol.

½	cup chopped walnuts	1	cup all-purpose flour
	Nonstick vegetable cooking spray	¾	cup yellow cornmeal
1	jar (16 ounces) cooked prunes in syrup	5	tablespoons sugar*
		½	teaspoon baking powder
	Grated zest of ½ lemon (yellow part of rind only)	¼	teaspoon baking soda
		⅛	teaspoon grated nutmeg
2	tablespoons lemon juice	⅔	cup buttermilk

1. Place the walnuts in a single layer on a paper plate or microwave-safe paper toweling. Microwave at full power, stirring once, for 2 minutes, or until the walnuts are toasted. Cool the walnuts completely.

2. Meanwhile, cut 4 circles of wax paper to fit the bottom of a 2-cup glass measure. Spray the measure with nonstick vegetable cooking spray. Place 2 of the wax paper circles in the cup and spray the bottom again.

3. Drain the prunes, reserving ½ cup of the syrup. Pit and chop the prunes. Combine the prunes and their reserved syrup with the lemon zest, lemon juice, walnuts, flour, cornmeal, sugar, baking powder, baking soda, nutmeg and buttermilk in a large bowl until the ingredients are well blended. Spoon half the batter into the prepared cup. Cover the top of the cup with microwave-safe plastic wrap, slightly vented in one place.

4. Microwave at half power, rotating the dish halfway through the cooking time, for 6 to 8 minutes, or until a thin skewer inserted in the center of the

Microwave Cookware

There's plenty of equipment designed specifically for microwave oven use, but you may be surprised at how well-stocked your kitchen already is with microwave-safe cookware, from coffee mugs to casserole dishes.

■ The first rule: Do not use metal in the microwave oven because metal reflects the microwaves. Not only will this prevent the microwaves from reaching the food they're supposed to be cooking, it can cause sparks ("arcing") that can damage the oven. Even dinnerware trimmed with a little gold or silver leaf can cause sparks.

■ Other types of cookware can be used as long as they do not become hot in the microwave. Good choices include heat-resistant glass or ceramic baking dishes, and nonmetallic mixing bowls, measuring cups, casserole dishes and custard cups. Most ordinary dinner plates will work well.

■ To test a dish to see if it is microwave-safe, put it in the microwave along with a water-filled glass measuring cup. Heat the water at full power for 1 minute. If the water in the cup becomes warm but the dish stays cool, the dish is microwave-safe. If the dish becomes warm, don't use it in the microwave.

❖   ❖   ❖

Steamed puddings and breads, such as our Fruit and Nut Bread, adapt superbly to microwaving.

Super Soup

Soup is like a parent's love — very forgiving. Unlike pastry, whose recipes must be followed to the letter, soup allows the cook tremendous flexibility. The microwave oven makes it easy to whip up good, homemade soup at a moment's notice.

■ In general, you should microwave soup in a container that can hold twice the volume of the soup. This will prevent the soup from boiling over. Microwave-safe large glass bowls are ideal for this. To hold in moisture and concentrate the flavors, cover the bowl with microwave-safe plastic wrap or a tight-fitting lid.

■ Feel free to substitute ingredients. Chicken broth will lighten the flavor in a soup that calls for beef broth, parsnips subtly vary the flavor of a soup that uses carrots, cooked rice or barley gives a new texture to a noodle soup. When you substitute ingredients that are very different from one another — if you use spinach instead of broccoli, for example — remember to alter the cooking time accordingly. If further cooking is needed, add time in small increments to avoid overcooking.

❖   ❖   ❖

bread comes out clean. Uncover the cup and let it stand directly on a heatproof surface for 10 minutes. Carefully loosen the bread from the cup with a knife, unmold the bread and cool it.
5. Repeat with the remaining batter.

Note: If the amount of sugar is increased from 5 tablespoons to ½ cup, the bread can double as a homey dessert pudding that's especially delicious topped with lemon curd or custard sauce.

SPLIT-PEA SOUP WITH HAM

A heart-warming soup for a cold winter's day. Just add a loaf of crusty bread and a green salad, and you have a satisfying meal.

LOW-CHOLESTEROL • LOW-FAT • MICROWAVE

Makes 4 servings.

Nutrient Value Per Serving: 355 calories, 25 g protein, 9 g fat, 45 g carbohydrate, 1,659 mg sodium, 29 mg cholesterol.

1 cup split peas	1 teaspoon dried thyme, crumbled
4 cups chicken broth	Freshly ground pepper
1 cup water	¼ cup chopped fresh parsley
1 carrot, peeled, trimmed and chopped	1 cup chopped cooked ham
1 medium-size onion, chopped	1 cup snow peas
1 large stalk celery, chopped	Microwave Croutons (recipe follows)

1. Rinse the split peas in a sieve, drain them and place them in a microwave-safe 3-quart glass bowl. Add 2 cups of the broth, the water, carrot, onion, celery, thyme, pepper and parsley. Cover the bowl tightly with microwave-safe plastic wrap.
2. Microwave at full power for 10 minutes. Carefully uncover the bowl. Stir the soup and cover the bowl again.
3. Microwave at half power for 30 minutes. Uncover, stir the soup and cover again. Microwave at half power for 15 minutes more, or until the split peas are tender.
4. Carefully uncover the bowl. Stir the soup to break up the split peas.
5. Stir in the remaining 2 cups of broth, along with half the ham and snow peas. Serve the soup. Top individual servings of the soup with the remaining ham and snow peas, and the Microwave Croutons.

Microwave Croutons:

Microwave 1 tablespoon of butter in a microwave-safe cup at full power for 30 seconds, or until the butter has melted. Trim the crusts from 2 slices of bread, and brush each slice on both sides with the melted butter. Cut the bread into cubes and place the cubes in one layer on a microwave-safe plate. Microwave at full power, stirring once or twice, for 3 to 4 minutes, or until the cubes are dry and golden.

CHICKEN NOODLE SOUP

MICROWAVE

Makes 4 servings.

Nutrient Value Per Serving: 392 calories, 32 g protein, 10 g fat, 43 g carbohydrate, 571 mg sodium, 76 mg cholesterol.

2	stalks celery, trimmed and sliced diagonally
3	small carrots, peeled and sliced diagonally
3	green onions, white and green parts, trimmed and sliced diagonally
½	teaspoon dried tarragon, crumbled
½	teaspoon salt

6	cups chicken broth
¼	pound rotelle pasta OR: other pasta, cooked according to package directions
2	cups cubed cooked chicken
1	cup frozen peas
¼	to ½ teaspoon freshly ground white pepper OR: to taste

1. Combine the celery, carrot, green onion, tarragon, salt and broth in a microwave-safe 3-quart glass bowl. Cover the bowl with microwave-safe plastic wrap or with a tight-fitting lid.

2. Microwave at full power for 12 minutes, or until the carrot slices are fork-tender.

3. Add the pasta, chicken, peas and white pepper to the bowl. Ladle the soup into 4 individual soup bowls, and serve the soup hot.

VEGETABLE SOUP WITH MEATBALLS

LOW-CALORIE • LOW-SODIUM • MICROWAVE

Makes 6 servings.

Nutrient Value Per Serving: 314 calories, 20 g protein, 15 g fat, 24 g carbohydrate, 129 mg sodium, 98 mg cholesterol.

1	pound ground round
1	egg
2	tablespoons dry red wine
½	cup soft bread crumbs
2	tablespoons finely chopped onion
2	tablespoons chopped fresh parsley
1	small clove garlic, finely chopped
	Salt and freshly ground pepper, to taste
6	cups beef broth
2	small carrots, thinly sliced
1	zucchini, cut into tiny cubes

6	fresh OR: canned plum tomatoes, chopped
2	medium-size leeks (white part only), trimmed, rinsed and chopped
1	clove garlic, chopped
4	leaves escarole, rinsed and cut crosswise into thin shreds
⅓	cup orzo OR: other tiny pasta
1	cup frozen green peas
	Grated fresh Parmesan cheese, for garnish
	Additional chopped fresh parsley, for garnish

Microwave Meatballs

Some tips for a favorite accompaniment to spaghetti and other dishes.

▪ Shape 1-inch meatballs for hors d'oeuvres and soups, 2-inch meatballs for main dishes. When cooking with a microwave, it's especially important to shape meatballs uniformly, for even cooking.

▪ To reduce the fat content, use ground beef round, turkey or veal; substitute egg white for the whole egg.

▪ Add chopped cooked vegetables or cooked grains to extend the meat and add flavor.

▪ For an extra treat, shape the meatball mixture around a tiny cube of cheese or an olive.

▪ Handle the meatballs as little as possible when shaping them, to avoid toughening them.

▪ Use a browning tray to help seal in the juices, or brown the meatballs on top of the stove, then continue cooking them in the microwave.

Soups in Seconds

Try these toss-together soups.

■ Cream of Tomato Soup: Place one 16-ounce can of crushed tomatoes in a microwave-safe 1½-quart casserole dish. Cover the dish. Microwave at full power for 5 minutes, or until the tomatoes boil. Carefully uncover the dish. Stir in ½ cup of sour cream or plain yogurt. Add chopped fresh dill, parsley or basil, if you have them on hand. Makes 3 servings.

■ Port and Lemon Squash Soup: Heat a 10-ounce package of frozen squash purée in a microwave-safe 2-quart bowl, following the package directions. Stir in 1 cup of heavy cream, 2 tablespoons of port wine, 1 tablespoon of lemon juice and a large pinch of nutmeg. Cover the bowl. Microwave at full power for 5 minutes, or until the soup boils. Makes 3 to 4 servings.

❖   ❖   ❖

Saucepan Substitutes

You can substitute microwave-safe bowls or casserole dishes to prepare foods that would conventionally cook in a saucepan on top of the stove.

The advantage of using a microwave-safe saucepan is that most of them have easy-grip handles and tight-fitting lids, which makes mid-cooking stirring and adding of ingredients much easier.

❖   ❖   ❖

1. Combine the ground round, egg, wine, bread crumbs, onion, the 2 tablespoons of parsley, the small clove of garlic and the salt and pepper in a bowl. Shape the mixture into 1-inch meatballs. Place half the meatballs in a ring around the edge of a microwave-safe 10-inch cake dish or 2-quart rectangular dish. Cover the dish with wax paper.
2. Microwave at full power for 5 to 7 minutes, turning over the meatballs and rotating the dish after 3 minutes. Drain off the excess fat. Remove the meatballs to a dish. Repeat with the remaining meatballs. Reserve any cooking juices from the meatballs.
3. Combine 4 cups of the broth with the reserved meatball stock, the carrots, zucchini, tomatoes, leeks and garlic in a microwave-safe 3-quart glass bowl. Cover the bowl tightly with microwave-safe plastic wrap.
4. Microwave at full power, rotating the bowl once, for 12 minutes, or until the vegetables are almost tender.
5. Uncover the bowl and stir in the meatballs, escarole, orzo or other pasta, green peas and remaining 2 cups of broth. Cover the bowl again.
6. Microwave at full power for 2 minutes more, or until the pasta is cooked. Ladle the soup into 6 individual soup bowls. Garnish the individual servings with the Parmesan cheese and the additional parsley.

CHILLED DILLED BEET SOUP

A cool, colorful soup to start off a meal. You can reduce the amount of sodium by using defatted homemade chicken broth.

LOW-CALORIE • LOW-CHOLESTEROL • LOW-FAT • MICROWAVE

Makes 8 servings.

Nutrient Value Per Serving: 80 calories, 5 g protein, 2 g fat, 12 g carbohydrate, 490 mg sodium, 4 mg cholesterol.

1¾ **pounds beets (about 8 medium-size beets), scrubbed**	⅛ **teaspoon freshly ground pepper**
3 **cups chicken broth**	**Additional plain nonfat yogurt OR: dairy sour cream, for garnish (optional)**
1¼ **cups buttermilk**	
1¼ **cups plain nonfat yogurt**	
1 **tablespoon chopped fresh dill**	**Dill sprigs, for garnish (optional)**
1 **tablespoon lemon juice**	

1. Trim the greens from the beets to about 1 inch. Scrub the beets well and place them in a microwave-safe 1½-quart casserole dish. Pour in ½ cup of water, and cover the casserole dish. Microwave at full power for 18 to 23 minutes, or until the beets are tender; if the beets vary in size, check periodically for the tenderness of the smaller ones. Let the beets cool slightly. Trim the ends and slip off the skins.
2. Coarsely chop the beets and place them in the container of an electric blender or food processor. Add 2 cups of the broth. Whirl until the mixture is a smooth purée.
3. Pour the purée into a large bowl. Whisk in the remaining 1 cup of broth, the buttermilk, the 1¼ cups of yogurt, the 1 tablespoon of dill, the lemon juice and pepper until the ingredients are well blended. Cover the bowl and chill the soup for several hours, or overnight.
4. To serve, whisk the soup a few times until it is blended and smooth. Pour the soup into 8 chilled individual soup bowls. If you wish, garnish each serving with a dollop of plain yogurt or sour cream, and a fresh dill sprig.

THE MAIN COURSE

The advent of the TV dinner in the 1950's ushered in a new era of "fast food" — though hardly a golden age of dining. The microwave oven changed that by making food fast and fantastic.

SHRIMP AND VEGETABLES WITH CHILI BEURRE BLANC SAUCE

LOW-CALORIE • LOW-FAT • MICROWAVE

Makes 2 servings.

Nutrient Value Per Serving: 214 calories, 29 g protein, 3 g fat, 19 g carbohydrate, 239 mg sodium, 186 mg cholesterol.

10	**large shrimp (about ⅔ pound), peeled and deveined, with tails left on if desired**
2	**carrots, trimmed, peeled and cut into thin julienne sticks**
¼	**pound snow peas, trimmed**
1	**large leek, trimmed, halved, well rinsed and cut into julienne sticks**
1	**cup shredded fresh spinach leaves**
	Chili Beurre Blanc Sauce (recipe follows)

1. Arrange the shrimp around the edge of a microwave-safe large plate, tails toward the center. Intersperse the shrimp with piles of the carrot sticks. Place a circle of the snow peas within the circle of carrot and shrimp. Scatter the leek, then the spinach, over the top. Cover the plate with microwave-safe plastic wrap.
2. Prepare the Chili Beurre Blanc Sauce.
3. Microwave the shrimp and vegetables at full power for 2 minutes and 30 seconds, or until the shrimp are opaque and pink; do not overcook.
4. Toss the shrimp and vegetables with the sauce.

CHILI BEURRE BLANC SAUCE

LOW-SODIUM • MICROWAVE

Makes about ½ cup.

Nutrient Value Per Tablespoon: 55 calories, trace protein, 6 g fat, 1 g carbohydrate, 2 mg sodium, 16 mg cholesterol.

1	**large dried ancho chili pepper**
½	**cup dry white wine**
¼	**cup white wine vinegar**
¼	**cup chopped onion**
¼	**teaspoon ground cumin**
¼	**cup (½ stick) unsalted butter**
1	**tablespoon chopped fresh parsley**

Seafood: A Microwave Success Story

■ Shellfish: Arrange clams, mussels or shrimp in a ring in a shallow, round dish. Cover and microwave at full power. Cook clams and mussels just until their shells open. Shrimp are done as soon as the flesh turns opaque; if you're preparing them unpeeled, cook them until the shells turn bright pink. Scallops do best arranged in a ring in a shallow dish, covered, and microwaved at half power.
■ Fish usually microwaves best tightly wrapped in plastic or parchment, or in a covered dish to help retain its moistness. To cook several fish fillets, arrange them spoke-style, with the thicker ends out. If cooking a single fillet, double over the thin end so the fish cooks evenly. Thin fillets, because of their greater surface area, cook more quickly than an equal weight of thicker fillets.
■ Fish steaks usually take slightly longer to cook than fillets; arrange them with the thinnest portions toward the center of the plate. If you don't have a carousel, rotate the dish once or twice during cooking. Start with the minimum recommended cooking time, test for doneness (fish should be barely opaque and flake easily with a fork) and add cooking time in half-minute increments.

Catch the Microwave

Microwaves reflect off the sides, top and bottom of the oven cavity, penetrating the cookware and causing the water molecules in food to vibrate rapidly (about 450 million times per second), which results in friction. The friction, in turn, creates heat and it is this internal heat that cooks the food.

❖ ❖ ❖

1. Place the chili pepper, wine, vinegar and onion in a microwave-safe 2-cup measure, and cover the measure with microwave-safe plastic wrap.
2. Microwave at full power for 5 minutes, or until the chili pepper is softened. Remove the chili pepper from the measure, and let the chili pepper cool.
3. Keep the wine mixture uncovered. Continue microwaving at full power until the wine mixture is reduced to an almost syrupy consistency, for about 5 to 7 minutes more. Add any liquid that has accumulated from the cooling chili pepper to the reduced wine mixture.
4. Meanwhile, seed and sliver the chili pepper.
5. Add the cumin to the reduced wine mixture. Microwave at full power for 1 minute, stirring once. Stir in the butter, half at a time. Stir in the chili pepper slivers and the parsley.

Shrimp and Vegetables with Chili Beurre Blanc Sauce cooks right on the serving plate.

MARINATED COD WITH SHIITAKE MUSHROOMS

Lime juice, teriyaki sauce and fresh gingerroot lend their distinctive flavors to fresh cod. We also like to use this marinade with chicken.

LOW-CALORIE • LOW-CHOLESTEROL • LOW-FAT • MICROWAVE

Makes 4 servings.

Nutrient Value Per Serving: 147 calories, 22 g protein, 1 g fat, 12 g carbohydrate, 551 mg sodium, 49 mg cholesterol.

3 dried shiitake mushrooms* (about ¼ ounce)	2 teaspoons honey
⅓ cup water	1 tablespoon cornstarch
1 pound fresh cod fillet	¼ teaspoon salt
1 strip (3 x ½ inch) lime zest (green part of rind only)	1 small sweet red pepper, cut lengthwise into thin strips
3 slices peeled fresh gingerroot (¼ inch thick)	4 cups Chinese (Napa) cabbage, sliced thinly
2 cloves garlic	2 green onions, sliced thinly on the diagonal
2 tablespoons lime juice	Cooked rice (optional)
2 tablespoons teriyaki sauce	

1. Combine the mushrooms with the water in a microwave-safe 2-cup measure. Microwave at full power for 1 minute and 20 seconds. Let the mushrooms stand until they are cool enough to handle. Cut off the tough stems of the mushrooms and discard them. Slice the mushrooms into slivers. Strain the mushroom cooking liquid through a double thickness of dampened cheesecloth or paper toweling. Set aside the cooking liquid.

2. Remove any fine bones from the cod fillet. Slice the cod on the bias into ¾-inch-thick slices. Place the cod in a microwave-safe bowl.

3. Combine 2 tablespoons of the mushroom cooking liquid with the lime zest, ginger, garlic, lime juice, teriyaki sauce, honey, cornstarch and salt in the container of an electric blender. Whirl until the ingredients are blended. Pour the marinade over the fish and turn to coat the fish. Let the fish stand in the marinade for 30 minutes.

4. Meanwhile, reserve some of the red pepper strips for garnish. Layer the cabbage, green onion and remaining red pepper strips in a microwave-safe 12 x 7½ x 2-inch baking dish.

5. Remove the cod from the marinade and arrange the cod over the vegetables in the baking dish.

6. Microwave the marinade in the bowl at full power for 1 minute and 15 seconds. Stir the marinade and spoon it over the cod.

7. Cover the baking dish with wax paper. Microwave at full power for 8 minutes, rotating the dish once. Garnish the cod with the reserved red pepper strips. If you wish, serve the cod with cooked rice.

*****Note:** *If shiitake mushrooms are unavailable, substitute ½ cup of sliced white mushrooms and omit Step 1. Substitute water for the 2 tablespoons of mushroom cooking liquid in Step 3.*

Fish in a Flash

Fish fillets, when they are cooked conventionally, can be prepared in minutes. But with the help of your microwave, they're practically an instant meal. Most individual fillets will be cooked if you microwave them, covered with microwave-safe paper toweling, at full power for 1 to 3 minutes. Microwave a pound of fillets at full power for 3 to 5 minutes. Then let the fillets stand for 5 minutes, which gives you enough time to make a sauce.

■ Top fish fillets with a mixture of fresh orange juice, grated orange zest and melted butter. Microwave, then sprinkle the fillets with chopped toasted walnuts.

■ Sprinkle fish fillets with finely chopped shallots and chopped mushrooms. Cover and microwave. While the fillets stand, drain off the cooking liquid into a glass measuring cup. Add a little sherry, heavy cream and, if you wish, a pinch of nutmeg to the cooking liquid. Microwave at full power until the sauce thickens.

❖ ❖ ❖

CHICKEN WITH MANGO CHUTNEY SAUCE

LOW-CALORIE • LOW-CHOLESTEROL • LOW-SODIUM
• LOW-FAT • MICROWAVE

Makes 4 servings.

Nutrient Value Per Serving: 166 calories, 28 g protein, 2 g fat, 8 g carbohydrate, 133 mg sodium, 68 mg cholesterol.

2	tablespoons mango chutney	2	whole chicken breasts, boned, skinned and cut in half
1	tablespoon coarse-grained mustard	½	cup chopped onion
2	teaspoons lemon juice	1	sweet red pepper, halved and sliced

1. Combine the chutney, mustard and lemon juice in a small bowl. Brush the chutney sauce onto the skinned side of the chicken.
2. Place the chicken, skinned side down, with the large parts facing out, in a microwave-safe 2-quart soufflé or casserole dish. Scatter the onion and half the red pepper over the chicken. Cover the chicken loosely with microwave-safe plastic wrap.
3. Microwave at full power for 9 minutes, or until the chicken is cooked, turning the pieces right side up and spooning more sauce from the bottom of the dish over them after half the cooking time.
4. Transfer the chicken to a serving platter and keep it warm.
5. Purée the sauce remaining in the dish in a food processor. If you wish, return the sauce to the soufflé dish and microwave at full power for 2 to 5 minutes to reduce and thicken the sauce.
6. Pour the sauce over the chicken. Garnish the chicken with the remaining red pepper.

SHREDDED CHICKEN FILLING

This moist and tender filling is perfect for tacos or enchiladas.

LOW-FAT • MICROWAVE

Makes 2 cups.

Nutrient Value Per ¼ Cup: 98 calories, 20 g protein, 1 g fat, 0 g carbohydrate, 145 mg sodium, 49 mg cholesterol.

1½	pounds boned, skinless chicken breast halves	1	bay leaf
¾	cup chicken stock OR: canned chicken broth	1	clove garlic, finely chopped
			Pinch of salt, to taste

1. Place the chicken in a microwave-safe 1- or 2-quart casserole dish. Add the stock or broth, the bay leaf and garlic. Cover the dish with heavy-duty plastic wrap, slightly vented in one place.
2. Microwave at full power for 5 minutes. Uncover the dish and turn over the chicken. Re-cover the dish and microwave for about 2 minutes more, or until the chicken is done. Let the chicken stand for 5 minutes.
3. When cool enough to handle, tear the chicken with your fingers into shreds and return it to the broth. Add the salt.

CORNISH GAME HENS WITH CURRANT COUSCOUS

A wonderfully flavorful way to serve game hens — perfect dinner party fare.

MICROWAVE

Makes 4 servings.

Nutrient Value Per Serving: 486 calories, 40 g protein, 18 g fat, 39 g carbohydrate, 709 mg sodium, 110 mg cholesterol.

Marinade:
- 2 green onions
- 2 tablespoons reduced-sodium soy sauce
- 1 tablespoon orange juice concentrate
- 1 tablespoon molasses
- 1 teaspoon dry mustard
- 1 tablespoon chopped, peeled fresh gingerroot

- 2 Cornish game hens, split in half

Currant Couscous:
- 2 cups reduced-sodium chicken broth OR: beef broth
- 1 cup couscous
- 3 tablespoons dried currants
- ½ teaspoon salt
- 1½ teaspoons cornstarch

1. Thinly slice the white ends of the green onions. Place the white slices in a large plastic food storage bag. Slice the green tops and reserve them for the couscous.

2. Prepare the Marinade: Add the soy sauce, orange juice concentrate, molasses, mustard, ginger and game hens to the plastic bag. Push out all the air from the bag, and secure the bag with a tie. Marinate the hens, refrigerated, for 2 to 24 hours, turning over the bag occasionally to marinate the hens evenly.

3. Prepare the Currant Couscous: Place the chicken or beef broth in a microwave-safe 4-cup measure. Microwave at full power for 5 minutes, or until the broth is boiling. Stir the couscous, currants and salt into the broth. Cover the measure with microwave-safe plastic wrap, slightly vented in one place. Microwave at full power for 1 minute and 30 seconds. Uncover the measure and stir in the reserved green part of the green onion. Cover the measure again, and let the couscous stand for 5 minutes.

4. Transfer the hens to a microwave-safe 13 x 9 x 2-inch baking dish, reserving the marinade. Fold under the wing tips and shield the ends of the wings with small pieces of aluminum foil. Cover the dish with microwave-safe plastic wrap, slightly vented on one side.

5. Combine the reserved marinade with the cornstarch in a microwave-safe 2-cup measure, and set the mixture aside.

6. Microwave the hens at full power for 14 minutes, or until the juices run clear when the hens are pierced between the thigh and breast meat.

7. Transfer the hens to a serving platter, and cover them to keep them warm. Degrease the cooking liquid in the baking dish. Add the degreased liquid to the marinade mixture to equal 1 cup; if you wish, you can use water in place of the cooking liquid. Stir the mixture to combine the ingredients.

8. Microwave the sauce at full power for 2 minutes, stirring once.

9. To serve, fluff the couscous with a fork. Divide the couscous, hens and sauce evenly among 4 individual dinner plates.

Microwave Do's

- Examine a new oven for shipping damage, and try all its special features immediately to catch problems while the warranty is in effect.
- Plug the oven into its own electrical circuit for maximum power output.
- Use potholders to remove food from the microwave.
- Microwave a liquid in a container that can hold twice the volume of the liquid to allow room for expansion.
- Buy boneless, uniformly shaped roasts for more even cooking. Some surface fat will ensure a nice browning effect.
- Cook ground beef in a microwave-safe colander set in another dish, to drain off fat.
- Heat baby food in a microwave-safe dish at half power. Always stir the food, and allow some standing time for heat to travel through the food. Then test the temperature of the food before feeding it to your child.
- Fold under thin edges of food such as fish fillets to get an even thickness all over. Place dense food, such as quiche, on a rack or inverted saucer.
- Pierce the skins of foods such as potatoes, squash, sausage and egg yolks to let steam escape and prevent bursting.
- Place a cake on a cutting board instead of a wire rack after microwaving, so the bottom will continue to cook.
- Rid odors by microwaving ½ cup of lemon juice with 1 cup of water for 3 minutes.

Microwave Don'ts

- Don't cook an egg in the shell. Steam builds up inside the shell, and will cause the egg to explode.
- Don't use the microwave for deep-fat frying (to avoid fires) or for canning (there's no way to tell if harmful organisms have been destroyed).
- Don't operate an empty microwave oven. Keep a cup of water in a microwavable container inside the oven to absorb the energy.
- Don't cook popcorn in containers other than microwave poppers. Instead, use packaged microwave popcorn and watch the popcorn carefully; kernels can scorch and catch fire.
- Don't microwave stuffed poultry. Uneven heating can cause salmonella growth.
- Don't warm a baby bottle in the microwave. When the bottle feels cool on the outside, the liquid inside still is very hot and could burn your baby severely.

POTATO TURKEY POCKETS FLORENTINE

The versatile cheese sauce in this one-dish meal also is delicious on top of broccoli, cauliflower or noodles.

MICROWAVE

Makes 4 servings.

Nutrient Value Per Serving: 427 calories, 36 g protein, 20 g fat, 26 g carbohydrate, 835 mg sodium, 122 mg cholesterol.

3	tablespoons butter
1	cup chopped onion
3	cloves garlic, chopped
1	package (10 ounces) frozen chopped spinach, thawed
1	pound potatoes
1	teaspoon Dijon-style mustard
¾	teaspoon salt
½	teaspoon dried dill
⅛	teaspoon freshly ground pepper
4	turkey cutlets, pounded thin (about 1 pound)

Cheese Sauce:

1	tablespoon butter
4	teaspoons all-purpose flour
⅔	cup milk
4	to 6 drops liquid red pepper seasoning
¼	teaspoon Worcestershire sauce
½	teaspoon Dijon-style mustard
¼	teaspoon paprika
½	cup shredded Cheddar cheese

1. Combine the 3 tablespoons of butter with the onion and the garlic in a microwave-safe 1-quart dish. Microwave at full power for 5 minutes, or until the onion is softened.

2. Drain the spinach in a colander and press out the excess liquid. Set aside the spinach.

3. Pierce the potatoes with a fork on all sides. Microwave at full power for 9 minutes, or until the potatoes are almost fork-tender. Let the potatoes stand for 5 minutes. Peel the potatoes and force them through a ricer or strainer into the onion-butter mixture. Add the 1 teaspoon of mustard, the salt, dill and pepper, and stir to combine the ingredients.

4. Lay the turkey cutlets on a piece of wax paper with the long sides facing you. Divide the spinach evenly among the cutlets, spreading it evenly over half the length of each cutlet. Spoon the potato mixture on top of the spinach, dividing it evenly and spreading it evenly. Fold the uncovered half of each cutlet over the half with the filling to make a pocket.

5. Arrange the pockets in a microwave-safe 10-inch pie plate so that the folded sides are against the side of the plate. Cover the plate with microwave-safe plastic wrap, slightly vented in one place. Microwave at full power for 6½ to 7 minutes, or until the turkey meat is opaque. Let the turkey pockets stand for 5 minutes while preparing the sauce.

6. Prepare the Cheese Sauce: Microwave the butter in a microwave-safe 2-cup measure at full power for 30 seconds, or until the butter is melted. Stir in the flour until it is blended. Add the milk, liquid red pepper seasoning, Worcestershire sauce, mustard and paprika. Stir to blend the ingredients well. Microwave at full power for 2 minutes, stirring twice. Stir in the Cheddar cheese until it is blended.

7. Spoon the sauce over the turkey pockets, and serve immediately.

FLANK STEAK ROLLS WITH HERBS AND VEAL

Packed with herbed croutons, veal and mushrooms, these rolled slices of beef are equally delicious warm or chilled.

LOW-CALORIE • LOW-SODIUM • MICROWAVE

Makes 8 servings.

Nutrient Value Per Serving: 299 calories, 21 g protein, 21 g fat, 6 g carbohydrate, 132 mg sodium, 104 mg cholesterol.

1	cup ½-inch bread cubes (5 slices, crusts removed)
5	tablespoons (½ stick) unsalted butter
½	teaspoon chopped fresh thyme OR: ¼ teaspoon dried thyme, crumbled
1	chopped fresh sage leaf OR: pinch of dried sage, crumbled
1½	teaspoons chopped fresh parsley
¼	cup (½ ounce) cubed wild mushrooms, such as shiitake, OR: white button mushrooms
1	large onion, finely chopped
1	small stalk celery, chopped

½	pound ground veal
1	egg, slightly beaten
	Salt and freshly ground pepper, to taste
1	flank steak (about 1½ pounds), trimmed of fat
½	teaspoon browning sauce
1	tablespoon all-purpose flour
1	large carrot, peeled and finely chopped
1	small clove garlic, chopped
1	bay leaf
1	small tomato, chopped
¼	cup beef broth
¼	cup dry red wine
	Additional chopped fresh parsley, for garnish

Taking the Chill Off: Defrosting

It is a myth that microwave ovens are good only for defrosting and reheating, but it is true that they perform these two functions very well.

■ Defrosting food in the microwave will save you a lot of time, especially on days when you forget to remove the dinner meat from the freezer before leaving for work. Some ovens come with programmed defrost functions which set time and temperature based on the weight of the food to be defrosted. When defrosting food, check it frequently — after the food defrosts, it will begin to cook. If your oven doesn't have a defrost program, use a low setting or follow the manufacturer's directions.

■ If you're defrosting something that's irregularly shaped, such as a whole chicken, shield the tips of the wings and the drumsticks with aluminum foil so they don't start to cook before the rest of the bird is thawed. You may have to shield the breast, too.

❖　❖　❖

Flank Steak Roll with Herbs and Veal is perfect make-ahead party fare. We serve it here with whole cranberry sauce and sliced loin of pork.

Made for Microwaves

To supplement your regular cooking equipment, you may decide to buy some cookware specifically made for microwave use. Microwave-safe plastic is an ideal material to choose, and several manufacturers offer microwave-safe products made of patented plastic materials. Products include potato bakers, vegetable steamers, cooking pouch holder/pourers and spatter screens.

■ The technology has advanced greatly in recent years, but most microwave ovens still have "hot spots." A good way to test for hot spots is to microwave a pastry shell without rotating it during cooking time; if you see darker areas interspersed throughout the cooked dough, these are the hot spots. To prevent food from cooking unevenly, you usually have to rotate the cooking dish. Wind-up turntables or carousels save you the trouble of opening the oven and turning the dish manually. Some ovens feature built-in carousels; before you buy one, make sure the larger dishes you plan to use will fit on the tray as it rotates.

1. Place the bread cubes in a single layer in a microwave-safe glass baking dish. Microwave at full power, stirring occasionally, for 4 to 5 minutes, or until the bread is dried. Combine 3 tablespoons of the butter with the thyme, sage and the 1½ teaspoons of parsley in a microwave-safe cup. Microwave at full power for 30 to 60 seconds, or until the butter is melted. Stir the butter mixture, then drizzle it over the bread cubes, tossing to coat the cubes well.
2. Combine 1 tablespoon of the remaining butter with the mushrooms, onion and celery in a bowl. Loosely cover the bowl and microwave at full power for 4 to 5 minutes, or until the vegetables are softened.
3. Combine the veal, egg and salt and pepper in a large bowl. Stir in the bread and mushroom mixtures.
4. With a mallet or the bottom of a small skillet, flatten the flank steak to about a 13 x 9-inch shape. Spread the veal mixture evenly over the steak leaving a ½-inch border around the edges. Fold over the lengthwise edges of the steak. Secure the folded steak with wooden picks, or tie the steak securely with kitchen twine.
5. Combine the remaining 1 tablespoon of butter with the browning sauce in a small custard cup. Microwave at full power for 30 seconds, or until the butter is melted. Brush the butter mixture over the steak roll.
6. Shake the flour in a 10 x 16-inch oven cooking bag, and place the bag in a microwave-safe 12 x 8 x 2-inch baking dish. Place the steak roll, seam side down, in the bag and add the carrot, garlic, bay leaf, tomato, broth and wine. Close the bag with a nylon tie, and make several 6½-inch-long slits in the top of the bag. Microwave at full power, rotating the dish occasionally, for 25 minutes, or until the steak is tender.
7. Carefully remove the steak roll from the bag. Skim the fat from the cooking liquid. Strain the cooking liquid and serve it with the steak. Garnish with the additional parsley. Or, if preparing the steak roll a day in advance, cool it in the cooking liquid. Refrigerate the roll, covered, in the cooking liquid overnight. Serve the roll cold without the cooking liquid. Or microwave the steak roll, covered, with the strained cooking liquid at full power for 3 minutes, or until the roll is warmed. Garnish the roll with the additional parsley.

THREE PEPPER BEEF ROLLS

A variation of the Japanese classic negamaki. The presentation of the rolls is enhanced by using strips of red, yellow and orange sweet pepper. The rolls can be assembled ahead of time, covered, refrigerated and cooked as needed.

LOW-CALORIE • LOW-CHOLESTEROL • MICROWAVE

Makes 4 servings.

Nutrient Value Per Serving: 229 calories, 26 g protein, 10 g fat, 7 g carbohydrate, 260 mg sodium, 68 mg cholesterol.

1 **pound top round beef, sliced very thinly as for sukiyaki***	1 **tablespoon reduced-sodium soy sauce**
4 **green onions, trimmed**	1 **teaspoon finely chopped fresh gingerroot**
12 **strips of sweet pepper, using red, yellow and orange peppers**	1 **clove garlic, finely chopped**
¼ **cup balsamic vinegar (see Tip, page 67)**	**Large pinch crushed red pepper flakes**
¼ **cup beef broth**	1 **teaspoon cornstarch (optional)**
1 **tablespoon honey**	

1. Divide the beef slices into 4 portions. For each roll, lay one portion of the beef slices, slightly overlapping, in a flat layer on a piece of wax paper. Place a green onion along the length of the beef slices, and arrange a red, a yellow and an orange pepper strip alongside the green onion. Using the wax paper to help you, roll the beef around the vegetables. Place the beef rolls, seam side down, in a microwave-safe, 2-quart rectangular glass baking dish.
2. Combine the vinegar, broth, honey, soy sauce, ginger, garlic and red pepper flakes in a cup, and blend the ingredients well. Pour the marinade over the beef rolls. Let the beef rolls stand for at least 10 minutes, or up to half an hour, spooning the marinade over the beef.
3. Microwave the beef rolls, uncovered, turning the rolls, repositioning them and spooning the marinade over them halfway through the cooking time, for 7 to 10 minutes, or until the vegetables are tender and the beef is cooked through. Remove the beef rolls from the dish to a cutting board.
4. If you wish, combine 1 teaspoon of cornstarch with 1 tablespoon of water, and stir the cornstarch mixture into the marinade. Microwave at full power, stirring once during the cooking, for 1 minute, or until the sauce thickens and bubbles. Brush the beef rolls with the marinade sauce.
5. Slice the beef rolls and serve them.

*Note: It's best to have your butcher cut the beef for this recipe, because an electric slicer produces the almost paper-thin results needed for this dish. If you cannot get very thinly sliced beef, plan to microwave the beef rolls, covered, at full power for 5 minutes, then at half power for about 30 minutes, turning over the rolls and repositioning them after 15 minutes.

Marinades

Marinades, pungent mixtures that usually contain oil and an acid such as wine or vinegar, add flavor and succulence to meats. Frequently they act as a tenderizer as well.
■ For quick absorption of the marinade's flavor, use smaller pieces of meat; the smaller the pieces, the shorter the marinating time.
■ Use a nonreactive container, such as a glass or plastic dish, for marinating because of the acid in most marinades.
■ For a marinating time of an hour or less, cover the marinating meat and leave it at room temperature. For longer marinating times, refrigerate the meat to avoid spoilage.
■ When you drain the marinade from the meat, reserve the marinade to use for basting or serving as a sauce.
■ To use a marinade as a sauce, heat it in the microwave until it comes to a simmer. Never serve a marinade uncooked.

❖ ❖ ❖

Take Cover!

A simple cover can intensify heat, speed cooking, prevent spattering, ensure moistness and retain nutrients. Different covers deliver different results.

■ Plastic wrap and microwave-safe lids are snug-fitting to conserve steam and tenderize food. Plastic wrap fits more tightly; some recipes call for folding back a corner to release steam. Remove plastic wrap from hot dishes by pulling the wrap away from your hands and face to avoid steam burns.

■ Wax paper makes a loose cover that holds in heat but lets steam escape to produce a crisper texture in recipes such as breaded chicken.

■ Microwave-safe paper toweling makes an absorbent, loose cover to soak up bacon grease, or excess moisture from breads.

■ When deciding whether or not to use a cover, the principles used in conventional cooking also apply to cooking in the microwave. Use a cover when you need to retain moist heat or stop evaporation, or when the food should make a lot of juice or sauce.

■ A cover has the additional advantage of holding in heat and distributing it more evenly throughout the dish.

❖ ❖ ❖

BEEF TOSTADA PIE CON QUESO

A hearty main dish sure to please any crowd. You can garnish the pie with lime wedges and fresh parsley, if you wish.

MICROWAVE

Makes 4 servings.

Nutrient Value Per Serving: 540 calories, 31 g protein, 28 g fat, 41 g carbohydrate, 1,169 mg sodium, 79 mg cholesterol.

¾	pound lean ground beef			Salt and freshly ground pepper, to taste
1	large onion, chopped		8	tostada shells, broken into quarters
1	clove garlic, finely chopped		1	can (16 ounces) pinto beans, rinsed and drained
1	can (16 ounces) whole tomatoes, packed in purée		1	can (4 ounces) diced green chili peppers, drained
½	teaspoon ground cumin		1	cup shredded Cheddar cheese
½	teaspoon dried oregano, crumbled			

1. Combine the beef, onion and garlic in a microwave-safe large, shallow dish, and cover the dish with wax paper. Microwave at full power, stirring once or twice, for 3 to 4 minutes, or until the meat no longer is pink. Drain the fat. Add the tomatoes with their purée, the cumin, oregano and salt and pepper. Cover the dish loosely with wax paper. Microwave at full power for 1 minute. Then microwave at half power, stirring twice, for 8 minutes, or until the meat filling is slightly thickened.

2. Arrange half the quartered tostada shells in a microwave-safe 9-inch round baking dish. Layer on half the pinto beans, half the meat filling, half the chili peppers and half the Cheddar cheese. Repeat with all the remaining ingredients except the Cheddar cheese.

3. Cover the dish with wax paper and microwave at half power for 5 to 6 minutes, or until the pie is heated through. Place the dish directly on a heatproof surface. Sprinkle the remaining ½ cup of Cheddar cheese on top. Let the pie stand for 5 minutes before serving it.

Note: *To make individual pies, place 4 whole tostada shells in a microwave-safe baking dish. Layer with half the meat filling, pinto beans, chili peppers and Cheddar cheese, and top with the remaining 4 whole shells. Repeat the layers, except for the Cheddar cheese. Microwave as directed in Step 3 above.*

PORK CHOPS CACCIATORE

If you like chicken cacciatore, you'll love this pork chop version.

MICROWAVE

Makes 4 servings.

Nutrient Value Per Serving: 618 calories, 31 g protein, 29 g fat, 57 g carbohydrate, 384 mg sodium, 79 mg cholesterol.

1   tablespoon olive oil
1   large onion, sliced into thin rings
1   large sweet red pepper, cut into ¼-inch strips
1   large sweet green pepper, cut into ¼-inch strips
1   clove garlic, finely chopped
1½ cups small mushrooms, quartered
2   teaspoons dried basil, crumbled

1   can (16 ounces) whole tomatoes in purée
¼   cup dry red wine OR: white wine
¼   teaspoon salt
4   center-cut ¾-inch-thick pork chops (about 1 pound total)
⅛   teaspoon freshly ground black pepper
½   pound penne, ziti OR: other pasta, cooked according to package directions

Split-Second Sauce

Dress up a plain presentation of chicken, fish, meat or vegetables in less than 5 minutes with one of these tasty sauces.

■ Sweet and Sour Sauce: Combine grated gingerroot, grated garlic, apricot preserves and mirin (Japanese rice wine vinegar). Microwave at full power until the sauce bubbles and thickens. Sweet and Sour Sauce is good with pork, poultry or scallops.

■ Cider Sauce: Peel, core and finely chop 1 tart apple. Combine the chopped apple with 1 finely chopped onion and a half cup of sweet apple cider. Season with a pinch of grated nutmeg. Microwave, covered, at full power, for 5 minutes. Purée the apple mixture, if you wish. Serve with pork.

■ Curried Orange Sauce: Microwave 1 finely chopped onion with a little curry powder to taste. Add orange juice, raisins and, if you wish, grated orange zest. This sauce is delicious with chicken or lamb.

❖   ❖   ❖

Mushrooms and sweet peppers enliven tomato sauce for Pork Chops Cacciatore. Arrange the chops with the meatiest portions toward the outer edge of the dish when microwaving.

Meaty Issues

■ Beef: The microwave oven will never replace the backyard grill for making delicious burgers, but it does a good job of cooking chili, meat loaf and similar dishes that use ground beef in combination with other ingredients. Similarly, don't expect to roast beef or steak other than conventionally. Stick to using the microwave for what it does best with unground beef: stewing and braising. Microwave recipes for these dishes usually use less liquid than their conventional counterparts. If you wish, you can brown the beef beforehand conventionally or on a microwave browning tray. As with conventional stews and braises, you'll probably achieve the most tender results if you start the dish on full power. Once the liquid boils, lower the power to keep the liquid just simmering.

■ Pork: Microwaved pork has the same strengths and limitations as beef does: fork-tender stews and braises, but save the browned roasts for the conventional oven.

■ When cooking several pork chops, arrange them in a ring, with the meatiest portions toward the edges of the dish. Use a browning tray, or cover the chops loosely with wax paper or with microwave-safe paper toweling.

❖　❖　❖

1. Combine the oil, onion, red and green peppers, garlic, mushrooms and basil in a microwave-safe medium-size bowl. Cover the bowl and microwave at full power for 5 minutes, or just until the vegetables are tender. Stir in the tomatoes with their purée, the red or white wine and the salt.
2. Arrange the pork chops in a microwave-safe shallow baking dish, with the meatiest portions pointed toward the outside of the dish. Sprinkle the chops with the black pepper. Pour the tomato mixture over the chops. Loosely cover the dish with wax paper to prevent spatters.
3. Microwave at full power for 5 minutes. Then microwave at half power for 15 minutes, or until the chops are tender and the meat near the bones no longer is pink.
4. Serve the pork chops and the sauce over the cooked pasta.

CONFETTI MEAT LOAF

By placing the meat mixture in a microwave-safe colander set in a glass pie plate, the excess fat can drain off during the cooking. We find that making a "well" in the loaf to create a ring shape allows for more even cooking.

LOW-CALORIE ● MICROWAVE

Makes 4 servings.

Nutrient Value Per Serving: 298 calories, 24 g protein, 17 g fat, 11 g carbohydrate, 270 mg sodium, 134 mg cholesterol.

½ cup chopped sweet green pepper	1 tablespoon chopped fresh parsley
1 small carrot, shredded (¼ cup)	½ teaspoon dry mustard
¼ cup chopped celery	¼ teaspoon salt
2 tablespoons chopped onion	¼ teaspoon freshly ground black pepper
2 medium-size tomatoes, cored, drained and chopped (1 cup)	1 pound lean ground beef Nonstick vegetable cooking spray
1 large egg	Fresh thyme and parsley sprigs, for garnish (optional)
1 cup fine soft bread crumbs (2 slices)	

1. Combine the green pepper, carrot, celery, onion and tomatoes in a microwave-safe 2-quart mixing bowl. Cover the bowl with wax paper.
2. Microwave at full power, stirring once, for 2 to 3 minutes, or until the vegetables are tender. Let the vegetables stand for 5 minutes, uncovered. Stir in the egg, bread crumbs, chopped parsley, mustard, salt and black pepper. Add the ground beef, mixing the ingredients well.
3. Spray the inside of a microwave-safe colander with nonstick vegetable cooking spray. Set the colander in a glass pie plate or casserole dish. Pack the meat mixture gently but firmly into the colander. Make a 1-inch-deep depression in the center of the meat loaf with the back of a spoon. Cover the colander with wax paper.
4. Microwave at half power for 6 minutes. Rotate the colander a half turn, and microwave at half power for 8 to 9 minutes, or until the loaf is set and the meat no longer is pink. The meat loaf will pull away from the side of the colander and may crack at the edges. Let the meat loaf stand, uncovered, for 3 to 4 minutes. Garnish with thyme and parsley sprigs, if you wish.

MIDDLE EASTERN LAMB STEW

Serve this savory stew over couscous or rice. Like most stews, its flavor improves if you prepare it the day before you plan to serve it.

LOW-CHOLESTEROL • MICROWAVE

Makes 6 servings.

Nutrient Value Per Serving: 448 calories, 21 g protein, 28 g fat, 29 g carbohydrate, 559 mg sodium, 72 mg cholesterol.

1	tablespoon butter	½	teaspoon ground cinnamon
1	tablespoon olive oil	½	teaspoon ground turmeric
1	large yellow onion, halved and thinly sliced	¼	teaspoon salt
1	clove garlic, finely chopped	⅛	teaspoon freshly ground pepper
1¼	pounds boneless lamb stew meat OR: sirloin steak, cut across the grain into ¼-inch-thick strips	3	fresh OR: canned plum tomatoes, chopped
3	tablespoons all-purpose flour	2	tablespoons raisins
		1	tablespoon capers (optional)
3	zucchini, trimmed, halved lengthwise and cut into ¼-inch chunks	1	can (16 ounces) chick peas, drained
1	cup chicken broth		Chopped fresh parsley (optional)

1. Combine the butter, oil, onion and garlic in a microwave-safe 2-quart casserole dish.
2. Microwave at full power for 2 to 4 minutes, or until the onion is tender.
3. Meanwhile, toss the lamb or sirloin, a few pieces at a time, with the flour in a bag until the meat is coated.
4. Stir the meat into the casserole dish. Cover the dish with wax paper.
5. Microwave at full power for 3 minutes, or until almost all the pink color is gone from the meat.
6. Stir in the zucchini, broth, cinnamon, turmeric, salt and pepper. Cover the dish tightly.
7. Microwave at full power for 8 minutes, or until the mixture just comes to boiling. Uncover the dish and stir in the tomatoes, raisins and, if you wish, capers. Cover the dish again.
8. Microwave at half power for 5 minutes, or until the tomatoes have broken down, the zucchini is almost cooked and the meat is tender.
9. Uncover the dish. Stir in the chick peas. Cover the dish and let the stew stand for 5 minutes. If you wish, sprinkle the stew with chopped parsley just before serving.

Microwave Techniques

If Albert Einstein were to come back to earth, he might well astound the world by developing a theory of microwave relativity, an easily stated universal truth about the relationship between food volume, density and microwave cooking time. Lacking one succinct formula, we'll explain the general principles of the microwave oven and let you proceed from there.

■ Cooking time in the microwave depends on the temperature, size, shape and density of the pieces of food, as well as the food's fat and liquid content, and the amount of food you wish to cook at one time. High-wattage ovens cook food faster than low-wattage models.

■ As with conventional cooking, very cold or frozen foods will take longer to heat through than room temperature foods. If your microwave oven has a defrost setting, use it to bring frozen foods to room temperature before cooking them. If your microwave doesn't have a defrost setting, make sure you allow enough time for foods to thaw thoroughly.

- Thicker, larger pieces of meat, fish, vegetables and other foods take longer to cook in the microwave than smaller pieces of food. For even cooking, it's particularly important to cut each ingredient into uniform pieces. If it's possible, arrange the ingredients in a single layer so they are not touching; they'll cook even faster.

- Because the microwave cooks food differently than a regular oven, new rules apply. Food placed on the outside of the cooking dish receives more microwave energy and therefore cooks faster. In most cases, food cooks most evenly if it's arranged in a ring near the outer edge of the dish. Zucchini sticks and other oblong-shaped foods can be set on the dish to resemble the spokes of a wheel. Thicker or slower-cooking parts, such as the meaty ends of drumsticks or the stems of broccoli, should face the outer edge of the dish.

- The lower energy received in the center is an advantage when you're cooking ingredients with varying cooking times. Put quick-cooking snow peas, for instance, in the center of the dish; arrange pieces of chicken around the perimeter.

❖ ❖ ❖

BROCCOLI-STUFFED BAKED POTATO

For a light main dish, these hearty, healthy potatoes can't be beat! And they're so easy to prepare, even your youngsters can whip them up. Just add a tossed green salad and you have a complete meal.

LOW-CALORIE • LOW-CHOLESTEROL • LOW-FAT • MICROWAVE

Makes 4 servings.

Nutrient Value Per Serving: 320 calories, 16 g protein, 10 g fat, 45 g carbohydrate, 215 mg sodium, 27 mg cholesterol.

4 baking potatoes (8 to 10 ounces each)	½ cup plain nonfat yogurt
1 bunch broccoli (1 pound) Salt and freshly ground pepper, to taste	4 ounces Monterey Jack cheese with peppers, shredded (1 cup)

1. Prick the potatoes several times with a fork. Place them directly in the microwave oven, leaving at least ½ inch between each potato. Microwave at full power, turning over the potatoes once, for 12 to 16 minutes, or until the potatoes are soft. Let the potatoes stand while you cook the broccoli.

2. Cut the flowerets from the broccoli stalks. Peel the stalks and cut them into ½-inch-thick pieces. Place the flowerets in the center of a microwave-safe 10-inch pie plate, and place the stalk pieces around the edge. Cover the plate with microwave-safe plastic wrap, slightly vented in one place. Microwave at full power for 6 minutes, or until the broccoli is barely tender.

3. Cut the potatoes lengthwise almost in half, leaving them slightly connected along one side. Season the potatoes with the salt and pepper. Spread the cut sides with the yogurt. Divide the broccoli among the potatoes and top with the Monterey Jack cheese. Place the potatoes on a microwave-safe dinner plate. Microwave, uncovered, at full power for 2½ to 3 minutes, or until the cheese melts, rotating the plate one quarter turn once. Serve the potatoes hot.

ACCOMPANIMENTS

The perfect side dishes for any meal, whether the main dish is microwaved or not—and they're ready in just minutes.

SCALLOPED POTATOES WITH LEEKS

A creamy side dish to complement any meal. To achieve a golden brown topping, you can place the casserole dish under the broiler for a minute or two just before serving.

MICROWAVE

Makes 4 servings.

Nutrient Value Per Serving: 354 calories, 14 g protein, 17 g fat, 38 g carbohydrate, 203 mg sodium, 56 mg cholesterol.

2 tablespoons butter	2 cups milk
2 leeks, trimmed, halved, well rinsed and chopped	¾ cup grated Gruyère cheese
2 tablespoons all-purpose flour	5 medium-size potatoes, peeled, if desired, and sliced ¼ inch thick
Salt and freshly ground pepper, to taste	Cooked leek strips, for garnish (optional)
Large pinch grated nutmeg	

1. Place the butter and the chopped leeks in a microwave-safe 2-quart glass measure.
2. Microwave, uncovered, at full power for 3 minutes.
3. Uncover the measure and stir in the flour, salt and pepper and the nutmeg. Pour in the milk, mixing it in with a wire whisk.
4. Microwave, uncovered, at full power, stirring every 2 minutes, for 5 minutes, or until the sauce thickens and bubbles. Stir in ½ cup of the Gruyère cheese.
5. Place half the potatoes in a microwave-safe 2-quart casserole dish. Top with half the cheese sauce. Repeat the layering. Cover the dish with microwave-safe plastic wrap, slightly vented in one place.
6. Microwave at full power for 15 to 20 minutes, or until the potatoes are tender and have absorbed the sauce, rotating the dish and gently stirring the potatoes after 10 minutes.
7. Sprinkle the remaining ¼ cup of Gruyère cheese over the top. Let the potatoes stand until the cheese melts. Garnish with strips of cooked leeks, if you wish.

Is It Soup Yet?

■ As with conventional cooking, only experience can tell you exactly when it is time to pull a dish out of the microwave oven. Microwave cooking is a little trickier than conventional cooking in that respect, because some of the usual clues—browned meat or dry cake tops, for instance—are absent. Also bear in mind that foods continue to cook once they're removed from the microwave oven.

■ Always start with the shortest recommended cooking time, and test for doneness frequently. This is especially true when you are preparing a new recipe, or getting used to your new microwave oven.

❖ ❖ ❖

"Dost thou love life? Then do not squander time; for that's the stuff life is made of."
—*Benjamin Franklin*

A Clean Machine

Baking soda safely cleans all the spatters and spills that can accumulate in a microwave. Just mix 2 tablespoons of baking soda with 2 cups of warm water, and sponge down the interior.

For stubborn stains, sprinkle on dry baking soda, rub lightly with a moist sponge, rinse and buff dry. Baking soda is an effective and non-abrasive cleanser; unlike many cleaning powders and liquids, it won't scratch or erode the delicate interior of the microwave. To neutralize food odors, leave a small dish of baking soda inside the microwave. Remember to remove the baking soda before using the oven.

BRAISED LEEKS IN CREAMY TOMATO SAUCE

Braising, a process of slow simmering, is the perfect way to bring out the delicate flavor of leeks. The creamy tomato sauce is made in the same pan to cut down on clean-up for you.

LOW-CHOLESTEROL • MICROWAVE

Makes 6 servings.

Nutrient Value Per Serving: 112 calories, 3 g protein, 5 g fat, 15 g carbohydrate, 311 mg sodium, 14 mg cholesterol.

4 large leeks (about 2 pounds)	3 cloves garlic, smashed
1 pound plum tomatoes, peeled and chopped	½ teaspoon dried basil, crumbled
1½ cups beef broth	¼ teaspoon fennel seeds
¼ cup chopped parsley	¼ cup heavy cream
1½ tablespoons chopped sun-dried tomatoes packed in oil, patted dry	2 teaspoons cornstarch

1. Trim the root ends of the leeks and trim off all but 2 inches from the green tops. Split the leeks lengthwise to within 1 inch of the root base, and rinse out the sand under running water.

2. Combine the plum tomatoes, broth, parsley, sun-dried tomatoes, garlic, basil and fennel seeds in a microwave-safe 13 x 9 x 2-inch baking dish. Add the leeks in a single layer, alternating the tops and bottoms. Cover the dish with microwave-safe plastic wrap, slightly vented on one side.

3. Microwave at full power for 20 minutes. Uncover the dish and turn over the leeks. Cover the dish again. Microwave at full power for 10 to 15 minutes, or until the leeks are fork-tender.

4. Transfer the leeks to a serving platter. Drain any cooking liquid back into the baking dish, and discard the garlic.

5. Stir together the cream and the cornstarch in a small bowl. Stir the cream mixture into the cooking liquid in the baking dish until the combined mixture is blended. Microwave at full power for 1 minute, or until the sauce comes to a boil and thickens.

6. Spoon the sauce over the leeks and serve.

TWO-WAY NEW POTATOES

LOW-CHOLESTEROL • LOW-SODIUM • MICROWAVE

Makes 6 servings.

Nutrient Value Per Serving: 345 calories, 15 g protein, 18 g fat, 5 g carbohydrate, 15 mg sodium, 0 mg cholesterol.

3	**pounds small new potatoes, scrubbed and dried**
10	**cloves garlic, mashed**
½	**cup extra-virgin olive oil**
	Salt and freshly ground black pepper, to taste

Chopped parsley (optional)
Classic Vinaigrette (optional; recipe, page 117)
Snipped fresh chives (optional)

1. Place the potatoes in a microwave-safe 14 x 11 x 2-inch dish. Stir in the garlic and the oil. Cover the dish.

2. Microwave at full power, shaking the dish twice, for 20 minutes, or until the potatoes are tender. Season with the salt and black pepper. If you wish, serve the potatoes hot, sprinkled with chopped parsley. Or cool the potatoes, cut them into chunks and serve them tossed with a vinaigrette dressing and snipped fresh chives.

TIAN OF WINTER VEGETABLES

A French classic updated for the microwave. The parsley topping is the winter equivalent of summer's pesto.

LOW-CHOLESTEROL • MICROWAVE

Makes 6 servings.

Nutrient Value Per Serving: 188 calories, 5 g protein, 11 g fat, 21 g carbohydrate, 108 mg sodium, 3 mg cholesterol.

2	**small acorn squash, halved crosswise, seeded and cut into ¼-inch-thick slices**
1	**small cauliflower, cored, divided into flowerets and sliced**
2	**medium-size zucchini, trimmed, halved lengthwise and cut into ¼-inch-thick slices**
2	**medium-size carrots, trimmed, peeled and sliced**
2	**small parsnips, trimmed, peeled and sliced**
2	**cloves garlic**

4	**strips lemon zest (yellow part of rind only)**
1	**tablespoon fresh rosemary (optional)**
½	**small red onion, quartered**
⅓	**cup grated Parmesan cheese**
1	**cup fresh parsley sprigs (no stems)**
¼	**cup olive oil**
	Salt and freshly ground pepper, to taste
1	**tablespoon dry white wine OR: lemon juice (optional)**

1. Arrange the acorn squash slices, cut sides in, around the outside rim of a microwave-safe 12- to 14-inch serving platter. Arrange the cauliflower slices in a circle within the squash. Add circles of the zucchini, carrot and parsnip in an attractive pattern.

2. With the motor running, drop the garlic though the feed tube of a food processor or the top of an electric blender, until the garlic is finely

Make It Snappy

Microwaved vegetables cook in little or no water, so their flavors remain intense and their textures do not become mushy. Water soluble vitamins, robbed by the cooking liquid when vegetables boil conventionally, are retained, and the colors stay vibrant.

■ When preparing vegetables for the microwave, remember that food cooks more quickly toward the edge of the dish.

■ Arrange beets, potatoes and other large vegetables you wish to cook whole in a single layer. Peas and green beans can cook in a glass measuring cup or serving bowl. Unevenly shaped vegetables, such as carrots, do best set on the dish to resemble the spokes of a wheel, with the thicker ends pointing toward the edge of the dish. Set broccoli and asparagus spears in a ring, with the flowerets and tips pointing toward the center.

■ When chopping vegetables to microwave, make the pieces as uniform in size as possible so they cook evenly. Arrange a combination of vegetables, such as the tian recipe, at left, so that thicker vegetables are around the edge of the dish.

■ For most green vegetables, add about a tablespoon or two of water to the dish, and cover the dish with a glass lid or microwave-safe plastic wrap. If you don't have a carousel, rotate the dish once or twice during the microwaving so the vegetables cook evenly.

> *"Come what come may, Time and the hour runs through the roughest day."*
> *—William Shakespeare*

chopped. Drop in the lemon zest, rosemary if you wish, and the onion. Stop the motor. Add the Parmesan cheese, parsley, oil and salt and pepper. Cover and pulse-chop until the ingredients are blended.

3. Spoon the parsley mixture over the vegetables on the platter. If you wish, sprinkle the 1 tablespoon of white wine or lemon juice on the vegetables. Cover the platter tightly with microwave-safe plastic wrap, slightly vented in one place.

4. Microwave at full power for 5 to 8 minutes, or until the squash slices are cooked, rotating the platter once halfway through the cooking time. Squash cooked in the microwave often is done before it appears to be, so pierce it with a fork to make sure.

5. Serve the vegetables, in their decorative pattern, directly from the cooking platter.

A colorful, delicious side dish for cold-weather months: Tian of Winter Vegetables.

HONEY-GLAZED CARROTS

Serve these with pork chops or ham. If you want to purée the cooked carrots, add ¼ cup of orange juice or water to the pan before cooking them.

LOW-CHOLESTEROL • LOW-SODIUM • LOW-FAT • MICROWAVE

Makes 4 servings.

Nutrient Value Per Serving: 103 calories, 1 g protein, 3 g fat, 19 g carbohydrate, 65 mg sodium, 8 mg cholesterol.

6 medium-size carrots (about 1 pound), peeled, trimmed and sliced into ¼-inch rounds	1 tablespoon butter
2 tablespoons honey	1 teaspoon ground cinnamon
	Pinch salt and freshly ground pepper, to taste

1. Combine the carrots, honey and butter in a microwave-safe 2-quart container. Cover the container tightly.

2. Microwave at full power for 6 to 8 minutes, stirring twice.

3. Uncover the container. Stir in the cinnamon and the salt and pepper. Toss to blend all the ingredients. Let the carrots stand, covered, for 2 minutes before serving them.

Standing Time

When food is removed from a microwave oven, it continues to cook because the heat generated in the outer layers continues to penetrate inward to the center by conduction. With some foods, the time it takes to carry them to the table is enough for proper heat redistribution. Dense foods may continue to cook for 15 to 20 minutes after they come out of the oven. Many microwave recipes account for this by recommending a specific standing time after cooking. During this period, cover the dish to retain heat and set the dish directly on a heat-proof surface. Some foods, including cakes and bar cookies, won't look quite right until they've had some standing time.

❖ ❀ ❖

Cinnamon and honey add a spicy sweet touch in Honey-Glazed Carrots.

Stirring Things Up

The center of a dish receives less microwave energy than the outside, so many recipes require stirring during the cooking time to redistribute food from the cooler center to the warmer outside. Many liquids also benefit from stirring to prevent lumps. It's easy to open the door and stir the dish without removing it from the oven. Just remember that the dish itself is likely to be very hot.

❖　❖　❖

Time on Your Side

Conventional ovens have thermostats to keep the temperature constant inside the oven no matter how you load up the shelves. Whether you're baking 2 potatoes or 22, the oven will maintain a more or less steady temperature, and the cooking time won't vary by much. In contrast, the microwave has only a certain amount of energy it can put out when it's operating at full power. If you cook one apple, for instance, all the microwave energy will be directed to the one piece of fruit. If you cook two apples instead, the oven will put out the same amount of energy, but that energy will get divided between the two apples. Each apple then will absorb less energy per minute while it's in the microwave, so the cooking time will be longer.

❖　❖　❖

SAVORY GREENS WITH BACON

LOW-CALORIE • LOW-CHOLESTEROL • LOW-FAT • MICROWAVE

Makes 4 servings.

Nutrient Value Per Serving: 97 calories, 3 g protein, 7 g fat, 7 g carbohydrate, 376 mg sodium, 8 mg cholesterol.

1 **pound fresh escarole** 　**OR: Swiss chard**	**Salt, to taste (optional)**
2 **slices bacon, chopped**	¼ **teaspoon freshly ground** 　**pepper**
1 **medium-size onion,** 　**chopped**	1 **tablespoon balsamic** 　**vinegar (see Tip, page 67)**
2 **cloves garlic, finely** 　**chopped**	2 **teaspoons Dijon-style** 　**mustard**
¼ **teaspoon finely chopped** 　**fresh rosemary** 　**OR: ⅛ teaspoon dried** 　**rosemary, crumbled**	**Freshly squeezed juice** 　**of ½ lemon (optional)**

1. Remove the tough stems, if any, from the greens. Rinse the greens well. If using the escarole, cut the leaves crosswise into ½-inch shreds. If using the chard, chop it into 1-inch pieces.
2. Combine the bacon, onion and garlic in a microwave-safe 3-quart dish.
3. Microwave at full power, stirring once, for 4 to 5 minutes, or until the bacon is almost completely cooked. Add the greens and the rosemary, and toss to coat them. Cover the dish tightly.
4. Microwave at full power, stirring once, for 5 to 7 minutes, or until the greens are cooked and tender.
5. Season with salt, if you wish. Add the pepper, vinegar and mustard. Sprinkle with lemon juice, if you wish.

SPICY STRING BEANS

LOW-CALORIE • LOW-CHOLESTEROL • MICROWAVE

Makes 6 servings.

Nutrient Value Per Serving: 50 calories, 2 g protein, 2 g fat, 7 g carbohydrate, 176 mg sodium, 0 mg cholesterol.

5 **cloves garlic, mashed**	1 **pound string beans,** 　**trimmed**
2 **slices peeled fresh** 　**gingerroot**	1 **tablespoon crushed red** 　**pepper flakes**
2 **green onions, trimmed and** 　**cut into ½-inch pieces**	1 **tablespoon soy sauce**
1 **tablespoon olive oil**	

1. Place the garlic, ginger, green onion and oil in the container of a food processor. Process until the mixture is finely chopped. Transfer the mixture to a microwave-safe 2-quart dish.
2. Microwave, uncovered, at full power for 2 minutes.
3. Add the string beans, red pepper flakes and soy sauce to the dish. Toss to coat the string beans well with the garlic mixture. Cover the dish with microwave-safe plastic wrap, slightly vented in one place.
4. Microwave at full power, stirring four times, for 8 to 11 minutes, or until the string beans are tender but still bright green.

VEGETABLE MICROWAVE COOKING TIPS

VEGETABLE	QUANTITY	WATER	PREPARATION TIPS	COOKING TIME (HIGH)	STANDING TIME
Acorn Squash	1 pound (1 whole)	——	Halve squash. Wrap halves tightly in plastic wrap.	6 minutes	1 minute
Asparagus Spears	1 pound	3 table-spoons	Snap off tough ends. Arrange tips toward center of the dish. Cover with plastic wrap.	5 minutes	5 minutes, covered
Beans (green or wax)	1 pound	½ cup	Snap off ends and pull off strings. Cover with plastic wrap.	12-15 minutes (stir every 5 minutes)	5 minutes, covered
Beets	6	1½ cups	Wash; do not peel. Cover with lid or plastic wrap.	8-10 minutes (rotate dish after 5 minutes)	4 minutes, covered
Broccoli Spears	1½ pounds	——	Place flowerets toward center of plate. Cover with lid or plastic wrap.	8-10 minutes (rotate dish after 5 minutes)	4 minutes, covered
Brussels Sprouts	1 pound	2 table-spoons	Cover with lid or plastic wrap.	6-7 minutes (stir once after 3 minutes)	3-5 minutes, covered
Cabbage	1 pound	¼ cup	Cut in wedges. Cover with lid or plastic wrap.	12-15 minutes (rotate dish after 6 minutes)	2 minutes, covered
Carrots	1 pound	¼ cup	Cut uniformly or leave whole. Cover with lid or plastic wrap.	6-7 minutes for slices; 8-9 for whole (stir or rotate halfway through cooking time)	5 minutes, covered
Cauliflower	1½ pounds	2 table-spoons	Remove outer leaves. Trim stem end. Separate flowerets or leave head whole. Cover with lid or plastic wrap.	6-8 minutes for flow-erets; 10-11 minutes for whole head (stir or ro-tate halfway through cooking time)	4-5 minutes, covered
Eggplant	1 pound, whole	——	Prick eggplant in several places. Set it on a layer or two of paper toweling.	6 minutes	1 minute
Greens (kale and mustard)	1¼ pounds	——	Rinse and coarsely chop. Cover with wax paper.	7-8 minutes (stir once after 3 minutes)	2 minutes, covered
Mushrooms	1 pound	2 table-spoons water or butter	Cut into even shapes. Cover with wax paper.	4-6 minutes (stir once after 3 minutes)	2 minutes, covered
Onions	1 pound	——	Remove root end and slice off top. Quarter, slice or leave whole. Cover with wax paper.	4-6 minutes (stir once after 2 minutes)	5 minutes, covered
Peas	2½ pounds (3 cups)	¼ cup	Shell and rinse. Cover with lid or plastic wrap.	9-13 minutes (stir once after 5 minutes)	5 minutes, covered
Spinach	1 pound	——	Rinse; shake off excess water. Cover with lid or plastic wrap.	5-7 minutes (stir once after 3 minutes)	2 minutes, covered

APPLE-STUFFED ACORN SQUASH

The fruit and nut filling bakes right along with the squash. This dish is a delicious accompaniment to roasted turkey or baked ham.

LOW-SODIUM • MICROWAVE

Makes 8 servings.

Nutrient Value Per Serving: 181 calories, 2 g protein, 8 g fat, 28 g carbohydrate, 63 mg sodium, 16 mg cholesterol.

2 Golden Delicious apples, quartered, cored and cut crosswise into ½-inch pieces	4 small acorn squash, halved crosswise and seeded (this is easier to do if the squash is placed on a towel)
¼ cup sugar	¼ cup (½ stick) butter, cut into 8 pats
¾ cup cranberries, divided	¼ cup finely chopped walnuts
1 teaspoon chopped fresh rosemary OR: ¼ to ½ teaspoon dried rosemary, crumbled	Additional sugar, for sprinkling
Large pinch grated nutmeg	Additional grated nutmeg, for sprinkling

1. Combine the apples with the ¼ cup of sugar, ½ cup of the cranberries, the rosemary and the pinch of nutmeg in a small bowl. Fill the squash cavities with the apple mixture. Top each squash half with a pat of butter. Wrap each squash half tightly with microwave-safe plastic wrap.

2. Place the squash in a ring around the inner edge of a microwave-safe 12-inch round platter. (If all the squash halves will not fit on the platter at once, prepare them half at a time.)

3. Microwave at full power for 10 to 15 minutes, or until the squash are tender. The squash may not look cooked, so pierce them with a fork to check for doneness.

4. Unwrap the squash. Sprinkle some of the walnuts and a few of the remaining cranberries into each squash cavity. Sprinkle with the additional sugar and nutmeg.

5. Microwave at full power for 1 minute, or until the cranberries on top are cooked but still retain their shape.

BROCCOLI MARINARA

LOW-CALORIE • LOW-CHOLESTEROL • LOW-FAT • MICROWAVE

Makes 4 servings.

Nutrient Value Per Serving: 51 calories, 4 g protein, 1 g fat, 11 g carbohydrate, 401 mg sodium, 0 mg cholesterol.

1 **head broccoli, trimmed and divided into flowerets**	1 **tablespoon finely chopped oil-cured olives (optional)**
1 **cup homemade tomato sauce OR: prepared tomato sauce**	1 **clove garlic, finely chopped**
1 **tablespoon lemon juice**	1 **teaspoon finely chopped fresh thyme OR: ½ teaspoon dried thyme, crumbled**
½ **teaspoon grated lemon zest (yellow part of rind only; optional)**	**Salt and freshly ground pepper, to taste**

1. Place the broccoli flowerets in a ring around the outside of a microwave-safe 12-inch round platter, leaving a space in the center.

2. Combine the tomato sauce, lemon juice, lemon zest, olives, garlic, thyme, salt and pepper in a 2-cup glass measure. Place the cup in the center of the platter. Cover the platter tightly with microwave-safe plastic wrap.

3. Microwave at full power for 5 minutes, or until the broccoli is crisply tender, rotating the dish once halfway through the cooking time. Pour the sauce over the broccoli, and serve.

Broccoli

A member of the Brassica family, along with cauliflower, Brussels sprouts, cabbage, kale and kohlrabi, broccoli are unopened flower buds that grow on thick stalks. Broccoli is believed to have originated in Italy; its name is derived from "brocce," meaning a branch. Italian immigrants first planted broccoli in America, but it wasn't until the 1920's that it was grown commercially.

■ This dark green vegetable is a good source of vitamins A and C. A serving of 3½ ounces, or 100 grams, is only 28 calories.

■ There are many varieties of broccoli. Some are dark green, others are purplish-green. Broccoli also is sold frozen as spears or chopped.

■ Select broccoli with tight, firm buds, no yellow flowers, and stalks that are not cracked or woody. Bunches can vary in size; a 2-pound bunch makes about 4 servings. Store broccoli in a plastic bag in the refrigerator crisper drawer.

■ Wash broccoli just before you use it. Cut a thin slice from the bottom of each stem or stalk. Discard the outer leaves and split the stalks lengthwise into ½-inch-thick pieces. Peel off the outer layer, beginning at the bottom and peeling to the base of the flowerets. If the spears are too long, cut them in half crosswise. For stir-frying, cut them into 2-inch lengths.

❖ ❖ ❖

Serve Broccoli Marinara over pasta as a main course.

Couscous

Couscous, a fluffy alternative to rice, is made from moistened semolina that is rolled into tiny, grainlike pieces and dried. It's available in both traditional and instant varieties.

■ The traditional variety of couscous is steamed over a simmering pot of stew. This stew also is called couscous.

■ The instant version of couscous is faster to prepare than rice or pasta, and is a perfect choice for cooking in the microwave. Just microwave the liquid and butter called for in the package directions. Stir in the couscous, and cover and let steam as directed.

■ If you have chicken or beef broth, tomato juice or a bit of wine on hand, add them as all or part of the liquid called for.

■ Use cooked couscous as a base for pilafs or stuffings.

■ Prepared with sweet spices, dried fruits and nuts, couscous can be served as a hot cereal with milk and honey.

COUSCOUS

A good alternative to rice, couscous actually is a pasta.

MICROWAVE

Makes 4 servings.

Nutrient Value Per Serving: 146 calories, 4 g protein, 6 g fat, 19 g carbohydrate, 338 mg sodium, 16 mg cholesterol.

1	small yellow onion, finely chopped	⅔	cup couscous
2	tablespoons unsalted butter	1⅓	cups chicken broth
			Salt and freshly ground pepper, to taste

1. Combine the onion and the butter in a microwave-safe 7 x 5-inch dish.
2. Microwave, uncovered, at full power for 2 minutes.
3. Add the couscous. Stir to combine all the ingredients and to coat the couscous. Add the broth and the salt and pepper.
4. Microwave, uncovered, at full power for 4 minutes. Fluff the couscous with a fork, and serve.

GINGERED SNOW PEAS

Any way you cook them, snow peas are ready in just minutes. Their bright green color and crisp taste are welcome additions to a meal.

LOW-CALORIE • LOW-CHOLESTEROL • LOW-SODIUM • MICROWAVE

Makes 2 servings.

Nutrient Value Per Serving: 82 calories, 3 g protein, 4 g fat, 9 g carbohydrate, 44 mg sodium, 10 mg cholesterol.

2	teaspoons butter	Salt and freshly ground pepper, to taste
1	teaspoon finely chopped fresh gingerroot	
½	pound snow peas, trimmed and strings removed, if necessary	

1. Place the butter and the ginger in a microwave-safe 14 x 11 x 2-inch baking dish.
2. Microwave at full power for 2 minutes, or until the butter melts and the ginger has released its flavor. Add the snow peas, and toss to coat them. Cover the dish tightly.
3. Microwave at full power, stirring once, for 3 minutes, or until the snow peas are barely crisp-tender; they'll continue to cook after removing the dish from the microwave.
4. Sprinkle with the salt and pepper, and serve.

Finishing Touches

7

There's something so satisfying about dessert—it adds a memorable finish to a menu, and leaves a lingering sweetness long after the meal is done. Some of our favorites are here in this chapter.

Fruit is an ideal base for dessert, because the results are light, not overly sweet—and wonderfully diverse. Stewed Apples in Creamy Rum Sauce (recipe, page 224) is a warming, one-skillet sensation, while our Raspberry Fool (recipe, page 227) is just the ticket for a summer's day.

If you like baked goods, you'll love our Baker's Oven section. You'll find some of our finest culinary treasures, such as an old-fashioned Bread 'n Butter Pudding with Raspberry Purée (recipe, page 230) and Apple Gingerbread with Nutty Cream Cheese (recipe, page 234). And if you haven't tried your hand at the "new-fangled" baker's oven—the microwave—let these recipes inspire you: Orange Banana Nut Cake (recipe, page 256), Mocha Brownies with White Chocolate Icing (recipe, page 259) and Hazelnut Cheesecake (recipe, page 261). Desserts have never been so deliciously quick and easy.

We know that making a fancy dessert can be a little intimidating. So we take you, step by step, through the making of Raspberry Cream Pouffs (recipe, page 240). We also offer more homey fare, such as Blueberry Buttermilk Cake (recipe, page 245) and Raspberry Jam Squares (recipe, page 248).

Because you don't always want to top off a meal with a rich sweet, and because many of us are watching our cholesterol and fat intake, we've collected some of our best "light" recipes, such as Plum Peach Sherbet, Mulled Wine Granita, and Orange-Zested Strawberries. Recipes for these guiltless wonders start on page 250.

When all is said and done, we hope our desserts add a sweet ending to your meals!

Lemon Walnut Cake (recipe, page 237) with Orange-Zested Strawberries (recipe, page 254)—a scrumptious dinner finale.

FESTIVAL OF FRUIT

Light and luscious, fruit is a wonderful way to end a meal. And, with these recipes, your family will clamor for more.

STEWED APPLES IN CREAMY RUM SAUCE

A great last-minute dessert for unexpected company. Your guests will love the rich rum-flavored sauce.

MICROWAVE

Makes 6 servings.

Nutrient Value Per Serving: 280 calories, 2 g protein, 18 g fat, 2 g carbohydrate, 87 mg sodium, 48 mg cholesterol.

1½ **pounds cooking apples** (3 to 4 large apples), such as Rome Beauty, Golden Delicious or Cortland	2 **tablespoons currants** OR: raisins
¼ **cup (½ stick) butter**	½ **cup heavy cream**
¼ **cup sugar**	2 **tablespoons dark rum**
½ **cup orange juice**	¼ **cup toasted slivered almonds (see Tip, page 130)**

1. Peel, quarter and core the apples. Cut each apple quarter into ½-inch-thick slices.

2. Melt the butter in a large skillet over medium heat. Add the apple slices and cook, turning them often, until they begin to turn golden, for about 5 minutes. Sprinkle the apple slices with the sugar. Increase the heat to medium-high, and continue to cook until the sugar melts and begins to caramelize, for about 5 minutes.

3. Add the orange juice and the currants or raisins to the skillet. Lower the heat and simmer, turning the apples often, until the sauce has thickened and the apples are almost tender, for about 7 minutes; the cooking time will depend on the type of apples you are using.

4. Add the cream to the skillet. Gently tip and roll the skillet until the cream is combined with the sauce and the apples are coated. Remove the skillet from the heat. Stir in the rum until it is well combined.

5. Divide the apples evenly among 6 warmed dessert dishes. Spoon the sauce over the apples. Garnish each serving with the toasted almonds.

"A" Is for Apples

There are over 300 varieties of apples; the varieties shown in the photo on page 225 are among those most widely available.

■ To keep fresh apples tasty, store them in the refrigerator crisper drawer, or in a plastic bag placed in the coldest part of the refrigerator.

■ To freeze apples, peel, core and slice them. Dip the slices in lemon juice, pack them closely in containers, and freeze them.

■ You also can dry apples: Peel, core and slice them, and dip the slices in lemon juice. Place the slices on screen racks, slotted pans or rack-lined trays, and put the trays in the hot sun or a low oven (between 105° to 150°). The fruit is dried when a slice that is cut in half and squeezed shows no moisture. Dried apples last for months if they are stored in an airtight container that is kept in a cool, dark place.

224

Winesap: Moderately tart; superb raw, cooked or baked.
Red Delicious: Sweetish, crunchy; best raw in salads, fruit cups or as snacks.
Golden Delicious: Sweeter than Red Delicious; an all-purpose variety.
McIntosh: Very juicy, slightly tart; great raw, baked or for use in sauces.
Cortland: Mild; excellent raw, or in pies and for use in cooking.
Granny Smith: Moderately tart; prized for snacks, salads and for use in cooking.
Rome: Slightly tart; the best choice for baking and cooking.
Crispin/Mutsu: Very crisp, sweet eating apple; sold under either of its names.

Microwave Instructions
(for a 650-watt variable power microwave oven)

Ingredient Changes: Reduce the butter to 2 tablespoons, and reduce the orange juice to 2 tablespoons.

Directions: Spread the almonds on the bottom of a microwave-safe 10-inch pie plate. Microwave, uncovered, at full power, stirring once, for 6 minutes to toast the almonds lightly. Remove the almonds and set them aside. Place the butter in the same pie plate. Microwave, uncovered, at full power for 1 minute to melt the butter. Add the apple slices and the sugar, and toss to mix them. Microwave, uncovered, at full power for 3 minutes, stirring once. Add the orange juice and the currants or raisins. Cover the plate with microwave-safe plastic wrap, vented in one place. Microwave at full power for 2 minutes. Stir in the cream. Microwave, uncovered, at full power for 1 minute. Stir in the rum. Spoon the apple slices into 6 warmed individual dessert dishes, spoon the sauce over them and sprinkle the tops with the toasted almonds.

Golden Delicious   **Rome**

Winesap   **Granny Smith**

FRESH BERRIES IN TUILES WITH CARAMEL SAUCE

A dessert that is as beautiful as it is delectable. Fresh berries in a sweet caramel sauce are served in a crisp cookie cup — the perfect ending to a summer feast.

LOW-SODIUM

Makes 8 servings.

Nutrient Value Per Serving: 235 calories, 1 g protein, 18 g fat, 19 g carbohydrate, 21 mg sodium, 66 mg cholesterol.

1 recipe Tuile Cookies (recipe, page 227)	**Caramel Sauce:**
1½ cups blueberries	1½ cups plus 2 tablespoons heavy cream
1 cup hulled and quartered strawberries	1 vanilla bean, split OR: ½ teaspoon vanilla extract
1 cup raspberries	⅓ cup granulated sugar
2 tablespoons 10X (confectioners' powdered) sugar	2 teaspoons lemon juice
	3 tablespoons water

1. Prepare the Tuile Cookies.

2. Combine the blueberries, strawberries, raspberries and 10X (confectioners' powdered) sugar in a medium-size bowl. Toss gently to mix the ingredients. Refrigerate the berry mixture.

3. Prepare the Caramel Sauce: Place 1½ cups of the cream along with the vanilla bean, if using, in a heavy, nonaluminum skillet. Cook the mixture over medium heat until it is reduced to 1¼ cups, for about 7 minutes. Remove the saucepan from the heat. Remove the vanilla bean and scrape the seeds into the mixture. Discard the vanilla bean. (You may wish to rinse the bean, dry it well and place it in a sugar canister to flavor the sugar.) If using the vanilla extract, stir it in now. Stir in the remaining 2 tablespoons of cream.

4. Combine the granulated sugar, lemon juice and water in a small saucepan, and stir to dissolve the sugar. Bring the mixture to boiling over medium-high heat. Cook, uncovered, without stirring, until the sugar mixture is pale amber in color, for about 5 minutes. Stir the sugar mixture into the cream mixture.

5. Gently stir the berry mixture into the warm sauce. Spoon the combined mixture into the tuiles. Serve immediately.

Fabulous Fruit: How to Pick a Winner

■ Blueberry: Most flavorful from June to August, the best blueberries are large, firm and unmarked. Refrigerate them for no longer than 2 days.

■ Mango: Fleshy mangoes come in many shapes and sizes, and range in taste from extra sweet to tart. They are available year round. Pick firm, semi-ripe mangoes. To ripen them fully, leave mangoes at room temperature. Refrigerate mangoes for up to two weeks.

■ Papaya: A tropical treat, papayas have a sweet pulp and a center cavity filled with black seeds. Available year round, papayas are at their peak in spring and fall. Buy fruit that just gives to the touch. Ripen papayas at room temperature; refrigerate papayas for up to two weeks.

■ Raspberry: This delicately flavored fruit peaks from June to August. Choose firm, dry berries. Refrigerate raspberries for up to two days.

■ Strawberry: Although they are available year round, the prime season for fresh strawberries is April to July. Select firm, dry, shapely, dark red berries. Refrigerate them for up to one week.

❖　❖　❖

Raspberries

Red raspberries are the most familiar variety of this berry, but there are black, amber, yellow and purple raspberries as well. Red and black raspberries are found growing wild in many parts of the country; the other varieties generally are grown in home gardens. The only variety of raspberry grown commercially are red raspberries.

■ Raspberries bruise easily, so they must be harvested by hand, which contributes to their expense when marketed fresh. Fresh raspberries are sold from mid-April to November, with peak supplies available from June to August.

■ Select raspberries that are firm, have a bright color and are well-shaped.

■ Before storing raspberries, sort them and place them in a single layer in a pan lined with paper toweling. Refrigerate the berries, and use them within 2 days of purchase.

■ Wash raspberries in a bowl of cold water just before using them; do not soak the berries. Use your hands to lift the berries gently out of the water, to avoid crushing them. Drain the berries on paper toweling.

❖   ❖   ❖

TUILE COOKIES

LOW-CALORIE • LOW-CHOLESTEROL • LOW-SODIUM

Bake at 400° for 5 minutes.
Makes 8 cookies.

Nutrient Value Per Cookie: 65 calories, 1 g protein, 3 g fat, 9 g carbohydrate, 25 mg sodium, 8 mg cholesterol.

	Nonstick vegetable cooking spray	½	teaspoon vanilla Pinch salt
1	egg white	2	tablespoons unsalted butter, melted
3	tablespoons granulated sugar	3	tablespoons all-purpose flour
1	tablespoon light brown sugar	1	tablespoon milk

1. Preheat the oven to hot (400°). Spray a large baking sheet with nonstick vegetable cooking spray, and set aside the sheet.
2. Mix together the egg white, granulated sugar, brown sugar, vanilla and salt in a small bowl with a wooden spoon until the mixture is smooth. Stir in the butter. Add the flour and stir until it is well combined. Pour in the milk and stir until the batter is smooth; the batter will be thin.
3. Using a measuring tablespoonful per cookie, spoon the batter onto the prepared baking sheet to make 2 cookies, leaving ample room between the cookies for spreading.
4. Bake one sheet at a time, in the preheated hot oven (400°) for 5 minutes, or until the cookies are browned around the edges. Immediately lift each of the cookies from the sheet onto the bottom of an inverted juice glass. Remove the cookies from the glasses when the cookies are cooled and crisp. Repeat with the remaining batter.

RASPBERRY FOOL

LOW-SODIUM

Makes 8 servings.

Nutrient Value Per Serving: 272 calories, 2 g protein, 18 g fat, 28 g carbohydrate, 22 mg sodium, 64 mg cholesterol.

4	cups raspberries (about 1 pint)	¼	cup 10X (confectioners' powdered) sugar
2	tablespoons red currant jelly	1½	cups heavy cream
3	tablespoons orange juice	¼	cup dairy sour cream
		⅓	cup honey

1. Combine the raspberries, red currant jelly, orange juice and 10X (confectioners' powdered) sugar in the container of a food processor or electric blender. Whirl until the mixture is puréed. Press the purée through a fine strainer with the back of a spoon, and discard the seeds. Refrigerate the strained purée until it is chilled, for about 2 hours.
2. Combine the heavy cream and the sour cream with an electric mixer in a small bowl. Beat until soft peaks begin to form. Gradually beat in the honey until stiff peaks form. Gently fold the raspberry purée into the whipped cream. Transfer the raspberry fool to a decorative serving bowl, and serve it immediately.

BANANA PUDDING

This creamy no-bake dessert is sure to be a family favorite. And it gives new meaning to the phrase "quick and easy."

LOW-CHOLESTEROL

Makes 12 servings.

Nutrient Value Per Serving: 364 calories, 5 g protein, 13 g fat, 60 g carbohydrate, 136 mg sodium, 23 mg cholesterol.

2	packages (3½ ounces each) vanilla instant pudding and pie filling mix	1	container (8 ounces) frozen nondairy whipped topping, thawed
1	can (14 ounces) sweetened condensed milk (not evaporated)	6	large bananas
		1	box (11 ounces) vanilla wafers

1. Prepare the pudding and pie filling, following the package directions. Let the filling stand until it is slightly thickened, for 3 minutes. Mix in the condensed milk and the nondairy topping.
2. Slice the bananas into ½-inch-thick rounds.
3. Layer the wafers, bananas and filling in a clear glass bowl or 13 x 9 x 2-inch glass dish. Serve the pudding immediately, or refrigerate it.

POACHED PEARS WITH GINGER

Simple poached pears are transformed into an exotic taste of the Far East by flavoring them with cinnamon, lemon and fresh gingerroot.

LOW-CHOLESTEROL • LOW-SODIUM • LOW-FAT

Makes 6 servings.

Nutrient Value Per Serving: 303 calories, 1 g protein, 1 g fat, 78 g carbohydrate, 2 mg sodium, 0 mg cholesterol.

4	cups water	6	slightly underripe Bosc OR: Anjou pears
1½	cups sugar		Lemon half
2	cinnamon sticks		
4	thin slices fresh gingerroot, crushed		**Garnish:**
2	strips lemon zest (yellow part of rind only)		Chopped candied gingerroot
			Thin lemon zest strips

1. Combine the water, sugar, cinnamon sticks, ginger and 2 strips of lemon zest in a large saucepan. Bring the mixture to boiling over high heat, stirring to dissolve the sugar. Reduce the heat to low and simmer the syrup, partially covered, for 20 minutes.
2. Peel the pears, and rub the peeled surfaces with the cut side of the lemon half to prevent discoloration. Core and seed the pears with a melon baller, leaving the stems on.

Go Bananas!

Bananas are a rich source of potassium, which is a mineral crucial to the normal functioning of muscles, including the heart. Bananas also are a good source of thiamine, riboflavin, niacin, and vitamins A and C.

❖ ❖ ❖

" The proof of the pudding is in the eating. "
—*Miguel de Cervantes*

Pears

Although there actually are thousands of pear varieties, only a handful are grown and marketed commercially.

■ Pears are harvested green because they develop a better flavor as the sugar content increases as a result of the conversion of starch to sugar. Pears to be used for cooking or baking should be firm and slightly underripe. Pears to be eaten out of hand or used fresh in salads and desserts should be fully ripe.

■ If pears are hard, let them ripen at room temperature until the fruits feel soft. Some green pears, such as Bartletts, will turn yellow when ripe, but others do not change color upon ripening.

■ Pears are available year-round because there are so many varieties. Most pears are grown in California, Oregon and Washington.

■ Pears provide a fair amount of vitamin C, some vitamin A, and B vitamins. A medium-size Bartlett pear has about 100 calories.

❖ ❖ ❖

3. Place the pears in the syrup, and bring the syrup to just under boiling over medium heat. Lower the heat and simmer, uncovered, for 10 minutes, or until the pears are slightly undercooked. Remove the saucepan from the heat. Let the pears stand in the syrup for 20 to 30 minutes.

4. Remove 1 cup of the syrup to a small saucepan. Boil the syrup to reduce it to ½ cup of sauce.

5. Remove the pears to a serving platter. Drizzle the pears with the sauce. Garnish with the candied gingerroot and the thin strips of lemon zest.

PEARS IN RED WINE SAUCE

A simple and elegant dessert that can be made in just minutes—this dish will "wow" your family and friends.

LOW-CHOLESTEROL • LOW-SODIUM • LOW-FAT

Makes 2 servings.

Nutrient Value Per Serving: 190 calories, 1 g protein, 6 g fat, 36 g carbohydrate, 2 mg sodium, 0 mg cholesterol.

1 tablespoon unsalted margarine	1½ tablespoons sugar
2 firm, ripe pears, peeled, cored and quartered	2 bay leaves
	¼ cup fruity dry red wine

1. Melt the margarine in a large skillet over medium-high heat. Add the pears, sugar and bay leaves, and sauté the mixture for 1 minute.

2. Add the red wine to the skillet. Bring the combined mixture to boiling and boil for 5 minutes, or until the sauce is slightly thickened and reduced by half.

3. Remove the bay leaves from the sauce. Divide the pears between 2 individual glass dessert dishes. Top the pears with the sauce.

THE BAKER'S OVEN

These old-fashioned desserts will fill your entire house with their delectable smells — and fill your family with delight.

BREAD 'N BUTTER PUDDING WITH RASPBERRY PURÉE

This dessert sensation can be made in a flat baking dish, or in a 10-cup mold, as pictured. If you use the 10-cup mold, soak the bread for 30 to 40 minutes in the custard mixture, pressing it down occasionally, as bread has a tendency to float to the top.

Bake at 375° for 1 hour.
Makes 12 servings.

Nutrient Value Per Serving: 388 calories, 10 g protein, 16 g fat, 50 g carbohydrate, 355 mg sodium, 246 mg cholesterol.

1	loaf (about 12 ounces) Italian bread	1	cup heavy cream
1	tablespoon butter or margarine, softened	1	teaspoon vanilla
5	eggs	2	tablespoons slivered almonds, toasted (see Tip, page 130)
4	egg yolks		Raspberry Purée (recipe follows)
1	cup sugar		Whipped cream (optional)
¼	teaspoon salt		
4	cups milk		

> **"** *B* read is the staff of life, but pudding makes a good crutch. **"**
> —*Scottish Proverb*

Treat your family to Bread 'n Butter Pudding with Raspberry Purée — and count on serving seconds. It's an irresistible combination of toasted almonds, rich custard and sweet-tart raspberries.

Eating Apples: Find Your Bite Style

- Munching around the core reveals a middle-of-the-roader; you're easy-going, easy to please.
- You eat in rows from top to bottom — indicating your logical, methodical approach to life.
- Do you peel your apple? You have a probing, analytical mind; no small talk for you.
- Nonconformist — that's your type if you slice against the grain.
- If you always cut an apple into wedges, you're neat, orderly and super-organized.

1. Preheat the oven to moderate (375°). Lightly butter a 10 x 2-inch round baking dish.
2. Slice the bread crosswise into twenty-four ½-inch-thick rounds. Very lightly butter one side of each slice.
3. Arrange the bread slices, buttered side up, in the prepared dish in a circular pattern, completely covering the bottom of the dish.
4. Beat together the eggs, egg yolks, sugar and salt in a large bowl. Beat in the milk, cream and vanilla. Pour the mixture through a strainer over the bread slices.
5. Set the baking dish in a larger pan. Fill the pan with about 1 inch of boiling water.
6. Bake the pudding in the preheated moderate oven (375°) for 1 hour, or until the center is almost set but still soft. Do not overbake the pudding; the custard will set as it cools.
7. Sprinkle the toasted almonds over the top. Remove the pudding from the water bath to a wire rack. Serve the pudding, warm or chilled, with the Raspberry Purée and, if you wish, whipped cream.

Raspberry Purée:

Place 1 package (12 ounces) of frozen dry-pack raspberries, partially thawed, in the container of a food processor or electric blender. Whirl at high speed until the berries are puréed.

CHUNKY APPLE CAKE

Bake at 350° for 1 hour and 15 minutes.
Makes 16 servings.

Nutrient Value Per Serving: 402 calories, 5 g protein, 23 g fat, 46 g carbohydrate, 203 mg sodium, 51 mg cholesterol.

1¼ cups corn oil	1 teaspoon ground cinnamon
1¾ cups sugar	3 medium-size apples (1¼ pounds), peeled and cut into chunks
3 eggs	
1 teaspoon vanilla	
3 cups all-purpose flour	1 cup walnuts, chopped
1 teaspoon baking soda	
1 teaspoon salt	

1. Preheat the oven to moderate (350°). Grease and flour a 9-inch angel food cake pan.
2. Beat together the oil and the sugar in a large bowl until the mixture is thick and creamy. Add the eggs and the vanilla, and beat until all the ingredients are well blended.
3. Sift together the flour, baking soda, salt and cinnamon onto wax paper. Stir the flour mixture into the egg mixture. Mix in the apples and the walnuts. Pour the batter into the prepared pan.
4. Bake the cake in the preheated moderate oven (350°) for 1 hour and 15 minutes, or until the cake is browned on top and the sides start to pull away from the pan. Cool the cake completely in the pan on a wire rack. Run a thin metal spatula around the edges and the center of the cake to loosen it. Invert the cake onto a serving platter.

APPLE RAISIN PIE

LOW-CHOLESTEROL

Bake at 425° for 55 minutes.
Makes 8 servings.

Nutrient Value Per Serving: 432 calories, 3 g protein, 20 g fat, 60 g carbohydrate, 291 mg sodium, 17 mg cholesterol.

1 package (11 ounces) pie crust mix

Filling:
1¼ pounds Golden Delicious apples (about 3 medium-size apples)
1¼ pounds Granny Smith apples (about 3 medium-size apples)
⅓ cup plus 1 tablespoon sugar
2½ tablespoons cornstarch
¾ teaspoon ground cinnamon
¼ teaspoon ground ginger

½ cup golden raisins
2 tablespoons frozen orange juice concentrate
2½ teaspoons lemon juice
1½ tablespoons unsalted butter

Glaze:
2 tablespoons heavy cream
1 teaspoon sugar
½ teaspoon cider vinegar

Crème fraîche
OR: whipped cream
(optional)

1. Preheat the oven to hot (425°).
2. Prepare the pie crust mix, following directions for a 9-inch double-crust pie. Roll the dough into a single crust, 12 inches in diameter. Fit the dough into a 9-inch pie plate, turn under the edges and form a high, free-form edge.
3. Prepare the Filling: Peel, quarter and core the apples. Cut them into ¼-inch-thick slices. Place the apple slices in a large bowl. Combine ⅓ cup of the sugar with the cornstarch, cinnamon and ginger in a small bowl. Sprinkle the cinnamon mixture over the apples, and toss gently to mix the ingredients. Let the apple mixture stand for 10 minutes.

An Apple a Day . . .

Recent research indicates there's more behind this old adage than we thought. Apples are low in calories (one medium-size apple has only 80), and high in fiber. They're a good source of vitamins A, B_1, B_2 and C, and the minerals potassium, phosphorus and calcium. What's more, they're virtually sodium- and fat-free. The latest health bulletin is the connection between apples and cholesterol. Apples contain no cholesterol themselves, but they also can help to prevent high cholesterol. Scientists have found that pectin, the form of dietary fiber found in apples, actually works to reduce the level of harmful cholesterol in the bloodstream, which can help lower the risk of heart disease.

Orange and ginger lend their wonderful flavors to our Apple Raisin Pie.

4. Combine the raisins, orange juice concentrate and lemon juice in a small bowl. Add the raisin mixture to the apple mixture, and stir to combine all the ingredients. Pile the filling into the crust and dot with the butter.

5. Prepare the Glaze: Combine the cream, sugar and vinegar in a small bowl. Brush the glaze on the pie crust rim. Place the pie on a baking sheet. Cover only the apple filling with a lightly buttered piece of aluminum foil, buttered side down.

6. Bake the pie on the middle rack in the preheated hot oven (425°) for 10 minutes. Cover the whole pie, including the crust, with the buttered foil. Bake for 40 minutes. Remove the foil. Sprinkle the top of the pie with the remaining tablespoon of sugar. Bake for 5 minutes more. If you wish, serve the pie with crème fraîche or whipped cream.

APPLE WALNUT TART

Bake at 350° for 45 minutes.
Makes 8 servings.

Nutrient Value Per Serving: 511 calories, 5 g protein, 28 g fat, 64 g carbohydrate, 197 mg sodium, 81 mg cholesterol.

1¼ **cups all-purpose flour**	¼ **cup (½ stick) butter,**
¾ **cup plus ½ cup firmly**	**melted**
packed light brown sugar	½ **cup walnut halves**
½ **cup (1 stick) butter**	**(optional)**
1 **egg, slightly beaten**	**Vanilla ice cream**
1 **cup walnuts**	**OR: whipped cream**
¼ **cup golden raisins**	**(optional)**
5 **cups ¼-inch-thick, peeled,**	
cored apple slices,	
Rome Beauty or Cortland	
(2 pounds)	

1. Combine the flour with ¾ cup of the brown sugar in a medium-size bowl. Cut in the ½ cup of butter and the egg with a pastry blender until the mixture is crumbly. Shape the dough into a disk, wrap it in plastic wrap and refrigerate it for 1 hour.

2. Preheat the oven to moderate (350°).

3. Flatten the dough with a rolling pin on a lightly floured board to a 12½-inch circle. Sprinkle with a little flour if the dough becomes too sticky. Transfer the dough to a 10 x 1-inch fluted tart pan with a removable bottom. Press and pull up the crust, making sure the dough is level with the top of the pan; like all sweet crusts, this one is difficult to work with. Press the dough firmly into the fluted side, keeping the dough a full ¼ inch thick; if the crust is thinner, it may slip down during baking. Place the tart shell in the freezer until it is very firm, for 20 to 25 minutes.

4. Grind the walnuts in a food processor for 2 seconds, or until they are coarsely ground. Sprinkle the ground nuts and the raisins onto the pie shell.

5. Toss the apple slices with the remaining ½ cup of brown sugar in a bowl. Arrange the slices in a circular pattern on top of the raisins and nuts in the tart shell. Drizzle the melted butter over the apples.

6. Bake the tart in the preheated moderate oven (350°) for 45 minutes, or until the apples are soft. Cool the tart on a wire rack. Remove the side of the pan. If you wish, arrange ½ cup of walnut halves around edge of the tart. Serve the tart with vanilla ice cream or whipped cream, if you wish.

Walnuts

The "English" walnut, also known as the California or Persian walnut, is the most common variety of walnut. "English" is a misnomer, because England does not produce walnuts commercially, but the name was given long ago to the walnuts native to ancient Persia. English trading ships transported Persian walnuts around the world, and thus promoted the mistaken belief that the nuts were grown in England. Spanish missionaries introduced walnuts to California, and by the 1800's the walnut industry there was established. Today, California is the leading producer of walnuts.

■ English walnuts are available shelled or unshelled. Shelled walnuts should be stored in an airtight container and refrigerated, or frozen for longer storage.

■ One ounce of English walnuts contains 186 calories and 4 grams of protein.

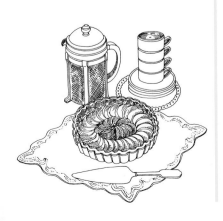

APPLE GINGERBREAD WITH NUTTY CREAM CHEESE

This gingerbread is made with cake flour to give it a moist, light texture.

Bake apples at 350° for 20 minutes; bake gingerbread at 350° for 30 minutes.
Makes 12 servings.

Nutrient Value Per Serving: 359 calories, 3 g protein, 19 g fat, 47 g carbohydrate, 269 mg sodium, 49 mg cholesterol.

1	**pound cooking apples (about 2 apples), peeled, cored and sliced**
2	**tablespoons butter, at room temperature**
¼	**cup firmly packed brown sugar**
1½	**cups sifted cake flour**
1½	**teaspoons baking powder**
¼	**teaspoon baking soda**
1½	**teaspoons ground ginger**
½	**teaspoon ground cinnamon**
½	**teaspoon salt**
⅓	**cup vegetable oil**
¼	**cup granulated sugar**

1	**egg**
½	**teaspoon vanilla**
½	**cup boiling water**
½	**cup dark molasses**

Nutty Cream Cheese:

4	**tablespoons butter, at room temperature**
½	**teaspoon vanilla**
4	**ounces cream cheese, at room temperature**
1	**tablespoon lemon juice**
1¾	**cups sifted 10X (confectioners' powdered) sugar**
½	**cup chopped walnuts**

1. Preheat the oven to moderate (350°).
2. Stir together the apple slices, 2 tablespoons of the butter and the brown sugar in a 9 x 9 x 2-inch square baking pan.
3. Bake the apples in the preheated moderate oven (350°) for 20 minutes, or until the apples soften. Leave the oven on.
4. Sift together the flour, baking powder, baking soda, ginger, cinnamon and salt onto wax paper, and sift again.
5. Beat together the oil and the granulated sugar in a large bowl with an electric mixer for 1 minute. Add the egg and ½ teaspoon of the vanilla, and beat for 2 minutes more, or until the egg mixture is light colored and thick.
6. Combine the boiling water with the molasses in a small saucepan, and stir the mixture well. Add the molasses mixture to the egg mixture alternately with the flour mixture. Pour the batter into the pan over the cooked apples.
7. Bake the gingerbread in the preheated moderate oven (350°) for 30 minutes, or until a wooden pick inserted in the center comes out clean. Cool the gingerbread in the pan on a wire rack.
8. Meanwhile, prepare the Nutty Cream Cheese: Combine the remaining 4 tablespoons of butter and ½ teaspoon of vanilla with the cream cheese, lemon juice and 10X (confectioners' powdered) sugar in a medium-size bowl and stir until the mixture is light colored and fluffy.
9. Spread the cream cheese mixture over the top of the gingerbread. Sprinkle the top evenly with the walnuts.

Apple Additions

There are all sorts of ways you can use apples to make dishes more interesting and appealing. Here are a few suggestions.

■ Grate apples into coleslaw for a snappy new taste.
■ Scoop out the centers and fill apples with tuna, chicken, salmon or fruit salads. Dice the scooped-out centers and mix them into the salads. Or serve ice cream or berries in the apple "bowls."
■ Pair apples with steamed vegetables in a salad. Combine equal parts of apple slices, sliced carrots, snow pea pods and green beans. Toss with French dressing, and chill.
■ Slice apples and top them with cheese, pâté or cooked sausage as hors d'oeuvres.
■ Chop apples and mix them with granola and lemon yogurt as a great snack.

FRENCH APPLE TARTE

LOW-CHOLESTEROL

Bake at 375° for 35 to 40 minutes.
Makes 6 servings.

Nutrient Value Per Serving: 312 calories, 2 g protein, 17 g fat,
38 g carbohydrate, 194 mg sodium, 16 mg cholesterol.

1	sheet frozen puff pastry (half of 17¼-ounce package), thawed	3	tablespoons unsalted butter, melted
2	medium-size Granny Smith apples (about 1 pound), peeled, halved, cored and thinly sliced	⅓	cup sugar Calvados Crème Anglaise (recipe, page 236; optional)

1. Cut an 8½-inch circle from the pastry. Place the circle on an aluminum foil-lined baking sheet with sides.

2. Preheat the oven to moderate (375°).

3. Starting ½ inch in from the pastry edge, layer the apple slices around the pastry in a circular pattern, covering the top of the pastry. Brush the slices with half the melted butter and sprinkle them with half the sugar.

4. Bake the tarte in the preheated moderate oven (375°) for 20 minutes. Remove the tarte from the oven. Brush it with the remaining butter and sprinkle on the remaining sugar.

5. Bake the tarte for 15 to 20 minutes more, or until it is browned on the edges. Serve the tarte warm, with Calvados Crème Anglaise, if you wish.

An elegant ending to any meal: Pumpkin Soufflé with Calvados Crème Anglaise (recipes, page 236), and French Apple Tarte.

235

PUMPKIN SOUFFLÉ

Bake at 375° for 50 minutes.
Makes 8 servings.

Nutrient Value Per Serving: 267 calories, 8 g protein, 17 g fat, 20 g carbohydrate, 191 mg sodium, 242 mg cholesterol.

½ **cup (1 stick) cold butter**
1 **cup all-purpose flour**
1⅓ **cups milk**
6 **eggs, at room temperature, separated**
½ **cup canned pumpkin**
½ **teaspoon ground mace**
½ **teaspoon ground ginger**
½ **teaspoon ground nutmeg**
½ **teaspoon ground cloves**
1 **teaspoon ground cinnamon**
1½ **teaspoons grated orange zest (orange part of rind only; 1 orange)**
2 **tablespoons honey**
10X (confectioners' powdered) sugar (optional)
Calvados Crème Anglaise (recipe follows)

1. Preheat the oven to moderate (375°). Grease and lightly flour a 1½-quart soufflé dish.
2. Break up the butter into 8 pieces in a large bowl. Add the flour. Cut in the butter with a pastry blender or 2 forks to form a dough.
3. Bring the milk to boiling in a small saucepan. Remove the saucepan from the heat. Whisk the dough into the milk until it is smooth. (The soufflé can be prepared earlier in the day up to this point, and refrigerated.)
4. Place the milk mixture in a large bowl. Add the egg yolks, pumpkin, mace, ginger, nutmeg, cloves, cinnamon, orange zest and honey, and mix until the ingredients are well blended.
5. Beat the egg whites in a large bowl until medium peaks form. Gently fold one third of the whites at a time into the pumpkin mixture. Pour the pumpkin mixture into the prepared soufflé dish.
6. Bake the soufflé in the preheated moderate oven (375°) for 50 minutes, or until the top is puffed and the center barely moves when it is shaken. Sprinkle with 10X (confectioners' powdered) sugar, if you wish. Serve the soufflé with the Calvados Crème Anglaise.

CALVADOS CRÈME ANGLAISE

LOW-SODIUM

Makes 8 servings.

Nutrient Value Per Serving: 94 calories, 2 g protein, 4 g fat, 13 g carbohydrate, 19 mg sodium, 140 mg cholesterol.

¾ **cup 10X (confectioners' powdered) sugar**
4 **egg yolks**
1 **cup milk**
½ **teaspoon vanilla**
1 **teaspoon Calvados OR: apple-flavored brandy**

1. Stir together the 10X (confectioners' powdered) sugar and the egg yolks in a medium-size bowl until they are well combined.
2. Combine the milk with the vanilla in a medium-size saucepan. Bring the mixture just to boiling.
3. Stirring constantly, add the milk mixture to the egg yolk mixture. Return the combined mixture to the saucepan. Cook over medium heat,

Sensational Soufflé

Soufflé is a light, puffy egg dish that can be either sweet or savory. The classic soufflé is baked and should rise above its dish. It must be served immediately. Baked soufflé can be flavored with cheese, vegetables, seafood, vanilla or chocolate. A chilled soufflé is made with gelatin to give it body. To give a chilled soufflé the appearance of having risen like a baked soufflé, a collar is wrapped around the dish. A gelatin-based soufflé is chilled until it is firm, and the collar is removed.

❖ ❖ ❖

stirring constantly, until the mixture is slightly thickened, for 2 to
3 minutes; do not boil it.
4. Pour the crème anglaise through a sieve into a large bowl to strain it.
5. Stir in the Calvados or apple-flavored brandy.

LEMON WALNUT CAKE

Bake at 350° for 50 to 60 minutes.
Makes 16 servings.

Nutrient Value Per Serving: 360 calories, 4 g protein, 21 g fat,
40 g carbohydrate, 154 mg sodium, 106 mg cholesterol.

2½ cups sifted cake flour
1 tablespoon baking powder
¼ teaspoon baking soda
¼ teaspoon salt
1 cup toasted walnuts,
   finely chopped
   (see Tip, at left)
1⅔ cups granulated sugar
1 cup (2 sticks) unsalted
   butter or margarine,
   softened
4 eggs, separated
2 tablespoons orange-
   flavored liqueur
1 teaspoon lemon extract
2 teaspoons grated lemon
   zest (yellow part
   of rind only)

1 tablespoon fresh
   lemon juice
1 container (8 ounces) dairy
   sour cream
⅛ teaspoon cream of tartar

Glazing Syrup:
½ cup 10X (confectioners'
   powdered) sugar
3 tablespoons fresh
   lemon juice
2 tablespoons orange-
   flavored liqueur
   OR: orange juice
½ teaspoon 10X
   (confectioners'
   powdered) sugar,
   for dusting (optional)

1. Preheat the oven to moderate (350°). Grease and lightly flour a 12-cup
Bundt® or tube pan.
2. Sift together the flour, baking powder, baking soda and salt onto wax
paper. Stir in the walnuts.
3. Beat together the granulated sugar and the butter or margarine until
light colored and fluffy in a large bowl with an electric mixer at high speed,
for about 2 minutes. Add the egg yolks, orange-flavored liqueur, lemon
extract, lemon zest and lemon juice, and beat for 1 minute. Reduce the
mixer speed to low, and mix in the sour cream just until it is blended. Stir in
the flour-walnut mixture in 3 additions, mixing after each until smooth.
4. Using clean beaters, beat the egg whites and the cream of tartar in a
medium-size bowl until soft peaks form. Stir one quarter of the beaten
whites into the batter. Fold in the remainder in 2 additions. Spoon the
batter into the prepared pan.
5. Bake the cake in the preheated moderate oven (350°) for 50 to
60 minutes, or until a wooden pick inserted in the center comes out clean.
Cool the cake in the pan on a wire rack for 10 minutes.
6. Meanwhile, prepare the Glazing Syrup: Combine the ½ cup of 10X
(confectioners' powdered) sugar with the lemon juice in a small pan. Bring
the mixture to boiling. Remove the mixture from the heat. Add the orange-
flavored liqueur or orange juice.
7. Invert the cake onto a wire rack placed over a piece of wax paper. Spoon
the syrup onto the cake while it is hot. Sprinkle the cake with ½ teaspoon of
10X (confectioners' powdered) sugar, if you wish. Serve the cake warm.

Toasting Walnuts

*To toast walnuts, spread them
in an even layer in a jelly-roll
pan. Bake them in a
preheated slow oven (325°),
stirring often, for about
20 minutes, or until the
walnuts are browned.*

❖ ❖ ❖

Zest for Cooking

*Lemons, limes and oranges
should be grated before being
squeezed when a recipe calls
for both grated rind and juice.
The same applies when zest is
called for in a recipe.
Carefully remove the zest,
using a very sharp paring
knife or a vegetable parer,
then squeeze for the juice.*

❖ ❖ ❖

BLUEBERRY ORANGE CUSTARD TART

You can prepare the orange pastry dough for the crust the day before you plan to bake this delectable tart.

Bake shell at 350° for 30 minutes; bake filled tart at 350° for 25 to 30 minutes.

Makes 8 servings.

Nutrient Value Per Serving: 407 calories, 6 g protein, 23 g fat, 46 g carbohydrate, 141 mg sodium, 193 mg cholesterol.

Orange Pastry:
- 1 cup unsifted all-purpose flour
- 1 teaspoon sugar
- ⅛ teaspoon salt
- 1 teaspoon grated orange zest (orange part of rind only)
- 5 tablespoons unsalted butter, cut into ½-inch slices
- 1 tablespoon vegetable shortening
- 2 to 2½ tablespoons cold orange juice

Orange Custard:
- ½ cup milk
- ½ cup heavy cream
- 4 strips (3 x 1 inch) orange zest (orange part of rind only)
- ½ vanilla bean, split lengthwise OR: ¼ teaspoon vanilla extract
- ⅛ teaspoon salt
- 6 tablespoons sugar
- 2 eggs, slightly beaten
- 1 egg yolk
- 2 teaspoons orange-flavored liqueur
- 2 cups blueberries
- 3 tablespoons red currant jelly
- ¼ teaspoon lemon juice

1. Prepare the Orange Pastry: Combine the flour, sugar, salt and orange zest in a large bowl. Cut in the butter and the shortening with a pastry blender or 2 knives until the mixture resembles coarse meal. Gradually add the orange juice, stirring with a fork until the dough leaves the sides of the bowl clean and can be gathered into a ball. Wrap the dough in plastic wrap and refrigerate it overnight.

2. Prepare the Orange Custard: Combine the milk, cream, orange zest, vanilla bean if using, and salt in a medium-size, nonaluminum saucepan. Heat the mixture over medium heat to scalding; small bubbles will appear on the milk around the edge of the pan. Remove the saucepan from the heat, cover it and let the milk mixture steep for 30 minutes. Remove and discard the orange zest. Remove the vanilla bean and scrape the seeds into the mixture. Discard the vanilla bean, or rinse the bean, dry it well and store it in a jar of sugar to flavor the sugar. If using the vanilla extract, add it after the milk mixture has steeped for 30 minutes.

3. Combine the sugar, eggs, egg yolk and orange-flavored liqueur in a medium-size bowl, and whisk to combine the ingredients. Gradually whisk in the milk mixture. Set aside the custard mixture.

4. Roll out the dough on a lightly floured surface to a 13-inch circle. Fit the dough into a 9-inch tart pan with a removable bottom so the dough fits evenly. Trim the edge, leaving a ½-inch overhang. Turn under the overhang to make a stand-up fluted edge. Chill the dough in the pan for 30 minutes.

5. Preheat the oven to moderate (350°).

Blueberries

Small, dark purple berries with very small seeds, blueberries are the fruit of a bush found in North America, Europe and Asia. In some parts of America they are called huckleberries, although huckleberries actually are a wild variety of blueberry found throughout New England, Pennsylvania and Virginia. They also are known as "bilberries," "whinberries" and "whortleberries"—but they're all varieties of the blueberry.

■ Fresh blueberries are marketed from May to August. Select plump, firm berries that are uniform in size. A dull appearance or soft, juicy berries indicate old berries.

■ Blueberries sometimes are covered with a waxy, white bloom that is a natural protective coating.

■ Blueberries have a short refrigerator life of 1 to 2 days, so use them quickly after purchasing them. Blueberries also can be frozen.

❖ ❀ ❖

Bake-A-Cake

To insure that a cake has the best possible texture, volume and shape, use the exact measurements, ingredients and pan size called for in the recipe. Follow the recipe directions to the letter.

■ Remember to preheat the oven for 10 minutes before putting the cake in it to bake.

■ The cake is done when:
—It shrinks slightly from the sides of the pan.
—The top of the cake springs back to shape when a fingertip is pressed lightly on it.
—A cake tester or wooden pick inserted near the center of the cake comes out clean, with no batter or moist particles clinging to it.

■ The cake may turn out heavy and soggy if the oven temperature is too low; the cake may fall if the the oven is too hot, if the oven door is opened too soon, or if there is not enough flour in the batter.

❖ ❖ ❖

" It's food too fine for angels, yet come take And eat thy fill! It's Heaven's sugar cake. "
—*Edward Taylor*

6. Line the dough with aluminum foil. Add dried beans to weight the shell.
7. Bake the shell in the preheated moderate oven (350°) for 15 minutes. Remove the foil and the beans. Bake for 15 minutes more, or until the shell is golden and set. Cool the shell in the pan on a wire rack.
8. Place the shell on a baking sheet. Pour the custard filling into the shell.
9. Bake the tart in the preheated moderate oven (350°) for 25 to 30 minutes, or until the custard is just set. Remove the tart to a wire rack to cool to room temperature.
10. Gently press the blueberries into the custard.
11. Melt the red currant jelly with the lemon juice in a small saucepan over medium heat. Brush the glaze over the blueberries. Serve the tart immediately.

CHOCOLATE ANGEL CAKE

A deliciously light and airy cake, with a wonderful chocolate flavor.

LOW-CHOLESTEROL • LOW-FAT
Bake at 375° for 30 to 35 minutes.
Makes 10 servings.

Nutrient Value Per Serving: 186 calories, 5 g protein, 0 g fat, 41 g carbohydrate, 390 mg sodium, 0 mg cholesterol.

¾ cup cake flour (not self-rising)
¼ cup unsweetened cocoa powder
1½ cups plus 2 tablespoons sugar
12 egg whites, at room temperature
1½ teaspoons salt
¼ teaspoon cream of tartar
2 teaspoons vanilla

1. Preheat the oven to moderate (375°). Line the bottom of a 10 x 4¼-inch angel food cake pan with wax paper, and set aside the pan.
2. Sift together the flour, cocoa and ¾ cup plus 2 tablespoons of the sugar onto wax paper. Set aside the flour mixture.
3. Beat together the egg whites, salt and cream of tartar in a very large bowl with an electric mixer until the mixture is foamy. Gradually add the remaining ¾ cup of sugar, 2 tablespoons at a time, beating at high speed, until stiff peaks form. Beat in the vanilla.
4. Sprinkle the flour mixture over the beaten egg white mixture, one third at a time, and gently fold it in. Spoon the batter into the prepared pan, smoothing the top.
5. Bake the cake in the preheated moderate oven (375°) for 30 to 35 minutes, or until the top of the cake springs back when lightly touched with your fingertip. Invert the pan onto a long-necked bottle or funnel, and cool the cake completely. When it is cool, turn the cake right side up. Run a thin metal spatula around the edges and the center of the cake to loosen it. Invert the cake onto a serving platter. Remove and discard the wax paper. Turn the cake right side up.

RASPBERRY CREAM POUFFS

Experiment with other fruits for the pouff filling—blueberries, strawberries, peaches, nectarines, bananas, mango or papaya. You also can flavor the whipped cream with almond or vanilla extract, if you wish.

Bake at 425° for 20 minutes.
Makes 10 servings.

Nutrient Value Per Serving: 521 calories, 7 g protein, 43 g fat, 29 g carbohydrate, 64 mg sodium, 372 mg cholesterol.

Crème Anglaise:
5	egg yolks
½	cup granulated sugar
2½	cups heavy cream, scalded in a saucepan
1¼	teaspoons vanilla

Pouff Shells:
¾	cup boiling water
1	teaspoon granulated sugar
¼	cup (½ stick) butter
¾	cup all-purpose flour
3	eggs
1	egg mixed with 1 teaspoon water

Chocolate Sauce:
½	cup heavy cream
2½	ounces semisweet chocolate, chopped

Raspberry Cream Filling:
1	cup heavy cream
4	tablespoons 10X (confectioners' powdered) sugar
½	pint fresh raspberries

1. Prepare the Crème Anglaise: Whisk together the egg yolks and the granulated sugar in a large bowl. Whisk in ½ cup of the hot cream. Stir the egg mixture into the scalded cream remaining in the saucepan. Stir the combined mixture over medium heat until it is thick enough to coat the back of a spoon, for 5 to 7 minutes; do not bring the mixture to a boil. Immediately pour the mixture through a strainer into a bowl to make the mixture smooth. Set the bowl in an ice water bath, and stir until the mixture is cool. Stir in the vanilla. Refrigerate the crème anglaise until you are ready to use it.

2. Preheat the oven to hot (425°). Lightly grease a baking sheet, and set aside the sheet.

3. Prepare the Pouff Shells: Combine the boiling water, granulated sugar and butter in a saucepan over medium-high heat until the butter melts. Remove the saucepan from the heat. Add the flour all at once, and beat the mixture with a wooden spoon to blend the ingredients. Return the saucepan to the heat and stir for 1 minute, or until a solid mass forms.

4. Add 1 of the eggs. Beat hard with the spoon until the mixture is smooth and well blended. Repeat with each of the 2 remaining eggs, then beat until the mixture is thick and shiny.

5. Using the spoon and a rubber spatula, form 10 equal mounds of dough and space them evenly on the prepared baking sheet. Brush the tops with the egg and water. Bake the pouffs in the preheated hot oven (425°) for 20 minutes, or until they are doubled in size and golden. Turn off the oven.

6. Pierce the sides of the pouffs with a small knife to release the steam. Return the pouffs to the turned-off oven for 2 to 3 minutes to dry out. Remove the pouffs to a wire rack to cool completely.

7. Cut off the top third from each pouff shell. With a fork, remove any portion of the insides that are damp.

8. Prepare the Chocolate Sauce: Heat the cream to simmering in a small, heavy saucepan. Remove the saucepan from the heat. Add the chocolate, and stir until the mixture is smooth. Keep the sauce warm.

9. Prepare the Raspberry Cream Filling: Beat the cream with 2 tablespoons of the 10X (confectioners' powdered) sugar in a bowl until the mixture is stiff. Fold in half the raspberries.

10. To serve, spoon ¼ cup of the crème anglaise on each of 10 individual dessert plates. Place a pouff on each plate. Spoon the filling into the pouffs. Place the remaining raspberries on the filling, dividing them equally. Replace the pouff tops. Drizzle the sauce over the crème anglaise on the plates in a decorative pattern *(see photo below)*. Sprinkle the pouffs with the remaining 2 tablespoons of 10X (confectioners' powdered) sugar.

6

7

8

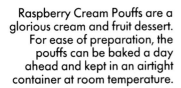

9

Raspberry Cream Pouffs are a glorious cream and fruit dessert. For ease of preparation, the pouffs can be baked a day ahead and kept in an airtight container at room temperature.

Mexican Chocolate Flan

Bake at 350° for 75 to 90 minutes.
Makes 12 servings.

Nutrient Value Per Serving: 313 calories, 8 g protein, 14 g fat,
43 g carbohydrate, 92 mg sodium, 217 mg cholesterol.

Caramel:
1   cup sugar
⅓   cup water

Custard:
1   quart milk
⅔   cup sugar
8   ounces Mexican chocolate
       OR: semisweet
       chocolate, chopped

9   eggs
1   teaspoon vanilla
1   tablespoon dark rum
       (optional)

Whipped cream, for
  garnish (optional)
Toasted almonds, for
  garnish (see Tip,
  page 130; optional)

1. Preheat the oven to moderate (350°). Place a 2½-quart, straight-sided soufflé dish nearby while preparing the caramel.

2. Prepare the Caramel: Combine the sugar with the water in a small, heavy-bottomed saucepan. Bring the mixture to boiling over medium-high heat. Cook for 10 to 12 minutes, or until the caramel is golden amber in color, brushing down the sides of the pan with water to prevent crystals from forming.

3. Pour the caramel immediately into the soufflé dish. Using potholders, carefully tilt the dish to coat the bottom and the sides.

4. Prepare the Custard: Combine the milk, sugar and chocolate in a medium-size saucepan. Bring the mixture to simmering over medium heat, stirring occasionally to dissolve the chocolate; if using the Mexican chocolate, it will not totally dissolve. Remove the saucepan from the heat.

5. Whisk together the eggs, vanilla and, if you wish, rum in a large bowl. Stir in about 1 cup of the hot chocolate mixture. Stir the egg mixture back into the saucepan. Strain the custard mixture immediately into a clean bowl.

6. Pour the custard mixture into the prepared dish. Place the dish in a larger baking pan, adding boiling water to the larger pan to a depth of 2 inches. Cover the soufflé dish lightly with aluminum foil.

7. Bake the flan in the preheated moderate oven (350°) for 75 to 90 minutes, or until the custard is slightly firm in the center and a knife inserted near the center comes out clean. Cool the flan in the water bath. Remove the soufflé dish from the water bath. Cover the soufflé dish, and refrigerate the flan overnight.

8. Run a thin knife around the edges of the flan to unmold it. Place a serving dish on top of the soufflé dish, and quickly invert the dishes over the sink, being careful not to spill any of the liquid caramel. Gently jiggle and twist the soufflé dish until the flan falls free. Remove the soufflé dish and scrape any remaining caramel from the soufflé dish onto the flan. To serve, cut the flan into wedges. Place a wedge of flan on an individual dessert plate, and spoon caramel sauce from the serving dish over the flan. Garnish each serving with whipped cream and toasted almonds, if you wish.

Individual Mexican Chocolate Flans

Individual flans are easy to make, and a lovely treat for dinner guests.

■ Pour about 1 tablespoon of the caramel mixture into each of twelve 5- to 6-ounce custard cups or straight-sided soufflé dishes, tilting the dishes to coat the sides (keep the caramel mixture in the saucepan over low heat so it will stay fluid while coating each dish).

■ Prepare the custard mixture as directed in Steps 4 and 5 at left. Carefully pour about ⅔ to ¾ cup of the custard mixture into each cup.

■ Place the custard cups in a large roasting pan or two 13 x 9 x 2-inch baking pans. Add boiling water to come halfway up the sides of the cups. Cover the cups lightly with a sheet of aluminum foil.

■ Bake the flans in the preheated moderate oven (350°) for 30 minutes, or until the custards are slightly firm in the centers and a knife inserted in the centers comes out clean.

■ Continue with Steps 7 and 8 at left.

❖   ❖   ❖

Bananas

Brought to the New World by the Spanish, bananas flourished in the lands bordering the Caribbean Sea. From there, bananas first were brought to the United States more than 150 years ago. At that time, they were considered solely a luxury fruit. Now available year-round, bananas are universally popular.

■ A 6-inch-long banana has about 85 calories. Bananas are a good source of potassium, thiamine, riboflavin, niacin, and vitamins A and C.

■ Buy firm, unblemished fruit. Store bananas at room temperature.

■ A quick banana guide:
1 pound = 3 medium-size bananas.
1 medium-size banana = ⅔ cup sliced, or ½ cup diced, or ⅓ cup mashed banana.

❖ ❖ ❖

BANANA CREAM PUFFS WITH COFFEE RUM SAUCE

Bake at 425° for 20 minutes.
Makes 8 servings (3 filled puffs with 2 tablespoons sauce per serving).
Nutrient Value Per Serving: 447 calories, 5 g protein, 28 g fat, 42 g carbohydrate, 66 mg sodium, 217 mg cholesterol.

Puffs:
1   **cup water**
½ **cup (1 stick) unsalted butter**
    Pinch salt
1   **cup all-purpose flour**
4   **eggs**

Banana Cream:
1   **cup heavy cream**
1½ **teaspoons banana extract**
2   **tablespoons 10X (confectioners' powdered) sugar**

Coffee Rum Sauce:
3   **tablespoons cold coffee**
2   **tablespoons cornstarch**
1½ **cups hot coffee**
1   **cup granulated sugar**
2   **tablespoons unsalted butter**
2   **tablespoons dark rum**

    10X (confectioners' powdered) sugar
1   **small banana, peeled and sliced, for garnish (optional)**

1. Preheat the oven to hot (425°). Lightly grease 2 baking sheets.

2. Prepare the Puffs: Combine the water, butter and salt in a medium-size saucepan. Cook the mixture over medium heat, stirring occasionally, until the butter melts. Remove the saucepan from the heat. Add the flour all at once. Return the saucepan to the heat. Mix for 1 to 2 minutes, or until the flour mixture pulls away from the sides of the pan. Remove the saucepan from the heat.

3. Beat in the eggs, one at a time, beating until the dough is smooth and shiny. Drop the dough, in about 1½-inch-diameter balls, onto the prepared baking sheets, leaving 2 inches between the balls.

4. Bake the puffs in the preheated hot oven (425°) for 20 minutes, or until the puffs are golden brown, reversing the position of the baking sheets once during the baking. Turn off the oven. Pierce each puff with the point of a knife. Let the puffs dry in the turned-off oven for 5 minutes. Cool the puffs on a wire rack. Cut off the top third from each puff, and set aside the tops.

5. Prepare the Banana Cream: Beat together the cream, banana extract and 10X (confectioners' powdered) sugar in a chilled, medium-size bowl until the mixture is stiff. Fill the puffs with the cream mixture. Replace the puff tops. Refrigerate the puffs while the preparing the sauce.

6. Prepare the Coffee Rum Sauce: Stir together the cold coffee and the cornstarch in a small saucepan until the mixture is smooth. Mix in the hot coffee and the granulated sugar. Cook over medium heat, stirring constantly, until the mixture boils and thickens. Remove the saucepan from the heat. Stir in the butter and the rum until the butter melts; you should have 2 cups of sauce. Cool the sauce slightly.

7. To serve, spoon 2 tablespoons of the sauce onto each of 8 individual dessert plates. Sprinkle the puffs with 10X (confectioners' powdered) sugar. Place 3 puffs on top of the sauce on each plate. Tuck a banana slice into each filling for garnish, if you wish.

COCONUT CREAM PIE

Toast coconut at 350° for 5 to 7 minutes; bake pie at 350° for 30 to 35 minutes.

Makes 8 servings.

Nutrient Value Per Serving: 543 calories, 5 g protein, 43 g fat, 38 g carbohydrate, 181 mg sodium, 186 mg cholesterol.

Crust:

5	slices (1 ounce each) firm white sandwich bread, quartered
3	tablespoons sugar
¼	cup (½ stick) butter, melted

Filling:

3	cups shredded fresh coconut OR: shredded unsweetened coconut*
1	cup heavy cream
⅔	cup sugar
2	tablespoons fresh coconut liquid* OR: water
3	egg yolks, at room temperature
1	teaspoon vanilla
⅔	cup Homemade Thick Cream (see Tip, at right)

1. Preheat the oven to moderate (350°). Lightly grease a 9-inch tart pan with a removable bottom.

2. Prepare the Crust: Combine the bread with the sugar in the container of a food processor or electric blender. Whirl until the bread is crumbled. Add the butter. Whirl just until the ingredients are combined. Spread the crust evenly in the prepared pan, and press out the crust to cover the bottom and sides of the pan. Refrigerate the crust.

3. Spread ½ cup of the coconut in an 8-inch square baking pan.

4. Toast the coconut in the preheated moderate oven (350°) for 5 to 7 minutes, or until it is golden. Reserve the toasted coconut for garnish.

5. Prepare the Filling: Combine the cream, sugar and coconut liquid or water in a small saucepan. Bring the mixture to boiling over medium-high heat. Reduce the heat to medium-low and cook the cream mixture for 15 minutes, or until it is reduced to 1 cup.

6. Pour the cream mixture into a large bowl. Stir in the remaining 2½ cups of shredded coconut, the egg yolks and vanilla until they are well blended.

7. Pour the filling into the prepared crust. Place the pan on a baking sheet.

8. Bake the pie in the preheated moderate oven (350°) for 30 to 35 minutes, or until the custard is set and golden brown. Cool the pie slightly on a wire rack.

9. Serve the pie warm with a dollop of the Homemade Thick Cream. Garnish with the reserved toasted coconut.

*__*Note:__ To shell a fresh coconut, pierce the eyes of the coconut with an ice pick or a nail hit with a hammer. Shake out the coconut liquid into a bowl and reserve it. Place the coconut in a baking pan. Bake the coconut in a preheated hot oven (425°) for 12 to 15 minutes, or until the shell begins to crack. When the coconut is cool enough to handle, break it open (you may want to wrap the coconut in a towel and hit it gently with a hammer). Pry off the hard shell with a blunt knife. Peel the brown skin off the coconut meat with a swivel-bladed vegetable peeler or small paring knife. Shred the coconut on a hand grater or in a food processor.*

Homemade Thick Cream

- Combine 1 cup of heavy cream with 2 teaspoons of buttermilk in a small, heavy-bottomed saucepan.

- Place the saucepan over low heat and heat until the cream mixture registers 95° on an instant-reading thermometer, or until the mixture feels lukewarm to the touch. Be careful not to heat the cream to too hot a temperature, or the culture will die.

- Pour the mixture into a clean glass jar with a lid. Place the lid on the jar, but do not tighten it. Place the jar in a warm (80°) spot, such as the top of the refrigerator. Cover the jar with a double thickness of paper toweling.

- Let the jar stand for 12 to 24 hours, or until the cream mixture is thickened.

- Remove the lid from the jar. Stir the cream mixture gently to combine it.

- Cover the jar and refrigerate the cream mixture for at least 4 hours to chill and thicken it further.

- Once ripened, the cream will keep for up to 1 week, refrigerated. Makes 1 cup.

Buttermilk

Originally, buttermilk was the liquid remaining after the fat was removed from the milk or cream used to churn butter.

■ Cultured buttermilk, found on supermarket dairy shelves, is made from pasteurized skimmed or partially skimmed milk inoculated with a suitable culture of lactic acid bacteria. It is left to ferment to a thickened consistency, at which time salt may or may not be added.

■ Buttermilk is a highly nutritious product. One cup (8 ounces) has 90 calories, 9 grams of protein and is a good source of calcium and riboflavin. A shelf-stable dried buttermilk powder is available as a convenient substitute.

❖ ❖ ❖

BLUEBERRY BUTTERMILK CAKE

Bake at 350° for 60 minutes.
Makes 12 servings.

Nutrient Value Per Serving: 350 calories, 5 g protein, 18 g fat, 44 g carbohydrate, 172 mg sodium, 83 mg cholesterol.

½ cup slivered almonds	½ cup firmly packed light brown sugar
2 tablespoons plus ¾ cup granulated sugar	2 eggs
2 cups plus 1 tablespoon unsifted all-purpose flour	1 teaspoon grated lemon zest (yellow part of rind only)
1½ teaspoons baking powder	¾ teaspoon vanilla
½ teaspoon baking soda	¼ teaspoon almond extract
¼ teaspoon salt	1 cup buttermilk
¼ teaspoon ground ginger	1 cup blueberries
14 tablespoons (1¾ sticks) unsalted butter, at room temperature	½ teaspoon lemon juice

1. Preheat the oven to moderate (350°). Generously grease a 10 x 4-inch kugelhof pan. Sprinkle the bottom of the pan with the almonds and 1 tablespoon of the granulated sugar.
2. Sift 2 cups of the flour with the baking powder, baking soda, salt and ginger onto wax paper. Set aside the flour mixture.
3. Beat together the butter, ¾ cup of the granulated sugar and the brown sugar in a large bowl with an electric mixer until the mixture is light colored and fluffy. Beat in the eggs, one at a time, beating well after each addition. Mix in the lemon zest, vanilla and almond extract.
4. Alternately fold the flour mixture and the buttermilk into the egg mixture, beginning and ending with the flour mixture.
5. Toss the blueberries with the lemon juice, the remaining 1 tablespoon of flour and the remaining 1 tablespoon of granulated sugar in a small bowl.
6. Pour the batter into the prepared pan and smooth the top. Scatter the blueberries over the top, and gently push them into the batter just so they are covered.
7. Bake the cake in the preheated moderate oven (350°) for 60 minutes, or until a cake tester inserted near the center comes out clean. Cool the cake in the pan on a wire rack. Run a thin knife around the edges of the cake to loosen it. Invert the cake onto a serving platter.

245

OATMEAL NUT SQUARES

These chewy squares are a taste of old-fashioned goodness.

Bake at 375° for 15 to 20 minutes.
Makes 16 squares.

Nutrient Value Per Square: 185 calories, 3 g protein, 11 g fat,
20 g carbohydrate, 96 mg sodium, 33 mg cholesterol.

1	cup all-purpose flour	1	egg
1	teaspoon baking powder	1	teaspoon water
½	teaspoon baking soda	½	teaspoon vanilla
¼	teaspoon salt	1	cup walnuts, chopped
½	cup (1 stick) unsalted butter, softened	¾	cup quick-cooking oats
¼	cup granulated sugar	½	cup chopped dried apple
¼	cup firmly packed dark brown sugar	¼	cup currants

1. Preheat the oven to moderate (375°). Grease an 8 x 8 x 2-inch baking pan. Stir together the flour, baking powder, baking soda and salt in a medium-size bowl.
2. Beat together the butter, granulated sugar, brown sugar, egg, water and vanilla in a medium-size bowl with an electric mixer until the mixture is smooth and creamy. Lower the mixer speed to low, and mix in the flour mixture until it is well blended. Stir in the walnuts, oats, apple and currants. Spread the batter evenly in the prepared pan.
3. Bake the cake in the preheated moderate oven (375°) for 15 to 20 minutes, or until the cake is lightly browned on top and the center feels firm when lightly touched with your fingertip. Cool the cake in the pan on a wire rack. Cut the cake into squares.

APPLE BLONDIES

In apples, the most intense flavor is just beneath the skin, so we used unpeeled apples in this recipe.

Bake at 350° for 30 minutes.
Makes 16 squares.

Nutrient Value Per Square: 180 calories, 2 g protein, 10 g fat,
23 g carbohydrate, 89 mg sodium, 50 mg cholesterol.

½	cup (1 stick) butter, softened	¼	teaspoon ground nutmeg
1	cup firmly packed dark brown sugar	⅛	teaspoon salt
2	eggs	1	large firm apple, such as Granny Smith or Golden Delicious
1	teaspoon vanilla	¼	cup coarsely chopped walnuts
¾	cup all-purpose flour	½	cup semisweet chocolate pieces
¼	teaspoon ground ginger		
¼	teaspoon ground cinnamon		

Oats

The grain of a grasslike plant in the cereal family, an oat grain generally is covered with a husk that is removed, although there are some varieties that are hull-less. Oats are used to make rolled oats and oatmeal.

■ To make rolled oats, the grains are cleaned, sorted, dried (to loosen the hulls and develop flavor), hulled and sterilized. The hulled, sterilized oat grains are flattened into flakes.

■ To make oatmeal, the hulled grains are cut into coarse to fine textures. The word oatmeal should be used for the ground meal of the grain, but it is used commonly to describe the cooked cereal.

■ Oats are available as rolled (also known as old-fashioned) oats, and as quick-cooking or instant oatmeal. Scottish oatmeal is made by cutting the oat grains with stone rollers, rather than steel rollers, which creates a coarse texture.

■ Oats cannot be used alone in making bread because they contain no gluten; they have to be combined with all-purpose flour for baking.

■ Oats are one of the most nutritious grains available, containing some protein and minerals, and they are an excellent source of fiber.

The Soft Touch

The best way to soften butter is to let it stand at room temperature. For faster softening, slice the butter and place the slices in a bowl. Then, for no more than 2 seconds at a time and stirring constantly, place the bowl of butter over a bowl of hot water; the butter should soften, not melt.

❖ ❖ ❖

Currants

Two different fruits are known as currants. One is a fresh red, black or white berry that grows on a shrub. The other is a dried, seedless grape.

■ Fresh currants are tiny, tart berries that grow in the northern United States and in northeastern Europe. Of these, red currants are the best known. In some markets, red currants are available fresh during the summer. Red currants primarily are made into jelly, preserves and syrup.

■ Black currants have a reddish flesh and are not as tart as the red. They're used to make the liqueur Cassis.

■ Dried currants look like tiny raisins. They are used in breads, cakes and pastries.

❖ ❖ ❖

1. Preheat the oven to moderate (350°). Grease and lightly flour a 9 x 9 x 2-inch square baking pan.
2. Combine the butter with the brown sugar in a large bowl. Beat with an electric mixer at low speed until the mixture is well combined, for about 2 minutes. Beat in the eggs, one at a time, until the mixture is very creamy. Stir in the vanilla.
3. Sift together the flour, ginger, cinnamon, nutmeg and salt onto wax paper. Sift the flour mixture again.
4. Add the flour mixture to the butter mixture, beating on low speed just to combine them.
5. Core the apple but do not peel it. Coarsely chop the apple. Fold the apple into the batter, along with the walnuts and the chocolate pieces. Scrape the batter into the prepared pan.
6. Bake the blondies in the preheated moderate oven (350°) for 30 minutes, or until the top is lightly browned and a wooden pick inserted in the center comes out clean. Cool the blondies in the pan on a wire rack. Cut the blondies in the pan into squares to serve.

Apple Blondies are packed with fruit, nuts and chocolate chips.

RASPBERRY JAM SQUARES

Bake crust at 400° for 5 minutes; bake squares at 350° for 25 minutes.
Makes 16 squares.

Nutrient Value Per Serving: 216 calories, 2 g protein, 10 g fat,
30 g carbohydrate, 72 mg sodium, 32 mg cholesterol.

½ **cup (1 stick) unsalted butter, cut into 4 pieces**
1½ **cups unsifted all-purpose flour**
⅔ **cup firmly packed light brown sugar**
⅓ **cup granulated sugar**
¼ **teaspoon salt**

½ **cup walnuts**
⅓ **cup dairy sour cream**
1 **egg**
½ **teaspoon vanilla**
½ **teaspoon baking soda**
½ **teaspoon ground cinnamon**
½ **cup raspberry jam**

1. Preheat the oven to hot (400°). Lightly grease an 8 x 8 x 2-inch square baking pan.

2. Combine the butter, flour, brown sugar, granulated sugar, salt and walnuts in the container of a food processor. Whirl to blend the ingredients. Measure out 1 cup of the walnut mixture for the crust, ½ cup for the topping, and leave the remainder in the processor.

3. For the crust, press the 1 cup of walnut mixture into an even layer on the bottom of the prepared pan.

4. Bake the crust in the preheated hot oven (400°) for 5 minutes.

5. Meanwhile, stir together the sour cream, egg, vanilla, baking soda and cinnamon in a small bowl. Add the sour cream mixture to the walnut mixture remaining in the food processor, and pulse just until the ingredients are blended.

6. Remove the pan from the oven. Reduce the oven temperature to moderate (350°). Spread the raspberry jam evenly over the crust to

Cinnamon

Cinnamon is the bark of several varieties of an evergreen tree native to Southeast Asia. True cinnamon is the Ceylon variety; other varieties of cinnamon are from the cassia trees.

■ Ceylon cinnamon is native to Ceylon and India. It has the mildest tasting bark and, for that reason, is not popular in this country. It is used extensively in Mexico. Americans tend to prefer the stronger taste of the bark from the cassia trees. One variety, the Saigon cassia, originated in China but now is grown extensively in Vietnam; this variety is ground. Another variety, the Batavia cassia, is rolled into sticks.

■ Cinnamon or cassia bark is harvested by cutting young shoots off the trees. The bark is stripped from the shoots and scraped. The inner bark, which is the fragrant layer, folds into itself when it begins to dry out, and looks like a roll of paper. It is rolled until it is about ½ inch in diameter, and it can be up to 3 feet in length.

■ Oil of cinnamon is extracted from the berries of the tree, and also from the residue of the bark.

✧ ✧ ✧

Sweet and chewy, Raspberry Jam Squares are a treat for adults and kids alike.

Raisins

Grapes were sun-dried into raisins as early as 1490 B.C. The word raisin is derived from "racemus," a Latin word meaning "a cluster of grapes or berries." Raisins were made accidentally when grapes could not be harvested, and the sun dried them. In losing their moisture, the grapes became sweeter and could be stored for longer periods of time.

■ Today, nearly half the world's supply of raisins is produced in California. Thompson Seedless, which are the familiar table grapes, and Muscat grapes are grown for raisins. They are harvested in late August or early September, and placed on trays to dry in the sun or are dried indoors with heat. It takes 2 to 3 weeks to dry grapes. About 4½ pounds of grapes are needed to make 1 pound of raisins.

■ Store raisins in a cool, dry place. Heat and air can cause them to dry out. After opening a package, place the raisins in an airtight container, or refrigerate them for long-term storage. If raisins become dry or form sugar crystals, rinse them with hot tap water or soak them briefly in water or cooking liquid.

❖ ❖ ❖

within ½ inch of the edges. Spoon the batter over the jam, and spread it in an even layer. Sprinkle with the remaining ½ cup of walnut mixture.

7. Bake the cake in the preheated moderate oven (350°) for 25 minutes. Cool the cake in the pan on a wire rack. Cut the cake into squares to serve.

CHOCOLATE-TOPPED APPLE RAISIN SQUARES

You'll get rave reviews from your family for these star-quality chocolate-covered bar cookies.

Bake at 350° for 25 to 30 minutes.
Makes 12 squares.

Nutrient Value Per Square: 465 calories, 7 g protein, 23 g fat, 61 g carbohydrate, 237 mg sodium, 69 mg cholesterol.

2½ **cups all-purpose flour**	½ **cup sugar**
2 **teaspoons baking powder**	2 **eggs**
1 **to 2 teaspoons ground cinnamon**	1¼ **cups unsweetened apple butter**
¼ **to ½ teaspoon ground nutmeg**	2 **teaspoons vanilla**
¼ **teaspoon ground cloves**	1 **cup raisins**
¼ **teaspoon salt**	1½ **cups coarsely chopped walnuts**
¼ **teaspoon baking soda**	1 **cup mini chocolate pieces**
½ **cup butter or margarine, softened**	

1. Preheat the oven to moderate (350°). Lightly grease a 13 x 9 x 2-inch baking pan.

2. Combine the flour, baking powder, cinnamon, nutmeg, cloves, salt and baking soda on a piece of wax paper.

3. Beat the butter or margarine with the sugar, eggs, apple butter and vanilla in a large bowl until the mixture is light colored and fluffy. Beat in the flour mixture until it is well blended. Stir in the raisins and 1 cup of the nuts. Spread the batter in the prepared pan.

4. Bake the cake in the preheated moderate oven (350°) for 25 to 30 minutes, or until a cake tester inserted in the center comes out clean.

5. Place the pan on a wire rack. Immediately sprinkle the top of the cake with the chocolate pieces. Let the cake stand for 5 to 7 minutes. With a thin metal spatula, spread the melted chocolate over the entire surface of the cake. Sprinkle with the remaining ½ cup of nuts. Cool the cake completely, and cut it into squares to serve.

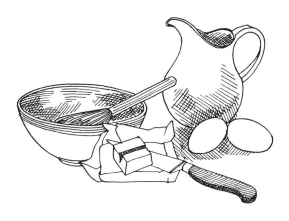

*L*IGHT DESSERTS

Refreshing delicacies that won't weigh you down.

PLUM PEACH SHERBET

LOW-CALORIE • LOW-CHOLESTEROL • LOW-FAT

Makes 10 servings.

Nutrient Value Per Serving: 133 calories, 3 g protein, 1 g fat, 30 g carbohydrate, 83 mg sodium, 3 mg cholesterol.

¾	pound fully ripe plums, halved, pitted and coarsely chopped	1	tablespoon lemon juice
		3	cups lowfat buttermilk
½	pound fully ripe peaches, peeled, pitted and coarsely chopped	1	cup sugar
		1	egg white

1. Combine the plums, peaches, lemon juice and ½ cup of the buttermilk in the container of an electric blender or food processor. Whirl until the fruit is puréed. Stir in the remaining 2½ cups of buttermilk, the sugar and egg white. Refrigerate the mixture, covered, until it is cold.
2. Prepare the sherbet in an ice cream maker, following the manufacturer's directions. Pack the sherbet into freezer containers and freeze it.

Plum Wonderful

Here are some tips for getting the most out of fresh plums.
■ For the best plums, select plump fruit, with the correct mature color for the variety of plum being purchased. To test for ripeness, press a plum gently with the palm of your hand — it should yield slightly.
■ Avoid plums with breaks in their skin, immature plums (comparatively hard, not fully colored) and overripe plums (very soft, leaking juice).
■ If you do buy firm, unripe plums, you can soften and ripen them in a loosely closed paper bag. Keep them in the bag at room temperature for 3 to 4 days, and check their progress daily. Refrigerate the plums when they are ripe.
■ One pound of fresh plums is equal to 6 medium-size (2-inch-diameter) plums, or 2½ cups sliced, or 2 cups diced, or 1¾ cups puréed plums.
■ Puréed plums are great for sauces. Or you can freeze the purée in ice cube trays to use in fruit drinks or club soda.

❖ ❀ ❖

Plum Peach Sherbet is a lusciously low-calorie delight.

CHOCOLATE GRANITA

A cool, refreshing ice made with low-calorie unsweetened cocoa.

LOW-CALORIE • LOW-CHOLESTEROL • LOW-SODIUM • LOW-FAT

Makes 6 servings.

Nutrient Value Per Serving: 108 calories, 1 g protein, 1 g fat, 23 g carbohydrate, 1 mg sodium, 0 mg cholesterol.

½ cup sugar	1 teaspoon vanilla
½ cup unsweetened cocoa powder	½ teaspoon ground cinnamon
2 cups water	1 teaspoon grated orange zest (orange part of rind only)
2 tablespoons crème de cacao liqueur	

1. Combine the sugar with the cocoa in a medium-size saucepan, stirring well to eliminate all the lumps from the cocoa. Slowly add the water, beating with a wire whisk until the mixture is smooth.

2. Bring the cocoa mixture to boiling over medium heat, stirring to dissolve the sugar. Lower the heat and simmer the mixture for 5 minutes. Remove the saucepan from the heat. Stir in the crème de cacao, vanilla, cinnamon and orange zest.

3. Pour the mixture into an 8- or 9-inch metal baking pan. Place the pan in the freezer and freeze the mixture until it is firm, but not solidly frozen. Break up the mixture into icy chunks with a fork. Return the pan to the freezer. Freeze the mixture for at least 3 hours, or until it is frozen solid.

4. At serving time, let the granita stand at room temperature for 5 minutes. Break up the granita with a fork. Spoon the chunks into 6 stemmed glasses, and serve.

MULLED WINE GRANITA

Serve this refreshing wine ice over slices of poached pear.

LOW-CALORIE • LOW-CHOLESTEROL • LOW-SODIUM • LOW-FAT

Makes 6 servings.

Nutrient Value Per Serving: 103 calories, trace protein, 0 g fat, 26 g carbohydrate, 3 mg sodium, 0 mg cholesterol.

1½ cups water	2 whole cloves
¾ cup sugar	2 strips orange zest (orange part of rind only)
1½ cups dry red wine	
1 cinnamon stick	

1. Combine the water, sugar, ¾ cup of the wine, the cinnamon stick, cloves and orange zest in a saucepan. Bring the mixture to boiling, stirring constantly; the sugar should dissolve. Reduce the heat and simmer for 3 minutes without stirring.

2. Allow the spiced syrup to cool. Strain the spiced syrup into a dish and stir in the remaining ¾ cup of wine. Freeze the syrup mixture for 3 to 4 hours, stirring every 30 minutes.

3. At serving time, let the granita soften a bit. Spoon the granita into 6 stemmed glasses, and serve.

COFFEE ALMOND FROZEN YOGURT

So delicious, your family will want this again and again. Chopped, blanched hazelnuts can be substituted for the almonds in this recipe, if you wish.

LOW-CALORIE • LOW-CHOLESTEROL • LOW-FAT

Makes 6 servings.

Nutrient Value Per Serving: 136 calories, 6 g protein, 3 g fat, 22 g carbohydrate, 75 mg sodium, 6 mg cholesterol.

3	tablespoons sugar	2	tablespoons finely
3	containers (8 ounces each) lowfat coffee yogurt		chopped, toasted almonds (see Tip, page 130) Few drops almond extract

1. Mix together the sugar, yogurt, almonds and almond extract in a medium-size bowl until the ingredients are well blended.
2. Transfer the mixture to an ice cream machine. Freeze the mixture, following the manufacturer's directions.

FRUIT COMPOTE WITH GINGERED ORANGE SAUCE

A wonderful combination of candied ginger and puréed oranges makes a perfect topping for fresh chopped pineapple and kiwifruit.

LOW-CALORIE • LOW-CHOLESTEROL • LOW-SODIUM • LOW-FAT

Makes 4 servings.

Nutrient Value Per Serving: 144 calories, 2 g protein, 1 g fat, 40 g carbohydrate, 6 mg sodium, 0 mg cholesterol.

2	oranges, peeled, seeded and chopped	1	pineapple, peeled, cored and chopped
1	teaspoon chopped fresh gingerroot	3	kiwifruit, peeled and chopped
1	tablespoon sugar		

1. Place the oranges and the ginger in the container of an electric blender or food processor. Whirl until the mixture is puréed.
2. Transfer the purée to a medium-size saucepan. Add the sugar. Cook the purée over low heat, stirring occasionally, until it is reduced to 1 cup of sauce, for about 20 minutes.
3. Combine the sauce with the pineapple and the kiwifruit in a decorative serving bowl, and serve.

The Scoop on Frozen Treats

These are a few of our favorite ways to enjoy frozen treats while keeping an eye on fat.

■ Slice the tops off small oranges or lemons; set aside the tops. Scrape out the pulp. Cut off a tiny slice from the bottom of each fruit so it will sit on a plate. Place a scoop of sherbet or frozen yogurt in each lemon or orange cup. Replace the tops, and place the fruit cups in the freezer. (Wrap the fruit cups individually in plastic wrap if you won't be serving them immediately.) At serving time, garnish each cup with a mint sprig.

■ For a beautiful frozen pie, spread layers of contrastingly colored softened sherbet, ice milk or frozen yogurt into a graham cracker crust; freeze each layer until it is firm before adding the next layer. Freeze the pie until it is solid. Serve wedges of the pie topped with fresh fruit or fruit purée.

Mangoes

A juicy, refreshing tropical fruit, mangoes are native to East India. They are flat or round in shape, and have yellow-orange to red skins when they are ripe.

■ Mangoes are in season from January to September. They are grown in southern Florida, California, Hawaii and Mexico. Mangoes are picked green, but will ripen if they are left at room temperature. The green skins turn yellow-orange when the mangoes are ripe. Once they are ripe, mangoes should be refrigerated.

■ In India, both green and ripe mangoes are used to make chutney and pickles.

■ To peel a mango, cut just the skin with the tip of a knife, starting from the stem and circling the fruit several times. Peel the skin in sections. The flesh will cling to the large, flat seed. Cut the flesh to free it from the seed, or scoop out the flesh with a spoon.

❖ ❖ ❖

BANANAS MARION

LOW-CALORIE • LOW-CHOLESTEROL • LOW-SODIUM • LOW-FAT

Makes 4 servings.

Nutrient Value Per Serving: 114 calories, 1 g protein, 3 g fat, 22 g carbohydrate, 35 mg sodium, 0 mg cholesterol.

1	tablespoon diet margarine Juice of 1 lemon OR: lime	4	walnut halves, chopped
2	bananas, sliced	1	tablespoon amaretto OR: Kahlúa
4	dates, chopped		Orange zest (orange part
1	teaspoon ground cinnamon		of rind only), for garnish

1. Melt the margarine with the lemon or lime juice in a medium-size skillet. Add the bananas, dates, cinnamon and walnuts, and sauté briefly. Sprinkle with the amaretto or Kahlúa.
2. Garnish with the orange zest, and serve.

MANGO LIME MOUSSE

LOW-CALORIE • LOW-CHOLESTEROL • LOW-SODIUM • LOW-FAT

Makes 6 servings.

Nutrient Value Per Serving: 133 calories, 4 g protein, 2 g fat, 25 g carbohydrate, 30 mg sodium, 8 mg cholesterol.

2	ripe mangoes, peeled, seeded and cut into chunks	2	envelopes unflavored gelatin
¼	cup 10X (confectioners' powdered) sugar	½	cup warm water (105° to 115°)*
2	tablespoons lime juice		Nonstick vegetable cooking spray
¾	cup sour half-and-half	6	strawberries, for garnish

1. Place a 9-inch round cake pan in the freezer.
2. Purée the mangoes in the container of an electric blender or food processor. Add the 10X (confectioners' powdered) sugar, lime juice and sour half-and-half, and process until the mixture is smooth.
3. Soften the gelatin in the warm water in a heat-proof, glass measuring cup for 1 minute. Place the cup over boiling water, and stir to dissolve the gelatin. Stir the gelatin into the mango mixture.
4. Spray the chilled cake pan with nonstick vegetable cooking spray. Pour the mango mixture into the pan, and refrigerate the mousse until it is set. Invert the mousse onto a serving platter. Garnish with the strawberries.

__Note:__ Warm water should feel tepid when dropped on your wrist.

POIRES CARDINALES

LOW-CALORIE • LOW-CHOLESTEROL • LOW-SODIUM • LOW-FAT

Makes 4 servings.

Nutrient Value Per Serving: 123 calories, 1 g protein, 1 g fat, 29 g carbohydrate, 41 mg sodium, 3 mg cholesterol.

4	gingersnap cookies (about 2 inches in diameter)	1	tablespoon 10X (confectioners' powdered) sugar
1	package (12 ounces) frozen dry-pack raspberries, thawed	2	fresh ripe pears
		1	lemon, cut in half Additional lemon juice, for sprinkling
4	teaspoons fresh lemon juice (1 lemon)	¼	teaspoon ground cinnamon

1. Place the gingersnaps in the container of an electric blender or food processor. Whirl until the cookies are crumbled. Remove the crumbs to a small bowl. Clean out the blender or food processor container.
2. Place the raspberries in the container of the blender or food processor. Whirl until the raspberries are puréed. Force the purée through a sieve with the back of a spoon into a second small bowl, and discard the seeds. Stir the 4 teaspoons of lemon juice and the 10X (confectioners' powdered) sugar into the purée. Cover the bowl and refrigerate the raspberry sauce.
3. Peel, halve and core the pears. Rub the peeled or cut surfaces with the cut sides of the lemon halves to prevent discoloration. Cut the pear halves into ¼-inch slices, and arrange the slices on 4 individual dessert plates. Sprinkle the slices with the additional lemon juice and the cinnamon.
4. Spoon the raspberry sauce around the pear slices, and sprinkle the gingersnap crumbs over the pears.

ORANGE-ZESTED STRAWBERRIES

LOW-CALORIE • LOW-CHOLESTEROL • LOW-SODIUM • LOW-FAT

Makes 8 servings.

Nutrient Value Per Serving: 61 calories, 1 g protein, 0 g fat, 13 g carbohydrate, 1 mg sodium, 0 mg cholesterol.

¼	cup sugar, or to taste	1½	tablespoons chopped orange zest (orange part of rind only)
¼	cup orange juice		
2	tablespoons dark rum	3	pints small strawberries

Combine the sugar, orange juice and rum in a large, self-sealing, plastic food storage bag. Add the orange zest and the strawberries. Seal the bag, pushing out all the air. Refrigerate the strawberry mixture for 2 to 4 hours, turning over the bag twice. Serve the strawberries with their sauce in 8 individual dessert dishes.

Picking Pears

Some major pear varieties:
■ Bartlett: Known as the summer pear, this variety is named for Enoch Bartlett, owner of the property on which the pear was developed in 1817. Over two thirds of the pears harvested in this country are Bartlett. Available from mid-July to October, Bartlett pears are bell-shaped, with fairly thin, clear yellow skins when ripe. The flesh is white, smooth and juicy. Bartlett is the only variety of pear that is commercially canned.
■ Anjou: Green, round and heart-shaped, this pear is available from October to May. Anjou pears are medium to large in size, with short necks. The flesh is yellowish-white, fine-textured, juicy and sweet. Color is not an indication of ripeness; when ripe, the pears yield to gentle pressure at the stem end.
■ Bosc: This variety has a long, tapering neck, a russet-brown skin and crunchy, white flesh. The fruit is medium to large in size. Bosc pears are available from September to March.
■ Comice: Medium to large in size, this fruit is almost round in shape. Comice pears are famous as gift fruits. The skin is yellow-green, often with a red blush. The flesh is very fine, juicy and not gritty. Comice pears are marketed from October to March.

❖ ❖ ❖

ALMOND COOKIES

LOW-CALORIE • LOW-CHOLESTEROL • LOW-SODIUM

Bake at 350° for 15 to 20 minutes.
Makes 2 dozen cookies.

Nutrient Value Per Cookie: 82 calories, 3 g protein, 6 g fat,
7 g carbohydrate, 18 mg sodium, 0 mg cholesterol.

9 ounces blanched whole almonds (about 1¾ cups)	2 tablespoons all-purpose flour
⅓ cup plus 2 tablespoons firmly packed light brown sugar	⅛ teaspoon salt
	2 egg whites

1. Preheat the oven to moderate (350°). Lightly grease a baking sheet.
2. Count out 24 almonds and reserve them. Place the remaining almonds in the container of a food processor, along with the brown sugar, flour and salt. Process until the almonds are fairly finely ground. Add the egg whites and process until the mixture comes together, for about 10 seconds; the mixture will not form a ball, but will stick together in a mass.
3. Place half the dough lengthwise down half the baking sheet. With moistened hands, pat out a 12 x 2-inch strip. Repeat with the remaining half of the dough down the other side of the sheet. Place the reserved almonds at 1-inch intervals along each strip.
4. Bake the strips in the preheated moderate oven (350°) for 15 to 20 minutes, or until they are crisped and lightly golden. Cool the strips on the baking sheet on a wire rack. When they are cool, slide a spatula under each strip to loosen it. Cut the strips into 24 cookies, using the almonds as portion guides. Store the cookies in an airtight container.

PEANUT BUTTER COOKIES

LOW-CALORIE • LOW-CHOLESTEROL • LOW-SODIUM

Bake at 375° for 10 minutes.
Makes 2 dozen cookies.

Nutrient Value Per Cookie: 92 calories, 2 g protein, 6 g fat,
9 g carbohydrate, 40 mg sodium, 18 mg cholesterol.

1¼ cups sifted whole wheat flour	⅓ cup unsalted butter, softened
1 teaspoon baking powder	¼ cup honey
½ cup natural peanut butter	1 egg yolk
	¼ teaspoon vanilla

1. Preheat the oven to moderate (375°). Grease 2 baking sheets.
2. Stir together the flour and the baking powder in a small bowl.
3. Beat together the peanut butter and the butter in a large bowl with an electric mixer at high speed until the mixture is light. Beat in the honey and the egg yolk. Continue beating until the mixture is light colored and fluffy.
4. Add the vanilla to the butter mixture, then the dry ingredients, stirring just to blend them.
5. Drop the batter by teaspoonfuls, 1 inch apart, onto the prepared baking sheets. Flatten each cookie slightly with a crisscross of fork tines.
6. Bake the cookies in the preheated moderate oven (375°) for 10 minutes, or until they are golden. Remove the cookies to a wire rack to cool.

The Cookie Store

Store soft cookies in an airtight container, along with a slice of apple on a piece of wax paper to keep the cookies soft and moist.

Store crisp cookies in a container with a loose fitting lid. If the cookies begin to soften, place them in a slow oven (300°) for a few minutes to make them crisp again.

255

MICROWAVE SWEETS

Use your microwave to make delectable desserts in no time at all!

SPICED BANANAS

LOW-CALORIE • LOW-CHOLESTEROL • LOW-SODIUM
• LOW-FAT • MICROWAVE

Makes 2 servings.

Nutrient Value Per Serving: 72 calories, 1 g protein, 0 g fat,
18 g carbohydrate, 5 mg sodium, 0 mg cholesterol.

3 tablespoons unsweetened apple OR: pear juice	⅛ teaspoon ground allspice
1 small banana, peeled and sliced	Pinch ground nutmeg
⅛ teaspoon ground cinnamon	Pinch ground cloves
	2 mint sprigs, for garnish

1. Combine all the ingredients in a microwave-safe dish, and toss them
gently to blend them. Microwave at full power for 1½ minutes, or until the
banana slices are hot and cooked through.
2. Divide the banana slices and cooking liquid between 2 individual dessert
plates. Garnish each plate with a mint sprig.

ORANGE BANANA NUT CAKE

A moist cake full of the zesty taste of fresh orange.

MICROWAVE

Makes 12 servings.

Nutrient Value Per Serving: 348 calories, 5 g protein, 16 g fat,
47 g carbohydrate, 86 mg sodium, 101 mg cholesterol.

¾ cup (1½ sticks) unsalted butter, softened	¼ teaspoon baking soda
1 cup granulated sugar	Pinch salt
½ cup firmly packed brown sugar	1 ripe banana
3 eggs	½ cup fresh orange juice
1 cup plain nonfat yogurt	1 tablespoon orange zest (orange part of rind only)
1¼ cups all-purpose flour	½ cup chopped pecans
2 tablespoons cornstarch	¼ cup corn syrup
½ teaspoon baking powder	Whole pecans, for decoration

1. Generously grease a microwave-safe Bundt® cake pan.
2. Beat together the butter, granulated sugar and brown sugar in a
medium-size bowl until the mixture is light colored. Beat in the eggs, one at
a time. Stir in the yogurt.
3. Sift together the flour, cornstarch, baking powder, baking soda and salt
onto wax paper.

Sweets in Seconds

*When it comes to the last
course, the microwave oven
can be a boon or a bane,
depending on the recipe
you're using. The microwave
is excellent for making moist
desserts, such as fudge
brownies, fruit compotes,
quick coffee cakes, cheese
cakes, flourless cakes, nut
cakes, custards, bar cookies
and steamed puddings. On the
other hand, crisp cookies,
soufflés, delicately textured
cakes and pastries are best
baked in a conventional oven.*

*Most baked desserts, whether
cooked in the microwave or
prepared conventionally,
share one common principle:
You must follow the
directions exactly. The size
and shape of the pan always
are important, but they are
especially important in
microwave baking, where the
baking process is very
different from that of a
conventional oven.*

Hold That Dessert!

For many desserts, a key "success factor" occurs after the baking. Conventionally baked desserts often are cooled on wire racks so that air can circulate around them and prevent their becoming soggy. Many microwave recipes, however, require a "standing time" on a flat, heatproof surface after the desserts emerge from the oven. This time is important for the desserts to finish cooking, and for any excess moisture to be absorbed.

4. Mash the banana with ¼ cup of the orange juice and the orange zest.

5. Add the banana mixture to the butter mixture alternately with the dry ingredients. Stir in the chopped pecans.

6. Pour the batter into the prepared pan. Set the pan on top of a microwave-safe bowl. Microwave, uncovered, at half power for 9 minutes, then at full power for 8 to 10 minutes, or until a wooden pick inserted near the center of the cake comes out clean. The top may still appear damp.

7. Cool the cake directly on a heatproof surface for 15 minutes. Turn out the cake onto a serving plate.

8. Meanwhile, combine the remaining ¼ cup of orange juice with the corn syrup in a microwave-safe glass measuring cup. Microwave at full power for 2 minutes, or until the mixture is warm and syrupy. Poke holes into the cake while it is still warm, and pour the syrup over the cake.

9. Decorate the cake with the whole pecans.

Orange Banana Nut Cake is sweet, moist and delicious.

DATE-FILLED OATMEAL SQUARES

These mouthfuls of chewy goodness are great to pop into someone's lunch bag—or to snack on any time at all.

MICROWAVE

Makes 24 squares.

Nutrient Value Per Square: 246 calories, 4 g protein, 9 g fat, 40 g carbohydrate, 55 mg sodium, 44 mg cholesterol.

Date Filling:
- 1 container (10 ounces) pitted dates
- ⅓ cup fresh orange juice
- ¼ cup sugar
- 1 tablespoon dark rum
- 4 2-inch strips orange zest (orange part of rind only)

Oatmeal Dough:
- 1 cup (2 sticks) unsalted butter
- 1½ cups firmly packed dark brown sugar
- 2 eggs
- 2 cups all-purpose flour
- 2 teaspoons baking powder
- 4 teaspoons ground cinnamon
- Large pinch salt
- 3 cups rolled oats

1. Prepare the Date Filling: Combine the dates with the orange juice in a microwave-safe, 1-quart glass measure. Cover the measure tightly with microwave-safe plastic wrap.

2. Microwave at full power, rotating the measure once or twice, for 5 minutes, until the juice bubbles and the dates are very soft.

3. Transfer the date mixture to the container of a food processor. Add the sugar, rum and orange zest. Process until the filling is smooth. Let the filling cool.

4. Meanwhile, prepare the Oatmeal Dough: Beat together the butter and the brown sugar until creamy in a large bowl with an electric mixer at high speed. Beat in the eggs. Lower the mixer speed to low. Beat in the flour, baking powder, cinnamon and salt. Beat in the oats.

5. Layer two thirds of the oatmeal dough in the bottom of a microwave-safe 9 x 13-inch baking dish. Spread the date filling over the top. Crumble the remaining oatmeal dough over the date filling, and press it in gently.

6. Shield the corners of the dish with aluminum foil to prevent the edges of the cake from overcooking.

7. Microwave at full power for 10 minutes, rotating the dish twice during the cooking time. Remove the dish from the oven to a heatproof surface. Let the cake cool. Cut the cake into squares with a serrated knife.

The Microwave Bakery

Turning out delicious baked products from a microwave oven probably is more a matter of expectation than expertise. If you know what to expect from the microwave, you can get the best results possible with no disappointments.

■ Use glass bakeware so that you can see the food as it cooks—you'll be able to check for doneness just by looking at the bottom.

■ In most cases, baked goods will be underdone at the center when they come out of the microwave; they will finish cooking and firm up during the standing time.

■ Cakes, whether from a mix or from scratch, tend to rise higher in the microwave than in a conventional oven. Underfill cake pans slightly, using the extra batter for cupcakes.

■ Avoid the urge to cut or slice baked goods until they are completely cooled.

■ For a "browner" look to baked goods, substitute brown sugar for some of the granulated sugar in most recipes, and whole wheat flour for not more than one quarter of the all-purpose flour.

Microwave Baking Dishes

Many manufacturers make microwave-safe dishes in shapes that are designed specifically for microwave baking. These dish shapes take into account the cooking pattern of the microwave. Food toward the center of a dish takes longer to cook in the microwave, so many foods cook best if arranged in a ring. Special microwave muffin pans have the cups arranged in a ring, instead of in the conventional line formation. Microwave cakes and meat loaves often benefit from being baked in ring-shaped pans instead of ordinary solid, round pans because the microwaves can reach the food through the center as well as the sides. Microwave Bundt® pans also are available; like the ring-shaped pans, they can be used for baking cakes as well as loaves made from ground meat and/or vegetables.

❖   ❖   ❖

MOCHA BROWNIES WITH WHITE CHOCOLATE ICING

Brownies that will satisfy the most intense craving—they're chocolate through and through, and topped with white chocolate icing!

MICROWAVE

Makes 16 brownies.

Nutrient Value Per Brownie: 215 calories, 3 g protein, 14 g fat, 22 g carbohydrate, 120 mg sodium, 50 mg cholesterol.

Mocha Brownies:
- 2 ounces semisweet chocolate, coarsely chopped
- 1 ounce unsweetened chocolate, coarsely chopped
- ½ cup (1 stick) butter, cut in half
- ½ cup all-purpose flour
- ⅓ cup whole wheat flour
- ½ teaspoon baking powder
- ¼ teaspoon salt
- ¾ cup firmly packed brown sugar
- 2 eggs
- 1 teaspoon vanilla
- ½ teaspoon espresso powder
- 1 cup toasted walnuts,* chopped

White Chocolate Icing:
- 1 ounce white chocolate, coarsely chopped
- ¼ cup 10X (confectioners' powdered) sugar
- 2 teaspoons milk

1. Prepare the Mocha Brownies: Combine the semisweet chocolate, unsweetened chocolate and butter in a microwave-safe, medium-size bowl. Microwave, uncovered, at full power for 1 minute and 15 seconds. Stir until the ingredients are blended. Cool the mixture until it is warm to the touch.

2. Meanwhile, stir together the all-purpose flour, whole wheat flour, baking powder and salt on a piece of wax paper.

3. Lightly grease a microwave-safe, 8-inch square baking dish.

4. Stir the brown sugar, eggs, vanilla and espresso powder into the chocolate mixture until the ingredients are well blended. Add the walnuts. Add the flour mixture, stirring just until it is combined. Pour the batter into the prepared dish and smooth the top.

5. Microwave, uncovered, at seven tenths power for 6 minutes, rotating the dish halfway through the cooking time. A wooden pick inserted in the center of the brownies should come out clean. Let the brownies stand for 10 minutes.

6. Meanwhile, prepare the White Chocolate Icing: Place the white chocolate in a microwave-safe small bowl. Microwave at full power for 90 seconds. Stir the chocolate. Add the 10X (confectioners' powdered) sugar and the milk, stirring until the icing is smooth. Drizzle the icing with a spoon onto the cooled brownies. Cut the brownies into squares. Serve the brownies immediately, or store them in an airtight container.

__Note:__ To toast walnuts in a microwave oven, place 1 cup at a time on a piece of microwave-safe paper toweling. Microwave at full power for 3 minutes, stirring halfway through the cooking time.

SPICY PEAR UPSIDE-DOWN CAKE

This is our favorite type of cake: showy to look at, but requiring a minimum amount of effort.

MICROWAVE

Makes 12 servings.

Nutrient Value Per Serving: 275 calories, 3 g protein, 11 g fat, 43 g carbohydrate, 177 mg sodium, 72 mg cholesterol.

1 **can (29 ounces) pears, packed in syrup**	¼ **teaspoon ground cardamom**
10 **tablespoons (1¼ sticks) butter, at room temperature**	¼ **teaspoon ground cloves**
	¼ **teaspoon ground cinnamon**
1 **cup firmly packed brown sugar**	¼ **teaspoon ground ginger**
1½ **cups all-purpose flour**	⅛ **teaspoon salt**
1 **teaspoon baking powder**	**Whipped cream**
2 **eggs**	**OR: vanilla ice cream (optional)**
Grated zest of ½ lemon (yellow part of rind only)	

1. Drain the pears, saving the syrup. Measure ⅔ cup of the pear syrup and reserve it. Cut the pears lengthwise into fourths.

2. Place 2 tablespoons of the butter in a microwave-safe, 9-inch round cake pan with straight sides. Microwave, uncovered, at full power for 50 seconds, or until the butter is melted.

3. Swirl the butter to coat the bottom of the pan evenly. Sprinkle ½ cup of the brown sugar evenly over the butter. Arrange all but 4 of the pear wedges in a circle around the outside of the pan. Place the remaining 4 pear wedges in the center of the pan.

4. Sift together the flour and the baking powder onto wax paper. Set aside the flour mixture.

5. Beat the remaining 8 tablespoons of butter with the remaining ½ cup of brown sugar in a small bowl with an electric mixer until the mixture is light colored and fluffy. Add the eggs, lemon zest, cardamom, cloves, cinnamon, ginger and salt. Beat the mixture at high speed for 2 minutes, or until the ingredients are well blended.

6. Reduce the mixer speed to low. Add the reserved ⅔ cup of pear syrup to the butter mixture alternately with the flour mixture, mixing just until the ingredients are blended. Pour the batter into the pan, covering the pear wedges, and gently smooth the top. Gently tap the pan on the counter a few times to remove any large air bubbles. Cover the pan with microwave-safe paper toweling.

7. Microwave at seven tenths power for 14 to 16 minutes, rotating the dish a half turn once during the cooking time. A wooden pick inserted in the center of the cake should come out clean. Let the cake cool in the pan on a wire rack for 10 minutes.

8. Invert the cake onto a serving plate. Serve the cake warm, with whipped cream or vanilla ice cream, if you wish.

Minted Mini S'Mores

Place 4 small imported wheatmeal biscuits face up on a piece of microwave-safe paper toweling in the microwave oven. Place 2 chocolate mint parfait wafers on each of 2 of the biscuits, and 1 chocolate drop (about 1 inch in diameter) on each remaining biscuit. Microwave at full power for 1 minute and 20 seconds, or just until the chocolate drops start to melt around the edges. Place a marshmallow on top of each parfait wafer. Microwave at full power for 30 seconds, or just until the marshmallows begin to puff.

Place a chocolate-drop biscuit, chocolate side down, on top of each marshmallow. Press down slightly to flatten the marshmallow to about a ¾-inch thickness. Let the s'mores stand for 3 minutes. Eat them warm.

❖　❖　❖

Hazelnuts

Widely grown and used in southern Europe, hazelnuts grow in clusters on shrubs and small trees. Hazelnuts are the fruit of the trees, and have a woody shell with a single seed or nut. The nut is round or oval, depending on the variety. In the United States, hazelnuts are grown commercially only in Oregon and Washington.

■ Hazelnuts also are called cobnuts or filberts. Filberts, which are cultivated hazelnuts, are so named because they ripen around St. Philbert's Day, August 22, when harvesting begins.

■ Hazelnuts are sold unshelled or shelled, but never are blanched. They may be used in candies, cakes, tortes, breads and cookies.

■ Store hazelnuts in a cool, dry place or refrigerate them.

■ When using hazelnuts in cooking, 1 pound of unshelled nuts equals 1½ cups of nuts; 1 pound of shelled nuts equals 3½ cups of nuts.

❖ ❖ ❖

HAZELNUT CHEESECAKE

This moist and creamy cheesecake cooks in less than 20 minutes. Cooking the bourbon removes the alcohol content and mellows the flavor.

MICROWAVE

Makes 8 servings.

Nutrient Value Per Serving: 575 calories, 10 g protein, 39 g fat, 48 g carbohydrate, 401 mg sodium, 233 mg cholesterol.

½	cup hazelnuts (2½ ounces)	1	cup lightly packed dark brown sugar
4	tablespoons butter		
1½	cups gingersnap crumbs (about twenty-four 2-inch cookies, 6 ounces)	4	eggs Grated zest of 1 lemon (yellow part of rind only)
¼	cup bourbon	1	tablespoon cornstarch
2	packages (8 ounces each) cream cheese	¾	cup dairy sour cream

1. Place the hazelnuts in a microwave-safe, 8-inch square baking dish or 10-inch pie plate. Microwave at full power for 2 minutes, stirring once. Rub the hazelnuts between paper toweling to remove their husks. Chop the hazelnuts, and set them aside.

2. Place the butter in the baking dish. Microwave at full power for 1 minute, or until the butter is melted. Add the gingersnap crumbs and ¼ cup of the chopped hazelnuts. Stir until the ingredients are blended.

3. Spread the gingersnap mixture evenly in the baking dish. Cover the mixture with plastic wrap. Press the mixture over the bottom and halfway up the sides of the baking dish. Remove the plastic wrap. Microwave at full power for 2 minutes.

4. Microwave the bourbon in a microwave-safe, 2-cup measure for 2 minutes, or until the bourbon is reduced by half.

5. To soften the chilled cream cheese, place it, uncovered, in a microwave-safe large bowl. Microwave at full power for 1 minute and 30 seconds.

6. Add the brown sugar to the cream cheese. Beat with an electric mixer for 1 minute, or until the ingredients are blended. Add the bourbon, eggs, lemon zest and cornstarch, and beat until the mixture is smooth. Blend in the sour cream on low speed just until it is combined.

7. Microwave the cream cheese mixture at full power for 5 minutes, or until it is thickened and the texture of sour cream, whisking twice during the cooking time until the mixture is smooth. Pour the batter into the prepared baking dish. Sprinkle the remaining ¼ cup of hazelnuts over the top of the batter.

8. Place the baking dish on an inverted microwave-safe plate in the microwave oven. Microwave at half power for 7 to 8 minutes, or until the cake is almost set in the center, rotating the dish a half turn once during the cooking time. Cool the cheesecake in the pan on a wire rack to room temperature. Refrigerate the cake for 6 hours, or overnight. Serve the cheesecake chilled.

BLUEBERRY CRUMBCAKE

A moist coffee cake that's significantly lower in saturated fat and sugar than traditional recipes; and it's been fortified with bran and wheat germ.

LOW-FAT • MICROWAVE

Makes 8 servings.

Nutrient Value Per Serving: 261 calories, 5 g protein, 8 g fat, 42 g carbohydrate, 157 mg sodium, 40 mg cholesterol.

1¾ cups unbleached all-purpose flour	¼ cup plus 2 tablespoons granulated sugar
¼ cup firmly packed light brown sugar	1½ teaspoons baking powder
1 tablespoon unsalted butter	½ teaspoon baking soda
1 tablespoon toasted wheat germ	¼ cup miller's (raw) bran
Grated zest (yellow part of rind only) and juice of ½ lemon	½ cup plain nonfat yogurt
	¼ cup lowfat milk
	1 large egg
½ teaspoon ground cinnamon	3 tablespoons safflower oil
	1 teaspoon vanilla
	¾ cup fresh blueberries

1. Lightly grease a microwave-safe, 8-inch round baking pan. For the crumb topping, combine 2 tablespoons of the flour with the brown sugar, butter, wheat germ, ⅛ teaspoon of the lemon zest and the cinnamon in a small bowl until the mixture is crumbly. Set aside the topping.

2. Sift all but 2 tablespoons of the remaining flour with the granulated sugar, baking powder and baking soda into a medium-size bowl. Add the bran and the remaining lemon zest. Toss the ingredients together.

3. Beat together the lemon juice, yogurt, milk, egg, oil and vanilla in a small bowl. Lightly dust the blueberries with the remaining 2 tablespoons of flour, shaking off any excess flour.

4. Add the yogurt mixture, then the blueberries, to the dry ingredients. Stir very gently with a large wooden spoon just until the mixtures are blended; don't overmix. Quickly pour the batter into the prepared pan and spread it evenly. Scatter the topping over the batter.

5. Microwave at full power for 12 to 13 minutes, rotating the pan every 3 minutes. Place the pan on a heatproof surface and let the cake cool. Cut the cake into 8 wedges, and serve. Or, if you wish, wrap each wedge in plastic wrap, and freeze the cake.

CARAMEL SAUCE

Rich and gooey—just like you remember it. This sauce is perfect over ice cream, or as a sweet topping for pound cake, custard or fruit compote.

LOW-SODIUM • MICROWAVE

Makes 10 servings.

Nutrient Value Per Serving: 164 calories, trace protein, 9 g fat, 21 g carbohydrate, 9 mg sodium, 33 mg cholesterol.

1 cup sugar	1 teaspoon vanilla
¼ cup water	1 teaspoon rum
1 cup heavy cream	

Yogurt

Wonderful by itself, with fruit stirred in, or in baking recipes such as our Blueberry Crumbcake (recipe, at left), yogurt has many nutritional benefits. One cup of lowfat yogurt provides a good amount of protein, zinc, folacin, B_{12} (important for healthy blood and skin tone) and riboflavin (important for providing energy to skin cells). Plus, a cup of nonfat yogurt provides 50 percent of your daily calcium requirement.

Sauces in Seconds

Here, some easy dessert toppings to whip up.

■ Minty Fudge Sauce: Stir 1 tablespoon of peppermint schnapps into fudge sauce.

■ Caramel Nut Sauce: Melt caramel candies in a glass measuring cup in the microwave at one quarter power. Thin the melted caramel with a little water, if necessary, and stir in chopped nuts. Serve the sauce immediately over pound cake or ice cream.

■ Cranberry Orange Sauce: Purée cranberry orange relish until it is fairly smooth. Heat the purée in the microwave at half power until it is warm. Stir in 1 tablespoon of orange-flavored liqueur and a dash of cinnamon. Serve Cranberry Orange Sauce over cheesecake or bread pudding.

■ Chocolate Shell Sauce: Melt chunks of semisweet chocolate in the microwave at half power. Pour the sauce over ice cream; it should harden immediately.

❖ ❖ ❖

" Sweets to the sweet: farewell!"
—*William Shakespeare*

1. Combine the sugar with the water in a microwave-safe, 8-cup measure. Cover the measure with microwave-safe plastic wrap, slightly vented in one place. Microwave at full power for 7 minutes, or until the syrup is golden colored, swirling the contents after 3 minutes. If the syrup is not golden colored after 7 minutes, microwave in 15-second increments until it is golden colored.
2. Remove the measure from the microwave oven. Stir in the cream, vanilla and rum. If the sugar crystallizes, microwave at full power for 15 seconds. Remove the measure from the oven, and stir the sauce.

Variations: Substitute another liquor or a liqueur for the rum.

APRICOT GLAZE

This one-step classic is easier than ever to make when you microwave it.

LOW-CHOLESTEROL • LOW-SODIUM • LOW-FAT • MICROWAVE
Makes 12 servings.

Nutrient Value Per Serving: 64 calories, trace protein, trace fat, 17 g carbohydrate, 3 mg sodium, 0 mg cholesterol.

1 jar (10 ounces) apricot preserves	2 tablespoons water

1. Combine the apricot preserves with the water in a microwave-safe, 1-quart glass measure or bowl. Cover the measure. Microwave at full power for 2 minutes to melt the preserves.
2. Pour the apricot mixture through a fine strainer into a bowl, and return the strained mixture to the measure. Microwave, uncovered, at full power for 1 minute more. Use the glaze while it is hot, or reheat it just before using it. Refrigerate leftover glaze, and reheat it in an uncovered microwave-safe glass jar.

RASPBERRY SAUCE

Raspberry sauce is one of the easiest ways to dress up a dessert, whether it's a charlotte, plain cake, vanilla ice cream or custard. Garnish with a few fresh berries, if you wish.

LOW-CHOLESTEROL • LOW-SODIUM • LOW-FAT • MICROWAVE
Makes 6 servings.

Nutrient Value Per Serving: 49 calories, trace protein, trace fat, 12 g carbohydrate, trace sodium, 0 mg cholesterol.

1 package (10 ounces) frozen raspberries in light syrup	1 tablespoon cherry-, raspberry-, or orange-flavored liqueur (optional)
1 tablespoon sugar (optional)	

1. Thaw the raspberries, following the package directions. Purée the raspberries in a food processor or electric blender. Press the purée through a fine strainer with the back of a spoon, and discard the seeds.
2. If you wish, stir in 1 tablespoon of sugar and one tablespoon of cherry-, raspberry- or orange-flavored liqueur.

EMERGENCY INGREDIENT SUBSTITUTES

WHEN THE RECIPE CALLS FOR:	YOU MAY SUBSTITUTE:
1 square unsweetened chocolate	3 tablespoons unsweetened cocoa powder plus 1 tablespoon butter, margarine or vegetable shortening
1 cup sifted cake flour	⅞ cup sifted all-purpose flour (1 cup less 2 tablespoons)
2 tablespoons flour (for thickening)	1 tablespoon cornstarch
1 teaspoon baking powder	¼ teaspoon baking powder plus ⅝ teaspoon cream of tartar
1 cup corn syrup	1 cup sugar and ¼ cup liquid used in recipe
1 cup honey	1¼ cups sugar and ¼ cup liquid used in recipe
1 cup whole milk	½ cup evaporated milk plus ½ cup water
1 cup buttermilk	1 tablespoon vinegar plus enough whole milk to make 1 cup
1 cup sour cream (in baking)	⅞ cup buttermilk or sour milk plus 3 tablespoons butter
1 egg (for custards)	2 egg yolks plus 1 tablespoon water
1 cup brown sugar (packed)	1 cup sugar or 1 cup sugar plus 2 tablespoons molasses
1 teaspoon lemon juice	¼ teaspoon vinegar
¼ cup chopped onion	1 tablespoon instant minced onion
1 clove garlic	⅛ teaspoon garlic powder
1 cup zucchini	1 cup summer squash
1 cup tomato juice	½ cup tomato sauce plus ½ cup water
2 cups tomato sauce	¾ cup tomato paste plus 1 cup water
1 tablespoon snipped fresh herbs	1 teaspoon dried herbs
1 tablespoon prepared mustard	1 teaspoon dry mustard
½ cup (1 stick) butter or margarine	7 tablespoons vegetable shortening

264

EMERGENCY
BAKING DISH AND PAN SUBSTITUTES

If you do not have the specific size of pan or mold called for in a recipe, substitute a pan of equal volume from the list below.

If the pan you are substituting is made of glass, reduce the baking temperature by 25°.

If you are substituting a pan that is shallower than the pan in the recipe, reduce the baking time by about one-quarter.

If you are substituting a pan that is deeper than the pan in the recipe, increase baking time by one-quarter.

HANDY CHART OF KITCHEN MATH
You'll never have a cooking crisis when you use our handy charts. Need a 4- or 6-cup baking dish? Will your fancy mold be the right size for the recipe? See below for the answers, plus much more!

COMMON KITCHEN PANS TO USE AS CASSEROLES WHEN THE RECIPE CALLS FOR:
4-cup baking dish:
  9-inch pie plate
  8 x 1¼-inch round layer-cake pan—**C**
  7⅜ x 3⅝ x 2⅝-inch loaf pan—**A**
6-cup baking dish:
  10-inch pie plate
  8 or 9 x 1½-inch round layer-cake pan—**C**
  8½ x 3⅝ x 2⅝-inch loaf pan—**A**
8-cup baking dish:
  8 x 8 x 2-inch square pan—**D**
  11 x 7 x 1½-inch baking pan
  9 x 5 x 3-inch loaf pan—**A**
10-cup baking dish:
  9 x 9 x 2-inch square pan—**A**
  11¾ x 7½ x 1¾-inch baking pan
  15½ x 10½ x 1-inch jelly-roll pan
12-cup baking dish and over:
  13½ x 8½ x 2-inch glass baking dish (12 cups)
  13 x 9 x 2-inch metal baking pan (15 cups)
  14 x 10½ x 2½-inch roasting pan (19 cups)
Three 8-inch-round pans:
  two 9 x 9 x 2-inch square cake pans
Two 9-inch-round layer-cake pans:
  two 8 x 8 x 2-inch square cake pans, or 13 x 9 x 2-inch pan
9 x 5 x 3-inch loaf pan:
  9 x 9 x 2-inch square cake pan
9-inch angel-cake tube pan:
  10 x 3¾-inch Bundt® pan, or 9 x 3½-inch fancy tube pan

TOTAL VOLUME OF VARIOUS SPECIAL BAKING PANS
Tube pans:

7½ x 3-inch Bundt® tube pan — **K**	6 cups
9 x 3½-inch fancy tube or Bundt® pan — **J** or **K**	9 cups
9 x 3½-inch angel-cake or tube pan — **I**	12 cups
10 x 3¾-inch Bundt® or Crownburst® pan — **K**	12 cups
9 x 3½-inch fancy tube mold — **J**	12 cups
10 x 4-inch fancy tube mold (Kugelhopf) — **J**	16 cups
10 x 4-inch angel-cake or tube pan — **I**	18 cups

Melon Mold:

7 x 5½ x 4-inch mold — **H**	6 cups

Springform Pans:

8 x 3-inch pan — **B**	12 cups
9 x 3-inch pan — **B**	16 cups

Ring Molds:

8½ x 2¼-inch mold — **E**	4½ cups
9¼ x 2¾-inch mold — **E**	8 cups

Charlotte Mold:

6 x 4¼-inch mold — **G**	7½ cups

Brioche Pan:

9½ x 3¼-inch pan — **F**	8 cups

A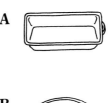

B

C

D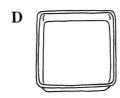

E

F

G

H

I

J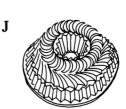

K

FOOD EQUIVALENTS

Berries, 1 pint ... 1¾ cups

Bread
    Crumbs, soft, 1 cup ... 2 slices
    Cubes, 1 cup ... 2 slices
    1 pound, sliced ... 22 slices

Broth
    Beef or
      Chicken, 1 cup ... 1 teaspoon instant bouillon or 1 envelope bouillon or 1 cube bouillon, dissolved in 1 cup boiling water

Butter or Margarine
    ½ stick ... ¼ cup or 4 tablespoons
    1 pound ... 4 sticks or 2 cups

Cream and milk
    Cream, heavy, 1 cup ... 2 cups, whipped
    Milk, evaporated, small can ... ⅔ cup
    Milk, instant, nonfat dry,
      1 pound ... 5 quarts, liquid skim milk
    Milk, sweetened condensed,
      14-ounce can ... 1⅔ cups

Cheese
    Blue, crumbled, 4 ounces ... 1 cup
    Cheddar or Swiss, 1 pound, shredded ... 4 cups
    Cottage, 8 ounces ... 1 cup
    Cream, 8-ounce package ... 1 cup
    Parmesan or Romano, ¼ pound grated ... 1¼ cups

Chocolate
    Semisweet pieces, 6-ounce package ... 1 cup
    Unsweetened, 1 ounce ... 1 square

Coconut
    Flaked, 3½-ounce can ... 1⅓ cups
    Shredded 4-ounce can ... 1⅓ cups

Cookies
    Chocolate wafers, 1 cup crumbs ... 19 wafers
    Vanilla wafers, 1 cup fine crumbs ... 22 wafers
    Graham crackers,
      1 cup fine crumbs ... 14 square crackers

Dried Beans and Peas
    1 cup ... 2¼ cups, cooked

Eggs (large)
    Whole, 1 cup ... 5 to 6
    Whites, 1 cup ... 7 to 8
    Yolks, 1 cup ... 13 to 14

Flour
    all-purpose, sifted, 1 pound ... 4 cups
    cake, sifted, 1 pound ... 4¾ to 5 cups

Gelatin, unflavored, 1 envelope ... 1 tablespoon

Nuts
    Almonds, 1 pound, shelled ... 3½ cups
    Peanuts, 1 pound, shelled ... 3 cups
    Walnuts, 1 pound, shelled ... 4 cups
    Pecans, 1 pound, shelled ... 4 cups

Pasta
    Macaroni, elbow,
      uncooked, 8 ounces ... 4 cups, cooked
    Noodles, medium width,
      uncooked, 8 ounces ... 3¾ cups, cooked
    Spaghetti, uncooked, 8 ounces ... 4 cups, cooked

Rice
    Enriched precooked rice,
      uncooked, 1 cup ... 2 cups, cooked
    Long-grain white rice,
      uncooked, 1 cup ... 3 cups, cooked

Sugar
    Brown, firmly packed, 1 pound ... 2¼ cups
    Granulated, 1 pound ... 2 cups
    10X (confectioners' powdered),
      sifted, 1 pound ... 3⅓ to 4 cups

Vegetables and Fruits
    Apples, 1 pound ... 3 medium size
    Bananas, 1 pound ... 3 medium size
    Cabbages, 1 pound, shredded ... 4 cups
    Carrots, 1 pound, sliced ... 2½ cups
    Herbs, chopped fresh,
      1 tablespoon ... 1 teaspoon dried
    Lemon, 1 medium size,
      grated ... 2 teaspoons lemon rind
    Lemon, 1 medium size,
      squeezed ... 2 tablespoons lemon juice
    Mushrooms, 1 pound, sliced ... 3 cups
    Onions, small white
      silverskins, 1 pound ... 12 to 14
    Onions, yellow cooking,
      1 pound ... 5 to 6 medium size
    Orange, 1 medium size,
      grated ... 2 tablespoons orange rind
    Orange, 1 medium size,
      squeezed ... ⅓ to ½ cup orange juice
    Peaches, 1 pound ... 4 medium size
    Potatoes, all-purpose, 1 pound ... 3 medium size
    Tomatoes, 1 pound:
      Large ... 2
      Medium size ... 3
      Small ... 4

MEASURING EQUIPMENT

MEASURING FLOUR
Measure the all-purpose flour called for in most of the recipes in this book by spooning flour from the bag or canister into a dry measuring cup, heaping slightly. (Note: The top of the cup is flat; there is no spout in a dry measure, as there is in a liquid measuring cup.)

Place the heaping cup of flour over the bag of flour or canister and run the flat side of a long knife across the top to level off the cup. (Note: Use this technique for granulated sugar too.)

MEASURING SHORTENING
Measure vegetable shortening by scooping it with a rubber scraper into a dry measuring cup; run the flat blade of a long knife over the top, then scoop it out of the cup with the rubber scraper into a mixing bowl.

Shortening can be measured before or after it is melted.

One stick of butter or margarine equals 4 ounces; 4 sticks equal 1 pound or 2 cups.

MEASURING LIQUID
Place a liquid measuring cup on a flat surface and stoop to be at eye level with the measuring cup; pour the liquid to the desired measure printed on the side of the cup. (Note: When measuring a syrup, such as molasses or honey, grease the cup with butter or margarine. Then the syrup will pour out easily.)

PACKING BROWN SUGAR
Measure light or dark brown sugar by packing it into a dry measuring cup, using the back of a tablespoon.

OVEN TEMPERATURES

Very Slow	250°-275°
Slow	300°-325°
Moderate	350°-375°
Hot	400°-425°
Very Hot	450°-475°
Extremely Hot	500°+

CASSEROLE MEASUREMENT CHART
Casseroles are international dishes. Recipes are imported from all over the world, and each country has its own system for measuring. The chart below will help you to convert your casserole's measurements from one system to another so you can be sure every recipe you make will turn out just right.

Cups	=	Pints	=	Quarts	=	Liters
1		½		¼		0.237
2		1*		½*		0.473
4		2*		1*		0.946
6		3		1½		1.419
8		4		2		1.892
10		5		2½		2.365
12		6		3		2.838

*In Canada, 1 pint = 2½ cups; 1 quart = 5 cups.

267

GLOSSARY

A

À la
In the manner of, as in *à la francaise:* in the style of the French.

Al dente
An Italian phrase used to describe pasta cooked to the perfect stage of doneness—tender, but firm enough to be felt between the teeth.

Antipasto
An Italian word meaning "before the meal." A selection of hors d'oeuvres, such as salami, marinated mushrooms, tuna or anchovies.

Au gratin
A dish, usually vegetables, cooked in a creamy sauce mixture, topped with bread crumbs and/or cheese and browned in the oven or broiler.

B

Blanch
To plunge foods quickly into boiling water, then into cold water, to loosen skins for easy removal. Also, a preliminary step in freezing vegetables.

Braise
To brown in fat, then to cook, covered, in a small amount of liquid.

C

Candy
A confection. Also, to cook fruit, fruit peel or gingerroot in a heavy syrup until it is transparent, and then drain and dry it. Also, to cook vegetables, such as carrots or sweet potatoes, in a sugar syrup or honey.

Caramelize
To cook sugar over low heat until it becomes a golden brown liquid.

Chorizo
A Spanish sausage, strongly flavored with paprika and garlic.

Coat the spoon
A term used to describe egg-based sauces or liquids (such as custard) when at their perfect consistency: When a metal spoon is dipped into the liquid and removed, it should be coated with a a thin, somewhat jelly-like film.

Confectioners' Powdered Sugar
Also known as 10X sugar. This is the finest grind of sugar available. A small amount of cornstarch has been added to the sugar to prevent it from lumping. Used for "dusting" desserts or in uncooked icings.

Crimp
To press the edges of pastry together with the tines of a fork or your fingertips to form a decorative edging or to seal in a filling.

Cut in
To blend shortening or other solid fat with a flour mixture by working them with a pastry blender or two knives until the combined mixture resembles peas or coarse meal.

E

Egg wash A whole egg or egg yolk, mixed with a little water or milk, that is brushed on bread dough before baking it to create a shiny crust.

Entrée A French term referring to the third course in a formal dinner. Also used to designate the main dish of a meal.

Evaporated milk Canned, unsweetened milk that has been slightly thickened by the removal of some of its water.

F

Fajitas A popular dish from the southwest. Pieces of skirt steak, usually marinated, are grilled, sliced and wrapped in flour tortillas. Fajitas also may be made from flank steak or boneless chuck, or even chicken or turkey.

Fillet A thin, boneless piece of meat or fish.

Flake To break up food, such as tuna, into smaller pieces with a fork.

Florentine In the style of Florence, Italy; usually served on a bed of spinach, topped with a cheese sauce and browned in the oven.

Flour, Cake Flour that is milled from soft wheat and containing less gluten-forming protein than all-purpose flour. Cake flour produces a lighter texture in cakes, cookies and pastries.

Flute To form a ruffled edge for a pie crust using your fingers and thumb.

Fricassee A dish consisting of meat cut into pieces, covered by a mixture of water, vegetables and, often, wine. The meat may be browned in butter or oil first. A gravy is made from the cooking liquid, and is served with the meat. Also the method by which this dish is prepared.

Frittata An unfolded omelet often containing vegetables or meat.

G

Garnish To decorate with colorful and/or elegantly cut pieces of food.

Glaze To coat food with honey, syrup or other liquid to create a shiny appearance.

Gluten The protein of wheat flour that forms the framework or structure of cakes, breads, cookies and pastries.

H

Hors d'oeuvres Any one of a variety of appetizers, such as olives, anchovies, canapés, etc., usually served at the beginning of a meal.

Hull To remove the caps and stems from fresh berries.

I

Ice   To cover with icing. Also, a frozen, water-based dessert.

Italienne, à l'   Served Italian style with pasta.

J

Julienne   To cut food into uniformly long, thin slivers (1½ x inches).

K

Kasha   Buckwheat groats that are braised or cooked in liquid. They usually are served as a starch in place of rice or potatoes.

Knead   To work dough with your hands until it is smooth and elastic. Kneading is necessary to develop the gluten in yeast breads, which gives them their framework and volume.

Kosher salt   A very coarse salt.

L

Liquid red pepper seasoning   The generic name for Tabasco® sauce.

M

Macerate   To let food, principally fruits, steep in wine or spirits to absorb flavor.

Maître d'hôtel   Simply cooked dishes seasoned with finely chopped parsley, butter and lemon. *Maître d'Hôtel* butter is a mixture of butter (or margarine), parsley, lemon juice and salt.

Marinate   To let food, principally meats, steep in an oil- or acid-based sauce prior to cooking. The marinade adds flavor and tenderizes the meat.

Marzipan   A confection made from almond paste, sugar and egg whites, which often is colored and shaped into tiny fruit and vegetable forms.

Mask   To coat foods with a sauce or aspic.

Mole   A sauce of Mexican origin, containing chili peppers, onion, garlic, and other ingredients, including bitter chocolate. It is the chocolate which gives mole sauce its distinctive flavor. The sauce is usually served over poultry.

Mousse   A rich, creamy dessert. Also, a hot or cold savory dish with a velvety texture, rich with cream and bound with eggs or, if cold, with gelatin.

Mull   To heat a liquid, such as wine or cider, with whole spices added to it.

N

Niçoise — Prepared in the manner of Nice, France — with tomatoes, garlic, olive oil and ripe olives.

Nouvelle Cuisine — A style of cooking developed in France which provides a lighter approach to classic French dishes and preparation techniques. The techniques have been adapted to many other types of cuisine.

O

Oil — To rub a pan or mold with cooking oil.

Orzo — Tiny, rice-shaped pasta.

P

Panbroil — To cook in a small amount of fat, pouring off drippings as they accumulate.

Parboil — To cook in boiling water until about half done; vegetables to be cooked in a casserole usually are parboiled first.

Pastry — A stiff dough that becomes flaky when baked, made from flour, water and shortening. Also, a rich dough used for desserts.

Pastry bag — A cone-shaped bag of fabric, parchment or plastic, with a hole at the end to which various tips are attached. Used to decorate various foods.

Pâté — A well-seasoned mixture of finely chopped or ground meats, and/or liver. *Pâté de foie gras* is made from goose livers and truffles.

Pectin — A water-soluble fiber, obtained from certain fruits and vegetables, which is manufactured in syrup form to use in the preparation of jellies and jams.

Penne — A type of pasta that has a short, quill- or slant-cut tubular shape.

Phyllo — A flaky, tissue paper-thin pastry used in many Greek dishes. Also, "fillo."

Pilaf — Rice cooked in a savory broth, often with small bits of meat or vegetables, herbs and spices.

Pinch — The amount of a dry ingredient that can be taken up between the thumb and index finger — about 1/8 teaspoon.

Pipe — To press a soft mixture through a pastry bag fitted with a decorative tip to create a garnish or fancy edging for a dish.

Plump — To soak raisins or other dried fruits in liquid until they are softened and almost returned to their natural state.

Poach — To cook food, such as fish fillets, in barely simmering liquid.

Purée — To reduce food to a smooth, velvety texture by whirling it in an electric blender or food processor, or by pressing it through a sieve or food grinder. Also, the food so processed.

R

Ragoût	A stew. (Pronounced rah-goo.)
Ramekin	A small, individual-size baking dish.
Reduce	To boil a liquid, uncovered, until the quantity is concentrated.
Render	To melt solid fat.
Rice	To press food through a container with small holes until it resembles rice.
Risotto	Rice that is browned in fat and cooked in chicken broth or other liquid until it is tender but firm. It is creamy in texture, not dry or runny.
Roast	To cook meat or poultry in the oven by dry heat.
Rotelle	A variety of pasta shaped like wagon wheels.
Roulade	A slice of meat rolled around any number of fillings. Also, a jelly-roll cake.
Roux	A cooked mixture of fat and flour used to thicken sauces and gravies.

S

Salsa	A number of sauces in Mexican and Southwestern cuisines, ranging from very spicy to very subtle. Also, an uncooked, seasoned tomato sauce served as a condiment and used to add flavor to other dishes.
Sauté	To cook food quickly in a small amount of hot fat in a skillet.
Scald	To heat a liquid just until small bubbles form around the edges of the pan, but not allowing the liquid to come to a boil.
Scallop	To bake small pieces of food in a casserole, usually in a cream sauce. Also, a thin, boneless slice of meat, such as veal.
Score	To make shallow, perpendicular cuts over the surface of a food with a knife.
Short	An adjective used to describe a type of bread, cake or pastry that has a high proportion of fat and is extremely tender or crisp in texture.
Shortening	A solid fat, usually of vegetable origin, used to add tenderness to pastry, bread, cakes or cookies.
Simmer	To cook in a liquid just below boiling.
Skewer	To thread food on a wooden or metal pin for cooking. Also, the pin itself.
Skim	To remove fat or film from the surface of a liquid or sauce.
Sliver	To cut in long, thin strips.
Steam	To cook in a covered saucepan in a steamer basket or on a trivet over a small amount of boiling water.
Steep	To soak food (such as tea) in liquid until the liquid absorbs its flavor.
Stew	To cook, covered, in simmering liquid.
Stir-fry	To cook food quickly over high heat in a small amount of oil, stirring or tossing constantly.
Stock	A liquid base for soups and sauces made by long, slow cooking of meat, poultry or fish with their bones. Stock may be brown or white, depending on whether the meat and bones are browned first.

T

Terrine A type of baking dish used to prepare dishes such as pâtés. Also, the dish so prepared.

Thicken To make a liquid more dense by adding flour, cornstarch or a beaten egg.

Thin To make a liquid less dense by the addition of more liquid.

Timbale A savory meat, fish, poultry or vegetable custard, baked in a small mold. Also, pastry shells made on special iron molds—i.e., Swedish Rosettes.

Torte A very rich, multilayered cake made with eggs and, often, grated nuts. The cake usually is filled, but frequently is not frosted.

Tortilla A thin pancake of unleavened cornmeal or wheat flour used in Mexican and Southwestern cooking. Usually served hot with a topping or a filling.

Truffles A type of underground fungi considered a delicacy. They are black, dark brown or white in color, and are quite expensive due to their rarity and the method used to obtain them. Also, an extremely rich, chocolate candy.

Truss To tie into a compact shape before roasting.

Turnover A circle or square of pastry folded over a sweet or savory filling, with the edges crimped together. Turnovers often are baked, but some are fried.

W

Whip To beat until frothy or stiff with an eggbeater or an electric mixer.

Wok A round-bottomed, bowl-shaped Chinese cooking utensil used for stir-frying.

Y

Yeast, Quick or Rapid-Rise A variety of yeast that causes doughs to rise in one half to one third less time than if using regular active dry yeast.

Z

Zest The oily, aromatic, colored part of the rind of citrus fruits.

INDEX

Italicized page numbers refer to photographs.